Islamic Finance in the Global Economy

Islamic Finance
in the Global Economy

SECOND EDITION

Ibrahim Warde

EDINBURGH UNIVERSITY PRESS

© Ibrahim Warde, 2000, 2010

First edition published by Edinburgh University Press in 2000
Reprinted 2001, 2005, 2006

Edinburgh University Press
22 George Square, Edinburgh
www.euppublishing.com

Typeset in Baskerville by
Koinonia, Manchester, and
printed and bound in Great Britain by
CPI Antony Rowe, Chippenham and Eastbourne

A CIP record for this book is available from the British Library

ISBN 978 0 7486 2776 9 (hardback)
ISBN 978 0 7486 2777 6 (paperback)

CONTENTS

ACKNOWLEDGEMENTS

This book builds on a number of academic and professional projects that I have been involved in over the years, some dealing with Islam and the Middle East, others with global finance and economics. I wrote the first edition of this book when I was still at the University of California at Berkeley. I have since moved to the Boston area, where I have had successive affiliations with the Center for Middle Eastern Studies at Harvard University, the Center for International Studies at the Massachusetts Institute of Technology, and the Fletcher School of Law and Diplomacy at Tufts University. I owe a debt of gratitude to Larry Michalak and the late George Lenczowski at Berkeley, Roger Owen and Thomas Mullins at Harvard, Philip Khoury and Richard Samuels at the Massachusetts Institute for Technology, and Leila Fawaz and Laurent Jacque at Tufts University.

In researching the first edition, I received assistance from Dr Samir Abid Shaikh, General Secretary of the International Association of Islamic Banks and from Dr Omar Hafiz, Deputy Director of the Islamic Research and Training Institute at the Islamic Development Bank.

Among those who have been most helpful for both editions, I would like to single out Professor Chibli Mallat, now at the University of Utah, on whose encyclopedic knowledge of Islamic law I relied extensively and Dr Muhammed Yunus, founder of the Grameen Bank, who has since received a richly deserved Nobel Peace Prize, and who deepened my understanding of the relationship between finance and development.

In this new edition, I have integrated ideas from Nassim Taleb, whose influential books, *Fooled by Randomness: The Hidden Role of Chance in Life and in the Markets* and *The Black Swan: The Impact of the Highly Improbable*, have rocked the complacent world of academic finance. His perspective on equity versus debt was especially relevant to this book. Geoffrey Gresh, a doctoral candidate at the Fletcher School, helped me update Chapters 6 and 11.

Most of my work on global economics and finance was published in *Le Monde diplomatique*, a stimulating publication – and a truly global one since it is now translated in twenty-five languages – that has challenged the "pensée unique" pervading the political-economic discourse. I would like to thank the editors for their help and guidance, in particular Alain Gresh, whose own work on Islam and the Middle East is invaluable, and Serge Halimi, now the director of *Le Monde diplomatique*, and whose editing skills and exacting standards have no doubt greatly improved my articles.

I have also been associated with academic initiatives focusing on Islamic finance. I have participated in a number of conferences sponsored by the Islamic Research and Training Institute (IRTI), the research arm of the Islamic Development Bank (IDB), and benefited from the important research being conducted there. I have also been closely involved with the two major research initiatives dealing with Islamic finance in American universities. The first is Harvard's Islamic Finance Project (IFP), formerly HIFIP, which has become, under the able leadership of Dr S. Nazim Ali, the premier research forum on Islamic finance. The second is that of the University of California Berkeley School of Law which started in 2008 and centers around the *Berkeley Journal of Middle Eastern & Islamic Law* (JMEIL) and the annual Islamic Finance Symposium. A number of dynamic law students, among them Hamada Zahawi, Khalil AbuGharbieh, and Amy Coren deserve a great deal of credit for starting this exciting project.

In 2007 I was selected as a Carnegie Scholar to work on "Financial Practices and Networks in Islamic Countries." Fieldwork in Malaysia, Egypt, the United Arab Emirates, and Bahrain was particularly useful as I worked on updating this book. I would like to thank the Dr Vartan Gregorian and the Carnegie Corporation for their confidence and support.

Few activities help to clarify one's ideas and stimulate one's thinking as much as lecturing. A great deal of learning occurs through the interaction between practitioners and students. I have been privileged to work as a consultant and lecturer to countless financial institutions – Islamic and conventional. Participants have often challenged my own views and broadened as well as deepened my understanding of the subject. I have also taught courses and seminars on Islamic finance in academic settings in the United States and in various countries. For a number of years now I have been teaching an annual course at the Fletcher School of Law and Diplomacy at Tufts University. I have also taught at the Massachusetts Institute of Technology's Sloan School of Management, and lectured to students in the Islamic Finance program at Strasbourg's École de Management, and to students in the Executive Master in Islamic Financial Management program jointly offered in Beirut by the École Supérieure des Affaires (ESA), and the Rotterdam School of Management (RSM).

Needless to say, any errors, omissions, and other shortcomings in the book are my responsibility alone.

A NOTE ON TRANSLITERATION AND DATES

Most scholarly works dealing with Islam use a transliteration system based on classical Arabic. However, in a book dealing with a variety of Islamic settings, many of them non-Arabic speaking, such transliteration would make no sense. Indeed, most common words dealing with the Islamic religion or tradition have their origin in the Arabic language but are written or pronounced differently. In a Turkish, Persian, Urdu, or Malay setting, the purist system of transliteration would be confusing, if not outright misleading. This book will, therefore, dispense in most cases with diacritical marks and common symbols – apostrophes, horizontal strokes, etc. – using instead a simplified system of transliteration. Thus, Koran will be used in preference to Qur'an and Shariah in preference to Shari'a. Only in a few cases (as in direct quotes) will such marks and symbols be used. When possible confusion may arise (Malaysians use Sariyah for Shariah, Iranians use zarura for darura), both transliterations will be used.

All dates are based on the Gregorian calendar.

ABBREVIATIONS

AAOIFI Accounting and Auditing Organization for Islamic Financial Institutes
ABC   Arab Banking Corporation
BCCI   Bank of Credit and Commerce International
BIMB   Bank Islam Malaysia Berhad
BIS   Bank for International Settlements
BMA   Bahrain Monetary Authority
BMI   Bank Muamalat Indonesia
BNI   Bank Negora Indonesia
BNL   Banca Nazionale del Lavoro
BNM   Bank Negara Malaysia
BSE   Bahrain Stock Exchange
CDS   credit default swops
CIA   Central Intelligence Agency
CIBAFI Council for Islamic Banks and Financial Institutions
DBS   Development Bank of Singapore
DIB   Dubai Islamic Bank
DIFC   Dubai International Financial Centre
DJIM   Dow Jones Islamic Market Index
DMI   Dar al-Maal al-Islami
EBRD   European Bank for Reconstruction and Development
ESIB   Egyptian-Saudi Investment Bank
FBSEA Foreign Bank Supervision and Enhancement Act
FDIC   Federal Deposit Insurance Corporation
FDICIA Federal Deposit Insurance Corporation Improvement Act
FIBE   Faisal Islamic Bank of Egypt
FIS   Front Islamique du Salut (Islamic Salvation Front – Algeria)
GCC   Gulf Cooperation Council
GDP   gross domestic product
GNP   gross national product
HIFIP   Harvard Islamic Finance Information Program (now Islamic Finance Project (IFP)
IAIB   International Association of Islamic Banks

IAS	International Accountancy Standards
IBP	Islamic banks' portfolio
ICIEC	Islamic Corporation for the Insurance of Investment and Export Credit
ICMI	Association of Moslem Intellectuals (Indonesia)
ICRIE	International Center for Research in Islamic Economics
IDB	Islamic Development Bank
IDS	Islamic debt securities
IFBS	Islamic Finance Services Board
IIBID	International Islamic Bank for Investment and Development
IICG	Islamic Investment Company of the Gulf
IIFM	Islamic International Financial Market
IIMM	Islamic Interbank Money Market
IIRA	Islamic International Rating Agency
IKIM	Malaysian Institute of Islamic Understanding
IMF	International Monetary Fund
IMMCs	Islamic Money Management Companies
IOFC	International Offshore Financial Center
IRTI	Islamic Research and Training Institute
ITFO	import trade financing operations
IUT	Islamic unit trusts
LMC	Liquidity Management Center
LME	London Metal Exchange
LTCM	Long-Term Capital Management
LTTFS	longer-term trade financing scheme
MESA	Middle Eastern Studies Association
MFI	micro finance institutions
MUI	Indonesian Ulemas Council
NATO	North Atlantic Treaty Organization
NEP	new economic policy (Malaysia)
NIEO	new international economic order
NIF	National Islamic Front
OBU	offshore banking units
OEC	Organization of Economic Cooperation
OECD	Organization of Economic Cooperation and Development
OIC	Organization of the Islamic Conference
OPEC	Organization of Petroleum Exporting Countries
PEP	politically exposed persons
PERLs	principal exchange rate linked securities
PKTCL	Pak-Kuwait Takaful Co. Ltd
PLS	profit-and-loss sharing
PSIA	profit-sharing investment accounts
RAVs	repackaged asset vehicles

INTRODUCTION:
ISLAMIC FINANCE IN THE GLOBAL ECONOMY

Much has happened since the publication of the first edition of this book in 2000. The Islamic sector has experienced tremendous growth, and has now reached an estimated $1,300 billion (a sixfold increase over the past decade).[1] No longer confined to the outer fringes of global finance, Islamic finance has also gone mainstream. Most major financial institutions are now involved in one way or another in Islamic finance, as are global consulting, accounting, and information companies. Islamic financial institutions now operate in at least 105 countries, and more countries have introduced (or are considering introducing) legislation designed to provide a regulatory framework for the industry.

Within the Islamic world, Islamic financial institutions have become major economic players. Five countries dominate Islamic banking: Iran with $345 billion in Islamic assets; followed by Saudi Arabia ($258 billion); Malaysia ($142 billion); Kuwait ($128 billion); and the United Arab Emirates ($112). A few non-Islamic countries, among them the United Kingdom and Singapore, have announced their intention of becoming hubs of Islamic finance, and others (such as Australia, France and South Korea) have altered their legislation to become more hospitable to Islamic finance.

A number of interrelated demographic, political, economic, and financial factors account for a boom in Islamic finance that shows no sign of abating. Initially scarce, Islamic financial products have multiplied in recent years, attracting a growing number of customers. Non-Islamic financial institutions that had previously ignored the Islamic market have started to pay close attention. With the rise in energy prices in the period between 2003 and 2008 further enhancing the economic importance of oil-producing Islamic countries, Islamic financial institutions received a further boost.

Especially notable is the appearance and growing popularity of *sukuk*, often described as Islamic bonds. Since 2002, corporations and government have been able to raise money in a Shariah-compliant way by issuing trust certificates that could be traded on the secondary market. Over a period of six years the market has skyrocketed to $100 billion.

Long criticized for being overly conservative when it came to financial innovation, Islamic institutions felt vindicated when the sub-prime crisis hit much of the conventional banking sector in 2007. In that year alone, the Islamic sector grew by

33 per cent. For a time, it looked like the sector would be spared the crisis, though in its later stages, especially as the financial crisis took its toll on the real economy, Islamic institutions were adversely affected: the year 2008 saw a sharp drop in the issuance of sukuk, and a few Islamic banks in the Gulf region suffered from the decline in real estate and stock market prices.[2]

A common mistake is to view Islamic finance as a monolith. Despite the growing harmonization of rules, there is a great deal of diversity within Islamic finance. As we look at the leading Islamic institutions, we notice the heterogeneity of Islamic banks: the top spots are held by the largest government-owned Iranian banks (led by Bank Melli, which is followed by Bank Saderat, Bank Mellat, Bank Tejarat, Bank Sepah, and Bank Keshavarzi) that are subject to sanctions and have few interactions with non-Iranian Islamic banks. Then there are Gulf Coopera-tion Council (GCC) banks such as Kuwait Finance House, Dubai Islamic Bank, Abu Dhabi Islamic Bank and Saudi Arabia's al-Rajhi, to which the more transna-tional Bahrain-based, Saudi-owned al-Baraka group could be added. The top ranks of Islamic banks also include two types of Malaysian banks: Islamic institu-tions, such as Bank Islam Malaysia Berhad (BIMB), and Islamic units of conven-tional banks such as Maybank Islamic Berhad. The largest Islamic institutions by assets also include Western-based institutions, such as the UK-controlled, but Dubai-based, HSBC Amana.

Another mistake is to assume that the Islamic sector has always existed in its current state, or that it appeared fully-formed at some point in the 1970s. In reality, Islamic banks have had their ups and downs, and have gone through constant change as a result of an evolving political-economic context and the dynamics of interaction with the conventional sector. In many respects, the Islamic sector is still a work in progress and the process of trial and error will continue for years to come.

The Evolution of Islamic Finance: A Three-Stage Analysis

This book helps the understanding of the current state of the Islamic sector by tracing its evolution through three distinct phases: the early years (1975–91); the era of globalization (1991–2001); and the post-September 11, 2001 period.

Islamic banks came into existence in the mid-1970s as a result of specific historical circumstances, the most significant element of which was the quadru-pling in the price of oil. The mood was then conducive to assertiveness and experimentation, and Islamic banks sought to establish an alternative to conven-tional banking: instead of functioning on the basis of interest, they would form partnerships based on profit-and-loss sharing with both depositors and would-be borrowers, through the traditional Islamic practice of *mudaraba* (commenda partnership or trusteeship finance).

The Islamic financial system was supposed to function according to the "double *mudaraba*" principle: on the liabilities side of the balance sheet, the depositor would be the financier and the bank the entrepreneur; on the asset side, the bank would be the financier and the person seeking funding the entrepreneur. Another product, the old Islamic sale-based technique of murabaha, was, in its updated form, expected to play a subsidiary role. Under the traditional murabaha, a buyer would ask a seller to buy a good on his behalf, and resell it to him after adding a pre-determined profit. The updated version added an element of financing to what was originally a spot transaction: the bank would still act as a merchant, purchasing the required goods directly from a supplier and selling them to the customer, but payment would be deferred. Since it lacked the element of profit-and-loss sharing and sought to mimic conventional finance by replacing the notion of interest with that of profit, the murabaha was not enthusiastically endorsed by religious scholars, but was considered an acceptable stop-gap that would allow modern Islamic institutions to build experience and resources while they developed a profit-and-loss-based financial system.

Another tenet of Islamic finance was that transactions had to be linked to the real economy. The first Islamic institutions were suspicious of all financial products whose links to the real economy were deemed tenuous, and thus preferred to invest in physical assets such as real estate or commodities. The performance of the first Islamic banks was disappointing: the profit-and-loss sharing model proved to be unworkable; the global recession and the sudden decline in oil prices in the early 1980s had a devastating effect on the physical assets in which they were heavily invested. Furthermore, the Islamic sector was negatively affected by financial scandals, such those of as Egypt's Islamic Money Management Companies (IMMCs) and the collapse of Bank of Credit and Commerce International (BCCI).

The second stage of Islamic finance (1991–2001) marked a departure from the early ideals. Islamic institutions moved toward more pragmatism and started focusing on ways of replicating conventional finance, albeit through Shariah-compliant contracts. Another significant factor was the rise of the Malaysian model of Islamic finance, which was more innovative and forward-looking (though religiously controversial).

Herein lay one of the many paradoxes of Islamic finance. Although Islam was often said to be incompatible with the new order that emerged with the end of the Cold War,[3] the age of globalization allowed Islamic finance to thrive. Skeptics could ask: how could a medieval economic system be relevant in a world of revolutionary, technology-driven global finance? And how could an interest-free system fit within the broader interest-based financial system? The fact is that financial deregulation allowed the creation of a wide range of new products. Just as it helped to create products presenting tax, legal, or financial advantages, financial engineering helped to devise products that would comply with religious precepts. Deregulation also had the effect of downgrading the role of interest: whereas conventional banks initially relied almost exclusively on "net interest income" (the difference between the interest charged to borrowers and the interest paid to depositors), they now relied on other sources of profits (from fees, proprietary trading, etc.) that were not directly linked to interest.

This growing convergence led to the creation of Islamic units by many conventional banks. Western banks, such as Citibank and HSBC, created Islamic banking subsidiaries, respectively, in Bahrain (1996) and in Dubai (1998). The late 1990s also saw the creation of the Dow Jones Islamic Market Index (DJIM), which tracked companies whose products and financial practices did not violate Islamic law.

The third phase in the evolution of Islamic finance started after the September 11, 2001 attacks. The "global war on terror" which became the overarching theme of international relations had a significant but paradoxical impact on Islamic finance. In the years following the attacks, the Islamic finance industry experienced dramatic growth and major transformations. The perception that Islam was under siege resulted in greater religiosity, which in turn drove an increase in demand for Islamic products.

Notable developments included countless new commercial and regulatory initiatives as well as the convergence of the Arab and the Malaysian models of Islamic banking. Coming under attack had the effect of greatly concentrating the minds of Islamic bankers and their regulators. As a result, efforts at international coordination and standardization grew more serious and better focused. The year 2002 alone saw the appearance of sovereign *ijara sukuk* and the creation of coordination and standard-setting mechanisms, such as the Islamic Finance Services Board (IFSB), the Islamic International Financial Market (IIFM), the Liquidity Management Center (LMC), and the Islamic International Rating Agency (IIRA). The Accounting and Auditing Organization for Islamic Financial Institutions (AAOIFI), though in existence since 1991, was greatly re-energized in its efforts to harmonize accounting and auditing rules and create standard Islamic contracts. The Arab–Malaysian convergence has recently accelerated with Arab Islamic banks, such as Saudi Arabia's al-Rajhi and the Kuwait Finance Houses starting to operate in the Malaysian market.

A Diverse and Complex Phenomenon

Despite such efforts at harmonization and streamlining there is still a great deal of diversity to the Islamic sector. Perceptions of Islamic finance in the West cannot be separated from general perceptions of Islam as a monolithic, unchanging and somewhat fossilized belief system. In reality, Islamic finance reflects the diversity of a fourteen-hundred-year-old, 1.2 billion strong religion spread over every continent. Islamic financial institutions come in all shapes and forms: banks and non-banks; large and small; specialized and diversified; traditional and innovative; national and multinational; successful and unsuccessful; prudent and reckless; strictly regulated and freewheeling, etc. Some are virtually identical to their conventional counterparts, while others are markedly different. Some are driven solely by religious considerations, others use religion as a way of side-stepping regulation, as a shield against government interference, as a tool for political change, or simply as a way of attracting customers. It should finally be noted that there are significant disagreements among Islamic scholars as to which new financial instruments (such as derivatives) are religiously acceptable.

In sum, the story of Islamic finance is a vastly complicated one, and cannot be captured without a full understanding of religion and finance, but also of history, politics, economics, business, and culture.

Book Outline

The book is divided into three parts. The first part provides background information on Islam and finance (Chapters 1 to 3). It debunks common myths about Islam and Islamic finance, traces the historical evolution of Islamic economics and finance, as well as the mechanisms by which Homo Islamicus and Homo Economicus were reconciled, and considers religious injunctions as they pertain to finance. By adoptive a comparative approach to religion and finance, we will see that all religions and even secular approaches (such as those of Greek philosophers) had misgivings about making money with money, and more specifically the notion of interest. Attempts to get around the prohibition of interest were certainly not unique to Islam. In medieval Christianity, the "*contractum trinius*" was a way of obtaining the same results as an interest-based loan by combining three separate contracts, each of them licit.

The second part of the book introduces and describes the world of Islamic finance (Chapters 4 to 7). It traces the birth and evolution of modern Islamic finance through the three phases described earlier, and places Islamic finance in its proper political and economic context. It accounts for the diversity of the industry by analyzing the ways different countries have introduced and dealt with Islamic finance, and by providing a detailed typology of Islamic financial products (*murabaha, mudaraba, musharaka, ijara, sukuk, takaful,* etc.).

The third part (Chapters 8 to 12) deals with the issues and challenges facing Islam from different vantage points. Chapter 8 looks at management, strategy, and culture (how the practices of Islamic financial institutions differ from those of conventional ones; the strategies developed by Islamic financial institutions to expand their markets; the managerial problems encountered by Islamic financial institutions; the problem of the "Islamic moral hazard;" the cultural barriers to the implementation of Islamic financial systems; the "different kind of bubble" unleashed by the recent financial meltdown). The following chapters deal, respectively, with economics (the mixed record of Islamic finance in mobilizing savings, allocating funds, promoting development, and alleviating poverty); regulation (the regulatory issues raised, domestically and internationally, by Islamic finance; the impact of the regulatory norms of the global economy on Islamic institutions); politics (the connection between Islamic finance and domestic politics; Islam in the new world order; the alleged ties of financial institutions with Islamic terrorism); and religion (the battles over religious interpretation; the current debates on the future of Islamic finance). The concluding chapter of the book addresses the impact of the global financial meltdown on Islamic finance.

Notes

1. This and other figures mentioned later are from the author's database.
2. See Chapter 8.
3. Samuel Huntington, *The Clash of Civilizations and the Remaking of World Order* (New York: Simon and Schuster Touchstone, 1997), p. 211.

I

ISLAMIC FINANCE IN THEORY AND PRACTICE

I Defining Islamic Finance

What is Islamic finance? Definitions range from the very narrow (interest-free banking) to the very broad (financial operations conducted by Muslims). A useful definition is the following: Islamic financial institutions are those that are based, in their objectives and operations, on Islamic law (the Shariah). They are thus set apart from "conventional" institutions, which have no such preoccupations. This definition goes beyond simply equating Islamic finance with "interest-free" banking. It allows operations that may or may not be interest-free, but are nonetheless imbued with certain Islamic principles to be taken into account: the avoidance of *riba* (in the broad sense of unjustified increase) and *gharar* (uncertainty, risk, speculation);[1] the focus on *halal* (religiously permissible) activities; and more generally the quest for justice, and other ethical and religious goals. Two aspects of Islamic finance must be singled out. First, the risk-sharing philosophy: the lender must share in the borrower's risk. Since fixed, predetermined interest rates guarantee a return to the lender and fall disproportionately on the borrower, they are seen as exploitative, socially unproductive, and economically wasteful. The preferred mode of financing is profit-and-loss sharing (PLS). Second, the promotion of economic and social development through specific business practices and through *zakat* (almsgiving). Most, but not all, Islamic institutions have a Shariah board – a committee of religious advisors whose opinion is sought on the acceptability of new instruments, and who conduct a religious audit of the bank's activities – as well as other features[2] reflecting their religious status. In sum, the defining difference is that while "conventional" finance usually seeks profit maximization within a given regulatory framework, Islamic finance is also guided by other, religiously-inspired, goals.[3]

No definition of Islamic finance is entirely satisfactory. To every general criterion – a financial institution owned by Muslims, catering to Muslims, supervised by a Shariah board, belonging to the International Association of Islamic Banks (IAIB) or the General Council for Islamic Banks and Financial Institutions (CIBAFI) – one can find some significant exception. Indeed, even the criterion of self-identification – that is, an Islamic institution is one that calls itself Islamic – would leave out the Turkish participation banks (previously called Turkish finance houses), or Saudi Arabia's Islamic banks, starting with the oldest one, al-Rajhi

Banking and Investment Company, which, for reasons discussed later in the book, do not refer explicitly to their Islamic character.

Most Islamic banks would in theory agree with a number of basic principles: the realm of finance should be linked directly to the real economy, and governed by the principles of risk sharing and profit-and-loss sharing; interest-based lending (generally considered to be riba) should be replaced by Islamic financing contracts based on equity, sale or leasing; transactions involving speculation or gharar (a notion encompassing excessive or avoidable risk, deceptive ambiguity, and risk shifting) should be avoided, as are transactions involving *haram* (religiously forbidden) activities and unethical behavior; transactions must be clear and transparent and must fulfill social and developmental goals; leverage should be limited; certain conventional practices (such as short-selling) are not allowed; and financial innovations must be monitored by religious scholars. This is, however, the theory or the ideal form of Islamic finance. The reality can best be understood in terms of the evolving context of the industry and its interaction with conventional finance.

Islamic finance also involves more than banking. It includes mutual funds, securities firms, insurance companies, and other non-banks. Where once – in the mid-1970s – Islamic banks were few in number and easily identifiable, the phenomenon has become quite amorphous with the proliferation of Islamic institutions and the blurring of the lines between traditional banking and other forms of finance. Another complicating factor is that a growing number of conventional financial institutions, both inside and outside the Islamic world, have in recent years been involved in varying degrees in Islamic finance, and most global conventional institutions offer a range of Islamic products.

For the outside observer the inevitable question is: how can a financial system operate without lending at interest? The answer is that other mechanisms are available: the Islamic bank can engage in equity-based transactions, or more commonly sell or lease the item that would normally be financed through an interest-bearing loan. In the age of financial deregulation and structured finance, many alternatives have been devised that are considered to be Shariah-compliant.[4]

II The Literature

Quantity, not quality, is the defining feature of writings on Islamic finance. The recent boom in Islamic finance has resulted in a flood of writings that add very little to our understanding of a complex and multifaceted phenomenon. Overall, scholarship is marred by four flaws: the "authorized" nature and pre-ordained conclusions of a significant portion of it; narrow geographic focus and lack of comparative analysis; reductionism (religious, financial, and legal); and faulty assumptions about the relation between theory and practice.

1 *The Problem of Authorized Literature and Preordained Conclusions*

Two types of literature, from opposite sides of the spectrum, have made it nearly impossible to have a nuanced or empirically-grounded understanding of Islamic finance and capture its evolutionary nature: one presents Islamic finance as a universal panacea; the other as a failure – at best an inconsequential phenomenon, at worst a fraud or a threat. A preliminary step to assessing the scientific validity of any type of research – whether on the health effects of cigarette smoking or on the therapeutic value of a new drug – is to know who financed it. Research sponsors usually have an agenda and expect the research to produce specific conclusions. From that standpoint, much of the research on Islamic finance should be used with caution.

In the early years of Islamic finance, a substantial literature was generated by promoters of the industry. The sudden emergence of Islamic finance had created a pressing need: Islamic economics was in its infancy and modern Islamic banking was a new concept, so substantial research was necessary. Islamic financial institutions have been very generous in funding research institutes and promoting publications, conferences, symposia, and seminars on Islamic finance. But the pressure to instantly generate a body of literature oriented toward positive conclusions explains both the vast output and its disappointing quality. Literally thousands of books, pamphlets, articles, and websites have been produced in the past few years on the subject, but very few rise to the level of serious, rigorous research. Over three dozen periodicals deal principally or even exclusively with Islamic finance. In addition, the business press – national, regional, and international – carries frequent articles on the subject, some of which are of an "advertorial" nature. Indeed, even in prestigious publications one can find, annually, and sometimes more often, the obligatory "sponsored section" on Islamic finance.

A more recent trend has been in the opposite direction, relentlessly criticizing and attacking all manifestations of Islamic finance. No less theological, apologetic, or exegetic than the previous literature, this one is rooted in a dogmatic, if not theological, approach to economics and finance.[5] (An additional set of critical writings, politically motivated, will be discussed in Chapter 11.) The economic perspective is implicitly rooted in two sets of views: one being that economics (and its finance sub-set) is a real science; the other being that the state of the art in finance, epitomized by the "Wall Street" model has achieved some level of platonic perfection. A number of writers have compared Islamic finance with its conventional counterpart and found the first wanting. Some have concluded that Islamic finance was thus bound to remain stunted. Countless writings (including within the Islamic banking profession) have expressed the view that the tests of maturity and success of the Islamic sector lies in exact replication by the Islamic sector of the conventional model.

Any differences between the two are considered to be market imperfections leading to loss of efficiency, which for many mainstream economists is a cardinal sin. A typical exercise is to compare the most common type of Islamic product, the *murabaha*,[6] with a conventional loan, and then wonder whether creating such a product is necessary, considering the extra costs (and thus loss of efficiency) it might entail.

Such an economic perspective misses the whole point of religiously-motivated behavior. It is unable to look beyond the bottom line and fails to appreciate the complexity of human motivations. A useful parallel is that of religiously-based dietary restrictions. Why do some people require their food to be, say, halal or kosher? Like the economist who is solely preoccupied with the bottom line, the professional nutritionist, concerned only with matters of nutrients and caloric intake would be at a loss to understand why people go out of their way (and probably pay more) to satisfy religious requirements. Yet the point is precisely that, for religiously-minded people, how the food is prepared – and similarly how the financial product is structured – is essential.

Thus, from opposite sides of the spectrum we can find an abundant literature that may be conducive to definitive sound bites or sweeping assertions though not to open-minded empirical inquiry.

2 The Geo-economics of Islam

Because of patterns of academic specialization, studies of Islamic economics and finance tend to be slanted toward the Arab or Persian world, and most classifications are derived from political as opposed to economic factors. In the academic world, the study of Islam usually falls under the Middle Eastern studies category. Yet Arabs represent only about 20 per cent of the Islamic world, and the Arab, Turkish, and Persian components of Islam taken together barely exceed one-third of Muslims worldwide. In the ranking of Muslim populations, Egypt, the most populous Arab country, comes in only eighth place after Indonesia, India, Pakistan, Bangladesh, Iran, Turkey, and Nigeria. In his 1994 Middle Eastern Studies Association (MESA) Presidential Address, Rashid Khalidi acknowledged that "we in Middle East Studies have frequently failed to reach beyond our own area of interest to make connections with those studying other regions, including neighboring ones with characteristics and problems quite similar to those of the Middle East – like Central Asia, Africa, South Asia and the Mediterranean."[7]

The political focus has another paradoxical consequence: those countries that are of political interest, such as Iran or the Sudan, have, because of sanctions and other political factors, also been somewhat isolated economically and relatively little attention has been paid to their economic evolution.

Such tropes have led many analysts of Islamic finance to dismiss developments that have occurred outside a limited number of Arab countries.[8] In reality, significant innovation has occurred throughout the Islamic world. In addition to pioneering countries such as Pakistan and Malaysia, there are Islamic experiments throughout the Islamic world, as well as within Islamic communities outside the Islamic world. By the same token, most Western perceptions of Islam are shaped by some of its most extreme political manifestations (principally Islamic radicalism) that are representative neither of the mainstream of the religion nor of its economic aspects. The geo-economics of Islam is indeed sharply different from its geo-politics. Not only are the largest communities outside the Middle Eastern core, but substantial Islamic middle classes have emerged in Asia, Africa, Europe, and the United States. Also central Asian countries which were once part of the Soviet Union – Azerbaijan, Kazakhstan, Turkmenistan, Uzbekistan, Kirgizstan, and Tajikistan – are poised to play, largely due to their oil, gas, or other natural resources, a growing role in the world economy. In addition, certain countries or communities – one thinks of the sultanate of Brunei or of the Ismaili sect – possess great wealth yet are politically insignificant. Any study of Islamic finance must acknowledge such geo-economic diversity.

3 Religious, Financial, and Legal Reductionism

Most writings on Islamic finance fall in one of three categories: theology, finance, and law. Theological writings tend to assume an ahistorical world where timeless religious principles apply. Writings by finance experts – of the kind found in the international business press and in finance textbooks – on the other hand, have little patience with the intricacies of religious tradition or the complex environment within which financial institutions operate.[9] They also have a tendency to parrot a conventional wisdom that was widely discredited with the 2008 financial meltdown. The richest and most rigorous writings on Islamic finance have been produced by legal scholars. The main flaw of such writings, however, is that they tend to define Islamic banking as "modern banking based on medieval Islamic legal doctrines as interpreted, modified, and implemented by competent Islamic legal authorities."[10] In other words, Islamic finance is all about law and it can be understood only by a return to *usul el fiqh* (principles of jurisprudence) and the rediscovery of the contracts of the classical age of Islam and their interpretation by the different schools of jurisprudence. Empirical studies of Islamic finance suggest that legalistic concerns are only one aspect, and probably not the most crucial one, of real-world Islamic finance (see, for example, Chapters 6 and 7).

In sum, the literature on Islamic finance is deeply disappointing principally because it is neither empirical (that is, based on the evidence) – nor interdisciplinary (that is, looking at all the facets of a complex and multidimensional phenomenon). The most learned volumes tend to wallow in endless hairsplitting: a proclivity common to jurists and theologians. The others tend to be shallow and faddish, focusing on the "emerging market" of the day, and on Islamic finance as either a hot or a fizzling new trend. Hence, their catechism-like flavor, offering a simple – often simplistic – perspective on a complex topic.

4 Islamic Banking between Ideal and Policy

One of the many paradoxes of Islamic finance is the contrast between the strong commitment of Islamist groups to the principle of Islamic banking and their lack of involvement in its implementation. On the one hand, Islamicizing the financial system is usually at the very top of the demands of Islamic groups. One reason is that the injunction against riba is a distinctive feature of Islam. Yet the practical implementation of Islamic finance is seldom part of the realm of "high politics," since Islamic movements rarely have a specific economic program for putting their ideals to work. They tend to talk in generalities about implementing the Shariah, but have no proposals for making the Shariah induce economic prosperity or true social justice. This is due to the ambiguity of Islamic economic norms, making a consensus on actual policy prescriptions elusive,[11] and also to the fact that economic policy is usually secondary to political or cultural issues. As Ayatollah Khomeini reportedly said, "The revolution is about Islam, not about the price of melons".[12]

Although theological and legalistic approaches assume that the Islamicization of finance proceeds according to a strict application of religious law, the empirical evidence tells us otherwise (see Chapter 6). Economic issues, and in particular the specific implementation of financial legislation, do not rank very high on the agenda of Islamic groups, and most headline-grabbing Islamic groups – such as the FIS, Hezbollah, or Hamas – have no clearly defined economic agenda.[13] On such matters as banking legislation, expediency is likely to prevail over "Islamic correctness." Typically, the wording of the legislation would conform to general principles but would be broad enough to accommodate a wide variety of inter-pretations. The general interest (*maslaha*) and overriding necessity (*darura*) – the need to achieve economic welfare and the requirements of a global economy – whether articulated or not, usually trump theological or legal concerns.

III Perceptions, Labels, and Classifications

1 Common Perceptions of Islam and Islamic Finance

Outside of a small circle of practitioners, Islamic finance remains little known. There are, however, within the general public, as well as within the smaller communities of scholars and financiers, broadly shared perceptions about Islam in general (and sometimes even about Islamic finance). If we consider the influ-ence of the likes of Francis Fukuyama or Samuel Huntington, we realize that lack of familiarity with Islam seldom deters people from making the kinds of sweeping pronouncements that soon become working assumptions in intellectual and policy debates. When Fukuyama discusses the timeless conflict between Islam and liberalism,[14] or when Huntington states that "in Islam, God is Caesar" or that "the Koran and the Shariah constitute basic law for Islamic societies,"[15] they are not only engaging in gross oversimplification, they are also making statements that do not stand up to rigorous historical or social-scientific analysis.[16]

Any religion that has survived for fourteen centuries, and that has some 1.2 billion followers spread in every part of the globe must have some measure of flexibility and diversity. Any such religion should be resistant to broad-brush generalizations. Statements to the effect that "Islam says …" "Muslims believe

..." must include significant qualifiers and caveats. Yet Islam is usually represented in terms of a monolithic *umma* (community of believers) and a fossilized belief system that has not changed since the seventh century. In that respect, Islam is unique: although every major religion has numerous, often contradictory, strands – intolerant and inclusive, moderate and radical, pietistic and political, obscurantist and progressive, peaceful and violent, mystical and worldly, etc. – not to mention its share of objectionable features and lunatic fringes, only Islam is likely to be systematically associated with its most extreme manifestations. An implicit assumption is that only the most backward form of the religion represents true Islam. John Esposito has observed that:

> non-Muslim scholars sound more like mullahs ... When faced with new interpretations or applications of Islam, they often critique them from the vantage point of traditional belief and practice. On the one hand, Islam is regarded as fixed, and Muslims are seen as too reluctant to accept change. On the other hand, when change occurs, it is dismissed as unorthodox, sheer opportunism, an excuse for adopting that which is outside Islam.[17]

In recent years, and especially since the September 11 attacks, the emblematic figures of Islam in the Western mind are radical fundamentalists who have come to "realize the wildest fantasies of Orientalism."[18] Sami Zubeida has noted the convergence "between the adherents of the Islamist movements and Westerners writing in the Orientalist tradition. Each postulates a cultural essence which underlies and unifies Islamic history and distinguishes it from an equally reductionist notion of the West."[19]

One of the more misleading generalizations is that Islam, unlike other religions, is a "complete way of life." For one thing, this could be said of any religion, since most enjoin virtuous behavior in everyday life. The implication is that the demands of Islam are not compatible with the requirements of modern life. Yet in many ways, Islam has less "structure" than other religions. What all Muslims share is a core of basic principles, the so-called "five pillars" of the faith.[20] Islamic clerics do not administer religious sacraments: they are more akin to religious/legal scholars who interpret the scriptures. Unlike other religions, the conversion process is simple: it comprises a witnessed profession of faith (*shahada*). Islam has no baptism or other initiation ceremony. Muslims do not belong to congregations. Mosques are open to all and do not maintain membership rolls. Islam also teaches that each person has a direct relationship with God and that no intermediary is needed. Many of the traditions associated in the Western mind with Islam (the use of the veil for women, for example) are not mandated by religion but can be explained either in terms of local customs or as "fundamentalist" reinterpretation of Islam.

The association of Islam with "a total way of life" leads to two common assertions with regard to politics and economics: one is that Islam prescribes very specific norms; the other is that Islam is inherently and primarily political. In reality, as will be seen throughout this book, Islamic norms on political and economic matters are broad and somewhat ambiguous, thus accommodating a wide variety of interpretations.[21] Many Islamic scholars actually draw a distinction between "political Islam" and "enlightened Islam."[22] As for the propagation of the Islamic faith, most of it is non-political – though the casual Western observer would not know it. Indeed, a number of students of Islam have noted that extremist political organizations – such as Hezbollah or Islamic Jihad – whose numbers run in the thousands or sometimes in the hundreds receive wide coverage, while apolitical organizations of a pietistic or missionary nature – such as Jamaat Tabligh – have millions of members yet are totally ignored by the media and the most widely quoted "experts" on Islam.[23]

2   The Diversity of Islam

Despite the prevailing clichés, a striking feature of Islam is its sheer diversity. Muslims constitute a majority of the population in some fifty-six countries in Africa, the Middle East, central, south and southeast Asia. They are a minority, often a fast-growing one, in most parts of the world, including Europe, Russia, the Americas, and Australia. The diversity is also religious, racial, ethnic, political, social, economic, and cultural. Despite the language of a unified umma, Islam is fragmented and decentralized, with no "clergy" and no centralized, "Vatican-like" church. Only a few countries – most prominently Iran – have a tradition of autonomous and hierarchically-structured clergy.

Most people are familiar with the Sunni–Shia divide. But there is a far greater diversity of religious groups, beliefs, and practices. Differences can be attributed to religious schisms, but more commonly to different historical paths as well as exposure to outside influences. In certain areas, such as what is now Saudi Arabia, there is a tradition of religious homogeneity (with the exception of a small Shia minority). A non-Muslim presence has been virtually absent and outside influence scant (the Ottoman influence was nominal and significant contacts with the West started only with the First World War). Being the birthplace of Islam is also, of course, a crucial element in the country's identity and religious beliefs and practices. But Saudi Arabia is a minority of the Arab world (18 million out of 200 million), which is itself a minority of the Islamic world (200 million out of about 1.2 billion).

In the Islamic world at large there are numerous traditions – Persian, Turkic, Indo-Pakistani, Indonesian, Malay, etc. – that have little in common with the experience of the Arabian Peninsula. The nature of the Islamic beliefs and traditions are shaped by numerous factors ranging from when and how the area was Islamicized, to the nature of pre-existing beliefs and institutions, to subsequent outside influences. In Indonesia and Malaysia, the Islamicization process occurred primarily around the fifteenth century. The local population was converted by merchants, not conquering armies. The brand of Islam that took root was mostly influenced by Sufism. It thus had a mystical foundation as opposed to the theological and literalist bias that could be found in some parts of the Islamic world. It was also cut off, for geographic and historical reasons, from the great Islamic empires. As a result, the brand of Islam that developed was idiosyncratic as well as syncretic, integrating a wide array of local and regional influences.[24]

In Eastern Europe and the former Soviet Union, Islam was long suppressed or ignored, only to re-emerge in a context of turmoil and foreign encroachments. In the Balkans today, some 8 million Muslims form a distant legacy of centuries of Ottoman rule. In the former Yugoslavia, much of Bosnia and Kosovo are Muslim. So are the majority of Albanians and a minority of Bulgarians. Within the Russian Federation, the Muslim Chechens, a long-persecuted minority, have engaged in a full war of secession against the Russian army. In the Caucasus, Muslim Azerbaijanis have a long historical enmity with Christian Armenians. In central Asia, Kazakhstan, Turkmenistan, Uzbekistan, Kirgizstan, and Tajikistan have either a majority or a plurality of Muslims. What all of these groups have in common is that they lived for decades under a political system that was anti-religious and sometimes engaged in aggressive religious suppression. In others, such as in the former Soviet Union, cultural and linguistic traditions persisted, but the role of religion was considerably reduced. In a post-Communist era, religion surfaced with a vengeance. Many communities which were only nominally Islamic found in Islam an essential component of a long-suppressed identity, and a number of Islamic countries – such as Turkey, Iran, and Saudi Arabia – have been attempting for a combination of political, economic, and religious reasons to export their own brand of Islam to that region.

Another phenomenon is the increased presence (mostly through recent immigration) of Muslims in non-Muslim lands. In the United States, Islam is expected to become in a few years the second largest religion. One-third of its 5 million adherents are black Americans. The others are mostly of Arab, Persian, or Pakistani-Indian ancestry.[25] Western Europe is home to some 14 million Muslims, although national origins, governmental policies, and degrees of assimilation differ greatly.[26] French Muslims are primarily from North Africa – Algeria, Tunisia, and Morocco – and are subjected to a specific mode of individual integration based on the tradition of "laïcité." In Germany, Muslims are usually from Turkey, and are subjected to different rules and practices. Their status, and that of their descendants is that of "guest workers" (making them ineligible for German citizenship). In the United Kingdom, Muslims are overwhelmingly from the Indian subcontinent and are integrated in British society "as a group and not as individuals."[27]

For all these reasons, one can identify a very broad range of Islamic beliefs and practices, that is in fact similar to what could be found in other religions such as Hinduism, Christianity, and Judaism. On one end of the spectrum, there are strict Muslims who would like religion to extend to all aspects of political and economic life.[28] Even within that category though, the understanding of religion and its tenets varies greatly, and there are significant disagreements as to how (and whether) Islamicization can be achieved.[29] On the other end of the spectrum, there are "nominal Muslims" or "sociological Muslims" who do not usually practice their religion and know little about it. Many Muslims around the world today have confined religion to the private domain of personal laws and separated it from economic and sociopolitical activities. In the words of Aziz al-Azmeh, "Islam is not a generic essence, but a nominal entity that conjoins, by means of a name, a variety of societies, cultures, histories and polities."[30]

3 "Fundamentalism" and other Labels

The dilemma of the researcher is that for purposes of description and comparison, labels are necessary, yet most of these labels belong to Western categories and perceptions. They are also frequently politically charged[31] and seldom fit Islamic realities. Labels used to describe different types of Islam – Islamism, fundamentalism, neo-fundamentalism, revivalism, modernism, traditionalism, liberalism, conservatism, Islamic totalism, establishment Islam, populist Islam, etc. – are to varying extents misleading.[32] Perhaps the most misleading of all, and the most overused, is the "fundamentalist" label. The word originated in connection with American Protestantism to signify a literal reading of the Bible. ("Intégrisme," its French counterpart was used to describe Catholic traditionalism.) In the Western mind, the word "conjures up images of mobs shouting 'death to America,' embassies in flames, assassins and hijackers threatening innocent lives, hands lopped off, and women oppressed."[33] In all too many instances, fundamentalism is used interchangeably with Islam and with radical extremism.

The "fundamentalist" label, which is supposed to have both religious and political overtones, has been applied to the governments of Libya, Saudi Arabia, Pakistan, Iran, and the Sudan, and to virtually every Islamic group and organization. In terms of both religion (the brand of Islam they follow, the role of clerics in the political leadership) and politics (the nature of political institutions, the ties with the West, the degree to which they want to export their institutions) the countries cited are sharply different. As for "fundamentalist" parties, they come in all shapes and forms. One study estimated that, as of the early 1990s, there were 175 Islamist groups (three-quarters of them "militant" or "radical") in the Middle East.[34] Another study found forty-five "Islamist" groups in Egypt alone.[35]

The confusion stems from the fact that the word can have different meanings. Ian Lustick's definition is that of an uncompromising political style characterized by (1) the motivation to achieve radical transformation of society, (2) according to directly felt transcendental imperatives, and (3) through political means.[36] Fundamentalism can also refer to those who want to return to early Islamic practices or who strive to adapt, sometimes but not always in a "radical" manner, the "fundamentals" of Islam to modern conditions, for example, by reinterpreting traditional Islamic concepts such as *shura* (consultation) and *ijmaa* (community consensus) in the light of modern realities. Fundamentalism is thus not necessarily the same as literalism, and modernism is not necessarily contradictory with a quest for authenticity.[37] A "fundamentalist" can, therefore, either be a traditionalist or a modernist, indeed, even a liberal. Leonard Binder has observed that "fundamentalist Islam and liberal Islam draw on the same religious sources, they often employ the same type of reasoning, they usually concentrate on the same authoritative pronouncements, and in some cases the differences between the two may be difficult to discern."[38]

Historical figures ranging from Ibn Taymiyya (1268–1328) to the Ayatollah Khomeini (1903–89) were at once fundamentalists and modernists. They were creatures of their respective eras who had internalized many of the "alien" beliefs of their contemporary setting yet fought against alien influences. In their desire to strip Islam of foreign influences and accretions and return to a pristine tradition, they often unwittingly innovated, if only by virtue of transposing ancient ideas, concepts, or institutions to a radically different environment. The Ayatollah Khomeini introduced and applied countless innovations to traditional Islamic doctrine.[39] He developed the concept of the rule of the pre-eminent jurist (*vilayat-e faqih*), and created a republic and a parliamentary democracy (both modern Western concepts) with a constitution based on an innovative, and sometimes controversial (including in traditional Islamic circles), application of Islamic principles.[40] By the same token, many of today's radical fundamentalists have internalized Rousseau, Fanon, or liberation theology and yet invoke authenticity.[41]

The great Islamic modernists of the "*salafiyya*" movement could also be characterized as fundamentalists.[42] Edward Mortimer noted that Rashid Rida (1865–1935) undertook the reinterpretation of Islam in the name of fidelity to the distant past (the *salaf*) and of strict adherence to the basic texts of Islam. He adopted a modernist interpretation of riba but was also an admirer of the militant Wahhabi puritans: "If "fundamentalism" means an effort to define the fundamentals of one's religion and a refusal to budge from them once defined, then Rida was a fundamentalist indeed. (But surely anybody with serious religious beliefs of any sort must be a fundamentalist in this sense?)." Mortimer concludes: "the precise meaning of (fundamentalism) when used in the context of Islam eludes me."[43] Similarly, John Esposito has noted that fundamentalism "tells us everything and yet, at the same time, nothing."[44] William Shepard summarized best the researcher's dilemma:

> On the one hand, such labels have undoubtedly often functioned as obstacles to understanding the actual people and tendencies involved, in part because they are frequently used without explicit definition, in part because they perforce lump together widely differing phenomena, and in part because they often convey an implicit bias or value judgment. In my view, this is particularly true of the label "fundamentalist." On the one hand, we cannot avoid labels if we are to talk about things, and we certainly cannot begin to make sense of an area as vast and complex as the modern Muslim world unless we can analyze its manifold phenomena into a manageable number of categories with suitable designations."[45]

Another source of confusion is that different groups of scholars have their own codes and conventions. In the French-language scholarship on contemporary Islam, a distinction is drawn between "Islamists," who have an explicitly political agenda and undertake "Islamicization from above," and "neo-fundamentalists," who are associated with "Islamicization from below" and are primarily concerned with Islamicizing society and promoting religiosity. Within that framework, "Islamists" and "neo-fundamentalists" would represent the more recent manifestations of Islam, while "fundamentalists" would refer to more traditional political movements, such as the Muslim Brothers.[46]

In this book, the word "Islamist" is used generically to encompass groups seeking to upgrade the role of Islam in political and economic life, and the word "radical" in reference to those, usually anti-Western, groups who seek to attain political power through the use of force. One cannot – despite all the reservations expressed – escape the use of the word "fundamentalist," if only in the broad sense of "seeking a return to the fundamentals of Islam." Whenever the word, and other comparable labels, is used in this book, the precise connotation will be circumscribed by context.

4 Traditionalism and Modernism

For the purpose of studying modern finance, a useful if imperfect dichotomy is that of "traditional" versus "modern" approaches, based respectively on the propensity, when it comes to financial products and concepts, to adopt a literalist, scholastic and legalistic approach, as opposed to the propensity to accept non-Islamic innovations based on an understanding of the "moral economy" of Islam (or sometimes simply to mimic conventional finance).

These are, of course, "ideal types", since things are far more complicated in practice. Toward the extremes of the spectrum would be, respectively, those who have no quarrel with interest rates and therefore see no need for Islamic banking, and those who on principle reject the very concept of banking because it does not go back to early Islam.[47] Most Islamic thinkers, however, fall outside such extremes and could be situated along the continuum. Different shadings and combinations of traditionalism–modernism produce infinite variations. Also, there is no agreement as to what constitutes "progress," and the old and the new are likely to coexist in unexpected ways. As discussions of Iran in this book show, many "modern" ideas were internalized by "traditional" clerics. Another illustration of selective adoption of innovations is, of course, the instrumental use made by Ayatollah Khomeini of modern technologies during his exile. At the time, audio-tapes of his fiery denunciations of the Shah's regime and of all things Western were duplicated and played throughout Iran.[48] Another, even more vivid example of the coexistence of the old and the new would be the use of the Internet to issue wholesale condemnations of modern finance. Thus, in a "cyberfatwa" titled "The Fallacy of the 'Islamic Bank'," Umar Ibrahim Vadillo writes: "The so-called 'Islamic bank' is a usurious institution contrary to Islam.

The "Islamic bank" is an absurd attempt to resolve, as was done in the case of Christianity, the unswerving opposition of Islam to usury for fourteen centuries. Since its origin, the 'Islamic bank' has been patronized and promoted by usurers." The author dismisses such a "usurious institution" as an invention of Western colonialism designed to incorporate the world's Muslims into the international financial and monetary system, adding: "In contrast to the modernist confusion, the position of the Shariah of Islam is clear and does not admit any controversy. From this it is clear that the Muslim must not only abandon usury but that he is also obliged to fight against usury."[49]

Still, for the purpose of analyzing the role of Islamic finance in the global economy, the traditionalist–modernist distinction is useful. Two strands can be found in the Islamic tradition. One is more "purist," and worried about foreign influences; the other is more cosmopolitan, more secular, and readier to accept the more admirable innovations of non-Muslims. Both strands, of course, claim authenticity.[50] As various sections of this book show, both have at various times and places been invoked to condone or prohibit certain economic practices. Given the decentralized nature of the religious hierarchy, especially in the Sunni world, virtually any position could be legitimated by some approving fatwa. As usually happens in religious controversies, each side will claim to represent "true" Islam, and bolster its position through the familiar game of quoting and counter-quoting. For the traditionalists, the words of the Koran and the *Hadith*, as well as classical *fiqh*, are sacred, and the interpretive leeway must be limited. Anything new or different is frowned upon. In contrast, modernists, insofar as they believe Islam to be fully compatible with progress, rationality, and science, do not feel it necessary to replicate the exact conditions of early Islam, but to find proper Islamic responses to new challenges.[51] They are likely to draw a distinction between God's law (as expressed in the Koran) and man-made law (the jurisprudence developed in the early years of Islam.[52] Their ideal is that of the time when Islamic cities were centers of learning and culture, and they praise the potential adaptability of Islam and the diversity of Islamic economic thought as "a manifestation of the inherent and natural potential of the divine Word of Allah, that is, its ability to be interpreted differently and to accommodate varying cultures."[53]

While the traditional strand may better fit Western stereotypes about Islam, the modern one is probably more common – and likely to achieve further gains in the future – in the areas of banking and finance. Consider, for example, new, complicated products such as derivatives. The traditional approach would consist in breaking them up into all their components and seeing what the schools of classical fiqh have to say about each of these components. The modern approach, relying on the basic principles and on the moral economy of Islam would probably be more useful in the global economy.

Or consider *zakat*. Traditionalists have argued that "no authority on earth has any right to alter the zakat rates."[54] They look upon the fiscal system established at the time of the Prophet and his immediate successors as a perfect and unchangeable system of redistribution that cannot be modified. Under that system, rates on certain livestock, fruits, and grain are specified with great care. For example, Caliph Umar decreed that dates and grapes were subject to zakat, while peaches and pomegranates were not. A strict application of such rules could have absurd results. And, indeed, over time, zakat became what Timur Kuran called an "ossified, dysfunctional ritual, increasingly divorced from its original purpose." Contemporary schemes to impose traditional zakat have resulted in farmers, many of whom lived under the poverty line, being subjected to the tax, while most property owners and wage earners were exempted.[55] A modernist approach would re-evaluate zakat and re-create it in the light of contemporary institutions and context, rather than simply replicate ancient practices.

5 Oversimplification and its Consequences

Assessments of Islamic banks tend to fall into one of two categories: excessive claims or outright dismissal. The authorized literature tends to paint an idyllic picture of Islamic finance and economics, a world where "no inflation, no unemployment, no exploitation and no poverty exist."[56] In contrast, many scholars have dismissed the Islamic banking phenomenon entirely. Most recent books on Islam have the requisite chapter (or paragraph, or sentence) on Islamic finance, usually containing sweeping and unsubstantiated generalizations about the phenomenon and its significance. One often encounters statements such as: "Economic Islam is nothing but 'rhetoric' dressing up either a socialist and Third World statism (Iran under Khomeini), or an economic liberalism oriented more toward speculation than toward production."[57] On the political implications of Islamic banking, one scholar sees in Islamic finance a potential tool for political transformation,[58] while another sees it as a "technocratic and non ideological" tool that is designed to adapt the financial sector to the global economy, while "leaving the social and political order unchanged."[59] On the issue of how Islamic banking is different from conventional banking, one encounters the same tendency toward soundbites and sweeping pronouncements. Islamic finance is either conventional finance by another name,[60] or a "financial system fundamentally different from the system currently dominant throughout the world."[61]

Such claims are not helpful in understanding a complex and multifaceted phenomenon. The Islamic banking system is by some measures a success, by others a failure. It is in some ways unique, but at the same time, most operations of Islamic banks tend to mirror those of conventional banks. A binary approach cannot capture the diversity and nuances of Islamic finance. On the issue of interest, one can be dismissive of all of Islamic finance because "time has a price measured by interest rates, and no economic system can ignore that."[62] The argument of Islamic scholars is more subtle. Islamic law, in fact, accepts the notion of the time-value of money or opportunity cost.[63] In the words of Fuad al-Omar and Mohammed Abdel-Haq: "The Shariah does ... recognize a difference in value due to a time element, and does not prohibit realizing the time-value of money. What is prohibited is any claim to the time-value of money as a predetermined quantity calculable at a predetermined rate."[64]

Similarly, on the issue of the role of Islam in the global economy and its compatibility with the "New World Order," a binary approach would be misleading. As this book shows, Islamic finance has thrived in the global economy just as it was denigrated culturally and politically.[65]

IV Capturing the "Big Picture" of Islamic Finance

This book does not purport to advocate a specific reading of the Shariah in regard to banking and finance. Rather it seeks to show how and why, at various times and places, interpretations and practices have differed. The purpose of the book is to dispel myths and stereotypes, and to present Islamic finance in all its complexity and diversity. Most broad questions on the subject (are Islamic banks successful? are they truly different from conventional banks? what is their political significance? etc.) can be answered only by "it depends" – surely a disappointing response for those accustomed to soundbites and definitive, if uninformed, opinions on the subject.

As already mentioned, most studies of Islamic finance are characterized by theological, financial, and legal reductionism. In addition, most have a strong case-study orientation, focusing on a single country, sometimes on a single bank, to draw broad conclusions. Such approaches give short shrift to the diversity and complexity of the phenomenon. They also prevent the capture of the "big picture" of Islamic finance – putting it in perspective and allowing a better understanding of the significance and likely evolution of the phenomenon. In order to counter the common monolithic, abstract, and dogmatic perspectives, this book will adopt, insofar as it is possible in a single volume, an empirical, historical, comparative, and interdisciplinary approach to shed light on a multi-dimensional topic.

1 An Emphasis on Context

Writings on Islamic finance tend to have an abstract, idealized character. Few facts are offered, and numbers are tortured till they confess. Little attention is paid to the actual experience of Islamic finance. Most studies assume that Islamic finance has always existed, or that it has appeared fully-formed at one point in time. In contrast this book pays close attention to the evolutionary nature of the Islamic sector, its dynamic nature, and the interaction of pioneers and scholars with their environment: historical; political; economic; social; and cultural. Modern Islamic finance did not come out of nowhere. It appeared in the 1970s as a result of specific historical circumstances; it later evolved as a result of a complex process of trial-and-error. This book recognizes the "path dependent" nature of this evolution, whereby past choices come to determine the range of available options for the future. It also underscores the diversity of Islamic finance.

Examples abound of how deeply embedded Islamic financial institutions are in their institutional and cultural framework. Saudi Arabia was founded as a "fundamentalist" Islamic state, in the sense that its society and institutions were based on a strict and "purist" interpretation of Islam. Paradoxically, this has made the issue of Islamic banking and finance politically sensitive. The reason is that by the time Islamic banks came into existence, Saudi Arabia was a wealthy state – to a large extent a rentier economy, living off its oil production and the substantial revenues from its foreign investment and interest income. Its economy was thus heavily dependent, directly and indirectly, on interest. Creating Islamic ("non-interest") banks would make existing banks un-Islamic, in a country where the rulers have repeatedly had to fend off accusations of impiety. One of the paradoxes discussed in the book is that Saudi Arabia played a central role in promoting Islamic finance, yet did not encourage the growth of Islamic institutions at home. It is only in recent years, mostly due to pressure from the customer base, that Islamic finance came to play a growing role in the national economy – making Saudi Arabia one of the late-comers in the Islamic sector.

In Egypt, the story of Islamic finance is equally complicated: in the late 1970s the government promoted Islamic banks as part its new alliance with Saudi Arabia and as a counterweight to left-wing and Nasserite opposition. Yet a disastrous experiment in the 1980s (the collapse of Islamic Money Management Companies [IMMCs])[66] transformed the context into one of suspicion, if not outright hostility to the Islamic sector. In secular, but cash-strapped, Turkey, Islamic banks (mostly from oil-rich Gulf states) were welcomed, but were not allowed to use the word Islam in their name, or to refer explicitly to their Islamic character. Initially called Special Finance Houses, they are now known as Participation Banks. In Jordan, the policy toward Islamic banks has reflected the accommodative policy toward Islamic groups in general. In Malaysia and Indonesia, Islamic finance has reflected the more syncretic brand of Islam, the developmental nature of government policies, as well as a variety of domestic considerations.[67]

In addition to discussing variations of Islamic finance based on different national contexts (Chapter 6), this book will explain the evolution of Islamic finance with reference to three distinct stages of development. The birth of Islamic finance is a product of the political-economy of the 1970s (the increase in oil prices and the new assertiveness of the South, the ascendancy of Saudi Arabia in regional politics and its control of the nascent pan-Islamic movement). Yet in later years, the international political economy changed beyond recognition. For lack of a better phrase, we will refer to the age of globalization, the widely used catch-all concept encompassing a wide range of phenomena: the end of the Cold War and the emergence of a unipolar world, deregulation and increased openness of markets, the growing role of finance, the acceleration of technological change, etc. The third stage is that of the post-September 11 era which created a new set of challenges for the Islamic sector.

2 An Historical Approach

Beyond looking at the impact of modern historical developments, it is essential to be aware of the broader historical backdrop. First, Islam developed in a commercial society: the Prophet Muhammed was a merchant, as were his four immediate "righteous" successors who shaped what came to be regarded as the ideal Islamic society; for centuries, major trade routes were under Islamic control; and merchants played a central role in spreading Islam to various parts of the world. Second, the history of Islam is one of constant adaptation and change. Indeed, "the history of Islam's early period contains valuable lessons concerning the need to devise new institutions to cope with new circumstances."[68] The law evolved,[69] as did rhetorical arguments on most issues.[70]

An historical perspective is also necessary to understand the changing nature of the relations between Islam and the West, and the consequences of the alternation of eras of growth and ascendancy with periods of stagnation and decline. At a time when Europe was still in the Dark Ages, culture and knowledge thrived in the Islamic world. Later, as the West went through its "great transformation,"[71] the Islamic world remained stagnant. By the nineteenth century, most of the Islamic world had been brought into a Western-imposed economic order for which it was ill-prepared. Between the golden age of Islam and this encounter, the world of ideas and institutions had changed dramatically. Most institutions with relevance to finance that exist today – capital markets, corporations, etc. – did not exist in the early days of Islam. Equally important, though less visible, were changes in mindsets – new understandings of cause-and-effect on matters of wealth creation; new empirical and normative perspectives on debt, risk, wealth, etc.

The modern "market system" revolutionized political, economic, social, and human relations. An intellectual and institutional revolution preceded and accompanied these changes.[72] The "modern" society was characterized by a different ethos, and different institutions and belief systems. The "science" of political economy, later "economics," based on the interaction of self-interested individuals in a world of scarcity dealt a blow to the communal bases to pre-modern or proto-economies. Although financial transactions had existed for a long time, there were, until the fourteenth century, no institutions exclusively devoted to banking. The birth of modern banking occurred in northern Italy and soon spread to all of Europe.[73] One intellectual development is especially worthy of mention in connection with modern financial instruments: new attitudes toward risk made possible by new discoveries in mathematics and probabilities in due course revolutionized finance.[74]

Along with economic and political transformations came new perspectives on debt and indebtedness. The long-held view could be summarized by the famous line from Hamlet (III:58):

> Neither a borrower, nor a lender be;
> For loan oft loses both itself and friend,
> And borrowing dulls the edge of husbandry.

Then, following the rise of capitalism, the industrial revolution, credit acquired a positive connotation. Walter Bagehot wrote in the nineteenth century: "In countries where there is little money to lend, and where that little is lent tardily and reluctantly, enterprising traders are long kept back, because they cannot at once borrow the capital, without which skill and knowledge are useless."[75]

In some respects, classical Islam anticipates modern finance. Islam innovated in its perspective on private property, its emphasis on written contracts, and more generally, its favorable view of business endeavors. Some Islamic business forms, such as the commenda partnership, have found their way in European legal codes. And when medieval Europe tried to circumvent its own restrictions on interest, it adopted certain Islamic *hiyals*.[76] Many of the advances in knowledge had an impact on future discoveries. In particular, the role played by the Arabic numbering system and other mathematical discoveries marked the crucial link between ancient Indian knowledge and discoveries of the modern age.[77] Many contributions proved critical to later advances in probabilities, statistics, and eventually risk analysis and modern financial tools. Omar Khayyam (1050–1130), best known as a poet and philosopher, was also a mathematician whose findings "formed the basis of concepts developed by the seventeenth-century French mathematician Blaise Pascal, one of the fathers of the theory of choice, chance and probability."[78] It should, therefore, not be surprising that the word hazard comes from the Arabic "*al-zahr*" (meaning dice), that the word algebra comes from "*al-jabr*" (meaning the assemblage of broken parts), or that the word algorithm (rules for computing) comes from al-Khawarizmi, a ninth-century mathematician. Also the word "cheque" comes from the Arabic *saqq*, and broker comes from *al-baraka* (via the Spanish *alboroque*, which is the gift or drink concluding a transaction).

Yet if throughout its golden age the Islamic world seemed to be on the cusp of great discoveries, the period between the fifteenth and the twentieth centuries was one of stagnation and decline. Mohammed Arkun noted that, during that period much of the Islamic world experienced a double break – with its own past (the classical era of the seventh through the fourteenth centuries), and with the West. In the field of knowledge, "a huge area was not thought about, and was thus unthinkable."[79] In Bernard Lewis' formulation, "The Renaissance, the Reformation, even the scientific revolution and the Enlightenment passed unnoticed in the Muslim world."[80] Hence, the discontinuity between the fifteenth and the twentieth centuries, and the need for Muslim revivalists to reconstruct, or reinvent, the Islamic past. In the words of Muhammed Arkoun, a "tinkered coherence was found based on arbitrarily selected fragments and traditions."[81] In terms of available financial instruments, the Islamic world was, at least until the thirteenth century, far more advanced than the West. Although banks did not exist (as noted by Udovitch, it was a world of "bankers without banks"), innovative financial instruments, many of which anticipated later conventional ones, were a part of commercial life.[82]

In Udovitch's interpretation, the reasons why banks did not develop in the

Islamic world had to do with the structure of economic life. For one thing, finance was never an autonomous activity; it was always a sub-set of commerce. And to a much greater extent than in the European economies of the late Middle Ages, financial relationships were embedded in personal and communal ties. Western banking arose as a combination of two factors: the generation of capital by means of deposits of the many, on the one hand, and money lending and the provision of credit for the few, on the other hand. In the Islamic world, there was a disconnect between deposit and credit, and financial intermediation (the conversion of deposits into loans) was therefore not necessary. Indeed, money in the Islamic world was deposited for safekeeping (al-wadiah) whereas in Europe, deposits could be used by the safekeepers.[83] In one case it was to be returned untouched, while in the other it could be used for credit purposes. In the Islamic world, credit and financing operations were conducted through transactions, usually involving profit-and-loss sharing, unrelated to safekeeping.

In addition, the need to aggregate small deposits and lend them was driven by the needs of perennially impecunious European princes. In Islam, advances of cash to the public treasury and ruling dynasties took the form of tax farming arrangements "in which individuals possessing liquid capital – presumably generated from commercial profits – advanced cash to the government in return for the right to farm the taxes of a given region for a given period."[84]

Such historical considerations are crucial to understand the evolution of Islam, and to extract the spirit or the moral economy of the religion, yet they are virtually non-existent in most writings on Islamic finance.

3 A Comparative Approach

In addition to historical references, there will be frequent comparative references (mainly in Chapters 3 and 12). Comparisons are, of course, necessary to put any phenomenon in its proper perspective, and draw useful parallels. In the case of Islam and Islamic finance, they are all the more necessary since the common myths evoked earlier need to be dispelled.

On the "uniqueness" of Islam as a "comprehensive way" of life, John Esposito wrote:

> What most forget is that all the world's religions in their origins and histories were fairly comprehensive ways of living. While the relationship of religion to politics has varied, religion is a way of life with a strong emphasis on community as well as personal life: the way of the Torah, the straight path of Islam, the middle path of the Buddha, the righteous way (dharma) of Hinduism. They provide guidance for hygiene, diet, the managing of wealth, stages of life (birth, marriage, death), and ritual and worship.[85]

On matters of economics and finance, the Bible has over 2,000 references to debt, saving, and charitable giving.[86] The Talmud provides detailed injunctions on all aspects of business behavior. The Canon law of the Christian Church discusses usury in excruciating detail. The Christian Church went through its own contortions – as discussed in conjunction with *contractum trinius*.[87] Nor are secular financial institutions necessarily divorced from religious considerations. In late nineteenth-century Germany, Frederic Raiffesen, a Protestant, and in early twentieth-century Canada, Alphonse Desjardins, a Catholic, created mutual savings societies out of a moral-religious impulse (neither of them was a banker) to save poor farmers from the clutches of money-lenders.[88] Today, a substantial amount of social investing is done by religious groups,[89] and on most issues of finance, ethical concerns (which are themselves heavily colored by religion) are ever-present. By the same token, the religious revivalism movement is not exclusive to Islam, though it is seldom discussed from a comparative perspective.[90]

4 An Interdisciplinary Approach

In order to capture the many facets of Islamic finance, an interdisciplinary approach is necessary. Most of the issues evoked can be looked at from different angles. Looked at from a purely economic angle, the riba debate may not seem like a big deal given that something equivalent to interest is likely to be devised, albeit under a different name. Yet this very issue, however, is quite consequential if considered from a marketing or from a religious standpoint. The economist may conclude that "there is no such thing as Islamic finance", while for a banking executive – considering that "product differentiation" is essential to strategy – devising and selling an "Islamic product" will be significantly different from devising and selling a "conventional product." Similarly, from a religious standpoint – that of a devout customer or that of religious authorities – differences that are invisible to the secular eye could be far from inconsequential. Five dimensions of the Islamic banking phenomenon are singled out for discussion in the last chapters of the book: management; economics; regulation; politics; and religion.

Notes

1. For more specific definitions, see Chapter 3.
2. For example, prayer rooms, business hours that do not conflict with prayer and other religious obligations.
3. A complicating factor in classification is that a distinction must be drawn between "Islamic financial institutions", whose entire product line is Islamic, and "Islamic products," increasingly offered by conventional institutions in addition to their conventional products.
4. See Chapter 7.
5. See Robert H. Nelson, *Economics as Religion: from Samuelson to Chicago and Beyond* (University Park, PA: Pennsylvania State University Press, 2001).
6. For details, see Chapter 7.
7. MESA Bulletin 29 (July 1995).
8. Nicholas Dylan Ray, *Arab Islamic Banking and the Renewal of Islamic Law* (London: Graham and Trotman, 1995), p. 3.
9. Frank E. Vogel and Samuel L. Hayes, III, *Islamic Law and Finance: Religion, Risk and Return* (The Hague: Kluwer Law International, 1998), p. 45.

10. Ray, *Arab Islamic Banking*, p. 3.
11. Karen Pfeifer, "Is there an Islamic Economics?," in Joel Beinin and Joe Stark (eds.), *Political Islam: Essays from Middle East Report* (Berkeley, CA: University of California Press, 1997), p. 161–2.
12. Alan Richards and John Waterbury, *A Political Economy of the Middle East* (Boulder, CO: Westview Press, 1996), p. 351.
13. See, for example, Hugh Roberts, "Doctrinaire Economics and Political Opportunism in the Strategy of Algerian Islamism," in John Ruedy (ed.), *Islamism and Secularism in North Africa* (New York: St. Martin's Press, 1994), p. 60.
14. Francis Fukuyama, *The End of History and the Last Man* (New York: Avon Books, 1993), pp. 46 and 217.
15. Samuel P. Huntington, *The Clash of Civilizations and the Remaking of World Order* (New York: Simon and Schuster, 1996), pp. 70 and 72.
16. Compare, for example, with Leonard Binder, *Islamic Liberalism: A Critique of Development Ideologies* (Chicago, IL: University of Chicago Press, 1988), and Olivier Carré, *L'Islam Laïque ou le retour à la Grande Tradition* (Paris: Armand Colin, 1993).
17. John L. Esposito, *The Islamic Threat: Myth or Reality?* (Oxford: Oxford University Press, 1992), p. 205.
18. Aziz al-Azmeh, *Islam and Modernities* (London: Verso, 1993), p. 140.
19. Sami Zubeida, "Is Iran an Islamic State?," in Beinin and Stork (eds.), *Political Islam*, p. 103.
20. See Chapters 2 and 12.
21. Timur Kuran, "The Economic System in Contemporary Islamic Thought: Interpretation and Assessment," *International Journal of Middle Eastern Studies*, 18 (1986), p. 140.
22. William E. Shepherd, "Muhammad Sa'id al-'Ashmawi and the Application of the Shari'a in Egypt," *International Journal of Middle Eastern Studies*, 28 (February 1996), pp. 39–58.
23. Esposito, *The Islamic Threat*, p. 202. See also Yahya Sadowski, "'Just' a Religion: For the Tablighi Jama'at, Islam is not Totalitarian," *Brookings Review*, Summer 1996, vol. 14, No. 3.
24. Bernard Botiveau and Jocelyne Cesari, *Géopolitique des islams* (Paris: Economica, 1997), pp. 40–1.
25. Yvonne Yazbeck Haddad (ed.), *The Muslims of America* (Oxford: Oxford University Press, 1993).
26. Rémy Leveau, "Maghrebi Immigration to Europe: Double Insertion of Double Exclusion?," in Charles E. Butterworth and I. William Zartman (eds.), *Political Islam, The Annals of the American Academy of Political and Social Science*, November 1992, pp. 170–80.
27. Botiveau and Cesari, *Géopolitique des islams*, pp. 84–90.
28. Carré, *L'Islam laïque ou le retour à la Grande Tradition*, p. 58.
29. See Chapter 12.
30. Aziz al-Azmeh, *Islams and Modernities* (London: Verso, 1993).
31. Some like "Islamo-fascism" are deliberately used to provoke.
32. William E. Shepard, "Islam and Ideology: Towards a Typology," *International Journal of Middle Eastern Studies*, 19 (1987), pp. 307–36.
33. Esposito, *The Islamic Threat*, p. 77.
34. R. Hrair Dekmejian, *Islam in Revolution* (New York: Syracuse University Press, 1995), p. 57.
35. Sana Abed-Kotob, "The Accommodationists Speak: Goals and Strategies of the Muslim Brotherhood of Egypt," *International Journal of Middle East Studies*, 27 August 1995, p. 322.
36. Ian S. Lustick, *For the Land and the Lord: Jewish Fundamentalism in Israel* (New York: Council on Foreign Relations, 1988), pp. 4–6.
37. Joel Beinin and Joe Stork, "On the Modernity, Historical Specificity, and International Context of Political Islam," in Joel Beinin and Joe Stork (eds.), *Political Islam*, p. 3.

38. Binder, *Islamic Liberalism*, p. 357.
39. Chibli Mallat, *The Renewal of Islamic Law: Muhammad Baqer as-Sadr, Najaf and the Shi'i International* (Cambridge: Cambridge University Press, 1993).
40. Sami Zubeida, Islam, *The People and the State: Essays on Political Ideas and Movements in the Middle East* (London: Routledge, 1989), p. ix.
41. Esposito, *The Islamic Threat*, p. 107. See also Gudrun Kramer, "Islamist Notions of Democracy," in Beinin and Stork (eds.), *Political Islam*, p. 76.
42. Malcolm Kerr, *Islamic Reform: the Political and Legal Theories of Muhammad 'Abduh and Rashid Rida* (Berkeley, CA: University of California Press, 1966).
43. Edward Mortimer, *Faith and Power: The Politics of Islam* (New York: Random House, 1982), p. 249.
44. Esposito, *The Islamic Threat*, p. 7.
45. William E. Shepard, "Islam and Ideology: Towards a Typology," *International Journal of Middle Eastern Studies*, 19 (1987), p. 307.
46. See, for example, Carré, *L'Islam laïque ou le retour à la Grande Tradition*; Gilles Kepel, *La revanche de Dieu: Chrétiens, juifs et musulmans à la reconquête du monde* (Paris: Editions du Seuil, 1991) or Olivier Roy, *L'échec de l'Islam politique* (Paris: Editions du Seuil, 1992).
47. Ray, *Arab Islamic Banking*, p. 8.
48. James A. Bill, *The Eagle and the Lion: The Tragedy of American Iranian Relations* (New Haven, CT: Yale University Press, 1989).
49. See http://www.geocities.com/Athens/Delphi/6588/bfallacy.html.
50. Fazlur Rahman, *Islam and Modernity* (Chicago, IL: University of Chicago Press, 1984).
51. Esposito, *The Islamic Threat*, p. 165.
52. Said al-Ashmawi, *L'Islamisme contre l'Islam* (Paris: La Découverte, 1990).
53. Mohamed Aslam Haneef, *Contemporary Islamic Economic Thought: A Selected Comparative Analysis* (Selangor, Malaysia: Ikraq, 1995), p. 140.
54. Timur Kuran, "The Economic System in Contemporary Islamic Thought: Interpretation and Assessment," *International Journal of Middle Eastern Studies*, 18 (1986), p. 148.
55. Kuran, "The Economic System in Contemporary Islamic Thought", p. 145.
56. Ahmed Abdel Aziz El-Nagar, *One Hundred Questions & One Hundred Answers Concerning Islamic Banks* (Cairo: International Association of Islamic Banks, 1980), p. 8.
57. Roy, *L'échec de l'Islam politique*, p. 10.
58. Clement M. Henry, *The Mediterranean Debt Crescent: Money and Power in Algeria, Egypt, Morocco, Tunisia and Turkey* (Tampa, FL: University Press of Florida, 1996), p. 22.
59. Roy, *L'échec de l'Islam politique*, p. 176.
60. Roy, *L'échec de l'Islam politique*, p. 10.
61. Ray, *Arab Islamic Banking*, p. 5.
62. Ibrahim Warde, "Perceptions of Islamic Banks among European and American Bankers," San Francisco: IBPC Working Papers, 1997.
63. Vogel and Hayes, *Islamic Law and Finance*, p. 2.
64. Fuad al-Omar and Mohammed Abdel-Haq, *Islamic Banking: Theory, Practice and Challenges* (London: Zed Books, 1996), p. 25.
65. See Chapter 11.
66. See Chapter 4.
67. Khoo Boo Teik, *Paradoxes of Mahathirism: An Intellectual Biography of Mahathir Mohammed* (Oxford: Oxford University Press, 1995).
68. Kuran, "The Economic System in Contemporary Islamic Thought," p. 149.
69. Vogel and Hayes, *Islamic Law and Finance*, p. 38.
70. Charles E. Butterworth, "Political Islam: The Origins," in Charles E. Butterworth and I. William Zartman (eds.), *Political Islam*, The Annals of the American Academy of Political and Social Science, November 1992, p. 28.
71. Karl Polanyi, *The Great Transformation: The Political and Economic Origins of Our Time* (Boston, MA: Beacon Press, 1957).

72. Albert Hirschman, *The Passions and the Interests: Political Arguments for Capitalism Before Its Triumph* (New Haven, CT: Princeton University Press, 1977).
73. Center of Medieval and Renaissance Studies, University of California, Los Angeles, *The Dawn of Modern Banking* (New Haven, CT: Yale University Press, 1979).
74. Peter L. Bernstein, *Against the Gods: The Remarkable Story of Risk* (New York: Wiley, 1996), p. 2.
75. Walter Bagehot, *Lombard Street: A Description of the Money Market* (Homewood, IL: Richard D. Irvin, 1962), p. 7.
76. Blaise Pascal, *Les Provinciales ou Les Lettres écrites par Louis de Montalte à un provincial de ses amis et aux RR. PP. Jésuites sur le sujet de la morale et de la politique de ces Pères* (Paris: Gallimard Folio, 1987), p. 131.
77. Bernstein, *Against the Gods*, pp. 32–3.
78. Bernstein, *Against the Gods*, p. 34.
79. Mohammed Arkoun, "Islam et modernité," in Alain Gresh (ed.), *Un péril islamiste?* (Brussels: Editions Complexe, 1994), pp. 205–6.
80. Bernard Lewis, *Islam and the West* (Oxford: Oxford University Press, 1993), p. 183.
81. Arkoun, "Islam et modernité", p. 208.
82. Yves Thoraval, *Dictionnaire de civilisation musulmane* (Paris: Larousse, 1995), p. 80.
83. Abraham L. Udovitch, "Bankers without Banks: Commerce, Banking, and Society in the Islamic World of the Middle Ages," *The Dawn of Modern Banking*, p. 259.
84. Udovitch, "Bankers without Banks," p. 260.
85. Esposito, *The Islamic Threat*, p. 198.
86. US News and World Report, April 27, 1998.
87. See Chapter 3.
88. Bernard Taillefer, *Guide de la Banque pour tous: Innovations africaines* (Paris: Karthala, 1996), p. 19.
89. See Chapter 7.
90. Among the exceptions are *The Fundamentalism Project*, a multi-volume book series edited by Martin E. Marty and R. Scott Appleby and published by the University of Chicago Press, and a few books such as Kepel, *La revanche de Dieu*.

2

ISLAM, ECONOMICS AND FINANCE

Any successful belief system, whether religious or secular, has seemingly contra-dictory characteristics: it is malleable enough to adapt to a variety of geographical settings and to survive the test of time, but it must also be able to maintain its specificity, or it would disappear or become fused with competing belief systems; it is idealistic, sometimes even utopian, yet capable of adjusting to human imper-fection and making the kind of compromises that are endemic to political and economic life. With this in mind we can better understand how a system rooted in the Middle Ages could survive, and thrive, in the global economy.

Following a broad overview of the parallel evolution of religion and history, this chapter explores the mechanisms by which Islam adapted to changing circumstances, and explains how Islam came to accommodate itself with modern economics and finance.

I Historical and Religious Background

The tenets of the Islamic religion can be conceived as a pyramid. At the top stands the Koran, considered by Muslims to be God's word as conveyed to the Prophet Mohammed. Below it are the *Hadith* and the *Sunna*. Often used interchangeably: the first, commonly translated as the Traditions of the Prophet, actually refers to his words and deeds, as reported by a chain of transmission going all the way back to the Prophet's companions; the second refers to the righteous path established by those words and deeds. In other words, the Hadith, in the form of a large and ill-defined number of short texts, relates stories about and sayings (specific pronouncements, deeds, or approvals of other people's actions) of the Prophet, whereas the Sunna consists of the practices and rulings deduced from such narratives.

As for issues and questions not addressed by those primary sources, the proper Islamic view can be obtained through *ijmaa* and *qiyas*. Ijmaa means consensus, and is based on the notion that the communal mind of Muslim scholars of a particular age provides an assurance of freedom from error. Qiyas refers to reasoning by analogy or by logical inference based on primary sources. Jurists, through devout and careful reflection and effort (*ijtihad*) can derive appropriate rulings, by ascertaining how the Prophet and his four immediate successors – the "right-guided caliphs" – would have acted, or what the accumulated wisdom of the community would prescribe. The Shariah, literally the path to water, is the divine law derived from all these sources. Though usually translated as Islamic law, the Shariah is in the eyes of certain scholars a broader term not designating law per se, but "designating good order, much like nomos."[1]

Indeed, in various matters, including economic ones, there are sharp disagreements as to what the Shariah dictates. The further down the pyramid, the broader the possible interpretations. The Koran, a short, specific text, is considered divine and eternal since it is the revealed word of God. The Hadith – a collection of narratives which were not set down in writing until two or three centuries later – provide a first area of controversy. A great number of Hadiths were deemed to be apocryphal, typically fabricated to support a particular political faction or opinion, and a long process of authentication did not dispel all doubts about the veracity of certain texts. Specific narrative are often characterized as strong or weak, depending on the nature of the prevailing consensus about their truthfulness.

Interpretations can still differ quite significantly, as different factions or traditions authenticate different Hadiths. In addition, Islamic groups over the ages have disagreed on the relative importance of the various tenets of the religion, some having called, for example, for reliance on the Koran only and disregarding the "man-made" elements of religion that developed over time.[2]

Such disagreements explain why different schools of jurisprudence (fiqh) developed over the years, each contributing different interpretations of the Shariah. By the tenth century, four main schools had emerged within the orthodox Sunni tradition (the Shia had their own, separate schools): Hanafi, Shafii, Maliki, and Hanbali. Every Sunni is in theory a follower of one of these schools. In classical Muslim society, four qadis (judges) in each major city would apply one of these four traditions in order to fill in areas of the law that were left undiscussed in the Koran and Sunna. Over the years, however, each school found particular favor in certain localities, hence, the geographical concentration of adherents that can be found nowadays. Hanbalis are primarily concentrated in Saudi Arabia; Malikis predominate in north and west Africa; Shafiis are a majority in Indonesia, Malaysia, east Africa, Yemen, and parts of Egypt; while the most widespread of the schools is the Hanafi, which was once the official school of the Ottoman empire, and is thus influential in Turkey as well as Egypt, Syria, Lebanon, Jordan, and Iraq. It is also adhered to in much of the Indian subcontinent.

The legal methodologies of these schools differ, combining different proportions of textual authority and analogical reasoning: the Hanbalis tend to adhere to strict interpretations of religious texts, while the Malikis and Hanafis allow wider discretion in the interpretations of such texts. On a specific issue, different schools may be clear, ambiguous, or silent; they also may be lenient or strict. In addition, individual countries differ in their eclecticism: in Algeria or Morocco, for example, only Maliki interpretations of the Shariah are allowed in court, while in Egypt interpretations based on any of the four schools are admissible.[3]

A combination of external influences and idiosyncratic evolution has led to significant diversity throughout the Islamic world, which in turn translated into growing doctrinal differences. All this, of course, runs counter to common generalizations. Thus, though the language of Islam emphasizes a unified umma (Islamic nation), the reality is far more complicated. A truly unified and coherent community existed only in the early years of Islam. The first schism occurred in 657, involving the Kharijites ("the goers-out"). An even more significant split occurred in 661, when followers of Ali refused to acknowledge the authority of Muawiyah (the founder of the Umeyyad dynasty) and his successors thus creating the Shia–Sunni divide. By the tenth century, with the appearance of rival caliphates in Egypt and in Spain, the notion of a unified umma became even more of a fiction.[4] In later centuries, such fragmentation increased significantly.

It is thus a mistake, common perceptions notwithstanding, to see Islam as a monolith. It follows that most facile generalizations deserve to be nuanced. For example, the extent to which Islam fuses mosque and state (din wa dawla) depends upon the period or the region under consideration. Under the Prophet Mohammed (622–32) as well as the first four (rashidun or "rightly-guided") caliphs (632–61) – Abu Bakr, Umar, Uthman, and Ali – temporal and spiritual power were inextricably linked. This period, which also coincided with remarkable territorial expansion, embodies the ideal of Islamic rule and social organization, a model that successive generations have striven to emulate.

However, soon afterwards, with the advent of the Umeyyad dynasty (661–750), some measure of separation of temporal and spiritual functions appeared. According to historian Philip Hitti, Muawiyah, by introducing "innovations" opposed by religious conservatives, by surrounding himself with non-Muslims, and by creating a hereditary dynasty, "secularized Islam and transformed the theocratic caliphate into a temporal sovereignty."[5] Nor is the impact of foreign influences on Islamic doctrines and practices sufficiently understood. Again, in the Umeyyad era, as explained by Albert Hourani, "The ruler, his governors and special deputies, the qadis, dispensed justice and decided disputes, taking into account the existing customs and laws of the various regions."[6] Further expansion and absorption of foreign influences occurred in the Abbassid era (750–1258). Although it was accompanied by bureaucratization, centralization, and attempts to reassert religious legitimacy, the cosmopolitan nature of the Abbassid empire further diluted the original Arab influence. In sum:

> Just as the Shariah had grown up by a slow and complicated process of interaction between the norms contained in the Koran and Hadith and the local customs and laws of the communities brought under the rule of Islam, so there was a continuing process of mutual adjustment between the Shariah, once it took its definitive form, and the practices of Muslim societies.[7]

The "definitive form" occurred in theory with the "closing of the gates of ijtihad." Yet when and why the gates were closed – and, most importantly, whether those gates were really ever closed – is still being debated.[8] One common explanation for the insistence that the Shariah had taken its final form is that with the increasing dilution of the original Arab-Islamic norms that occurred with the gradual weakening of the Abbassid empire, culminating with the Mongol invasion of Baghdad in 1258, Muslim jurisprudents, fearing that alien customs and norms would subvert the Islamic legal system, arrived at a consensus: from then on, no new laws would be produced.[9] With the formal collapse of the Abbassid empire, the centers of power moved further away from the Arab core toward the Turkic world, and the Islamic world grew ever more diverse and fragmented.

Though the rhetoric of the unity of spiritual and temporal power remained, secularist trends have been on the rise since the tenth century. In the words of Edward Mortimer:

> In a sense …, all genuine political authority in the mainstream Muslim tradition was secular after the loss of effective power by the Abbassids in the tenth century AD. Virtue and justice were no longer regarded as indispensable qualifications of a ruler. Full enforcement of the Shari'a came to be seen as an ideal rather than a necessity. Political power was no longer the instrument through which the ideal community could be realized, but merely a prosaic necessity for the maintenance of order and security, and thus of the minimum conditions in which the faith could be practiced and the Muslim community survive.[10]

Similarly, Olivier Carré has argued that after the tenth century, the "great tradition" and the "real orthodoxy" of Islam separated politics and religion. Divine law was limited to improving a government's policies by prescribing certain social correctives.[11]

Throughout its golden age (roughly the seventh to the tenth century in the Middle East, and the eleventh to the fourteenth century in North Africa and Spain), the Islamic world did not fit the image of a narrow-minded theocracy. Great libraries and translation centers were established where the great works of philosophy, literature, medicine, and science from East and West were collected and translated. Such knowledge was improved upon and formed a necessary link to later advances in the West. Bernard Lewis has noted that in that golden age Europe looked to the Islamic world "as central Africa looked to Victorian England."[12]

So where does the persistent image of an Islam incapable of separating mosque and state – indeed, incapable of dealing with modernity and change – come from? The answer lies in the parallel evolutions (and occasional clashes) of Islam and the West starting with the end of the Islamic golden age. In the later Middle Ages, while Islamic culture and civilization still thrived elsewhere (in North Africa and Spain, for example), the birthplaces of Islam and of the early Islamic empires had entered a long period of stagnation. In later centuries, with a few exceptions, the Islamic world stagnated, while European powers forged ahead. A well-known chain of historical events – the Renaissance, the Reformation, the Enlightenment, the Industrial Revolution, imperialism – created an unprecedented economic, political, cultural, and intellectual gap between the Islamic world and the West. Characteristically, the Ottoman Empire, the last great Islamic empire, once feared by the Christian West, was considered, for at least its last 200 years, "the sick man of Europe," an ever-weakening entity susceptible to all forms of encroachments by foreign powers.

Of particular interest to us are the political, economic, and cultural impacts of the Western ascendancy on the Islamic world, throughout the colonial – or "modern" – era, generally dated from Napoleon's 1798 Egyptian campaign. Until then, much of the Islamic world had lived in relative isolation and kept to its traditional ways. While certain Islamic societies had proven to be quite dynamic, others had remained stagnant for generations. In those communities, there was a deep-seated suspicion of innovation (*bidaa*). Yet in a changing world, the habit of condemning absolutely every practice that did not go back to the time of the Prophet could not be sustained. Innovations would be analyzed on the basis of their intrinsic merits. In the confrontation with a strong and assertive Europe bent on exporting its ideas and institutions, certain scholars were more inclined than others to adopt alien ideas and customs. Hence, the disagreements between those who favored *taqlid* (imitation) and those who advocated *islah* (reform) or *tajdid* (renewal).[13]

By the late nineteenth century, most countries followed a path of Westernization and secularization that led them to adopt, under foreign tutelage, Western models in politics, economics, law, and education. Muslims were divided. While some did not see a necessary contradiction between Islam and Westernization, a number of political and religious movements emerged throughout the Islamic world, calling for a return to Islamic values and traditions. There was no clear consensus, insofar as some wanted a return to the past, while others called for an update of Islamic doctrine. Islamic modernists shared with traditionalist Islamic groups the belief that the ills of society were caused by the betrayal of Islamic ideals. While they shared with secularists the embrace of reason, science, and progress, what set Islamic modernists apart was their belief that political liberalization and intellectual reawakening could be, indeed had to be, rooted in a return to Islam. The Wahhabis of Saudi Arabia, the Mahdists of the Sudan, the Sanussis of Libya, and other "fundamentalist" movements that emerged in the eighteenth and nineteenth centuries drew their rhetoric and their ideals from the early Islamic age. The "new" ideology, seeking to blur the lines between religion and politics, has been characterized by Olivier Carré as a "deviant orthodoxy."[14]

Another characteristic of many such fundamentalist movements was their anti-Western character, which worked in perfect symbiosis with the anti-Islamic bias of certain Westerners, justifying and reinforcing stereotypes. A whole tradition of Orientalist writers posited axioms that later came to shape common perceptions of Islam.[15] Writer Ernest Renan proclaimed the Muslim to be "incapable of learning anything or of opening himself to a new idea."[16] As for Lord Cromer, who ruled Egypt in the late nineteenth century, he argued that "Islam's gradual decay cannot be arrested by any modern palliatives however skillfully they are applied."[17]

There were, nonetheless, from the nineteenth century, significant attempts to modernize Islamic doctrine. Perhaps the most influential movement was the Salafiyya, founded in Egypt in 1883 by the pan-Islamic forerunner, Jamal al-Din al-Afghani (1839–97), a Persian whose influence was felt throughout the Islamic world. Through their journal, *al-Manar*, al-Afghani and his disciples, the Egyptian, Muhammad Abduh (1849–1905) and the Syrian, Rashid Rida (1865–1935), sought to bring about political, legal, and intellectual reform.[18] The movement encapsulated the complexity of the phenomenon. Edward Mortimer saw in al-Afghani "an example of three types of Muslim response to the West: the defensive call to arms, the eager attempt to learn the secret of Western strength, and the internalization of Western secular modes of thought."[19] In sum, modernity – undertaking a radical reinterpretation of Islam to suit modern conditions – is not easy to dissociate from a quest for authenticity. And fundamentalism – if defined as the effort to return to the fundamentals of the religion – is not necessarily the same as literalism.

Among social scientists, there is a venerable tradition, going back at least to Max Weber, that looks at Islam as a closed system, whose essence is inhospitable to development and modernity. Yahya Sadowski observed:

> When the consensus of social scientists held that democracy and development depended upon the actions of strong, assertive social groups, Orientalists held that such associations were absent in Islam. When the consensus evolved and social scientists thought a quiescent, undemanding society was essential to progress, the neo-Orientalists portrayed Islam as beaming with pushy, anarchic solidarities. Middle Eastern Muslims, it seems, were doomed to be eternally out of step with intellectual fashion.[20]

Such perspectives came back with a vengeance following the September 11, 2001 terrorist attacks when a climate of Islamophobia revived negative stereotypes about Islam.[21]

II Islamic Economics

Commerce is central to the Islamic tradition. The Prophet Mohammed was himself a merchant. Born in the Banu (sons of) Hashim clan of the Quraysh tribe, Mecca's leading traders, he was orphaned in childhood and raised by his uncle, Abu Talib, who taught him the caravan trade. In his twenties, he became the commercial agent of a rich widow whom he later married. It should, therefore, come as no surprise that in the early Islamic literature, merchants were glorified, or that commercial profit is sometimes referred to as "God's bounty." Whereas it took Christianity centuries before it stopped regarding business as a degrading occupation,[22] Islam from its inception explicitly legitimized private property, business enterprise, and profit. As long as the merchant fulfills his religious duties, he is rewarded spiritually as well as materially (Koran 2:198, 73:20).[23] Unlike the Jewish and the Christian Sabbaths, Friday is not a full day of rest: before and after the religious gathering, Muslims are expected to carry on their worldly activities (Koran 62:9–10).[24] Another illustration of the close connection between commerce and religion is that the Islamic religion was spread in many parts of the world (such as Africa and the Far East) by proselytizing merchants.

In Prophet Mohammed's day, Mecca, then western Arabia's wealthiest city, depended heavily on trade and revenues from pilgrims. The continuous spread of Islam soon brought the region's lucrative trade routes, previously controlled by Byzantium and Sassanid Persia, under Islamic control. Muawiyah and his Umayyad successors expanded the empire from their new capital, Damascus, into Europe and to the borders of India and China, inaugurating a new era of prosperity. The Abbassid caliphate, based in Baghdad, established links between the Mediterranean basin and the Indian Ocean, creating a single trading system that brought about significant changes in agriculture and crafts, and the emergence of great cities.[25]

As the economy became increasingly complex, a number of previously unknown questions – about administering an empire, regulating trade, taxation, etc. – had to be addressed. Institutional innovation occurred, for example, with the creation of *hisbah*, an office in charge of supervising markets, providing municipal services, and settling petty disputes.[26]

The Islamic literature on such subjects as contract law grew to account for every possible eventuality. As for more theoretical issues dealing with economics, they were largely ignored by the fuqaha of the classical age.[27] There were however a few thinkers who dealt with economic issues, the most famous of whom is Ibn Khaldun (1332–1406). Best known for his pioneering work in history and sociology, he also wrote about supply and demand, capital formation, trade cycles, and the theory of value. Still, Ibn Khaldun, usually considered to be the greatest economist of Islam, was writing in the period immediately preceding the great transformation of the world economy, on the eve of the era of major discoveries, which was to be followed by the rise of capitalism and the Industrial Revolution. More importantly for our purpose, banks and other modern-style financial institutions had not yet come into existence. When they did, Islamic scholars had to struggle to reconcile a scholarly and legal tradition rooted in the medieval age with the exigencies of the modern world.

In the colonial era, most constitutions and legal codes invoked the Shariah, although in practice references to Islam were limited (for example, stating that the state religion would be Islam, that the head of state would be a Muslim, and that the Shariah would be a source of law). Most areas of the law (with certain exceptions, such as family law) were inspired directly or indirectly by Western models. For example, Egypt under Mohammed Ali was directly inspired by the French Napoleonic Code. (By later using Egypt as a model, other Islamic countries were indirectly influenced by French ideas.) In addition, with the importation of Western models, the role of the *ulema* (learned men and scholars) was reduced, and that of elected representatives enhanced. Thus, even where the Shariah may have been the "the principal source of all legislation," elected representatives had wide discretion to use other sources of legislation as well.[28]

As the colonial era came to an end, newly independent states came to reassess their economic policies. The 1950s and 1960s saw the advent of economic nationalism, with its emphasis on the role of the state as an engine of growth and development.[29] Neither this statism nor the later liberalization would be significantly challenged on strictly religious grounds. Indeed, in economics as in politics, Islam does not provide an explicit blueprint. Two strands of Islam could be used to justify one or the other set of policies. Liberals played up Islam's accent on property rights and the glorification of profit to advocate *laissez-faire*. Socialists emphasized the Koran's focus on justice (*adl*) and compassion toward the needy to justify state intervention as well as redistributive policies.[30]

But although the process of economic decision making was significantly secularized, references to Islam were seldom absent. Thus, Nasserite Egypt founded the Islamic Congress (in conjunction with Saudi Arabia and Pakistan)[31] and created the Supreme Council of Islamic Affairs which published *Minbar al-Islam* (The Pulpit of Islam). And in pursuing controversial policies on matters such as nationalization, land reform, or family planning, Islamic symbols and references were occasionally used, and the government was careful to obtain approving *fatwas* (legal opinions).[32]

However, since Ibn Khaldun the Islamic world had not really produced any prominent economist.[33] The ideological debates of the modern era had been framed according to Western norms. Muslims who studied Western-style economics (and related fields) tried to transpose that knowledge to the Islamic world. With decolonization and the nascent trend toward a return to Islam, religious scholars attempted to rethink economics and the social sciences in the light of their religious training, with the goal of creating an "authentic" or at least indigenous brand of economics.[34] Rather than simply asserting claims based on divine revelations, and which human beings cannot refute, since the 1970s Islamic economists have gone to great lengths to buttress their case with logic, scientific theory, and empirical evidence.[35] Rodney Wilson observed in 1997 that "there has been more written on Islamic economics in the last two decades than in the previous fourteen hundred years."[36] Yet in the words of Chibli Mallat: "Many of the works tend to dabble in generalities and to err in a lack of rigor which prevents the emergence of a serious and systematic literature. The recent 'fad' of 'Islamic economics' has impressed the production with an urgency that has kept the literature produced so far to a superficial and repetitive standard."[37] It is usually agreed that the most important work is that of Mohammed Baqer as-Sadr, whose book *Iktissaduna* ("our economy") is a far-reaching critique of both capitalism and Marxism, and an attempt to develop an Islamic approach to economics.

For Baqer as-Sadr, "Islamic economics is not a science (*ilm*)," but simply a doctrine (*madhab*). In other words, it is not designed to explain why economic events occur, but to show the path to follow. It is based principally on the idea of justice, which is by essence a matter of "ethical appreciation." It is subordinated to a totality ultimately determined by religion. The three basic principles of the Islamic system are "multifold property," "limited economic freedom," and "social justice." As for dealing with scarcity and wealth creation, Baqer as-Sadr focuses on distribution, "before and after production." A distribution system must be established based on the moral principle of "general insurance and social solidarity," and taking into account labor, need, and Islam's original view of property.[38] Although critical of capitalist and socialist ideologies, it incorporated elements of both, showing that Islam was not incompatible with modern economics.

With the new-found wealth of oil-producing countries and the rise of Islamic militancy, the need to promote further thinking on economic matters gained new urgency. The proliferation of research institutes and fiqh academies, and the encouragement of an ijtihad designed to update Islamic beliefs resulted in countless attempts at defining a system that would be at once internally consistent, faithful to Islamic principles, and adapted to the contemporary world. The quest for ijmaa was, however, elusive. Unable to speak with a single voice, Islamic scholars have often settled for majority-based decisions.

In 1976, the First Islamic Conference on Islamic Economics was held in Mecca. For the first time in Islamic history, a high-level conference dealt exclusively with economic matters. Concrete steps were taken to survey the field and promote Islamic economics as an academic discipline. In 1979 King Abdul Aziz University established the International Center for Research in Islamic Economics (ICRIE) to conduct and support theoretical and applied research in various sub-fields.[39] The number of research institutes increased throughout the 1980s and 1990s, and more universities expanded their teaching of Islamic economics.[40] Starting with Pakistan in the late 1970s, a growing number of countries sought to Islamicize their economic systems. Islam would typically be presented as offering a "third way" between capitalism and socialism that would not only be different, but also superior to, and no less efficient than, the other two. In a few instances – as in Libya where Moammar Qaddhafi's "Green Book" presented an idiosyncratic brand of radical socialism – the system proposed was closer to the socialist end of the continuum.[41] But as later sections will show, since the late 1980s, the "third way" has reflected the global neo-liberal trend, and was in most Islamic countries far closer to the capitalist end of the continuum.

III Adapting to Changing Circumstances

As already mentioned, no belief system that has flourished over a long period of time and in a variety of places could have done so without some measure of adaptability. Even a scholar with the unimpeachable Islamic credentials of Mohammed Baqer es-Sadr noted that the texts of the Koran and the Sunna "do not manifest – generally – their legal or conceptual content in a clear precise manner."[42] In drawing up the economic rules, more effort – more ijtihad – is needed. And if we consider the institutions created by the Iranian revolution, the most significant Islamic revolution in modern times, a substantial amount of innovation has taken place.

It should be noted at the outset that Islamic commandments are not as unbending as they would superficially appear. Traditional Islamic injunctions are not framed as simple dichotomies, but along a continuum, thus allowing significant flexibility and pragmatism. In the early Islamic community, an action (either for the community as a whole, or for every single member of it) could be regarded as obligatory (*wajib*), meritorious (*mustahabb*), morally neutral (*mubah*), reprehensible (*makruh*), or forbidden (*haram*). Also, most injunctions contain dispensations and exceptions. On the subject of fasting during Ramadan, the sick and travelers could postpone their fasting, and those for whom it would cause hardship could dispense with fasting, compensating instead with a good deed, such as feeding a poor person (Koran 2:184–5).[43]

As Islam expanded, it was brought into contact with different cultures and this made it necessary for Islamic jurisprudence to produce legislation on problems for which there were no clear legal precedents to follow. The principles of Islamic jurisprudence (*usul el fiqh*) provide for a set of elaborate rules with which to interpret the Shariah. But the existence of such complex rules did not preclude adaptive mechanisms. The principle of *talfiq* (patching) would, for example, authorize judges to choose an interpretation from schools of jurisprudence other than their own if it seemed to fit the particular circumstances of the case.

Furthermore, there is a central distinction in Islamic law between *ibadat* (acts of worship) and *muamalat* (transactions). Ibadat refer to relations between man and God, such as prayer and fasting, and are immutable, whereas muamalat which refer to relations between man and man, and are open to evolution and change. Thus, in the realm of muamalat, which is, of course, that of economic and financial dealings, there is considerable room to develop and change the law, albeit within limits and based on principles discussed in the following pages, to facilitate human interaction and promote justice and prosperity.

More generally, three principles allow for departures from existing norms: local custom (*urf*), the public interest (*maslaha*), and necessity (*darura*). The Shariah can thus be accommodated to societal developments, and allow for innovation, exceptions and loopholes – provided that they are properly justified.

We have already seen how in administering justice during the Umayyad era, the governors took into account the existing customs and laws of newly conquered territories, and how the cosmopolitanism of the Abbassid era resulted in considerable diversity. With the weakening of Arab influence in later centuries, syncretism was unavoidable. To put it differently, the farther removed in time and space from early Islam and its birthplace, the stronger the likely influence of indigenous customs.

And as Islam encountered new challenges, especially following its nineteenth century encounters with capitalism and the West, the concept of maslaha, translated as the general good or public interest, was frequently invoked. Based on that classical principle, a jurist confronted with rival interpretations of a passage from the Koran or the Hadith can choose the one he deems to be most conducive to human welfare. Islamic modernists, such as Mohammed Abduh and Rashid Rida, made maslaha the key principle for deciding the law where the Koran and the Hadith gave no clear guidance. The principle of talfiq, combined with independent ijtihad, was extended to allow a systematic comparison of all classical schools of laws and reach a synthesis that would combine their most appropriate features. Some fuqaha have even argued that the general interest could even override a revealed text.[44] So regardless of how far they have been willing to go, Muslim thinkers have had wide latitude to reason independently from first principles, and a modern Muslim nation could thus enact "a system of just laws appropriate to the situation in which its past history has placed it."[45]

A related concept is that of darura, or overriding necessity. Otherwise questionable innovations could be justified by the notion, tacitly accepted by all fiqh schools that "necessity permits the forbidden" (al-darura tubih al-mahzurat). In its dietary injunctions, for example, the Koran specifically authorizes transgressions caused by necessity (2:173).[46] On various occasions, the Koran has disavowed any divine intent to cause hardship (2:286).[47] The doctrine originally related to individual behavior. For example, a person who would otherwise starve could be allowed to eat pork. A version of the doctrine holds that a mere "need" (haja), if it affects many, may be treated like a dire necessity affecting only one.[48] In post-revolutionary Iran, the scope of darura was considerably expanded. It has been invoked to waive the primary rulings of Islam if the very existence of the state was threatened, or, in the words of the Ayatollah Khomeini, in instances where inaction would lead to "wickedness and corruption."[49]

Frequent departures from doctrine have occurred since and considerable interpretive leeway was allowed to religious overseers. Consider the case of private property. The Iranian constitution requires property to meet three conditions: that ownership must "not go beyond the bounds of Islamic law;" that the property itself "should contribute to the economic growth and progress of the country;" and that the property must not "harm society." The crucial matter is one of interpretation as to what "contributes to economic growth and progress" or to "what harms society." On such issues, wide latitude was left to the Majlis (Parliament), which remains in a position to confiscate property arbitrarily.[50]

The landmark "temporary cultivation agricultural land" bill transferring ownership of properties from their legal owners to those who had seized them following the revolution, was justified on the grounds of zarura (Persian transliteration of darura). The bill acknowledged that the government would be dispossessing those who had legal title to the land, but this was justified because the alternative was even less satisfactory. In the debate, necessity itself (the impracticality of removing farmers from the land they occupied) was often conflated with criteria such as fairness and justice and with political considerations such as retribution against the ancien régime.[51]

In a global economy, the overriding necessity of "the markets" has often prevailed over doctrine and tradition. In Saudi Arabia, for example, religious courts had tended to side with defaulting borrowers against creditor banks, especially when the borrowers claimed that since their contracts involved riba, they ought to be voided. So Saudi banks, invoking the credibility of the country in international financial markets, arranged that many such matters involving banks be dealt through administrative bodies. Such measures reassured both domestic and international financiers. Subsequently, Saudi Arabia used this reputation for pragmatism and fair play to borrow heavily on international markets.[52]

In financial matters, darura has been invoked to justify many departures. For instance, when pricing their products by relying on interest-based benchmarks, the argument was that Islamic banks, given their small size relative to conventional banks were price-takers and not price-makers. Many other practices, including charging interest on certain loans, could be rationalized on the ground that Muslims had to be able to compete with other peoples who were not bound by the same strictures.[53] Keeping interest-bearing balances in foreign banks could also be justified since such were the norms and practices of the international economy. Similarly, the "necessity" of economic development has been invoked in the controversial Egyptian fatwas authorizing interest.[54] Typically, however, those fatwas invoking darura add that certain types of unlawful profit should be "purified," that is, used for religiously meritorious purposes, that Muslims should work toward finding an Islamically-acceptable alternative, and that when this is accomplished, the raison d'être for granting a dispensation will be extinguished.

IV Reconciling Homo Islamicus and Homo Economicus

The most important difference between Homo Islamicus and Homo Economicus is the assumption of altruism. As with other pre-capitalist systems, Islam is preoccupied with the welfare of a community where every individual behaves altruistically and according to religious norms.

One of the most significant intellectual developments of the modern era was the new thinking that accompanied and inspired capitalism and the Industrial Revolution, and came to constitute the basic proposition of the "science" of political economy in the eighteenth and nineteenth centuries – and later of the discipline of economics. At a time when the Christian ethic emphasized the pursuit of private virtue and the merits of selfless behavior, a number of thinkers turned the logic on its head: acknowledging the "dark side" of human nature, they argued in favor of "pitting greed against greed", of "turning private vices into public virtues" and of letting "interests" rather than "passions" rule.[55] In dealing with the age-old issue of scarcity, this intellectual movement stressed the role of selfish and rational individuals. The central proposition of free market economics is that by pursuing their own self-interest, people confer countless benefits on one another. In the famous formulation of Adam Smith (1723–90), "It is not from the benevolence of the butcher, the brewer, or the baker, that we can expect our dinner, but from their regard to their own interest."[56]

For its critics, the major flaw of Islamic economics is the assumption of altruism. In the words of Timur Kuran:

> The primary role of the [behavioral norms of Islam] is to make the individual member of Islamic society, homo islamicus, just, socially responsible, and altruistic. Unlike the incorrigibly selfish and acquisitive homo economicus of neoclassical economics, homo islamicus voluntarily foregoes temptations of immediate gain when by doing so he can protect and promote the interests of his fellows.[57]

The core problem of political economy, that of scarcity in a world of self-interested actors is abolished by assumption since it is solved by the diffusion of selfless behavior. Alan Richards and John Waterbury write: "The Islamist position is that harmony and social order will be achieved by the promotion of individual virtue – by individuals' altering their behavior to conform with Divine Revelation."[58] Insofar as God has created everything in the right amounts to meet human needs, scarcity is an unnatural condition caused by greed and avarice. Under normal circumstances, altruism, sobriety, and virtue are expected, all the more so since the human being is God's "Khalifah," or vicegerent on earth (Koran 2:30)[59] and the resources at his disposal are only a temporary trust (Koran 57:7).[60] In other words, what is "economically correct" is not "Islamically correct," and vice versa. Where one approach sees man as inherently selfish, the other considers him altruistic and virtuous. For economists, Islam does not have a realistic view of human behavior; for Islamists, economics is founded on the principle of individual self-interest and as such, it glorifies greed and is immoral.

In reality, however, the gap between Homo Economicus and Homo Islamicus has proven to be easy to bridge. For one thing, there is an original area of convergence in that, in some respects, "Homo Islamicus is a modern incarnation of 'the Protestant ethic': an entrepreneur who works hard for material gain and is spiritually pure will be rewarded here on earth in the form of shared profits and social recognition."[61] In certain Islamic communities, sanctification through hard work is at the core of religion. In Senegal, for example, this has been a defining characteristic of the two–million strong Mouride brotherhood. Some of the injunctions of that community are reminiscent of Calvinism as described by Max Weber: "Let us reject jihad [holy war] and wage jihad against our souls," and "Work as if you were never going to die, and pray as if you were going to die tomorrow."[62] The attempts by Malaysia to harness Islam to the goal of economic development are part of the same logic.[63]

As for modern Islamic economics, distinctions should be drawn between early and later writings, on the one hand, and between abstract, theological treatises and more pragmatic, policy-oriented writings, on the other hand. The critique by Timur Kuran refers primarily to writings of the 1976–81 period.[64] These were the early years of modern Islamic economics, when most approaches were utopian and theoretical. The sobering Pakistani and Iranian experiments had by then barely started; they were driven by political and cultural factors, with economics appearing as an afterthought. The confident tone of the early Islamic economics literature owes as much to the untried nature of the solutions proposed as to the euphoric mood of the years following the oil boom, when a new international economic order seemed to be within reach.[65] As the abstract views collided with a harsh reality, Islamic economics became more pragmatic. Subsequent writings on Islamic economics, while not very original, have generally shed their utopian expectations and built bridges to conventional economics. As the case studies in Chapter 6 show, experiments in Islamic economics were influenced more by "situational factors" than by ideology proper. One recent textbook in Islamic economics offers the following comparison of capitalism and the Islamic economic system:

- under capitalism, human beings are selfish; under the Islamic economic system, human beings are selfish as well as altruistic;
- under capitalism, materialism is the supreme value; under the Islamic economic system, materialism should be controlled;
- capitalism favors absolute private ownership; the Islamic economic system favors private ownership within a moral framework.[66]

In sum, far from being inherently contradictory and irreconcilable, Islamic and conventional economics differ primarily in the extent to which the former adds an ethical and social dimension that the latter usually lacks. Another example of the convergence is the fact that rather than some heavenly ideal, it is *falah* (best translated as "well-being") which is increasingly at the center of Islamic economics.[67] By one definition, "Islamic economics aims at the study of human falah achieved by organizing the resources of the earth on the basis of cooperation and participation."[68]

This more pragmatic brand of Islamic economics, incorporating moral as well as material well-being, is not fundamentally different from "Keynesian" approaches (which in a broad sense include socio-economics, institutionalism and other approaches seeking to alleviate the excesses of the market through state intervention), or from attempts by Christian, Jewish, or even secular thinkers to inject an ethical dimension to freemarket economics by tempering the unbridled pursuit of self-interest with certain social and moral values. At a time when unfettered free markets have triumphed, attempts at "balance" (between state and market, between individual rights and social obligations),[69] as well as the preoccupation with ethics, have the potential to form the basis for an Islamic alternative.

Contemporary debates on political economy can be situated on a continuum where the two extremes are a pure free market and absolute government control. Most ethical and religious systems reject this polarization and invoke a "third way" or a "middle ground." History has shown that such a "middle ground" can accommodate a range of opinions. The Catholic Church has historically been able to accommodate both left-wing "liberation theology" and right-wing conservatives. In recent years, with the triumph of the free market ideology, many religious thinkers have seen no contradiction between religious teachings and the defense of the free market. Catholic theologian, Michael Novak, has launched a strong moral defense of capitalism, noting that, "like prudence in Aristotelian thought, self-interest in democratic capitalist thought has an inferior reputation among moralists." Arguing that "self-interest" is not synonymous with greed or acquisitiveness, he proposed a definition that would encompass "religious and moral interests, artistic and scientific interests, and interests in peace and justice," as well as concern for the well-being of one's family, friends, and country.[70]

Islamic economic thinking has evolved along a similar tack. Whereas in the 1960s, many Islamic intellectuals stressed the compatibility of Islam with socialism (based on the preoccupation with justice or adl), and for some even with Marxism, many influential economists today emphasize the affinities between Islam and the free market ideology. Since dubious intentions[71] could combine to produce beneficial results – welfare and especially progress toward meeting the needs of the poor[72] – the system could be morally justifiable, and, indeed, perhaps morally superior to well-meaning but ineffectual policies.[73] It is revealing that the first major attempt at full Islamicization of an economy – in Pakistan under President Zia in 1977 – was part of a neo-liberal economic package. Even more striking, in the Sudan during 1992–3, Islamists openly and unapologetically embraced the most extreme form of neo-liberalism under the stewardship of Abdul Rahim Hamdi, Minister of Finance (and Islamic banker), who was influenced by the ideas of Milton Friedman. He defended free market rules on the ground that "this is how an Islamic economy should function." He even argued that "the population accepts these hardships because it supports Islam and us."[74]

In sum, the Homo Economicus versus Homo Islamicus contrast is now largely irrelevant. Both represent, if not a utopia (literally meaning "no place"), then at least an ideal.[75] Both are normative rather than descriptive. Homo Islamicus states what people should strive toward, as opposed to how people are likely to behave (the "ought" as opposed to the "is").[76] Homo Economicus similarly represents an idealized free market, one that works only under certain assumptions. As noted by Richards and Waterbury, "It is well to remember that policymaking practice *never* conforms to rigorous theory."[77] Much to the dismay of fundamentalists of all stripes, the "real economy," though it may be inspired by a given ideology is also likely to stray from that ideology.

In fact, insofar as the economic profession can be regarded as a learned class devoted to the defense of the free market system,[78] one could see obvious parallels between the guardians of the dogma in both Islam and economics: intolerance toward dissident or "incorrect" views; territoriality; focus on arcane and sterile debates, etc. Reading certain economists' denunciations of the sins committed against the free market, one recognizes a tone that the Western press usually associates with "ayatollahs."[79] One can even see religious overtones in "economic fundamentalism."[80] Rodney Wilson wrote about the preoccupation of economists with "pure" equilibrium: "The economic order is ... permanent, and should reflect the divine order ... Some of the language and symbolism – perfect markets, the concept of equilibrium, efficiency in transactions which implies perfect knowledge – all perhaps unconsciously, could be viewed as striving for some heavenly ideal."[81] And Bernard Maris remarked that abstract economics possesses "the same essence as theology insofar as both are based on compilation and gloss, commentary and the deepening of commentary."[82] Just as those who inhabit a highly formalized world of perfect competition, perfect information and perfect rationality seek to eliminate imperfections (such as the existence of a public sector, which in most countries accounts for nearly half of the gross domestic product (GDP), so do Islamic purists who seek to establish a world dominated by altruism and virtue. Just as one can find absurd prescriptions in the writings of religious fundamentalists, one can find equally absurd policy prescriptions made by economic fundamentalists.[83] If nothing else, the financial meltdown of 2007–8 has proven the dangers of such ideological hubris.

V Reconciling Islam and Finance

The Koran states that despite their superficial resemblance, profits from commerce are fundamentally different from profits from money-lending (2:275).[84] Unlike Christians, who have usually denigrated all business endeavors, Muslims have traditionally looked favorably at commerce, while being suspicious of finance. As Chapters 3 and 12 show, the reconciliation between Christianity and finance, and for that matter between Christianity and business in general, was long-drawn and fraught with theological and philosophical disputes.

In Islam, although riba would occasionally be interpreted not as interest, but as usury (or excessive interest), strict definitions have typically prevailed. But as its economy grew more complex, the Islamic world was able to find proper substitutes, justifications, or subterfuges. In the early years of Islam, jurists devised an impressive array of contracts designed to circumvent riba, the most important ones being profit-and-loss sharing contracts (*mudaraba* or *qirad*).[85] Some of these contracts were, in fact, so clever as to be considered hiyal (singular: hila), meaning ruses or wiles: that is, lawful means used, knowingly and voluntarily, to reach an unlawful objective. Provided that certain formalities were used, interest, albeit by a different name, could be charged and paid. Certain schools of jurisprudence – in particular the Hanafis and Shafiis – took a tolerant view of such hiyal,[86] and entire treatises were written detailing how Muslims could use such contrivances while staying on the right side of the Shariah. It was thus a form of casuistry (looking at a specific "case" to prove that the general rule of behavior does not apply). One of those hiyals, the "*mohatra* contract," is mentioned in Blaise Pascal's eighth *Lettre Provinciale* (1656) as representative of the casuistic reasoning of Jesuits.[87] The mohatra refers to the ancient double sale also known as *ina* or *mukhatara*, where a borrower and a lender arrange to sell and then resell between them a trivial object once for cash and once for a greater sum on credit, with the net result being a loan with interest.[88] There is disagreement among scholars as to how common such devices were. Maxime Rodinson has found them to be very common, while others argue that he overstated the case.[89] Then, of course, there was the possibility of circumventing riba by dealing with non-Muslims (mostly Jewish) money-lenders; a common practice since the Abbassid era.[90]

Modern finance entered the Islamic world alongside Western colonial expansion.[91] Foreign banks financed trade and development and, in due course, Islamic governments, strapped for cash, had become debtors, therefore paying interest to foreign creditors. The Ottoman Empire issued interest-bearing treasury bond from 1840,[92] but it is in Egypt that foreign bankers played a crucial role.[93] Egypt's role in legitimizing modern finance cannot be overemphasized. It was the first Islamic country to possess indigenously-controlled banks. The National Bank of Egypt was created in 1898 with mixed capital (50 per cent was in Egyptian hands). In 1920, Banque Misr was established, the first ever to be formed exclusively with local capital. Egypt's thriving stock market made it a favorite among early twentieth century "emerging" markets. (At one point in the highly unusual context of the period following the end of the Second World War, Egypt had the third largest stock market in the world.[94]) Egypt's legal code, which was French inspired and allowed interest not exceeding 7 per cent, served as a model for many Arab codes. Perhaps most importantly, it is in Egypt that interest was legitimated by religious authorities in 1904. In a famous, if controversial, fatwa, mufti Sheikh Mohammed Abduh, a leading figure of Islamic reform, cautiously legitimated interest generated either by savings bank accounts or by insurance policies.[95]

The riba controversy was temporarily ignored but not put to rest. Many legal codes adopted by Islamic countries observed an "eloquent silence" – to use Maxime Rodinson's formulation – on the issue of interest-bearing loans. Overall, interest was tolerated, although it was not uncommon for devout Muslims to refuse interest on their savings. The world of finance took a new turn with the end of colonialism. Newly independent states established national monetary authorities and central banks, and issued local currencies. Control over the credit system, and thus over interest rates, was perceived as a crucial part of development and economic policy, especially where banks had been nationalized (in countries such as Egypt, Syria, Iraq, Algeria, South Yemen, Libya, and the Sudan). In short, until recent attempts at "Islamicizing" economic systems, all countries, regardless of ideological leanings, learned to live with interest and with modern finance. Custom, necessity, and the public interest helped to overcome the age-old suspicion toward debt and practices such as insurance.[96] With the advent of Islamic finance, the prevailing consensus among Islamic scholars was that dealing with conventional banks was acceptable if Islamic institutions were not accessible to them. As for the issue of Muslims or Islamic institutions benefiting from interest, opinions and practices have varied. Some Islamic institutions have steadfastly refused to receive interest, whereas others, including the Islamic Development Bank and the Faisal Islamic Bank of Egypt (FIBE) have always placed their excess funds in interest-bearing accounts, usually overseas.[97] Three theological arguments have typically been invoked to justify receiving interest. One was the overriding necessity argument: given the developmental needs for Muslims, taking interest was justified. Another was based on the old distinction between *Dar al Harb* (literally the "realm of war"), that is, non-Muslim countries, and the realm of Islam ("Dar al Islam"). It would then be permissible to profit from interest in dealings with "Dar al Harb," especially since this would strengthen the relative position of "Dar al Islam." A third, more frequent, position was that income from interest could be accepted, but that it should be "purified," that is, earmarked for charitable purposes.

Islamic revivalism has to some extent led, along with the Islamicization of economic systems (in Pakistan, Iran, and the Sudan), to a re-examination of riba and gharar. But as Chapter 6 shows, even those countries that have "eliminated interest" have developed interest-like mechanisms, and still have significant components of their economies operating on the basis of conventional interest. The transformation of modern finance that has taken place in recent years has also reopened the debate about the acceptability of new financial instruments and about such issues as leverage.[98] The trend has been toward new religious interpretations that would allow, within bounds, the creation of instruments adapted to new financial needs.[99]

Notes

1. Aziz al-Azmeh, *Islam and Modernities* (London: Verso, 1993), p. 12.
2. At one extreme end of the spectrum, some have gone as far as far to argue that only the Meccan part of the Koran was binding. See William E. Shepard, "Islam and Ideology: Towards a Typology," *International Journal of Middle Eastern Studies*, 19 (1987), p. 312.
3. See Nicholas Heer (ed.), *Islamic Law and Jurisprudence* (Seattle, WA: University of Washington Press 1990); Wael B. Hallaq, *A History of Islamic Legal Theories: An Introduction to Sunni Usul al-Fiqh* (Cambridge: Cambridge University Press, 1997); C. G. Weeramantry, *Islamic Jurisprudence: An International Perspective* (New York: St. Martin's Press 1988).
4. Henri Laoust, *Les Schismes dans l'Islam* (Paris: Payot, 1965).
5. Philip K. Hitti, *Syria: A Short History* (New York: Macmillan 1959), p. 115.
6. Albert Hourani, *A History of the Arab Peoples* (Cambridge, MA: Harvard University Press, 1991), p. 66.
7. Hourani, *A History of the Arab Peoples*, p. 161.
8. Wael B. Hallaq, "Was the Gate of Ijtihad ever Closed?," *International Journal of Middle Eastern Studies*, 16 (1984), pp. 1–33.
9. Joseph Schacht, *An Introduction to Islamic Law* (Oxford: Oxford University Press, 1964), p. 70.
10. Edward Mortimer, *Faith and Power: The Politics of Islam* (New York: Random House, 1982), p. 37.
11. Olivier Carré, *L'Islam laïque ou le retour à la grande tradition* (Paris: Armand Colin, 1993).
12. Bernard Lewis, *Islam and the West* (Oxford: Oxford University Press, 1993), p. 13.
13. John O. Voll, "Renewal and Reform in Islamic History: *Tajdid* and *Islah*," in John L. Esposito (ed.), *Voices of Resurgent Islam* (Oxford: Oxford University Press, 1983), pp. 32–47.
14. Carré, *L'Islam Laique ou le retour à la grande tradition*.
15. Edward Said, *Orientalism* (New York: Random House, 1979).
16. Albert Hourani, *Europe and the Middle East* (Berkeley, CA: University of California Press, 1980), p. 10.
17. John O. Voll, *Islam: Continuity and Change in the Modern World* (Boulder, CO: Westview

Press, 1982), p. 33. See also Roger Owen, *Lord Cromer: Victorian Imperialist, Edwardian Proconsul* (Oxford: Oxford University Press, 2004).

18. Malcolm Kerr, *Islamic Reform: the Political and Legal Theories of Muhammad 'Abduh and Rashid Rida* (Berkeley, CA: University of California Press, 1966).

19. Mortimer, *Faith and Power*, p. 115.

20. Yahya Sadowski, "The New Orientalism and the Democracy Debate," in Joel Beinin and Joe Stork (eds.), *Political Islam: Essays from Middle East Report* (Berkeley, CA: University of California Press, 1997), p. 43.

21. See Chapters 4, 5 and 11.

22. Max Weber, *The Protestant Ethic and the Spirit of Capitalism* (Upper Saddle River, NJ: Prentice Hall 1980).

23. 2:198 "It is no sin for you that you seek the bounty of your Lord. So when you press on from Arafat, remember Allah near the Holy Monument, and remember Him as He has guided you, though before that you were certainly of the erring ones." (reference to commercial activities in Mecca during Pilgrimage). 73:20 "Thy Lord knows indeed that thou passes in prayer nearly two-thirds of the night and [sometimes] half of it, and [sometimes] a third of it, as do a party of those with thee. And Allah measures the night and the day. He knows that [all of] you are not able to do it, so He has turned to you [mercifully]; so read of the Koran that which is easy [for you], keep up prayer and pay the poor-rate and offer to Allah a goodly gift. And whatever of good you send on before hand for yourselves, you will find it with Allah – that is best and greatest in reward. And ask forgiveness of Allah. Surely Allah is forgiving, merciful."

24. 62:9 "O you who believe, when the call is sounded for prayer on Friday, hasten to the remembrance of Allah and leave off traffic. That is better for you, if you know." 62:10 "But when the prayer is ended, disperse abroad in the land and seek Allah's grace, and remember Allah much, that you may be successful."

25. Ira M. Lapidus, *Muslim Cities in the Later Middle Ages* (Cambridge, MA: Harvard University Press, 1967).

26. Muhammad Akram Khan, *An Introduction to Islamic Economics* (Islamabad: International Institute of Islamic Thought and Institute for Policy Studies, 1994), p. 83.

27. Chibli Mallat, *The Renewal of Islamic law: Muhammad Baqer as-Sadr: Najaf and the Shi'i International* (Cambridge: Cambridge University Press, 1993), p. 111.

28. William E. Shepherd, "Muhammad Sa'id al-'Ashmawi and the Application of the Shari'a in Egypt," *International Journal of Middle Eastern Studies*, 28 (1996), pp. 39–58.

29. Myron Weiner and Samuel P. Huntington (eds.), *Understanding Political Development* (Boston, MA: Little, Brown, 1987).

30. Timur Kuran, "Economic Justice in Contemporary Islamic Thought," *International Journal of Middle East Studies*, 21:2 (May 1989), pp. 171–91.

31. In those years competition between pan-Arabism and pan-Islamic usually pitted Egypt against Saudi Arabia (see Chapter 5), although there were periods of "rapprochement" between the two countries.

32. John L. Esposito (ed.), *Voices of Resurgent Islam* (Oxford: Oxford University Press, 1983), p. 9.

33. Khalid M. Ishaque, "The Islamic Approach to Economic Development," in John L. Esposito (ed.), *Voices of Resurgent Islam* (Oxford: Oxford University Press, 1983), pp. 268–76.

34. See Chapter 5.

35. Timur Kuran, "The Economic System in Contemporary Islamic Thought: Interpretation and Assessment," *International Journal of Middle Eastern Studies*, 18 (1986), p. 135.

36. Rodney Wilson, *Economics, Ethics and Religion: Jewish, Christian and Muslim Economic Thought* (New York; New York University Press, 1997), p. 115.

37. Mallat, *The renewal of Islamic law*, p. 111.

38. See al-Sayyed Muhammad Baqer as-Sadr, *Iqtissaduna*, Dar al-Taaruf wal Matbuaat Beirut (n.d.), pp. 279–310. See also Mallat, *The Renewal of Islamic Law*, pp. 117–20.

39. Traute Wohlers-Scharf, *Arab and Islamic Banks: New Business Partners for Developing Countries* (Paris: OECD, 1983), p. 91.

40. Khan, *An Introduction to Islamic Economics*, p. 30.

41. John L. Esposito, *The Islamic Threat: Myth or Reality?* (Oxford: Oxford University Press, 1992), p. 80.

42. Mallat, *The Renewal of Islamic law*, p. 125.

43. 2:184: "But whoever among you is sick or on a journey, (he shall fast) a like number of other days. And those who find it extremely hard may effect redemption by feeding a poor man. So whoever does good spontaneously, it is better for him; and that you fast is better for you if you know." 2:185 "The month of Ramadan is that in which the Koran was revealed, a guidance to men and clear proofs of the guidance and the Criterion. So whoever of you is present in the month, he shall fast therein, and whoever is sick or on a journey, (he shall fast) a (like) number of other days. Allah desires ease for you, and He desires not hardship for you, and (He desires) that you should complete the number and that you should exalt the greatness of Allah for having guided you and that you may give thanks."

44. Carré, *L'Islam laïque ou le retour à la Grande Tradition*, p. 15.

45. Mortimer, *Faith and Power*, p. 244.

46. 2:173 "Allah has forbidden you only what dies of itself, and blood, and the flesh of swine, and that over which any other name than that of Allah has been invoked. Then whoever is driven by necessity, not desiring, nor exceeding the limit, no sin is upon him. Surely Allah is forgiving, merciful."

47. 2:286 "Allah imposes not on any soul a duty beyond its scope. For it is that which it earns (of good) and against it that which it works (of evil). Our Lord, punish us not if we forget or make a mistake. Our Lord, do not lay on us a burden as Thou didst lay on those before us. Our Lord, Impose not on us afflictions which we have not the strength to bear. And pardon us! And grant us protection! And have mercy on us! Thou art our Patron, so grant us victory over the disbelieving people."

48. Frank E. Vogel and Samuel L. Hayes, III, *Islamic Law and Finance: Religion, Risk, and Return* (The Hague: Kluwer Law International, 1998), p. 38.

49. Shaul Bakhash, "The Politics of Land, Law, and Social Justice in Iran," *Middle East Journal*, 43:2 (Spring 1989), p. 196.

50. Jahangir Amuzegar, *Iran's Economy Under the Islamic Republic* (London: I. B. Tauris, 1993), pp. 21–8.

51. Bakhash, "The Politics of Land, Law, and Social Justice in Iran."

52. Kiren Aziz Chaudhry, *The Price of Wealth: Economies and Institutions in the Middle East* (Ithaca, NY: Cornell University Press, 1997), p. 37.

53. Mortimer *Faith and Power*, p. 245.

54. Michel Galloux, *Finance islamique et pouvoir politique: le cas de l'Egypte moderne* (Paris: Presses Universitaires de France, 1997), p. 43.

55. Albert Hirschman, *The Passions and the Interests: Political Arguments for Capitalism Before Its Triumph* (Princeton, NJ: Princeton University Press, 1977).

56. Adam Smith, *An Inquiry into the Nature and Causes of the Wealth of Nations* (Chicago, IL: University of Chicago Press, 1977).

57. Timur Kuran, "The Economic System in Contemporary Islamic Thought: Interpretation and Assessment," p. 136.

58. Alan Richards and John Waterbury, *A Political Economy of the Middle East* (Boulder, CO: Westview Press, 1996), p. 354.

59. 2:30 "And when thy Lord said to the angels, I am going to place a ruler in the earth, they said: Wilt thou place in it such as make mischief in it and shed blood? And we celebrate Thy praise and extol Thy holiness. He said: Surely I know what you know not."

60. 57:7 "Believe in Allah and His Messenger and spend of that whereof He has made you heirs. So those of you who believe and spend – for them is a great reward."

61. Karen Pfeifer, "Is there an Islamic Economics?," in Joel Beinin and Joe Stark (eds.), *Political Islam: Essays from Middle East Report* (Berkeley, CA: University of California Press, 1997), p. 163.
62. Sophie Bava and Danielle Bleitrach, "Islam et pouvoir au Sénégal: Les mourides entre utopie et capitalisme," *Le Monde diplomatique*, November 1995.
63. See Chapter 6.
64. Timur Kuran, "The Economic System in Contemporary Islamic Thought: Interpretation and Assessment," pp. 135–64.
65. See Chapter 5.
66. Khan, *An Introduction to Islamic Economics*, p. 26.
67. Khan, *An Introduction to Islamic Economics*, pp. 34–44.
68. Khan, *An Introduction to Islamic Economics*, p. 33.
69. See Ellen Frankel Paul, Fred D. Miller, Jr., and Jeffrey Paul (eds.), *Ethics and Economics* (London: Basil Blackwell, 1985), Amitai Etzioni, *The Moral Dimension: Towards a New Economics* (New York: Free Press, 1988).
70. Michael Novak, *The Spirit of Democratic Capitalism* (Lanham, MD: Madison Books, 1991).
71. The notion of intent (*niyya*) is often introduced to judge an action, with different schools of jurisprudence having different positions on evaluating it.
72. Michael Novak, *The Catholic Ethic and the Spirit of Capitalism* (New York: Free Press, 1993), Richard John Neuhaus, *Doing Well and Doing Good* (New York: Doubleday, 1993).
73. See, for example, Khan, *An Introduction to Islamic Economics*, pp. 33–90.
74. Judith Miller, *God Has Ninety-Nine Names: A Reporter's Journey through a Militant Middle East* (New York: Simon and Schuster, 1996), p. 144.
75. It is also the title of the famous book by Thomas More (1516) about an imaginary island that represented moral, political, and social perfection.
76. Mohammed N. Siddiqi, *Muslim Economic Thinking* (Leicester: The Islamic Foundation, 1981), p. 69.
77. Richards and Waterbury, *A Political Economy of the Middle East*, p. 356.
78. Peter E. Earl, "A Behavioral Theory of Economists' Behavior," in Alfred S. Eichner (ed.), *Why Economics is not yet a science* (Armonk, NY: M. E. Sharp, 1983).
79. Robert J. Barro, *Markets and Choices in A Free Society* (Cambridge, MA: MIT Press, 1996), and Milton Friedman, *Capitalism and Freedom* (Chicago, IL: University of Chicago Press, 1963).
80. Robert H. Nelson, *Economics as Religion: from Samuelson to Chicago and Beyond* (Philadelphia, PA: The Pennsylvania State University Press, 2001).
81. Rodney Wilson, *Economics, Ethics and Religion: Jewish, Christian and Muslim Economic Thought* (New York: New York University Press, 1997), p. 45.
82. Bernard Maris, *Des Economistes au-dessus de tout soupçon, ou la grande mascarade des prédictions* (Paris: Albin Michel, 1990), p. 57.
83. Ibrahim Warde, "La vie, la mort, le marché," *Le Monde diplomatique*, June 1998.
84. See Chapter 3.
85. Abraham Udovitch, *Partnership and Profit in Medieval Islam* (Princeton, NJ: Princeton University Press, 1970).
86. Nabil A. Saleh, *Unlawful gain and Legitimate Profit in Islamic Law: Riba, Gharar and Islamic Banking* (Cambridge: Cambridge University Press, 1986).
87. Blaise Pascal, *Les Provinciales ou Les Lettres écrites par Louis de Montalte à un provincial de ses amis et aux RR. PP. Jésuites sur le sujet de la morale et de la politique de ces Pères* (Paris: Gallimard Folio, 1987), p. 131.
88. Vogel and Hayes, *Islamic Law and Finance: Religion, Risk, and Return*, p. 39.
89. Galloux, *Finance islamique et pouvoir politique*, p. 18; Maxime Rodinson, *Islam and Capitalism* (London: Penguin, 1978), p. 144.
90. Whereas a hila is considered illicit, the more benign *makhraj* (literally "way out" and sometimes translated as "solution") is licit.

91. Charles Issawi (ed.), *The Economic History of the Middle East 1800–1914* (Chicago, IL: University of Chicago Press, 1966), pp. 10–11.

92. Historians, however, disagree on the amount of interest charged. Estimates vary between 8 and 12 per cent.

93. David Landes, *Bankers and Pashas: International Finance and Economic Imperialism in Egypt* (Cambridge, MA: Harvard University Press, 1958).

94. *Worth*, December 1996–January 1997.

95. Chibli Mallat, "The Debate on Riba and Interest in Twentieth Century Egypt," in Chibli Mallat (ed.), *Islamic Law and Finance* (London: Graham and Trotman, 1988), pp. 69–88.

96. Mortimer, *Faith and Power*, p. 238.

97. Elias Kazarian, *Islamic Versus Traditional Banking: Financial Innovation in Egypt* (Boulder, CO: Westview Press, 1993), p. 225.

98. See Chapter 7.

99. Vogel and Hayes, *Islamic Law and Finance*, pp. 235–95.

3

RIBA, GHARAR, AND THE MORAL ECONOMY OF ISLAM IN HISTORICAL AND COMPARATIVE PERSPECTIVE

Most definitions reduce Islamic banking to "interest-free" banking. While the injunctions against riba are indeed the cornerstone of Islamic finance, debates persist as to the exact significance of the word. Since the early days of Islam, the majority of scholars have adopted a restrictive definition: any form of interest constitutes riba. The debate is nonetheless still lively. This chapter starts with the riba debate, its origin, and significance. It later discusses gharar, a lesser known yet in the contemporary world of finance equally significant prohibition; the moral economy of Islam; a broader approach focusing on the spirit, as opposed to the letter of Islam; and the religious versus secular approaches to these issues. The final section places the money and religion debate in comparative and historical perspective.

I Riba

Riba means increase. Given that definition, there is in riba both more and less than meets the eye. Riba is not necessarily about interest as such, and it certainly is not exclusively about interest. It really refers to any unlawful or undeserved gain derived from the quantitative inequality of the counter-values. Interest or usury (that is, reimbursing more than the principal advanced) would then be only one form of riba. Imposition of late fees would be an example of non-interest riba.[1]

The Koran declares that those who disregard the prohibition of riba are at war with God and his Prophet. That prohibition is explicitly mentioned in four different revelations of the Koran (2:275–81, 3:129–130, 4:16, and 30:39), expressing the following ideas: despite the apparent similarity of profits from trade and profits from riba, only profits from trade are allowed; when lending money, Muslims are asked to take only the principal and forgo even that sum if the borrower is unable to repay; riba deprives wealth from God's blessings; riba is equated with wrongful appropriation of property belonging to others; and Muslims should stay away from it for the sake of their own welfare.[2] But the Koran does not elaborate further. A few of Prophet Mohammed's companions even expressed frustration at the vagueness of the definition.

The Hadith, however, is more specific, distinguishing two types of riba: *riba al-fadl*, which is produced by the unlawful excess of one of the counter-values;

and *riba al-nasia*, which is produced by delaying completion of the transaction in exchange for an increase of the counter-value. Early Islamic scholars also mentioned a third type of riba, *riba al-jahiliyya* (or pre-Islamic riba), which occurs when the lender gives the borrower at maturity date a choice between settling the debt or doubling it. The process of doubling and re-doubling would continue and would end with the enslavement of the defaulting borrower.

The riba debate has been approached from many angles. One set of discussions contrasts "interest," that is, a moderate, economically justified remuneration of capital, with "usury," that is, an excessive, sometimes extortionate rate. In the same vein, some have argued that the Koranic prohibition was aimed only at the common pre-Islamic practice of riba al-jahiliyya. The majority of Islamic scholars still consider that any increase in the amount of money returned by a borrower constitutes riba and is, therefore, prohibited.

Another angle is the requirements of the modern economy. In recent decades, darura, maslaha, as well as existing practices and customs have been repeatedly invoked by Islamic modernists.[3] In the words of Fazlur Rahman, "As long as our society has not been reconstructed on the Islamic pattern, it would be suicidal for the economic welfare of the society and the financial system of the country and would also be contrary to the spirit and intentions of the Quran and Sunna to abolish bank-interest."[4] By the same token, some have raised the issue of the inflationary nature of the contemporary economy. The prohibition of riba would then apply to real interest (that i, the interest rate minus the rate of inflation) as opposed to nominal interest. Otherwise, the absence of interest in an inflationary period would amount to negative real interest, which would penalize lenders and subsidize borrowers.[5]

In the same vein, some have argued that the concept of riba has been misunderstood, misinterpreted, and misapplied. Mohammed al-Ashmawi makes three arguments to show that a sweeping prohibition against interest is unwarranted. First, in his view, the riba referred to in the Koran was the riba al-jahiliyya (see below), which refers to the common pre-Islamic practice of doubling the principal[6] in exchange for more time, and which resulted in the enslavement of the borrower if in the end he could not pay. Second, riba-based on a widely quoted Hadith – specifies six commodities, and should apply only to these six, and not to modern currency.[7] Third, a distinction should be drawn between economically useful loans, such as those taken by businesses and institutions for the purpose of investing and making a profit, and exploitative loans, such as those made to poor individuals to help them meet immediate basic needs.[8] In contrast, certain scholars have claimed that a modern economy could bypass riba altogether by devising appropriate mechanisms.[9]

It is generally agreed that the Prophet's view evolved from exhortation against riba in his "Mecca period" to outright prohibition in his "Medina period." Different explanations have been advanced as to why riba is condemned. A few have to do with expediency, but most were related to economic and ethical norms. Historian Philip Hitti has, for example, suggested that Mohammed's injunctions against usury were aimed at the Jews of Medina: he badly needed their financial support when they were keen on charging interest on these loans.[10] Yet the very persistence of the prohibition, well beyond Mohammed's life suggests concerns beyond mere expediency.

Islamic scholars have insisted that the prohibition of riba as not an isolated religious injunction but "an integral part of the Islamic economic order with its overall ethos, goals and values."[11] One needs, therefore, to look at the "moral economy" of a "pre-modern" economic system, where transactions involved various forms of barter and exchange, often completed over time. From such a perspective, one can find striking parallels between early Islam and contemporaneous ethical and religious systems.

The controversy over riba shows no sign of abating. Some have condemned attempts to even discuss the matter. One scholar wrote: "If Quranic theories come into conflict with the modern scientific theories, I find no reason to trouble my conscience. I firmly believe that the sciences of today may become the mythology of tomorrow and what Quran has said, we may not understand it today, but it is likely to become quite clear to us tomorrow."[12] At the other end of the spectrum, a few have dismissed the "entire medieval notion of riba as an obsolete idea."[13]

Rather than resolving the issue, a number of fatwas have perpetuated the controversy. In 1904, in a context of rapid economic change, Egypt's *mufti* (chief religious cleric), the reformer Muhammad Abduh, issued by request of the government a controversial fatwa on the Egyptian Savings Fund (Sanduq al-Tawfeer) created by the Postal Administration. In exchange for cash deposits, the Egyptian Savings Fund had issued savings "certificates" which yielded depositors a fixed and pre-determined rate of return on their money. The Savings Fund used such deposits for various small investments. The fatwa adopted, albeit carefully, a tolerant view of fixed and pre-determined rates.[14] Ambivalence and hedging have since characterized such decisions. As was observed by Chibli Mallat;

> Egyptian muftis writing in the 20th century acknowledge that they are treading a delicate path and are dealing with powerful economic actors and institutions that have strong supporters in new, as well as in established, commercial sectors. Because a fatwa that unilaterally condemned interest-bearing transactions would be totally ineffective, most muftis have taken care to formulate their opinions in language that is either cautious or ambiguous."[15]

Despite attempts at "balance," disagreements have not subsided. In 1986, the Fiqh Academy of the Islamic Conference supported the restrictive interpretation of early jurists, condemning all interest-bearing transactions as void.[16] But in 1989, while an economic and rhetorical argument between Islamic financial institutions and conventional banks was raging (in the wake of the collapse of the Islamic Money Management Companies [IMMCs]),[17] the Mufti of the Egyptian Republic (later Sheikh of al-Azhar), Muhammad Sayyed Atiyya Tantawi, issued what he considered to be his most important fatwa, one legitimizing "capitalization certificates" (*shahadat al-istithmar*), which are interest-bearing government bonds underwritten by Egyptian banks. To justify his position, he cited jurists as well as bankers and secular experts. He argued "that the determination of the profit in advance is for the sake of the owner of the capital (that is deposited) and is done to prevent a dispute between him and the bank."[18] In addition, since the certificates were issued in connection with the state's financing of a development plan to encourage the population to increase its level of savings, legally the certificates are not loans, but deposits. Despite the traditional pre-eminence of Egyptian grand muftis within the Islamic – especially Sunni – world, many leading figures in the Islamic world remained unconvinced. Thus, a decision of the Federal Shariah Court of Pakistan dismissed the fatwa in 1992 as the "solitary opinion of Shaikh Tantawi of Egypt."[19]

In 2002, Tantawi reiterated his views in a similar fatwa. He has also on many occasions launched frontal attacks against Islamic banks, accusing them of hypocrisy and of using the word "Islam" misleadingly in their appellation. In a 1995 speech, he criticized Western-style banks which established "Islamic" subsidiaries to meet the growing demand for such services. He said that there was little difference between Western-style banks, which offer fixed interest rates, and Islamic banks, in which depositors share the risk of investing in projects, for Islam simply requires financial transactions to be marked by "clarity and justice." Even more provocatively, he argued that "banks which set fixed interest are closer to Islam because they make clear people's entitlement."[20]

Tantawi's successor as mufti, Sheikh Nasr Farid Wassel, took the same position, declaring: "I will give you a final and decisive fatwa: so long as the banks invest the money in halal, then the transaction is halal." He called for an end to the controversy about bank interest, adding that "there is no such thing as an Islamic and non-Islamic bank."[21]

Egypt is in a singular position in the Islamic world. On the one hand, it played a pioneering role in Islamic finance and hosts some of the earliest Islamic institutions. Also, most of its conventional banks offer Islamic products. Yet the country's top religious establishment has legitimated moderate interest and in effect considers Islamic institutions superfluous and questionable. Not surprisingly, Islamic finance had, as of early 2009, achieved only moderate growth.

In conclusion, it could be said that, although the riba debate still preoccupies religious scholars, it is of little import in the actual operations of Islamic banks. Indeed, with financial deregulation, banks can largely bypass interest-based products. Although Islamic financial institutions usually price their products on the basis of interest-based benchmarks,[22] they engage in transactions that do not involve riba. In contrast, it is the concept of gharar that has now come to play a central role in Islamic finance.

II Gharar

The question of gharar was generally ignored in the early writings on Islamic finance. It was only in the 1980s, with the pioneering work of Nabil Saleh and a handful of other specialists, that serious work started appearing on this fundamental though ill-understood, concept.[23] Unlike riba, which has parallels in all major religious traditions, gharar is unique to Islam[24] – a religion steeped in commerce. It is also particularly relevant in today's financial environment.

The word gharar itself is not mentioned in the Koran, though etymologically related words, meaning deception or delusion with a connotation of peril, risk, or hazard, are.[25] It is, however, frequently mentioned in the Hadith. As in the case of riba, the prohibition is unequivoca, though the concept lends itself to different interpretations. In most works on Islamic finance, it is translated as uncertainty, risk, or speculation. Equating gharar with risk, or uncertainty can be misleading, since it would be nonsensical, especially in a society of merchants to prohibit such things which are beyond human control. Furthermore, Islam does not even advocate the avoidance of risk. Indeed, incurring commercial risk is approved, even encouraged, since it provides the justification for profit. The question of gharar refers to aleatory transactions, or transactions conditioned on uncertain events.

Qadi Iyad, the eleventh century Maliki scholar, defined gharar as "that which has a pleasant appearance but a hated essence."[26] When it comes to commercial transactions, many deals look seductive but are fraught with hidden flaws. It is hard to resist the lure of easy money, hence the temptation to seek short cuts and misrepresent to others (and often to oneself) the pitfalls of uncertain transactions. Such built-in ambiguities in turn lead to disputation and discord within the community. In the Hadith a range of transactions are forbidden: selling a fish in the sea; what is in the wombs and the contents of the udders; a runaway slave, etc. When it comes to foodstuffs, grapes cannot be sold until they become black, nor can grain be sold until it is strong. Merchants must be in possession of foodstuffs before selling them, at which time they must weigh them. There are also prohibitions against the "sale of gharar." Among such transactions are the "sale of the pebble" (the sale of an object determined by the throwing of a pebble), or the stroke of the diver.[27] Based on these Hadiths, Frank Vogel has arranged those prohibitions in a spectrum, according to the degree of risk involved: pure speculation; uncertain outcome; unknowable future benefit; and inexactitude. He concluded that:

> a possible interpretation of the gharar hadiths is that they bar only risks affecting the existence of the object as to which the parties transact, rather than just its price. In the hadiths, such risks arise either (1) because of the parties' lack of knowledge (*jahl*, ignorance) about that object; (2) because the object does not now exist; or (3) because the object evades the parties' control. Therefore the scholars might use one of these three characteristics to identify transactions infected by the type of risk condemned as gharar.[28]

As explained by Maxime Rodinson:

> Any gain that may result from chance, from undetermined causes, is here prohibited. Thus, it would be wrong to get a workman to skin an animal by promising to give him half the skin as reward, or to get him to grind some grain by promising him the bran separated out by the grinding process, and so on. It is impossible to know for certain whether the skin may not be damaged and lose its value in the course of the work, or to know how much bran will be produced.[29]

In sum, a distinction is drawn between the risk connected to normal business transactions, and the kind of uncertainty that can be used by one party to take advantage of another. Classical Islam also distinguished major and minor gharar,[30] and certain schools of fiqh tolerate gharar in case of need (haja) and when it cannot be avoided without great difficulty.[31]

Clearly, since the early days of Islam, the worlds of commerce and finance have changed considerably, though human nature – with its ever-present temptation to get something for nothing - has not. In today's financial environment, gharar is pervasive since it encompasses deceptive ambiguity, asymmetrical information, risk-shifting strategies, and all forms of excessive and unnecessary risk-taking which are akin to betting and speculation.

To quote Nassim Taleb, "the glib snake oil façade of knowledge" promoted by finance professionals in a way designed to obfuscate and encourage investors to take risks that they do not understand.[32] George Akerlof's "lemon theory" discuses the consequences of asymmetrical information – an endemic problem in finance since those who devise and sell complex instruments have an edge over those who buy them. Former business school professor, John Kay, noting that "it became increasingly hard to understand the nature of the underlying risk" of such instruments, describes the gulf between the theory and the reality. He writes:

> The financial economics I once taught treated risk as just another commodity. People bought and sold it in line with their varying preferences. The result, in the Panglossian world of efficient markets, was that risk was widely spread and held by those best able to bear it. Real life led me to a different view. Risk markets are driven less by different tastes for risk than by differences in information and understanding. People who know a little of what they are doing pass risks to people who know less. Since ignorance is not evenly distributed, the result may be to concentrate risk rather than spread it.[33]

As for shifting risk to others (or to society at large) and the tendency to privatize profits and socialize losses, it was a fixture of the scandals revealed by the financial meltdown of 2008, when years of accumulated profits and bonuses resulted in the near collapse of the global economy. A famous exchange from a few years earlier reveals the gap between the authorized discourse on risk-taking and the "greater fool" reality. Following a $200-million settlement obtained by the New York State Attorney-General against Merrill Lynch for biased research, Stan O'Neal, the head of the investment banking giant stated: "If we attempt to eliminate risk – to legislate, regulate, or litigate it out of existence – the ultimate result will be economic stagnation, perhaps even economic failure." To which the then Attorney-General, Eliot Spitzer, responded: "Indeed, you did not want to tolerate risk. Because what you did was shift the risk to unknowing investors while you got the fees up front."[34]

Finally, gharar incorporates the prohibition of the kind of risk that is akin to outright speculation. Indeed, unlike conventional economics which has a benign attitude toward speculation, Islam forbids speculation and gambling (qimar). Three passages in the Koran prohibit Maysir,[35] a game of chance played in pre-Islamic days (2:219, 5:90, and 5:91).[36] In every instance, the prohibition is associated with that against wine drinking. The primary reason for condemning Maysir was that it caused enmity and distracted the faithful from worship.

All this explains the importance in the Shariah of seeking clarity, simplicity and avoiding unnecessary complexity. As for necessary and unavoidable risk-taking, it must be based on equitable sharing among those involved.

III Contemporary Interpretations: Religious and Secular Experts

At a time of revolutionary changes in international finance, it was inevitable that literal, scholastic and legalistic interpretations of the Shariah would clash with pragmatic interpretations focusing on the spirit of Islam, and likely to invoke maslaha and darura. Where traditionalists are likely to defer to fiqh scholars, modernists will seek the advice of secular experts. In reality, the world of finance has grown so complicated that secular experts must be called upon to explain certain instruments and practices, leaving it to Shariah Boards and Islamic financiers to decide whether certain products and practices conform to the spirit of Islam.

In that regard, the 1989 Tantawi fatwa broke new ground. Chibli Mallat explains how the mufti based his decision, "on the basis of the Koran and Hadith, the obligation of wise men to search for the truth, the principle of ijtihad, the virtue of avoiding fanaticism, and *the importance of expertise to unravel arcane subjects*" (my emphasis). Tantawi cited the Koran's injunction to "ask the ahl al-dhikr if you do not know" (21:7), with *ahl al-dhikr* defined as "the people of expertise and experience in all science and art." The mufti further added: "in medicine you ask physicians, in fiqh the fuqaha, and in economics you ask economists."[37]

In what Mallat emphasized was a "significant and unusual move," the mufti conceded he could not answer questions that fell beyond his area of expertise – he specifically wrote that expertise in the Shariah does not imply familiarity with arcane financial matters – without consulting experts on banking: "Scientific trust requires (the mufti) not to issue a fatwa in such matters before asking those who are knowledgeable and possess expertise in these matters, because ruling on an issue requires (the mufti) to fully understand it (literally: ruling on a matter is part of imagining it)."[38] Accordingly, Tantawi sent detailed questions to the chairman of the board of Egypt's Ahli Bank, and inserted in his fatwa lengthy quotes from secular specialists. Not only were the opinions of secular experts a factor in the fatwa, but the mufti promised that in the future such consultations would occur to unravel financial matters.[39]

As already noted, the Tantawi fatwa was controversial in the Islamic world. Considering that modern economic and financial orthodoxy has turned old axioms on their heads, we can appreciate the range of controversy among scholars – and better understand the diversity of Islamic finance. Examples of the clash between secular financial orthodoxy and traditional Islamic injunctions on finance abound. On the topic of speculation, the early Islamic tradition roundly and unambiguously condemned gharar. Yet in recent centuries, new approaches toward risk have emerged: by relying on the past and using probabilities and other quantitative techniques, risk could be measured and to some extent tamed.[40] In areas such as insurance or financial derivatives, risk management has become crucial. So, rather than a wholesale condemnation of aleatory transactions, a more subtle and sophisticated approach to risk is called for in the light of recent intellectual advances.[41]

Put differently, rather than avoiding risk, financiers must learn to control it. But the danger of over-reliance on secular experts is that of falling into the trap of "market fundamentalism."[42] Economics textbooks usually explain that speculators play a "positive and necessary" role in the economy. The benefits of debt and the advantages of using "OPM" (other people's money) are highly touted. Finance professors have routinely justified egregious behavior[43] and glorified dubious characters such as "junk bond king," Michael Milken.[44] There is even an Orwellian tinge to the language of finance. Thus "hedge funds," whose purpose as suggested by their name is theoretically to mitigate risk, have become instruments of the riskiest form of speculation.[45]

Nor is there a credible consensus among secular experts. To be sure, the dominant economic orthodoxy assumes that a minimally regulated finance sector is good for the general welfare, and that the financial economy is a reasonably accurate reflection of the underlying real economy.[46] Yet other scholars have noted the disconnect between the financial economy and the real economy. Susan Strange, for example, has described as the erratic, volatile world of "casino capitalism," that bears little resemblance to the textbook universe of finance.[47] The international financial crisis of 1998 has shown that the leading experts of secular finance – Myron Scholes and Robert Merton who won the Nobel Prize in economics in 1997 for their contribution to the pricing of options and yet whose Long-Term Capital Management hedge fund collapsed the following year – can have it wrong.[48]

One could, therefore, see how, by relying on the rationalizations of certain experts, virtually any financial transaction could be justified. One manifestation of the range of disagreement is the "fatwa wars," which can only intensify as finance gains in complexity, whereby financial institutions would compete to find scholars that would tell them what they want to hear.[49]

IV The Moral Economy of Islam

Joan Robinson identified the three prerequisites for an economic system as being "a set of rules, an ideology to justify them, and a conscience in the individual which makes him strive to carry them out."[50] The ethical dimension is all too often forgotten, though it exists, as we shall see later, in any society.[51] This section explores the moral economy, or ethical framework, of Islam.[52]

Hard work and participation in economically creative activity is obligatory for every Muslim (Koran 62:10).[53] The importance of productivity has been justified as follows:

> Economic activity is not to be confined to earning or producing enough to meet one's personal needs only. Muslims are expected to produce more because they cannot participate in the process of purification through providing security to others (zakat or alms tax) unless they produce more than what they themselves consume. The most recommended use of fairly earned wealth is to apply it to procuring of all means to fulfill a Muslim's covenant with Allah.[54]

The broad ethical-economic system emphasizes fairness and productivity, honesty in trade and fair competition (Koran 17:35; 26:181–3),[55] the prohibition of hoarding wealth and worshipping it (Koran 104:2–4),[56] and the protection of human beings from their own folly and extravagance. Such a system, although rooted in an ancient tradition, is not, at least in its broad outlines, far removed from many contemporary approaches to ethical business practices.

As for the ethical-economic justification for the prohibition of riba, it is three-pronged: riba is unfair, it is exploitative, and it is unproductive. Under a traditional interest-based relation between borrower and lender, the borrower alone either incurs the losses or reaps disproportionately high benefits. Conversely, the lender makes money irrespective of the outcome of the business venture. Islam prefers that the risk of loss be shared equitably between the two. In other words, rather than collecting a "fixed, predetermined" compensation in the form of interest, lenders should be entitled to a share of any profits from a venture they have helped to finance. The broader argument is that any profit should be morally and economically justified. Hence, the injunctions against aleatory contracts and gharar where gain is the result of chance, or undetermined causes. As in other religions, riba was also seen as exploitative, since it tended to favor the rich, who were guaranteed a return, at the expense of the vulnerable, who assumed all the risk.

Significantly, the issue of fairness is not unrelated to issues of productivity and efficiency. Earning a profit is legitimate when one is engaged in an economic venture and thereby contributes to the economy. By certain accounts, Meccan merchants in the days of the Prophet routinely engaged (usually in between arrivals and departures of caravans) in interest-based lending, speculation and aleatory transactions.[57] This would account for the sharp distinction drawn in the Koran between profit from trade and profit from riba. While the former benefited the community and enhanced welfare, the latter diverted resources toward non-productive uses and contributed to illiquidity and scarcity.[58] The modern-day equivalent of that debate contrasts the real, productive economy with the financial, speculative one. Some Islamic economists have also argued that an interest-based economy is inherently inflationary and causes unemployment and poverty because the creation of money is not linked to productive investment.[59]

V An Historical and Comparative Approach

There are striking similarities between the spirit and often the letter of all Abrahamic religions on economic matters. All three emphasize justice through just wages and just prices, criticize speculation and wasteful consumption, and advocate moral behavior in commerce. This section considers primarily the attitudes towards interest. While injunctions were often identical in the pre-capitalist world, changes in the Western world, in particular since the sixteenth century, have led to new intellectual and theological attitudes. After the idea of a moderate, legally capped interest had replaced the previous ban on usury gained ground, there was a movement to eliminate such ceilings and let "the market" determine interest rates.

Moral qualms about money were common in the pre-capitalist world. In ancient Mesopotamia, the Hamurabi code (1800 BC) placed limits on interest rates and banned compound interest (interest on the interest). Aristotle provided the most influential argument about the "barrenness" of money: it should be a means of exchange and should not be allowed to multiply. The Romans allowed interest but regulated interest rates.[60]

The scholastic tradition among Christian theologians made the Aristotelian case that money was a "sterile commodity." The long-standing rule was *pecunia pecuniam non parit*, or money does not make money. The canon (which was not necessarily shared by the classical scholars of Islam) also considered the "pricing of time" illegitimate, since "time belongs to God." Unlike the farmer or the craftsman who actually produced something, money-lenders did not.[61]

Judaism, Christianity, and Islam considered that the lender, by definition, possessed a store of capital that exceeded his requirements, while the borrower lacked the resources to satisfy his immediate needs. It would thus be unfair and even immoral for a needy borrower both to repay the capital and to increase the lender's wealth still further by paying him interest, especially since the additional amount must be taken from the fruit of the borrower's industry. All three religions preached that the prosperous had a duty to assist the needy, if not by gifts, at least through interest-free loans.[62]

Importantly, however, if these religions were very similar, they were not identical. The Jewish tradition generally prohibited interest (Leviticus 25:36).[63] A loophole, however, allowed for interest on money lent to non-Jews (Deuteronomy 19:19–20).[64] The Christian gospels do not mention interest specifically, though they repeatedly denigrate money-making and economic pursuits.[65] As is the case with Judaism and Islam, the Christian tradition recommends that lenders should be prepared to forego parts of their loans to the poor (Luke 6:34–5).[66] Later Christian tradition provided for something called "antidora," a spontaneous and unforced gift of the borrower to the lender to thank him for his loan. Unlike conventional interest, it was not obligatory, pre-determined and fixed, but voluntary and in an amount left to the discretion of the borrower.[67]

In Christianity, as in Islam, there is also the principle of purification of ill-gotten gains. It was common in the Christian Middle Ages, for money lenders to lighten their guilt "by including in their will a token bequest to a charity and calling it restitution of any 'ill-gotten' money."[68] Money-lenders were sinners, but they were not beyond salvation: "Indispensable but malodorous, they were deliberate public sinners, likened to prostitutes, and hence tolerated on earth but earmarked for hell unless they repented, and made full restitution of their accursed gains."[69] Historian, Jacques Le Goff, draws interesting connections between the invention of the concept of purgatory in the second half of the twelfth century and money-lending. In his words, "the birth of purgatory is also the dawn of banking."[70]

Economic transformations created new financial needs and typically resulted in an intensification of the debates over usury.[71]

> The more frequent practices contrary to doctrine become," wrote Maxime Rodinson, "the more the ideological authorities (if they want to retain, on the one hand, some influence over society, and, on the other, some degree of coherence in their intellectual system) are led to theorize with finesse and subtlety, to allow for cases, exceptions, degrees of guilt and of innocence, means of atoning more or less fully for one's offences, and to work out a graduated scale of penalties and tolerances. It, therefore, seems quite in order that, in mediaeval Christian society as in Muslim society, it was at the very moment when capitalistic practices implying the need for interest were developing with the greatest vigor that the theologians and religious lawyers took the greatest trouble to theorize about the prohibition of interest, justifying it, explaining it and allowing for cases and exceptions."[72]

Similarly, Abraham Udovitch noted: "The frequent, copious, and vehement reiteration of the prohibition against usury in medieval Islamic religious writings has been interpreted by some scholars as indirect testimony to its equally frequent violation in practice."[73]

In medieval Europe, the ban on usury was repeatedly reaffirmed: the Council of Reims (1069) and the Second Lateran Council (1139) condemned usury.; the Third Lateran Council (1179) excommunicated usurers; the Fourth Lateran Council (1215) permitted Jews to practice it; and the Council of Lyon (1274) reiterated the condemnation and marked the first official recognition of salvation by purgatory. The arguments of the scholastics and other canonists remained virtually unchallenged throughout the thirteenth and fourteenth centuries. Like the Third Lateran Council, the Second Council of Lyon in 1274 proclaimed that Christians who lent at interest would be excommunicated.[74] In 1311 the Council of Vienna declared that secular legislation that did not prohibit interest was invalid and that anyone who asserted otherwise was a heretic who would be punished accordingly.

While those theological discussions were taking place, new institutions and practices were created to circumvent the Church's prohibition of usury. One of the best-known innovations was *contractum trinius*, a contract combining three separate contracts: one of partnership; one of sale of profit; and one of insurance. The lender would invest money with a merchant on a profit-and-loss sharing basis, insure himself against a loss of capital, and sell back to the merchant any profit above a specified amount. Each of the components was considered permissible; combining them was tantamount to lending money at a pre-arranged guaranteed fixed rate of return.[75] In the fifteenth and sixteenth centuries, increasing attention was devoted to the question of the licitness of such practices.[76]

It was only in 1515 that the Church, at the Lateran Council, legitimated interest on secured loans. Although it still took a long time before the idea was fully accepted, new and increasingly subtle approaches to money-lending (often inspired by the Islamic hiyals) had been gaining ground. There were a number of ways of circumventing prohibitions on usury, which in its canon law definition meant "whatever is added to the principal."[77] One was the traditional "free and loving loan" (*mutuum gratis et amore*), a loan with a built-in, concealed interest."[78] Perhaps the most significant invention in that respect was the "letter of exchange."[79] As a first step, the idea of a small interest for certain purposes was accepted. The Jesuits, for example, approved of commercial credit.[80]

A counter-theory of usury appeared with the Protestant Reformation. The reformers, no longer bound by canon law, engaged in significant innovation on matters of political economy and money. Martin Luther (1483–1546) urged Christians to participate fully in the world and challenge the Church's teachings. John Calvin (1509–64) argued that religious fulfillment came from hard work and not merely from prayer and spiritual contemplation. In his famous "Letter on Usury" (1545), Calvin stated that usury is licit, but "not everywhere, nor always, nor in all goods, nor from all." He used the golden rule as a guide: usury is sinful only if it hurts one's neighbor, and charity and natural equity alone can decide in what particular cases a charge for a loan does hurt a neighbor since each believer is guided by his own conscience. For example, lending to the poor in order to achieve a profit is wicked, but in lending to the rich, a modest profit is acceptable. The ministers of the gospel could lend to merchants, but in such a way that their profit is not certain.[81]

The Calvinist bankers in Geneva were thus free to develop their financial interests without any feelings of guilt, provided that they observed the Christian

teaching on justice to the poor, and that they were totally honest in their dealings.[82]
In time, some of Calvin's followers sought to eliminate some of the "exceptions"
that Calvin had provided for. In 1630 Calvinist classicist, Claude Saumaise (1588–
1653), took the defense of usurers who lent to the poor. In his view, the moneylender performs a highly useful service, as does anyone who provides a means
for meeting a great public need. His views, as summarized by John Noonan, are:
"If it is licit to make money with things bought with money, why is it not licit to
make money from money? Everyone makes his living from someone else; why
should not the usurer? The seller of bread is not required to ask if he sells it to a
poor man or a rich man. Why should the moneylender have to make a distinction?" Saumaise also defended high interest charges, which he saw as beneficial
in stimulating the borrowers to repay more quickly. In his view, it was negligence,
inertia, and prodigality that were the real enemies of the poor, not the usurer.[83]

Such views become common, especially in England, with the advent of industrialization and the triumph of the capitalist ideology. In letters written in 1787 "in
defence of usury," Jeremy Bentham made the case for the "the liberty of making
one's own terms in money bargains."[84] He noted the mischief of anti-usurious
laws, principally "that of precluding so many people, altogether, from the getting
the money they stand in need of, to answer their respective exigencies," and
"the distress it would produce, were the liberty of borrowing denied to every
body."[85] Bentham objected in particular to the differentiation made between
money-lending and other forms of commerce: "Why a man who takes as much
as he can get, be it six, or seven, or eight, or ten per cent for the use of a sum of
money, should be called usurer, should be loaded with an opprobrious name, any
more than if he had bought a house with it, and made a proportionable profit by
the house, is more than I can see."[86]

In sum, the history of ideas in relation to money had gone through three
stages. In the first, usury was generally forbidden. In the second, a small rate of
interest, regulated by the state, was permitted. In the theological debate, a new
emphasis was placed on those passages of the gospels that stressed the need for
wealth to fructify. Thus, the parable of the talents stresses the need to be productive (Matthew 25:14–30). In another parable, a nobleman calls ten of his servants
before a long journey, giving them a pound each saying, "Trade with this while
I'm away." Upon his return, the servants who used the funds which their master
had provided to make additional money were praised, whereas the servant who
merely returned the money without gain is condemned (Luke 19:22–6).

Catholic countries were somewhat slower in formally endorsing this view.
Thus, in France interest-based loans were only formally legalized in October
1789 (and later incorporated in the Napoleonic Civil Code).[87] The Egyptian code
(as well as other codes in the Islamic world that were influenced by it), inspired
by the French code, also adopted the view that interest was legal provided that
it was limited by law. In the third stage, the prevailing view was that existing
ceilings were too low and that they should either be significantly increased or
removed altogether. In line with the free-market ideology, they argued that it was

up to the market to determine interest rates. Nowadays, and especially with the deregulation movement of the 1980s, while most countries still have laws on the books against usurious rates and against extortionate lending, it is a Benthamite logic that prevails, as usury ceilings have been allowed to rise significantly or to be overridden under most circumstances.

Despite this evolution, misgivings about finance and about the "unearned" quality of financial profits have not subsided. There is a considerable literature on predatory and unproductive finance, ranging from critiques of rentier economies and parasitic groups, to the pernicious effects of debt, to scathing portraits of the misdeeds of financiers.[88] In the United States, despite the dominance of the free market ideology, there is a long history of suspicion of banks and financiers. At the time of the controversy over the chartering of the Bank of the United States, Thomas Jefferson had argued that it was only "the speculators, the creditors, and the wealthy bank stockholders who benefited from a public debt" and that "the bankers had no stake in general prosperity or public well-being except insofar as they generated tax revenues to pay the interest charges that enriched them."[89] At times of economic hardship – for example, in the 1890s and 1930s – bankers and financiers were the designated culprits.[90] During the Great Depression, bank robbers became folk heroes. In the 1980s and 1990s, just as financial deregulation started spreading all over the world, "paper entrepreneurs" were occasionally attacked for shuffling assets without creating value,[91] just as "Wall Street" (at the time announcements of layoffs would invariably boost a company's stock value) was criticized for having interests that were antithetical to those of "Main Street."[92] It took the near meltdown of global finance in 2008 to bring the excesses of finance into the political and economic mainstream.[93]

Notes

1. In the early years of modern Islamic finance, Islamic institutions did not assess late fees, which created a moral hazard: it would make financial sense for debtors to be systematically late in their payments. A compromise was soon found: Islamic institutions would impose late fees as a means of imposing on-time payment discipline, but the proceeds from such late fees would go to a charitable fund. In many instances such funds are tapped to help distressed borrowers.

2. 2:275 "Those who swallow riba cannot rise except as he arises whom the devil prostrates by [his] touch. This is because they say, 'Trading is only like riba. And Allah has allowed trading and forbidden riba. To whomsoever then the admonition has come from his Lord, and he desists, he shall have what has already passed. And his affair is in the hands of Allah. And whoever returns [to it] – these are the companions of the Fire' therein they will abide." 2:276 "Allah will blot out riba, and He causes charity to prosper. And Allah loves not any ungrateful sinner." 2:277 "Those who believe and do good deeds and keep up prayer and pay the poor-rate – their reward is with their Lord; and they have no fear, nor shall they grieve." 2:278 "O you who believe, keep your duty to Allah and relinquish what remains (due) from riba, if you are believers." 2:279 "But if you do (it) not, then be apprised of war from Allah and His Messenger; and if you repent, then you shall have your capital. Wrong not, and you shall not be wronged." 2:280 "And if (the debtor) is in straitness, let there be postponement till (he is in) ease.

And that you remit (it) as alms is better for you, if you only knew." 2:281 "And guard yourselves against a day in which you will be returned to Allah. Then every soul will be paid in full what it has earned, and they will not be wronged." 3:129–30 "O you who believe, devour not riba, doubling and redoubling and keep your duty to Allah, that you may be successful. And guard yourselves against the fire which has been prepared for the disbelievers." 4:161 "And for their taking riba – though indeed they were forbidden it – and their devouring the property of people falsely. And We have prepared for the disbelievers from among them a painful chastisement." 30:39 And whatever you lay out at riba, so that it may increase in the property of men, it increases not with Allah; and whatever you give in charity, desiring Allah's pleasure – these will get manifold."

3. Edward Mortimer, *Faith and Power: The Politics of Islam* (New York: Random House, 1982), p. 245.

4. Fazlur Rahman, "Riba and Interest," *Islamic Studies: Journal of the Central Institute of Islamic Research*, Karachi, 3: 1 (1964), p. 42.

5. See David Baldwin and Rodwey Wilson "Islamic Finance in Principle and Practice, with special reference to Turkey," in Chibli Mallat (ed.), *Islamic Law and Finance* (London: Graham and Trotman, 1988).

6. Hence, the Koranic verse 3:129 "O you who believe, devour not riba, doubling and redoubling and keep your duty to Allah, that you may be successful."

7. The Hadith, in its abbreviated form: The Prophet said: "[Exchange] gold for gold, silver for silver, wheat for wheat, barley for barley, dates for dates, salt for salt, measure for measure and hand-to-hand If the [exchanged] articles belong to different genera, the exchange is without restraint provided it takes place in a hand-to-hand transaction." Nobil Saleh, *Unlawful Gain and Legitimate Profit in Islamic Law* (Cambridge: Cambridge University Press, 1986) (2nd edn., 1992, Kluwer Law International).

8. William E. Shepherd, "Muhammad Sa'id al-'Ashmawi and the Application of the Shari'a in Egypt," *International Journal of Middle Eastern Studies*, 28 (1996), p. 46.

9. Chibli Mallat, *The renewal of Islamic Law: Muhammad Baqer as-Sadr, Najaf and the Shi'i International* (Cambridge: Cambridge University Press, 1993), pp. 162–84.

10. Philip Hitti, *Islam: A Way of Life* (Oxford: Oxford University Press, 1970), p. 23.

11. Fuad al-Omar and Mohammed Abdel-Haq, *Islamic Banking: Theory, Practice and Challenges* (London: Zed Books, 1996), p. 9.

12. Anwar Iqbal Qureshi, *Islam and the Theory of Interest* (Lahore: Ashraf, 1974), p. 4.

13. Ziaul Haque, *RIBA: The Moral Economy of Usury, Interest, and Profit* (Selangor, Malaysia: Ikraq, 1995).

14. Chibli Mallat, "The Debate on Riba and Interest in Twentieth Century Egypt," in Mallat (ed.), *Islamic Law and Finance*, p. 69–88.

15. Mallat, "The Debate on Rib".

16. Fuad al-Omar and Mohammed Abdel-Had, *Islamic Banking: Theory, Practice and Challenges* (London: Zed Books, 1996), p. 8.

17. See Chapter 4.

18. Chibli Mallat, "Tantawi on Banking," in Muhammad Khalid Masud, Brinkley Messick and David S. Powers (eds.), *Islamic Legal Interpretation: Muftis and their Fatwas* (Cambridge, MA: Harvard University Press, 1996), pp. 286–96.

19. Mallat, "Tantawi on Banking."

20. Reuters, May 30, 1995.

21. Agence France-Presse, August 22, 1997.

22. The justification is that Islamic banks, by virtue of their relative size in the global banking system must conform to established pricing mechanisms. They compete against conventional institutions and operate within a global interest-based system. In economic terms, they are price-takers and not price-makers.

23. See Saleh, *Unlawful Gain* and Frank E. Vogel and Samuel L. Hayes, III, *Islamic Law and*

Finance: Religion, Risk and Return (Cambridge, MA: Kluwer Law International, 1998).

24. Outside of religion, a number of philosophical systems have nonetheless advocated comparable principles. Roman Stoic, Seneca, wrote about the need to avoid "things that are the gift of chance. Whenever circumstance brings some welcome thing your way, stop in suspicion and alarm … They are snares … We think these things are ours when in fact it is we who are caught. That track leads to precipices; life on that giddy level ends in a fall."

25. 31:33 "Let not this world's life deceive you, nor let the great deceiver (the devil) deceive you about Allah."

26. Quoted in *A Mini Guide to Islamic Banking and Finance* (Kuala Lumpur: Cert Publications, 2006), p. 21.

27. Vogel and Hayes, *Islamic Law and Finance*, pp. 87–8.

28. Vogel and Hayes, *Islamic Law and Finance*, pp. 89–90.

29. Maxime Rodinson, *Islam and Capitalism* (London: Penguin, 1978), p. 16.

30. Mahmoud A. El-Gamal, *Islamic Finance: Law, Economics, and Practice* (Cambridge: Cambridge University Press, 2006), p. 59.

31. Saleh, *Unlawful Gain*, p. 53.

32. Nassim Nicholas Taleb, "The Fourth Quadrant: A Map of The Limits of Statistics," *The Edge*, September 15, 2008, available at: *http://www.edge.org/3rd_culture/talebo8/talebo8_index.html*. See also Nassim Nicholas Taleb, *The Black Swan, The Impact of the Highly Improbable* (New York: Random House, 2007) and *Fooled by Randomness: The Hidden Role of Chance in Life and in the Markets*, 2nd edn. (New York: Random House, 2008).

33. John Kay, "Same Old Folly, New Spiral of Risk," *The Financial Times*, August 13, 2007.

34. Paul Krugman, "The Acid Test," *The New York Times*, May 2, 2003.

35. A game of chance played by Arabs. The derivation is either from *yusr* (facility or ease, that is, ease with which wealth could be attained) or from *yasara* (dividing anything into parts or portions).

36. 2:219 "They ask thee about intoxicants and game of chance. Say: in both of them is a great sin and (some) advantage for men, and their sin is greater than their advantage. And they ask thee as to what they should spend. Say: what you can spare. Thus does Allah make clear to you the messages that you may ponder." 5:90 "O you who believe, intoxicants and games of chance and (sacrificing to) stones set up and (dividing by) arrows are only an uncleanliness, the devil's work; so shun it that you may succeed." 5:91 "The devil desires only to create enmity and hatred among you by means of intoxicants and games of chance, and to keep you back from remembrance of Allah and from prayer. Will you then keep back?"

37. Mallat, "Tantawi on Banking," pp. 286–96.

38. Mallat, "Tantawi on Banking," pp. 286–96.

39. Mallat, "Tantawi on Banking," pp. 286–96.

40. Peter L. Bernstein, *Against the Gods: The Remarkable Story of Risk* (New York: Wiley, 1997).

41. See Chapter 2.

42. See Chapter 2.

43. Benjamin J. Stein, *License to Steal: The Untold Story of Michael Milken and the Conspiracy to Bilk the Nation* (New York: Simon and Schuster, 1992).

44. Ibrahim Warde, "Michael Milken, ange et martyr," *Le Monde diplomatique*, August 1993.

45. Ibrahim Warde, "La grande kermesse de l'économie financière," *Le Monde diplomatique*, June 1993.

46. Ibrahim Warde, "La tyrannie de l'économiquement correct," *Le Monde diplomatique*, May 1995.

47. Susan Strange, *Casino Capitalism* (Oxford: Basil Blackwell, 1986).

48. Ibrahim Warde, "Le système bancaire dans la tourmente" and "LTCM, un fonds au-dessus de tout soupçon," *Le Monde diplomatique*, November 1998.

49. Michel Gallois, *Finance islamique et pouvoir politique: le cas de l'Egypte moderne* (Paris: Presses universitaires de France, 1997).
50. Joan Robinson, *Economic Philosophy* (London: C. A. Watts, 1962), p. 13.
51. James C. Scott, *The Moral Economy of the Peasant: Rebellion and Subsistence in Southeast Asia* (New Haven, CT: Yale University Press, 1976).
52. On that subject, see also Charles Tripp, *Islam and the Moral Economy: The Challenge of Capitalism* (Cambridge: Cambridge University Press, 2006).
53. 62:10 "But when the prayer is ended, disperse abroad in the land and seek Allah's grace, and remember Allah much, so that you may be successful."
54. Khalid M. Ishaque, "The Islamic Approach to Economic Development," in John L. Esposito (ed.), *Voices of Resurgent Islam* (Oxford: Oxford University Press, 1983), p. 271.
55. 17:35 "And give full measure when you measure out, and weigh with a true balance. This is fair and better in the end." 26:181–3 "Give full measure and be not of those who diminish. And weigh with a true balance. And wrong not men of their dues, and act not corruptly on earth making mischief."
56. 104:2–4: "Woe to who amasses wealth and counts it. He thinks that his wealth will make him abide. Nay, he will certainly be hurled into the crushing disaster."
57. Henry Lammens, *La Mecque à la veille de l'Hégire* (Beirut: Imprimerie catholique, 1924).
58. Traute Wohlers-Scharf, *Arab and Islamic Banks: New Business Partners for Developing Countries* (Paris: OECD, 1983), p. 75.
59. Ahmed Abdel Aziz El-Nagar, *One Hundred Questions & One Hundred Answers Concerning Islamic Banks* (Cairo: International Association of Islamic Banks, 1980), p. 8.
60. Hamid Algabid, *Les banques islamiques* (Paris: Economics, 1990), pp. 48–50.
61. John Noonan, *The Scholastic Analysis of Usury* (Cambridge, MA: Harvard University Press, 1957).
62. J. Pierre V. Benoit, *United States Interest Rates and the Interest Rate Dilemma for the Developing World* (Westport, CT: Quorum Books, 1986), pp. 34–55.
63. 25:36: "You shall not charge your brother interest on a loan, either by deducting it in advance from the capital sum, or by adding it on repayment."
64. 19:19: "Do not charge your brother interest, whether on money or food or anything else that may earn interest." 19:20. "You may charge a foreigner interest, but not a brother Israelite, so that the Lord your God may bless you in everything you put your hand to in the land you are entering to possess."
65. 16:13 "No servant can be the slave of two masters; for either he will hate the first and love the second, or he will be devoted to the first and think nothing of the second. You cannot serve both God and Money." 18:22 "Sell everything you have and distribute to the poor, and you will have riches in heaven." 18:24–25 "How hard it is for the wealthy to enter the kingdom of God! It is easier for a camel to go through the eye of a needle than for a rich man to enter the kingdom of God."
66. 6:34–5 "And if you lend to those from whom you expect to receive, what credit is that to you? Even sinners lend to sinners, to get back the same amount. But love your enemies, and do good, and lend, expecting nothing in return, and your reward will be great, and you will be sons of the Most High, for he is kind to the ungrateful and the evil."
67. Bartolomé Clavero, *La Grâce du don: anthropologie catholique de l'économie moderne* (Paris: Albin Michel, 1997).
68. Robert Lopez, in *The Dawn of Modern Banking*, Center of Medieval and Renaissance Studies, University of California, Los Angeles (New Haven, CT: Yale University Press, 1979), p. 7.
69. Lopez, in *The Dawn of Modern Banking*.
70. Jacques Le Goff, "The Usurer and Purgatory," in *The Dawn of Modern Banking*, p. 52.
71. Robert Heilbroner, *The Making of Economic Society* (Englewood Cliffs, NJ: Prentice Hall, 1993), pp. 35–49.

72. Rodinson, *Islam and Capitalism*, p. 48.
73. Abraham L. Udovitch, "Bankers without Banks: Commerce, Banking, and Society in the Islamic World of the Middle Ages," in *The Dawn of Modern Banking*, p. 257.
74. Center of Medieval and Renaissance Studies, University of California,*The Dawn of Modern Banking*, pp. 291–9.
75. John F. Chown, *A History of Money: From AD 800* (New York: Routledge, 1997), p. 121.
76. Benoit, *United States Interest Rates*, p. 47.
77. Noonan, *The Scholastic Analysis of Usury*, p. 365.
78. Robert Lopez, in *The Dawn of Modern Banking*, p. 17.
79. Jean-François Bergier, "From the Fifteenth Century in Italy to the Sixteenth Century in Germany: A New Banking Concept?," in *The Dawn of Modern Banking*, p. 106.
80. Noonan, *The Scholastic Analysis of Usury*, p. 221.
81. Noonan, *The Scholastic Analysis of Usury*, p. 365–7.
82. Benoit, *United States Interest Rates*, p. 88.
83. Noonan, *The Scholastic Analysis of Usury*, p. 371.
84. Jeremy Bentham, *Defence of Usury: Shewing the Impolicy of the Present Legal Restraints on the Terms of Pecuniary Bargains* (London: Payne and Foss, 1816), p. 1.
85. Bentham, *Defence of Usury*, p. 45.
86. Bentham, *Defence of Usury*, p. 14.
87. Hubert Bonin, *La banque et les banquiers en France du Moyen-Age à nos jours* (Paris: Larousse, 1992), p. 19.
88. See, for example, Richard Farnetti, *Le Royaume Désuni: L'économie britannique et les multi-nationales* (Paris: Syros, 1995); Connie Bruck, *The Predators' Ball: The Inside Story of Drexel Burnham and the Rise of the Junk Bond Raiders* (New York: Simon and Schuster, 1988); James Stewart, *Den of Thieves* (New York: Simon and Schuster, 1991).
89. Mansel G. Blackford and K. Austin Kerr, *Business Enterprise in American History*, 2nd edn. (Boston, MA: Houghton-Mifflin, 1990), p. 71.
90. William Greider, *Secrets of the Temple: How the Federal Reserve Runs the Country* (New York: Simon and Schuster, 1986).
91. Robert Reich, *The Next American Frontier* (New York: Time Books, 1983).
92. Marie-Agnès Combesque and Ibrahim Warde, *Mythologies américaines* (Paris: Editions du félin, 1996), pp. 227–8, and Doug Henwood, *Wall Street: How It Works and for Whom* (London: Verso, 1997).
93. See, for example, Charles R. Morris, *The Trillion Dollar Meltdown: Easy Money, High Rollers, and the Great Credit Crash* (New York: Public Affairs, 2008).

4

THE EVOLUTION OF MODERN ISLAMIC FINANCE

Following a few pioneering experiments, modern Islamic finance started in earnest in the 1970s. Largely driven by the oil boom, it was bound to be transformed by the collapse of oil prices in the 1980s, and more generally by changes in the global political and economic system. In that respect, it is useful to think in terms of three distinct stages: the early years (1975–91); the age of globalization (1991–2001); and the post-September 11, 2001 period.

I Precursors

The idea of modern Islamic finance is usually traced to Indian Muslims in the 1940s. As they pondered their future in the final years of British colonial rule, they discussed the ways in which old Islamic practices could be revived. Abul Ala Mawdudi (1903–79), who created the Jamaat-i Islami, popularized the notion of Islamic economics. In his view, Islam is not simply about religious beliefs and rituals. It is a complete way of life that should include economics and finance. Though short on specifics, Mawdudi argued in favor of constraining market processes through behavioral norms based on the Islamic tradition. In the same vein, following the partition of 1947 and the creation of the state of Pakistan ("land of the pure"), Pakistani scholars addressed the feasibility of a financial system that would conform with the Shariah and eliminate riba. However, these debates remained mostly theoretical, and it took a number of political and economic developments, more specifically the advent of pan-Islamism and the rise in oil prices, before such ideas were put into practice.[1]

A few pilot experiments preceded the formal start of modern Islamic banking. In the Indian subcontinent, loan cooperatives, influenced by European mutual loan experiments[2] and infused with religious and ethical ideals, were started in the 1940s.[3] At least one experiment took place in Pakistan in the late 1950s, when rural landlords created an interest-free credit network.[4] In Malaysia, the Muslim Pilgrims Savings Corporation was set up in 1963 to help people save toward performing their religious pilgrimage (haj). It later evolved into the Pilgrims Management and Fund Board, or the Tabung Haji as it is now popularly known – an Islamic savings bank of sorts which invested the savings of prospective pilgrims in accordance with the Shariah.[5]

The highest profile experiment was conducted in Egypt between 1963 and 1967, in Mit Ghamr in the Nile Delta. The founder, Dr Ahmed Naggar (who would later become Secretary of the International Association of Islamic Banks [IAIB]), had been educated in West Germany and was greatly influenced by the mutual savings schemes he discovered there. With capital supplied by West German banks, he obtained the support of the Egyptian government. At its peak, the bank had nine branches in operation, 250,000 depositors and close to 2 million Egyptian pounds in deposits. Although its charter made no reference to Islam or the Shariah, the bank neither paid nor charged interest. It earned profits by engaging in trade and industry directly or in partnership with others, and to a lesser extent by financing business on a profit-sharing basis.[6] The circumstances of its closure are somewhat obscure. By certain accounts the bank had encountered severe financial problems. Others suggest that the bank was commercially successful but was closed for political reasons, which ranged from fear of Islamic fundamentalism to disagreements over how the bank should be regulated.[7]

In 1971, as part of Anwar Sadat's policy of co-opting Islamic groups in his fight against leftist elements, the Egyptian government created the Nasser Social Bank. The official goals were to "broaden the base of social solidarity among citizens" and to "provide aid to needy citizens." As with the previous experiment, there was no direct reference to religion, but the bank's operations were based on mudaraba and the collection and distribution of zakat.[8]

Finally, a few experiments involving Islamic money management took place around the same period. In Egypt, Abd al-Latif al-Sharif, who at one time had to flee to Saudi Arabia to avoid Nasser's persecution of the Muslim Brothers, founded the al-Sharif company in the 1960s.[9] The company would gain notoriety in the 1980s as one of the leading Islamic Money Management institutions.

II The First Stage (1975–91)

1 The First Islamic Banks

The aggiornamento of Islamic doctrine on banking matters occurred under the auspices of the Organization of the Islamic Conference (OIC), then largely dominated by Saudi Arabia. Most accounts suggest that the turning point occurred when, in the early 1970s, King Faisal of Saudi Arabia was sold on the idea of the creation of a pan-Islamic bank. These were heady days for oil-producing countries, many of which had already moved to take control of their economic destiny by progressively nationalizing the "commanding heights" of their economies, including oil industries and financial institutions.[10] The quadrupling of oil prices in 1973–4 marked a watershed, leading many to believe that it had ushered in, if not a New International Economic Order (NIEO), then at the very least a new era in North–South relations.[11] Under those circumstances, an Islamic banking system held the promise of more control over the Islamic world's political and economic destiny. It was also assumed that idle funds that had stayed away from the conventional (or interest-based) banking system would flock to a system devised according to Islamic precepts.

As the issue moved to the forefront of the Islamic agenda, the challenge was to devise a system that would be at once consistent with religious precepts and also viable in a modern economy. Hence, an unprecedented ijtihad that built on earlier attempts to redefine financial concepts and practices. At the Third Islamic Conference, held in Jeddah in 1972, a comprehensive plan to reform the monetary and financial systems according to Islamic ethics was presented to the foreign ministers of participating countries.[12]

The 1974 OIC summit in Lahore voted to create the inter-governmental Islamic Development Bank (IDB), which was expected to become the cornerstone of the Islamic banking system. In addition to injecting funds into the regions where they were most needed and providing fee-based financial services and profit-sharing financial assistance to member countries – in the spirit of the NIEO and of Southern solidarity – the new institution was to promote through direct participation, training and advice, and the creation of additional Islamic institutions. It would also manage the income from interest received from non-Muslim countries, as well as from zakat funds, finance reciprocal trade and serve as a clearing house for international payments between Muslim countries. Forty-four countries were founding members of the bank, the largest shareholders being Saudi Arabia (25 per cent), Libya (16 per cent), the United Arab Emirates (14 per cent) and Kuwait (13 per cent).

The Dubai Islamic Bank, created in 1975, is considered to be the first modern, non-governmental, Islamic bank. Before the decade was over, similar banks had sprouted up throughout the Islamic world: the Kuwait Finance House (1977); the Faisal Islamic Bank of Egypt (1977); the Islamic Bank of Sudan (1977); the Jordan Islamic Bank for Finance and Investment (1978); the Bahrain Islamic Bank (1978); and the Islamic International Bank for Investment and Development in Egypt (1980). In addition, a handful of international investment banks were created, such as the Islamic Investment Company in Nassau (1977), the Islamic Investment Company of the Gulf in Sharjah (1978), the Sharia Investment Services in Geneva (1980), and the Bahrain Islamic Investment Bank in Manama (1980).[13] Those developments would not have been possible without the influence of a handful of pioneers, chief among them Prince Mohammed al-Faisal al-Saud (a son of King Faisal), whose role as entrepreneur, lobbyist and proselytizer will be further discussed in the following pages. Another early pioneer was Sheikh Saleh Kamel, a self-made Saudi businessman and founder of the Dallah al Baraka group. According to Clement M. Henry, "Each was a determined and principled innovator, noted for his piety as well as his entrepreneurship."[14]

The paradigm of modern Islamic banking was established in those years, through what Monzer Kahf called "the new alliance of wealth and Shariah scholarship."[15] Since riba was defined as interest, Islamic banking became synonymous with interest-free banking. The prevailing belief was that interest-based banking would be primarily replaced by profit-and-loss sharing (PLS) schemes.

Many questions, however, were left unresolved, for example, whether banks could invest in bonds or debentures, earn interest on their balances with conventional banks, or be involved in commodity trading and similar operations that could involve uncertainty or speculation. Yet the oil bonanza as well as the novelty of the concept allowed wide latitude for experimentation. Funds were plentiful for the handful of Islamic institutions which were in a position to share a monopoly on the small but growing niche of clients looking for Islamically-correct investments. Many depositors did not seek any remuneration, thus providing banks with the cheapest possible funding.

Despite the early enthusiasm, the initial evolution of Islamic finance led to disappointment in many quarters. Banks concentrated on trading, investment in physical assets such as commodities and real estate, and a variety of mark-up schemes. Profit-and-loss sharing arrangements – which were expected to be the main financial instruments – proved to be far more complicated to put together. Whenever banks ventured into that terrain, they lost money. Banks preferred less risky alternatives. Murabaha, which was initially looked at as a stop-gap instrument, soon became the product of choice. Perhaps the most common criticism was that interest-free banking was really an exercise in semantics. To many critics, Islamic banks were in reality quite similar to conventional banks since something resembling interest, albeit under a different name, was in the end paid to most depositors and charged to most borrowers. It should be remembered that the 1970s were a decade of high inflation worldwide, and concerns about maintaining purchasing power were paramount.

In their own defense, Islamic financiers argued that the system was still in its infancy. Governments, and most significantly private-sector pioneers, put a lot of effort and money into helping to fine-tune Islamic banking concepts and practices. The creation in 1977 of the International Association of Islamic Banks (presided over by Prince Mohammed) provided an additional coordination and advice mechanism for the new banks. Among the IAIB's first initiatives was the publication of the *Handbook of Islamic Banking*.[16] Written in Arabic by leading Islamic scholars, this "scientific and practical encyclopedia for Islamic bankers" was designed to become the definitive reference for Islamic institutions.

Conceptual and practical issues were to be further clarified under the auspices of the IAIB and other pan-Islamic organizations. At the meeting of the Governors of Central Banks and Monetary Authorities of the Islamic Conference held in Riyadh in 1980, Prince Mohammed presented a progress report on Islamic banking. On the same occasion the Islamic Investment Company submitted proposals for Model Islamic Banks and a Model Law for the Establishment, Organization, Regulation, and Control of Islamic Banks. Countries were invited to adapt such guidelines to their individual requirements.[17]

The period saw the proliferation of research institutes dedicated to Islamic economics and finance.[18] One example was the Saleh Kamel Center for Islamic and Commercial Research created in 1979 at the al-Azhar University. Funded by the founder of the Dallah al-Baraka group, its goals were:

to favor comparative research on Islamic and Western thought in economics, management, and accounting; advise Islamic financial institutions; organize training sessions for their executives, as well as conferences and symposia; publish the *Review of Islamic Commercial Studies*; and revive the cultural heritage of Islam, though the translation and publication of ancient works.[19]

In 1979, Pakistan became the first country to embark on a full Islamicization of its banking sector.[20] The following years saw a number of important developments. One was the rapid expansion of transnational networks; the most significant of which was the "Prince Mohammed group," comprising Islamic banks and investment companies promoted by the Saudi prince. The group included national Islamic banks which provided finance to the general public at local level as well as internationally-oriented Islamic investment and holding companies. In addition to the Islamic Investment Company in the Bahamas (with its wholly-owned subsidiaries, the Islamic Investment Company of the Gulf and a service company, the Sharia Investment Services company in Geneva), in 1981 Prince Mohammed set up the most ambitious Islamic project ever, Dar al-Maal al-Islami (the DMI Group), with a targeted capitalization of $1 billion.[21]

DMI was a potent mix of finance, politics, and religion. The founding members – a who's who of Islamic political and religious leaders – signed the "appeal of the Islamic Umma". Shareholders belonged to sixteen countries: seven countries were represented by their rulers; the others by prominent business, political, and religious leaders. The list included ten Saudi princes; two Kuwaiti princes; the Emir of Bahrain; the Emir of Abu Dhabi (and leader of the United Arab Emirates); Sheikh Zayed Bin Sultan al-Nahyan; Guinean President, Ahmed Sekou Toure; Pakistani leader, Zia ul-Haq, and even the exiled King Fuad II of Egypt (who signed the manifesto from his residence in Monaco). The Sudanese signatories were the President, Jaafar al-Nimeiri; the Prime Minister, Sadiq al-Mahdi; and Hassan al-Turabi, president of the National Islamic Front. Egyptian signatories included, in addition to the former king, Ibrahim Kamel, a pioneer of Islamic banking; and Omar Abdul Rahman.[22] DMI was registered as a trust under the laws of the Bahamas and managed by an eighteen-member board. Its wholly-owned operating company, DMI S.A. was registered in Geneva. A six-member Religious Supervision Board was to ensure that operations were conducted in accordance with the Shariah.

The very name of the group evokes the golden age of Islam, since Dar al-Maal was the organization in charge of public finance and almsgiving. As for being headquartered in non-Islamic tax and regulatory havens, the internal information bulletin of the group explained that it was "for reasons of neutrality and political security." The bulletin added that "given the Islamic nature of the enterprise and the desire to promote unity inside the Islamic umma," the founders hoped that "in the nearest possible future, a company would be created within the legal framework of an Islamic state, whose headquarters would be in Mecca, thus emphasizing its pan-Islamic character." The statement also said that "this transformation should not affect the economic interests of the DMI shareholders."[23]

From the outset, DMI had ambitious expansion plans: financing development and setting up a worldwide network of subsidiary Islamic banks, investment and insurance companies in the "Umma West" (Africa), the "Umma Center" (the Persian Gulf, North Africa, and Turkey), the "Umma East" (Pakistan, Bangladesh, Malaysia) and even outside the Islamic world, in the Americas, Europe, and the Far East.[24] With such political and financial firepower, backed up by religious credentials, the group was in a position to enter most markets it targeted, often on favorable terms.

The early 1980s also saw further "full Islamicizations" of banking systems (the Sudan and Iran in 1983). Other notable developments, and harbingers of future evolution, were the decision by Danish authorities to authorize the creation of the Islamic Bank International, which would operate according to the Islamic Shariah without any special concessions or exceptions granted,[25] and the creation in 1979 by Egypt's Banque Misr, one of the oldest and best-known Middle Eastern institutions, of a dedicated Islamic unit.

The price of oil peaked in 1981 and started a slow process of decline. The political and economic context of the mid-1980s was thus quite different from that of the previous decade, and, as discussed later in this chapter, it challenged many of the early assumptions of Islamic finance. At the same time, other factors gave Islamic finance a second wind. In November 1985, the Islamic Fiqh Academy, meeting in Jeddah made an appeal to all Islamic countries to facilitate the creation of Islamic banks. It also decided to forbid Muslims from using a conventional bank if an Islamic bank was available in their area.[26] Needless to say, neither injunction had any immediate results. At the very least, however, it marked a further commitment of the Islamic community to the cause of Islamic finance, and made outright governmental opposition to Islamic finance difficult.

The collapse of oil prices caused sharp decreases in the revenues of oil-rich states, with attendant economic, political, social, and religious consequences throughout the Islamic world: cancellation of contracts; reduction of subsidies and public expenditures; a drop in foreign workers' remittances; political and social unrest; and growing Islamic militancy. Other major political economic and financial changes were taking place in the world at large – the winding down of the Cold War, the spread of neo-liberal ideology and deregulation and privatization policies, and the transformation of finance[27] – which in due course profoundly affected the Islamic world.

These developments did not hinder the growth of Islamic financial institutions. In fact, non-oil countries welcomed the major Islamic groups. In Turkey, for example, the creation of the "Special Finance Houses" (Islamic banks) occurred in 1983 under a temporary military dictatorship which paradoxically "supported secularism with a zeal reminiscent of Muslim 'fundamentalism.'"[28] But since the country was in the midst of a financial crisis, its secular leaders courted Islamic banking groups, granting them unprecedented privileges. In those years, Turkey also obtained substantial aid from other Arab and Islamic sources, particularly the IDB. The decree that established the "Special Finance Houses" gave them rights and privileges that were not available to their conventional competitors. It reserved to the Prime Minister's office the right "at all times" to supervise them. After the al-Baraka and Faisal groups opened their banks, a special law specifically exempted them from the provisions of existing banking legislation. The new institutions were required to keep only 10 per cent of their current accounts and a mere 1 per cent of their much larger participation accounts as reserves with the Central Bank (in contrast to the 10–15 per cent reserve requirement to which conventional banks were subjected). The "Special Finance Houses" were also authorized to deal in commodities and were exempted from lending limits and deposit insurance requirements to which other commercial banks were subjected. And despite a 1984 ban on television advertising for banks (in the wake of the brokerage houses crisis) they were given permission to advertise on state television. According to a Turkish journalist, all these privileges amounted to a new "form of capitulation."[29]

In sum, because of the financial crunch experienced by governments, the bargaining power of Islamic bankers grew and they were able to keep on expanding. Another notable development, though one barely noticed at the time, was the first Malaysian banking legislation on Islamic finance in 1983 which created Bank Islam Malaysia Berhad (BIMB), a fully-fledged commercial bank controlled by the government and in which the Tabung Haji had a 12.5 per cent participation. Unlike countries such as Pakistan, Iran, or the Sudan, Malaysia did not seek to Islamicize its financial sector, but rather to encourage a dual banking structure whereby an Islamic sector would coexist with the conventional one. Unlike other developments discussed earlier, it was not primarily driven by the pioneers of Islamic finance but by the developmental goals of the Malaysian government. The Islamic sector would greatly expand in later years, albeit with little interaction (until the post-September 11 era) with the Gulf-centered Islamic banks. (In the next few pages and in Chapter 6, we will draw a distinction between the Arab or Gulf model and the Malaysian model of Islamic finance.)

Yet with the dramatic economic transformations, many of the assumptions, indeed, the founding principles, underlying the 1970s ijtihad crumbled. In particular, the world of international finance, which had not changed much between the 1950s and the 1970s, underwent a veritable revolution in the 1980s; one that has accelerated since.[30] The *Handbook of Islamic Banking* thus left out a wide range of financing techniques and instruments, and adopted what in hindsight appears to be an unduly restrictive position on many products that later gained great currency. For example, the *Handbook* stated that transactions involving financial derivatives such as futures and options were forbidden,[31] as were purchases of government bonds and fixed-return securities.[32] Also, Islamic banks could not purchase stocks or commodities for short periods of time solely to make a profit. (Such transactions also had to be aimed at promoting investment.[33])

A new ijtihad was progressively taking place in order to deal with the changing position of Islamic finance within the international political economy and the new world of deregulated finance. Islamic finance grew more decentralized, diverse, and pragmatic. As the following section shows, new forms of Islamic finance also came into existence outside the networks created by the first Islamic banks.

2 New Forms of Islamic Finance

Unrelated to this small network of Islamic banks, other financial companies appeared here and there. Egypt, for example, saw the proliferation of *sharikat tawzif al-amwal al-islamiyya* or Islamic Money Management Companies (IMMCs). With the exception of the al-Sharif group mentioned earlier, these companies appeared in the early 1980s, and came to dominate Egyptian finance, and even the country's economics and politics throughout the 1985–88 period.[34]

The emergence of IMMCs was the result of a combination of factors: the loopholes in the *infitah* (open door) policies; the growth of labor remittances; the rigidities of the banking system; the drop in government revenues; and, of course, the rise of Islamism. The policy of infitah, inaugurated in the early 1970s by Anwar Sadat, and pursued under the Mubarak regime despite substantial changes, did not do away with some of the essential characteristics of pre-infitah policies. As Yahya Sadowski noted:

> *Infitah* has often been misrepresented by its advocates and its opponents, as marking a change from a state-directed to a free-market economy in Egypt. It unquestionably led to important changes in economic structure, but fostered only limited liberalization. It legalized a wide range of imports, but kept tariff barriers high. It promoted private banking, but kept interest rate regulations intact. It left most price controls in place and expanded consumer subsidies. It created a more liberal economy, but one whose basic features were still clearly *dirigiste* (original emphasis).[35]

The integration of Egypt within the regional economy (in addition to the massive aid received from the United States following the Camp David Agreements) transformed Egypt's financial situation. Migrant workers, who needed to repatriate their hard currency, found few outlets for their savings. Credit and interest rates were tightly regulated, and cumbersome and outdated rules and regulations still prevailed. As a result, interest rates offered by banks did not even compensate for inflation, and most of the available credit went to finance short-term trading, established businesses, or collateralized transactions. Clearly, the official banking system was unable to cope with the demands of the new economy.

A parallel financial sector was quick to emerge. It started with the black market for foreign exchange. Currency traders suddenly became among the richest businessmen in the country. The government tolerated this black market, "viewing it as a safety valve that lubricated the wheels of trade and encouraged the flow of dollars into Egypt."[36] As foreign exchange restrictions were partially lifted, many such dealers evolved into full-service financial institutions. Rather than offering traditional savings accounts, they purported to manage the public's money. And rather than offering traditional loans, they engaged in profit-and-loss sharing arrangements, as well as a variety of mark-up schemes. To their depositors, they issued "investment certificates." [37] Since "dividends" paid under *musharaka*, mudaraba, or murabaha were not technically interest, they were not subject to the government regulations controlling interest rates. And since these companies were not really banks, they were not subjected to costly and stifling regulations or to reserve requirements. They were not even bound by law to disclose financial statements, hold annual meetings, or keep detailed records of transactions. Neither were the IMMCs subjected to any coordinated religious supervision (although most employed religious figures and used their fatwas to justify their practices).

IMMC drew huge deposits by offering attractive dividends, typically 25 per cent, more than double what official banks offered, and became the preferred channel for the remittances of Egyptians working abroad. In a typical "euphoric episode,"[38] Egyptians accustomed to negative interest rates and unresponsive banks experienced something unprecedented: their savings were rapidly increasing in value; to boot, the companies were offering an unprecedented level of service. Religion was a strong selling point. Vigorous marketing campaigns warned against the ills of "usurious interest," and associated their success with their religious orientation. One of the advertising slogans of al-Rayyan was *al-baraka waraa al najah* or "the blessings behind success."

Although the companies made heavy use of religious language and symbolism, they do not seem to have had significant ties to political organizations. There were a few exceptions, such as the al-Sharif group, which had long-standing ties to the Muslim Brothers.[39] Still, the possible political implications of an alliance with anti-governmental groups did not escape the government.[40]

Obviously, given the large number of such firms – about 200 at their peak – generalizations are hazardous: some were serious about their religious character, while others used it primarily as a marketing ploy. Some made legitimate and "productive" investments, while others were essentially speculative ventures. A few were from the start fraudulent operations.[41] The best-known and largest IMMC was al-Rayyan (named after one of Islam's heavenly gates), which was fronted by a religious figure, but in reality controlled by the shady Abdul-Fattah brothers. Its early income had come from money changing, black-market currency trading, as well as a few high profile commercial and industrial ventures, but it increasingly engaged in financial speculation. Such a mix of activities was typical of most IMMC: the visible investments were in the productive sectors of the Egyptian economy (manufacturing, tourism, etc.), but the hidden ones involved speculation – primarily in gold, foreign currency, and commodity markets. In addition, it looked like many deposits found their way into bank accounts abroad.

By 1985, the role of the IMMCs in the economy became critical. The government was then in the middle of a fiscal crisis, the official economy was in a recession, and the official banks were experiencing a shortage of funds. So, on the one hand, their role seemed salutary: they mitigated the effects of the economic crisis, providing the much-needed basic services that the official banking sector was unable to offer. On the other hand, the government realized that the IMMC were a time-bomb that was waiting to explode. Central Bank governor, Ali Negm, was especially vocal in criticizing the companies and warning their depositors. Yet the companies remained defiant. In November 1986, following news reports about heavy losses incurred by al-Rayyan, a run on deposits occurred. Al-Rayyan withstood the panic (reportedly with help from local banks and possibly from Saudi banks), but not without launching a counter-campaign against the government. In advertisements in Egyptian publications, it accused the government of plotting against it. When in the following days, the Central Bank governor was replaced, al-Rayyan claimed victory (though it was unclear whether the two events were connected).[42]

Yet despite the inability (or unwillingness) of the government to move decisively against the IMMCs, their dividend policy was clearly unsustainable. And, indeed, as the competition heated up, they had to increase their "dividends" (some offered over 3 per cent a month). It was a matter of time before many simply became huge pyramid, or Ponzi, schemes.[43]

Egyptian society was deeply polarized. The "new bourgeoisie" that emerged from the infitah, as well as returning migrant workers, were the beneficiaries of the new system. The traditional business establishment in contrast viewed the IMMCs as dangerous upstarts and as a potentially destabilizing force in the economy. Other splits occurred along religious and political lines. The more secularly-inclined Egyptians viewed the IMMCs as a vehicle for further Islamicization of Egyptian society. A number of prominent political figures were now on the payroll of the major IMMCs; some were offered even more attractive "dividends" than typical depositors. By the same token, certain segments of the media were kept at bay since they were increasingly dependent on large advertising and printing contracts. A propaganda war erupted between the official banking sector and the IMMC, which were accused of making false promises to investors and of being hypocritical, since they were using religion to enrich themselves. The IMMCs retorted that the official banks were simply jealous of their success, and that they were spreading rumors intended to cause their downfall. Throughout the 1985–8 period, despite a string of failures, politicians were unable to agree on the regulation of IMMCs.[44]

The official banking sector was strongly opposed to these new rivals. Its main argument was that the unregulated IMMCs engaged in unfair competition against the regulated banking system, and that their practices threatened the entire financial system. It should be noted that in the confrontation between the IMMCs and the official banks, Islamic banks, such as the Faisal Islamic Bank of Egypt, were on the side of the official banks, of which they were part. (Tocomplicate things further, a number of conventional Egyptian banks had since the early to mid-1980s created Islamic branches of their own.) Still, on a number of occasions, IMMCs attempted to cross over into the official banking sector. Apparently, the only successful attempt was the acquisition by the al-Sharif company of 30 per cent of the shares of the International Islamic Bank for Investment and Development (IIBID).[45] The al-Rayyan group tried unsuccessfully to become a member of the International Association of Islamic Banks.

By 1988, the majority of IMMCs were facing problems of liquidity. Many of their owners fled the country. Under pressure from the International Monetary Fund, the government finally reined in the IMMCs, requiring them to maintain a capital-to-deposit ratio of 10 per cent, channel their accounts through commercial banks, and publish audited financial statements. But it was too late. By then a large number of Islamic companies had failed, or were beyond rescue. It was a matter of months before al-Rayyan encountered the same fate. The impact on the Egyptian economy was considerable. By some estimates, $3 billion – 15 per cent of Egypt's GNP – had evaporated.[46]

Soon afterwards came the 1989 Tantawi fatwa, which was a mixed blessing for both conventional and Islamic finance.[47] It legitimated interest, and in the long-standing battle between Islamic and conventional banks, stood on the side of conventional banks. But from an Islamic banking standpoint, it helped ease the suspicions that had long surrounded all areas of finance. In particular, it drew attention to the role of secular experts and to the need for religious scholars to pay heed to them.[48] Thus, although controversial in the Islamic world, it was a milestone in the evolution of Islamic finance. Challenging the dogmatic fixation on riba-as-interest, it allowed for a new pragmatism and set the stage for a growing convergence between Islamic and conventional finance.

III The Second Stage (1991–2001)

A useful, if arbitrary, turning point is the year 1991, which started with the first Gulf War, during which talks of a New World Order started, and ended with the collapse of the Soviet Union, which sealed the end of the Cold War. That year was also dominated by the Bank of Credit and Commerce International (BCCI) scandal which (unfairly) tainted the Islamic finance industry. The following years were marked by the quest for a new, post-Cold War paradigm. Many of the grand visions, whether "the end of history" or the "clash of civilizations" posited a sharp ideological break with the past and new attitudes toward Islam.

1 The Growing Pains of Islamic Banks

The forays of the first Islamic banks into profit-and-loss sharing proved to be disastrous. It is questionable whether equity-based banking was viable to begin with,[49] but the economic downturn consecutive to the sudden fall in oil prices certainly did not help. The early Islamic banks in their desire to focus on real assets invested heavily in gold, real estate, or commodities – investments that proved to be dubious in the changing macro-economic environment of the 1980s. Many took note of the irony that sticking to the letter of Islamic law could violate its spirit: Islamic banks were invested in real assets all right, but their contribution to productivity or to the real economy was dubious. In many respects, such investments could be seen as outright speculative. Many bankers invoked the lack of suitable investments, especially given the worldwide recession, as well as the paucity of truly Islamic products. Some Islamic banks were on the brink of insolvency. Thus, the IIBID incurred heavy losses speculating in US commodities markets and was temporarily taken over by the Egyptian Central Bank.[50]

Another setback was the collapse of the BCCI in 1991. Although not itself an Islamic bank, BCCI had in 1984 set up an Islamic Banking Unit in London, which at its peak had $1.4 billion in deposits, and had generally made heavy use of Islamic rhetoric and symbolism.[51] More importantly, however, the scandal brought Islamic institutions into the international limelight and raised questions about the management and regulation of transnational banks. The PriceWaterhouse report commissioned in the wake of the bank's closure revealed that of BCCI's $589 million in "unrecorded deposits" (which allowed the bank to manipulate its accounts) the major part – $245 million – belonged to the Faisal Islamic Bank of Egypt (FIBE). This amount was supposed to be used for commodity investments, though there was no evidence that such investments were ever made.[52] Similarly, the Dubai Islamic Bank (DIB) had placed $86 million with the bank. Although neither the FIBE nor the DIB was suspected of wrongdoing, the image of Islamic banks suffered a blow. Islamic banks came under closer scrutiny, and post-BCCI international regulation tightened the screws on transnational banks, thus complicating the strategies of the main Islamic banking groups, Dallah al-Baraka and DMI.[53]

The proliferation of problems highlighted the flaws in the Islamic banking system and the need for sound management practices. It also had a demonstrative effect that strengthened the "modernist" interpretation of the Shariah: the literal-legalistic interpretation – that is, focusing on an unduly restrictive reading of the Shariah, focusing on the prohibition of interest – can lead to a large number of possibly worse transgressions such as fraud (ghosh) or speculation (gharar). It was thus a combination of internal problems and external events that led to a transformation of Islamic finance.

2 Islamic Banks in the Age of Globalization

By the late 1980s, the global political economy had undergone a profound transformation which posed new challenges to Islamic finance. Old hierarchies and political alignments crumbled and a new economic order emerged; the world of finance was unrecognizable. The attempt to create a new, fundamentally different financial order based on profit-and-loss sharing had failed. Islamic banks had instead been achieving the same goals as conventional banks, albeit through Islamic contracts and within the limits imposed by religious advisors. This new phase can be defined by its pragmatism, diversity, multi-polarity, and convergence with conventional finance.

The early Islamic banks, organized under the umbrella of the IAIB had a virtual monopoly on Islamic finance. By the early 1990s, it constituted only one part of a much broader and much more diverse groups of companies, most of which do not belong to the IAIB. New poles of influence appeared. One such pole is Malaysia, whose political-economic profile and religious traditions were quite different from those of the countries involved in the aggiornamento of Islamic finance (Persian Gulf states, Egypt, and Pakistan). Malaysia was a "model" economy, with a thriving middle class and growth rates approaching the double digits. Mahathir Mohammed, Malaysia's long-serving prime minister, harnessed Islam to his goal of economic growth through the embracing of high-technology and modern finance. His approach to Islamic finance was highly pragmatic. Rather than using what was historically acceptable as a starting point, he adopted the opposite approach, challenging the Malaysian ulema to an ijtihad designed to generate new ideas. Rather than being an obstacle to change, religion was to be an engine of growth and modernization and a tool to promote financial innovation. An Islamic financial system that could offer a growing array of sophisticated financial services was part and parcel of the effort to turn Kuala Lumpur into a leading regional, if not international, financial center.

The Malaysian model came into its own in the 1990s. The dual banking logic, as well as other Malaysian innovations such as Islamic insurance, had taken root (though not necessarily as a result of self-conscious or systematic imitation of the Malaysian model). Another singular characteristic of the Malaysian system is that Islamic products were geared to Muslims as well as to non-Muslims. Muslims would have the opportunity to invest according to their religious beliefs, while non-Muslims, especially for the Chinese minority which controls most of the country's wealth, would have an extension of choice in money management. The message of Malaysian leaders was that industrialization and productivity were fully compatible with piety, and that welfare in this world was fully compatible with salvation in the next. Arab and Malaysian Islamic banks evolved along separate paths, and had minimal interaction. Scholars in the Arab world considered their Malaysian counterparts to be too lax in their religious interpretations. They often referred to the Islamic sector of that country simply as "Malaysian finance."[54]

Behind the differences in interpretations and practices were significant political-economic and religious factors. From a political-economic standpoint, the Gulf ijtihad was primarily driven by the surpluses generated by the oil boom of the mid- to late 1970s, whereas the Malaysian effort was driven by the developmental imperative, combined with domestic political factors such as the promotion of the (Muslim) Malay majority. In other words, the first was concerned with asset management, while the second focused on generating financing for the economy and transforming the country from an agricultural backwater to an industrializing nation. Another fundamental difference between the two systems is that the Arab model had evolved in somewhat haphazard fashion, whereas the Malaysian model was clearly based on a directive, top-down, approach. Whereas the Shariah guidance model was fragmented and decentralized, Malaysia sought consistency by centralizing the process at its Central Bank.

A number of Islamic research centers and universities engaged in a vast effort to legitimate modern finance, and in particular an "Islamic capital market" using specially designed interest-free bonds and other securities.[55] Many Malaysian "innovations" were not deemed acceptable to Shariah boards in more conservative Arab states, in particular the widespread use of *bay' al 'ina* and *bay' dayn* (sale of debt).

In the 1990s, most Islamic countries – and quite a few non-Islamic ones – had encouraged the creation of Islamic financial institutions. But in devising a legal framework for their Islamic institutions, those countries were no longer relying primarily on the guidance of the IAIB or the IDB, but on national interest considerations, with positioning in the global economy being a key factor. Domestic factors and the diversity of national circumstances (including, of course, the impact of indigenous forms of Islam) have inevitably added to differences across countries. While paying lip service to the need for harmonization and consistency, the diversity of interpretations increased.

As for the convergence between Islamic and conventional finance, it is highlighted by five phenomena. First, a growing number of conventional banks opened Islamic subsidiaries and/or "Islamic windows," offering their customers a choice between Islamic and conventional products. Following a well-established trend, the Arab Banking Corporation, the largest Middle Eastern bank (which was founded jointly by Kuwait, Libya, and the United Arab Emirates in 1980) announced in late 1997 the creation of an Islamic unit. Virtually every conventional bank in the Middle East and the Islamic world now offers at the very least some Islamic investment options.

Second, financial institutions from outside the Islamic world started creating Islamic subsidiaries or offering Islamic products. Financial firms that aspired to become global brands – Citicorp, HSBC – had long-standing ties with Persian Gulf states, but felt the need to upgrade their involvement in Islamic finance through the creation of dedicated Islamic units. In later years, virtually all major global financial firms would have some involvement in Islamic finance.

Third, many Islamic institutions aimed their increasingly sophisticated and diverse products at non-Muslims. Financial institutions started creating Shariah-compliant products as an alternative to conventional products. Such products would be intrinsically attractive to many customers, including non-Muslims. The Malaysian example (where the majority of clients are non-Muslims) is especially striking. In some cases, the financial criteria would be decisive. In the words of Majed al-Refai, chief executive of the Bahrain-based First Islamic Investment Bank: "Our aim is to create credit-rated medium- to long-term investment tools which are comparable with existing conventional products, so that financial advisors can advise their clients to invest with us on the basis of returns, rather than because they are Islamic."[56] In other cases (for example, in the case of Islamic mortgages or Islamic mutual funds), ethical considerations are paramount.

Fourth, a growing number of Islamic banks have been established outside the Islamic world in order to cater to local Islamic communities. Since the 1980s, such institutions have been created in Europe, the Americas, and Australia. Today, Islamic banks exist in virtually all parts of the world. Certain products and practices (again such as mortgages or mutual funds) have often originated in countries such as the United Kingdom or the United States.

Fifth, much of the new ijtihad on Islamic finance has been conducted by Shariah advisors in cooperation between conventional and Islamic institutions, often outside the Islamic world. Perhaps the most ambitious research on Islamic finance is now conducted at Harvard University, which in December 1995 started the Harvard Islamic Finance Information Program (HIFIP), which was later renamed the Islamic Finance Program (IFP) and now operates as part of the Harvard Law School. The program is "committed to the collection, analysis and dissemination of information on the Islamic financial sector" and aims to "promote research and development in the field of Islamic finance, sponsor research projects which investigate new trends, strategies, and methods in Islamic finance" with "particular emphasis given to studies which investigate how existing financing methods available in conventional finance can be applied to Islamic finance and vice versa."[57]

3 Islamic Banks, Conventional Banks and the New World Order

The rhetoric and certain analyses notwithstanding, Islamic finance was firmly embedded within the international political and economic order. The world of banking and finance is by nature status quo-oriented. It craves stability and abhors uncertainty. In every new market they penetrated, Islamic banks have typically established links with the local power structure, and have worked within established oligopolies.[58] At the international level, the major Islamic banking groups, rather than trying to establish a global Islamic network that would rival the global banking system were keen to remain embedded within that system. Indeed, in their transnational operations, Islamic banking operated more out of London or Geneva, than out of the major Islamic capitals. As for the IDB, its statutes provided for coordination and collaboration with the International Monetary Fund (IMF) and other international organizations.[59]

In the 1970s, and as summarized by Anwar Sadat, there was a "commonality of interests between the Islamic states and the West: oil in exchange for technology and the common interest against the Soviet threat."[60] Ideologically, both liberalism and economic Islam were driven by their common opposition to socialism and economic dirigisme.[61] With the elimination of the Soviet threat, a New World Order has emerged, and with the exception of a few "rogue" states which remained at the fringes of that system,[62] most countries involved in Islamic finance were active participants, and in some cases major beneficiaries, of the new system.[63] The seminal event of the New World Order was the 1991 Gulf War, and most Islamic states were part of the US-led coalition.

Geopolitical factors were reinforced by economic and business considerations. After the oil shocks of the 1970s, the "recycling" of petrodollars was undertaken by Western, and primarily American, banks. More generally, many countries involved in Islamic finance – especially those in the Persian Gulf – belong in the "coupon-clipper" category, and have a stake in the stability of international markets in which they are heavily invested.[64] Paradoxically, the paucity of acceptable Islamic products has also led Islamic banks to be heavily invested in foreign currencies, to have a large percentage of their deposits abroad,[65] and to work closely with international banks and the London Metal Exchange in *tawarroq* (commodity bought on credit and immediately resold for cash) transactions.

The international banking system was also instrumental in the very creation of Islamic banks. The fledgling Islamic banks, lacking experience and resources, had little choice but to rely on the expertise of their international counterparts. And as Islamic banks gained experience, the world of finance was undergoing major transformations. So rather than being phased out, the cooperation with Western banks – in the form of joint ventures, management agreements, technical cooperation and correspondent banking – was stepped up leading to a significant web of relationships between conventional and Islamic finance.

IV The Third Stage (After 2001)

1 The September 11 Effect

This integration was temporarily set back by the attacks of September 11, 2001. The attacks against the World Trade Center and the Pentagon, instantly interpreted as an "act of war," reordered political priorities and transformed international relations. The "global war on terror" had a significant but paradoxical impact on Islamic finance. In the years following the attacks, the Islamic finance industry experienced dramatic growth and major transformations. The perception that Islam was under siege resulted in greater religiosity, which in turn drove an increase in demand for Islamic products. Criticisms of Islamic banks were no doubt an important factor in the serious effort at rationalizing and streamlining Islamic finance. Sheikh Saleh Kamel went as far as to call for a repatriation of Islamic funds, declaring that: "The West has always been hostile to Islamic banking, and 10 years ago, al-Baraka Bank was even closed down in London. Therefore, it is time Muslim financial institutions and individuals bring back their money from the West to invest in Muslim countries and develop this industry in our region."[66] The calls for repatriation of funds did not go unheeded. Islamic institutions suffered a short-lived blow, but nevertheless they were on the cusp of yet another period of unprecedented expansion. After a short lull, demand for Islamic products accelerated, and the number of conventional institutions creating Islamic units or offering Islamic products kept growing, both inside and outside the Islamic world.

Notable developments included countless new commercial and regulatory initiatives as well as the convergence of the Arab and the Malaysian models of Islamic banking. Coming under attack had the effect of greatly concentrating the minds of Islamic bankers and their regulators. As a result, efforts at international coordination and standardization grew more serious and better focused. In 2002 alone, there was the appearance of sovereign *ijara sukuk* and the creation of coordination and standard-setting mechanisms such as the Islamic Finance Services Board (IFSB), the International Islamic Financial Market (IIFM), the Liquidity Management Center (LMC), and the Islamic International Rating Agency (IIRA). The Accounting and Auditing Organization for Islamic Financial Institutions (AAOIFI), though in existence since 1991 was greatly re-energized in its effort to harmonize accounting and auditing rules and create standard Islamic contracts. In 2005, International Islamic Center for Reconciliation and Commercial Arbitration for Islamic Finance Industry was launched in Dubai in order to settle financial and commercial disputes.

Another significant development of the post-September 11 era was the growing convergence of the Arab and Malaysian models. The freezing of the assets of prominent Saudis and the crackdown on Islamic financial institutions and charities led many Muslim investors to take a significant chunk of their assets out of the United States. Home markets could not absorb all those withdrawals (estimated at about $200 billion) and the quest for a new diversification strategy led more or less naturally to Malaysia, a Muslim country which had achieved an impressive level of economic development. Other forms of political and economic interaction also intensified. Malaysian Prime Minister Mahathir Mohammed's stature grew in the Islamic world as he took a strong stand against those aspects of the global war on terror that he considered as unfairly targeting Muslims. There was also a significant increase in trade and tourism (many Gulf Arabs chose to vacation in Malaysia rather than in the United States or Europe). As a way of promoting its own viewpoint, Bank Negara Malaysia is spending $57 million to invite Islamic scholars from around the world to Kuala Lumpur for a "Shariah dialogue" program.[67]

Earlier misgivings about diverging interpretations of the Shariah gave way to a quest for common ground. The most dramatic example was the 2002 sovereign Malaysian sukuk, which explicitly targeted Gulf investors (for that issue, Malaysian as well as Arab Shariah scholars gave their endorsement). Soon afterwards, those ijara sukuk formed the template for a number of Arab sukuk issues. The new web of institutions linking Arab and Malaysian institutions proved to be quite effective.

Malaysia started working closely with Arab regulators, especially those of Bahrain and the United Arab Emirates on matters of Islamic finance. The Dubai Financial Services Authority (DFSA) entered into a memorandum of understanding with Bank Negara Malaysia, committing both parties to the further development of international Islamic finance markets. As a result of the joint initiative, the Dubai International Financial Center (DIFC), domestic funds will be the first foreign funds permitted to be sold into Malaysia.

The relatively closed Malaysian market has also progressively opened its doors to Arab Islamic banks. In 2002, the Malaysian government established the first IIFM at its Labuan International Offshore Financial Center (IOFC), where foreign Islamic institutions were encouraged to establish branches. The Malaysian Central Bank introduced tax incentives to encourage overseas institutions to enter or expand in Islamic banking, insurance, and fund management.[68] Foreign institutions can now hold up to 49 per cent of the Islamic banking units of Malaysian banks.

Most significantly, since 2006, three Arab Islamic banks have been authorized to operate in Malaysia: Kuwait Finance House; Saudi Arabia's al-Rajhi; and the Asian Finance House. The first two powerhouses of Islamic finance had initially been major players confined to their home markets, while the third is a joint venture of the Qatar Islamic Bank and other Middle Eastern investors. Saudi-based al-Rajhi, whose Malaysian operations have a four-member Shariah Board consisting of two Saudis and two Malays, has experimented with products inspired by Malaysian practices before trying to re-export them to its home market. One example is a profit-and-loss sharing account whose remuneration, like those of a conventional savings account, is fixed and predetermined (thanks to a profit reserve account which allows the bank to cover fluctuations in its profits and losses).[69] Another interesting development is the broadening of Shariah boards of Malaysian banks to Arab scholars.[70]

The Arab–Malaysian integration was part of a broader phenomenon of regionalization of Islamic finance. The Dubai Islamic Bank, the first Islamic bank, has also recently expanded its operations to Pakistan. As for Singapore, it has announced its intention to become a hub of Islamic finance. The Development Bank of Singapore (DBS) has recently established, in association with Arab investors, the Islamic Bank of Asia, to focus on wealth management and capital market instruments for corporate and private banking clients in the Middle East and Asia.

2 The Financial Meltdown and Islamic Finance

By 2008, Islamic finance had become part of the mainstream of global finance. The trend was driven primarily by a desire on the part of global financial institutions to tap the wealth of the Islamic world, as opposed to a genuine admiration for the merits of Islamic finance, let alone as part of the quest for an alternative form of finance. Indeed, in the first years of the new millennium, the paradigm of global finance, as epitomized by major Wall Street firms with their focus on financial innovation, commanded near-unanimous support where it mattered: that is, among financial regulators, economics and finance professors, the financial community at large, and the media. In those years, Islamic banks were usually on the receiving end of lectures essentially asking them to become more like mainstream finance.[71] The discourse was dutifully repeated within the Islamic world.[72]

This discourse proved to be spectacularly wrong, starting with the US sub-prime crisis of 2007. The following year, only a massive government bail-out saved the financial markets, which were assumed to be all-knowing and self-correcting, from collapse. Financial innovation was supposed to improve efficiency and liquidity, yet the state-of-the-art in financial innovation brought forth an outright credit freeze. Risk management was dealt with as if it was an exact science, yet as critic Robert Kuttner observed, "Supposedly, these derivatives on top of derivatives 'spread risk,' but in truth they spread risk the way an epidemic spreads diphtheria."[73]

A number of statements by the Alan Greenspan, the high priest of unfettered capitalism and the man dubbed "the maestro,"[74] captured the prevailing conventional wisdom as the bubble was inflating. In 2002, just as he lowered interest rates, he claimed that "bubbles cannot be prevented or defused by financial regulators." In 2004 he asserted that "a national severe price distortion seems most unlikely in the United States, given its size and diversity." In 2005 he added that a decline in home prices "likely would not have substantial macroeconomic implications." That year he also observed that "increasingly complex financial instruments have contributed to the development of a far more flexible, efficient, and hence resilient financial system than the one that existed just a quarter-century ago." In 2006, shortly after he left the chairmanship of the Federal Reserve Board and on the eve of the bursting of the bubble, Greenspan said: "I think the worst of this may well be over."[75]

The deluge of books praising the magic of the market was suddenly replaced by works chronicling the disastrous mistakes made by financial "geniuses." (Often, the same authors who sang the praises of the infallible market later engaged in a critique of the arrogance of financial theory.[76]) Even Alan Greenspan changed his tune, conceding that he had "found a flaw" in his bedrock belief of "40 years or more" that markets would regulate themselves. "I made a mistake," he said.[77]

The recent financial crisis could be divided into three phases. In the first, the decline in US real estate prices drew attention to sub-prime loans, which it turned out had, through the miracle of securitization, found their way onto the balance sheets of major international financial institutions. In the second phase, losses suffered by such institutions triggered claims for which major Wall Street firms and other companies such as insurer AIG were utterly unprepared. Indeed, through highly lucrative and unregulated credit derivatives known as "credit default swaps," high-flying financial firms had in effect insured countless institutions (and one another) against defaults, and now they had to pay up. As the world's leading global financial institutions discovered the time-bombs on their balance sheets (in the form of toxic assets and unfunded liabilities), they realized that they were essentially insolvent: the ensuing credit freeze caused a global financial meltdown which soon spread to the real economy. The third phase of the financial crisis was thus a global economic recession – which would have turned into a depression were it not for massive government intervention worldwide. It is only then that Islamic banks started to feel the effects of the meltdown.[78]

Why did Islamic institutions escape the first two phases relatively unscathed? Quite simply because many of the practices that caused the financial freeze would not pass muster with Shariah Boards. Indeed, neither the securitization of sub-prime loans (which is a sale of debt) nor credit default swaps (which are the sale of promises and are rife with gharar) are acceptable. Similarly, negative Islamic attitudes toward short-selling were vindicated by the role short-selling played in many aspects of the financial crisis[79] and subsequent limits placed on short-selling of financial stocks in London, New York and elsewhere. Some old-fashioned principles such as the distrust of excessive leverage and of open-ended innovation proved well-founded. As for the systematic vetting of new products by Shariah advisors, it could be looked at as a system of checks and balances, a useful corrective to the groupthink that had overtaken conventional finance.[80]

When the financial tsunami hit, bringing conventional finance to its knees, there was a mood of soul searching within mainstream finance. In parallel, there was a sense of triumphalism among promoters of Islamic economics and finance. Some did not hesitate to present Islamic finance as a panacea that would solve all the world's economic ills, and as the model that conventional banks had to adopt to get out of their predicament.[81] Yet soon afterwards, the extension of the crisis from the financial realm to the real economy exposed the vulnerability of a sector that is mostly asset-backed,[82] though its inherent conservatism somewhat mitigated the effects of the economic downturn.[83] This showed that Islamic finance was not after all a panacea, and that a faith-based system is not automatically immune to the vagaries of the financial system.

On balance, however, the Islamic sector weathered the financial meltdown better than the conventional sector. If nothing else, there was an acknowledgment within conventional circles that the principles and strictures of Islamic finance were not without merit. This in turn created a renewed sense of self-confidence within the Islamic sector, which also weakened the hand of those who equated progress with uncritical imitation of conventional banks.

Notes

1. See Chapter 5.
2. Bernard Taillefer, *Guide de la Banque pour tous: Innovations africaines* (Paris: Karthala, 1996).
3. Stéphanie Parigi, *Des Banques Islamiques* (Paris: Ramsay, 1989), p. 35.
4. Rodney Wilson, *Banking and Finance in the Arab Middle East* (New York: St. Martin's Press, 1983), p. 75.
5. Rodney Wilson, "Islamic Development Finance in Malaysia," in Saad al-Harran (ed.), *Leading Issues in Islamic Banking and Finance* (Selangor, Malaysia: Pelanduk Publications, 1995), p. 65.
6. Michel Galloux, *Finance islamique et pouvoir politique: le cas de l'Egypte moderne* (Paris: Presses universitaires de France, 1997), p. 24.
7. See, for example, Galloux, *Finance islamique et pouvoir politique*, pp. 35–6, Adnan M. Abdeen and Dale N. Shook, *The Saudi Financial System* (New York: John Wiley, 1984), p. 165, Timur Kuran, "The Economic Impact of Islamic Fundamentalism," in Martin Marty and R. Scott Appleby (eds.), *Fundamentalism and the State: Remaking Polities, Economies, and Militance* (Chicago, IL: University of Chicago Press, 1993), p. 313, Fuad al-Omar and Mohammed Abdel-Haq, *Islamic Banking: Theory, Practice and Challenges* (London: Zed Books, 1996), p. 21, and Parigi, *Des Banques Islamiques*, p. 170.

8. Galloux, *Finance islamique et pouvoir politique*, pp. 28–9.

9. Galloux, *Finance islamique et pouvoir politique*, p. 90.

10. Daniel Yergin, *The Prize: The Epic Quest for Oil, Money and Power* (New York: Simon and Schuster, 1991), pp. 563–87.

11. Joan Edelman Spero, *The Politics of International Economic Relations*, 4th edn. (New York: St. Martin's Press, 1990), pp. 170–1.

12. Conference of Foreign Ministers of Islamic States, "The Institution of an Islamic Bank, Economic and Islamic Doctrine", Jeddah, February 29, 1972.

13. Traute Wohlers-Scharf, *Arab and Islamic Banks: New Business Partners for Developing Countries* (Paris: OECD, 1983), p. 80.

14. Clement M. Henry, *The Mediterranean Debt Crescent: Money and Power in Algeria, Egypt, Morocco, Tunisia and Turkey* (Gainesville, FL: University Press of Florida, 1996), p. 124.

15. Monzer Kahf, "Islamic Banks: The Rise of a New Power Alliance of Wealth and *Shari'a* Scholarship," in Clement M. Henry and Rodney Wilson (eds.), *The Politics of Islamic Finance* (Edinburgh: Edinburgh University Press, 2004).

16. *Al Mausua al Ilmiya wa al Ammaliya lil Bunuk al Islamiya (The Handbook of Islamic Banking*, 6 vols (Cairo: International Association of Islamic Banks, 1977–86) (in Arabic). For a compact, English-language publication of the IAIB see Ahmed Abdel Aziz al-Nagar *et al.*, *One Hundred Questions & One Hundred Answers Concerning Islamic Banks* (Cairo: International Association of Islamic Banks, 1980).

17. Wohlers-Scharf, *Arab and Islamic Banks*, p. 78.

18. See Chapter 2.

19. Galloux, *Finance islamique et pouvoir politique*, p. 45.

20. See Chapter 6.

21. Wohlers-Scharf, *Arab and Islamic Banks*, p. 81.

22. Parigi, *Des Banques Islamiques*, p. 128.

23. Quoted in Galloux, *Finance islamique et pouvoir politique*, p. 102.

24. Wohlers-Scharf, *Arab and Islamic Banks*, p. 98.

25. The bank, however, shut down after a few years.

26. Galloux, *Finance islamique et pouvoir politique*, p. 162.

27. See Chapter 5.

28. Henry, *The Mediterranean Debt Crescent*, p. 124.

29. Henry, *The Mediterranean Debt Crescent*, p. 125.

30. François Chesnais, *La mondialisation financière: Genèse, coût et enjeux* (Paris: Syros, 1996).

31. *The Handbook of Islamic Banking*, vol. 5, pp. 429–33.

32. *The Handbook of Islamic Banking*, pp. 435–7.

33. *The Handbook of Islamic Banking*, p. 427.

34. Mahmud Abd al-Fadel, *The Biggest Financial Swindle: The Economy and Politics of Money Management Companies* (Cairo: Dar al-Mustaqbal al-Arabi, 1989) (in Arabic), p. 66.

35. Yahya M. Sadowski, *Political Vegetables? Businessman and Bureaucrat in the Development of Egyptian Agriculture* (Washington, DC: The Brookings Institution, 1991), p. 104.

36. Sadowski, *Political Vegetables?*, p. 226.

37. Galloux, *Finance islamique et pouvoir politique*, p. 80.

38. See John Kenneth Galbraith, *A Short History of Financial Euphoria* (New York: Viking, 1990).

39. *Al-Ahram al-Iqtissadi*, July 18, 1988.

40. Sadowski, *Political Vegetables?*, p. 238.

41. Parigi, *Des Banques Islamiques*, pp. 83–105.

42. Henry, *The Mediterranean Debt Crescent*, p. 267.

43. Charles Ponzi developed a scheme in Boston in 1919 and 1920 in which he would promise an "investor" high rates on his money (40 per cent for 45 days), then would borrow larger sums from later investors, take a cut, and use the remainder to pay the interest to earlier investors.

44. The only exception was Law 89, which regulated new money management companies, but did not affect existing ones. See Henry, *The Mediterranean Debt Crescent*, p. 267.
45. Henry, *The Mediterranean Debt Crescent*, p. 262.
46. *Forbes*, April 17, 1989.
47. See Chapter 3.
48. Chibli Mallat, "Tantawi on Banking," in Muhammad Khalid Masud, Brinkley Messick and David S. Powers (eds.), *Islamic Legal Interpretation: Muftis and their Fatwas* (Cambridge, MA: Harvard University Press, 1996), pp. 286–96.
49. See Chapter 7.
50. Henry, *The Mediterranean Debt Crescent*, p. 264.
51. Ibrahim Warde, "BCCI: Perspectives from North and South," University of California, Berkeley: Center for Middle Eastern Studies, 1991.
52. Mark Potts, Nicholas Kochan and Robert Whittington, *Dirty Money: BCCI: The Inside Story of the World's Sleaziest Bank* (Washington, DC: National Press Books, 1992), pp. 77–8.
53. See Chapter 10.
54. Especially contentious were the issues of *bay' dayn* (sale of debt) and *bay' al 'ina*, which were essential building blocks to Islamic corporate debt. Outside Malaysia, most scholars consider the sale of debt to be un-Islamic. As for Bay' al 'Ina (under which somebody sells a good for cash and then buys it back from the same person at a higher price in exchange for deferred payment), most schools of Islamic jurisprudence consider it a hila (ruse or legal artifice) to get around the prohibition of riba, though the Shafii school generally regards it as acceptable.
55. See Chapter 6.
56. Inter Press Service, English News Wire, November 26, 1996.
57. Available at: http://www.hifip.harvard.edu.
58. Henry, *The Mediterranean Debt Crescent*, p. 125.
59. Hamid Algabid, *Les banques islamiques* (Paris: Economics, 1990), p. 122.
60. Ali E. Hillal Dessouki (ed.), *Islamic Resurgence in the Arab World* (New York: Praeger, 1982), p. 91.
61. Emmanuel Sivan, "La revanche de la société civile," in Alain Gresh (ed.), *Un péril islamiste?* (Brussels: Editions Complexe, 1994), p. 28.
62. See Chapter 11.
63. Ibrahim Warde, "Les dividendes de l'opération bouclier du désert," *Le Monde diplomatique*, November 1990.
64. Alan Richards and John Waterbury, *A Political Economy of the Middle East* (Boulder, CO: Westview Press, 1996), p. 71.
65. Galloux, *Finance islamique et pouvoir politique*, p. 63.
66. *Gulf News*, November 12, 2001.
67. Yaroslav Trofimov, "Borrowed Ideas: Malaysia Transforms Rules For Finance Under Islam; In a Lesson to Arabs, Asian Bankers Mix Religion, Modernity," *The Wall Street Journal*, April 4, 2007.
68. Roula Khalaf, Gillian Tett and David Oakley, "Eastern Promise turns to Western Delight," *The Financial Times*, January 18, 2007.
69. Trofimov, "Borrowed Ideas," *The Wall Street Journal*, April 4, 2007.
70. "CIMB appoints Sheikh Nizam Yaqubi to Syariah body," *The Edge*, July 11, 2006.
71. See, for example, Jay Collins, "The Road Ahead for Islamic Finance," in *Integrating Islamic Finance into the Mainstream: Regulation, Standardization and Transparency* (Cambridge, MA: Harvard Law School, 2007), and Robert Merton's keynote address at the Eighth Harvard University Forum On Islamic Finance, "Innovation and Authenticity," April 18–20, 2008.
72. See fraud.
73. Robert Kuttner, "Back-to-Basics Banking," *The Boston Globe*, October 11, 2008.

74. Bob Woodward, *Maestro: Greenspan's Fed and the American Boom* (New York: Simon and Schuster, 2000).
75. See Ibrahim Warde, "Fannie et Freddie tombent à l'eau …," *Le Monde Diplomatique*, October 2008.
76. Compare, for example, Eric Briys and François de Varenne, *The Fisherman and the Rhinoceros: How International Finance Shapes Everyday Life* (New York: Wiley, 2000) and Henri Bourguignat and Eric Briys, *L'arrogance de la finance: Comment la théorie financière a produit le krach* (Paris: La Découverte, 2009).
77. "Rescuing Capitalism," *The New York Times*, October 25, 2008.
78. See Chapter 8.
79. Stephanie Kirchgaessner and Greg Farrell, "Fuld says Lehman Victim of Short Sellers," *The Financial Times*, October 6, 2008.
80. See Conclusion.
81. See, for example, P. K. Abdul Ghafour, "Islamic Finance Panacea for Global Crisis: Chapra," *Arab News*, October 23, 2008 and Robin Brant, "Is Islamic Finance the Answer?," BBC News, May 11, 2009.
82. See Chapter 8.
83. Andrew Wood, "Islamic Finance Escapes Worst of Crisis", *The Financial Times*, June 7, 2009.

5

ISLAMIC FINANCE AND THE GLOBAL
POLITICAL ECONOMY

In the three eras identified in the previous chapters, the evolution of Islamic finance was nothing if not paradoxical. The creation of the first Islamic banks could be seen, especially in the context of the oil crisis and the calls for a New International Economic Order as a challenge to the existing political-economic order. In reality, the first Islamic banks were firmly embedded within the existing Western financial system. By the same token the age of globalization allowed a financial system rooted in the Middle Ages to thrive. Even more striking, amid the Islamophobia generated by the September 11 attacks and the "Global War on Terror," Islamic finance experienced its most dramatic growth in the first years of the twenty-first century. These paradoxes can be understood only in connection with the evolution of global political economy during those three periods.

I The Political and Economic Context of the Birth of Modern Islamic Finance

Modern Islamic banking would probably not exist were it not for two political-economic developments: pan-Islamism and the increase in oil prices. At the center of both was Saudi Arabia's King Faisal. It is thus appropriate that the leading network of Islamic banks be named after him, even though the Faisal Bank is still not allowed to operate as a commercial bank in Saudi Arabia.

1 Pan-Islamism

For all the talk throughout Islamic history about the "umma" (the Islamic nation, or the community of believers), pan-Islamism as a modern political movement began in earnest in the 1960s at the time of the "Arab Cold War."[1] Egypt's President Gamal Abdel Nasser was then a champion of the Third World's struggle against Western colonialism. His brand of nationalism, secularism, and socialism was embraced by other newly independent Islamic states such as Algeria and Indonesia. The relations between Egypt and Saudi Arabia had its ups and downs, but for most of the 1960s, the two countries were at odds. Saudi Arabia was a conservative, Islamic monarchy with strong ties to the West. It served as a sanctuary for many of the Muslim Brothers leaders who suffered from the repression of Nasser's regime. Egypt reciprocated by offering asylum to insubordinate members of the Saudi royal family. The Yemeni civil war (1962–7), during which both countries fought on opposing sides, became the focal point of the "Arab Cold War."

King Faisal sought to trump Nasser's pan-Arabism by founding a pan-Islamic movement, the Muslim World League, and used the pilgrimages to Mecca to forge ties with Islamic leaders, both inside and outside the Arab world. To oppose Nasser's message of Arab and Third World solidarity, he proclaimed the doctrine of Islamic solidarity.[2] In addition, he extended substantial amounts of aid to non-Arab Islamic countries in Asia and Africa, and embarked on a series of high profile visits to Islamic capitals. Upon one such visit to the Shah of Iran in December 1965, the Saudi king was accused by the Egyptian press of using Islam "as an instrument to combat Arab unity."[3]

A number of events set the stage for an Islamic renewal, thus enhancing Faisal's position. The most dramatic was the Six-Day War of June 1967. Significantly, in his first speech following the crushing Arab defeat, a humbled Nasser made a specific reference to religion.[4] In the soul-searching that followed, many of the principles that had governed Egypt's policy were called into question. It became common to say that the Arabs were punished for straying from the path of true Islam.[5] Egypt embarked on a more moderate course and Saudi Arabia's stature within the Islamic world grew. Then in 1969, a deranged Australian set fire to the al-Aqsa mosque in Israeli-occupied Jerusalem. In the aftermath, King Faisal, by then the unquestioned leader of the nascent pan-Islamic movement, called for an Islamic summit in Rabat, Morocco, at which it was agreed to form a permanent Islamic organization. The Organization of the Islamic Conference (OIC) was born in 1970, the same year Nasser died. And unlike the June 1967 war, which was fought in the name of Arab nationalism, the October 1973 war (known as the Ramadan War in Arab countries and as the Yom Kippur War in Israel) was full of religious symbolism. It was, for example, code-named "Badr" – the name of Prophet Muhammed's first decisive victory over the Meccans.

By the mid-1970s, pan-Islamism had become a powerful movement, helped in no small part by the new-found wealth of Saudi Arabia. In such countries as Turkey and Pakistan, which until then had limited ties to the Arab world, Islamic solidarity became an important foreign policy theme "as the Muslim oil-producing states of the Middle East become important markets (especially for manpower) and important sources of economic aid."[6] The rapprochement between Pakistan and Persian Gulf states was especially significant since, as we saw, it was in Pakistan that the bulk of the early research on Islamic banking had been conducted. Throughout the 1970s, "while Saudi Arabia and other Gulf states provided the cash, Pakistan has provided much of the manpower, and much of the zeal, for the network of supranational 'Islamic' institutions that has developed … under the umbrella of the Organization of the Islamic Conference."[7] Interestingly, it all occurred during the rule of Zulficar Ali Bhutto – to whom the labels of "secular" and "socialist" are usually affixed –

who made numerous trips to oil-producing countries, emphasized the theme of Islamic brotherhood in his speeches, and hosted the Islamic summit conference in Lahore, during which the idea of the creation of an Islamic bank was adopted. (That summit was also that of the reconciliation between Pakistan and the newly-created Bangladesh, following an appeal in the name of Islam by Egyptian President Anwar Sadat.)[8]

2 The Petrodollar Windfall

Although Nasser's policies following the 1967 war were marked by relative moderation and pragmatism, it was under his successor, Anwar Sadat, that Egypt, timidly at first and then increasingly boldly, embarked on a new course: an Egypt-first stance that meant the abandonment of Nasser's "meddling" in other countries' affairs; distancing from the Soviet Union (Soviet advisers were expelled in 1972, but the Soviet Union nonetheless supported Egypt during the 1973 war); and a de-Nasserization policy at home, which meant primarily the abandonment of socialism and embarking, especially after 1974, on a policy of infitah (open door).

All those policies were welcomed by Saudi Arabia, and the two countries entered into an era of close cooperation. King Faisal granted generous financial assistance to Egypt, recognized Egypt's military role as the main confrontation state vis-à-vis Israel, and coordinated his oil policy with President Sadat. Cooperation on military and oil matters was crucial since the embargo and oil price increases of 1973–4 were closely linked to the Arab–Israeli war of October 1973.

By the early 1970s, the balance of power between oil producers and consumers and between governments and oil companies had shifted. Because of uninterrupted economic growth and the increased reliance on oil – at the expense of other energy sources – worldwide demand was very strong. Oil producers realized that with high inflation and a falling dollar, their oil receipts were steadily dwindling. (In real terms, the price of oil, which had remained stagnant for decades, was going down.) At the same time, oil-producing countries had become more assertive and better equipped to negotiate with oil companies: they now had nationals who had studied petroleum engineering, law, or business administration in Europe and the United States; they had also accumulated enough financial reserves to enable them to survive a showdown with oil companies. In the period between 1970 and 1973, they were thus able to obtain better terms: greater control over oil policy, higher prices, greater share of receipts, and even gradual nationalization, which increasingly transformed the role of foreign oil companies from all-powerful intermediaries and owners or part-owners of oil resources, to mere service providers hired at the discretion of governments to explore for, extract, refine, and sell the oil.[9]

So, just as King Faisal was kept apprised of war preparations, Anwar Sadat was strongly pressing him to use the "oil weapon": that is, to create a linkage between the price, indeed, the availability, of oil, and the Arab–Israeli conflict.[10] A conjunction of political and economic factors led to the oil embargo in October

1973 against countries supporting Israel (including the United States), and the quadrupling of the price of oil between October and December of that year. In what is commonly considered to be one of the most massive transfers of wealth in modern times, the mid-1970s were dominated by talk of a New International Economic Order (NIEO), more specifically of new relations between North and South and of Southern and particularly Islamic solidarity. In that context, Islamic banking went from a vague, somewhat utopian, idea to reality.

3 Relations with the United States and the West

In 1975 Hans Morgenthau, then the leading American theorist of international relations said:

> The control of oil, the lifeblood of an advanced industrial state, by poten-
> tates who have no other instrument of power and who are accountable to
> nobody, morally, politically, or legally, is in itself a perversity. It is a perver-
> sity in the sense that it defies all rational principles by which the affairs of
> state and the affairs of humanity ought to be regulated to put into a few
> irresponsible hands power over life and death of a whole civilization.[11]

The tone of Morgenthau's statement, and others by similarly learned people – let alone those of less learned ones – suggests an unwarranted attempt to somehow cripple if not destroy "the free world" and its economy.

The great paradox of the developments presented in the previous pages is that the main players involved – Anwar Sadat, King Faisal, the Shah of Iran – happened to be the strongest supporters of the United States and the West, all keen on having their national economies firmly embedded within the US-centered international economic framework. Sadat and Faisal felt that the "oil weapon" was a means to break a political deadlock and achieve a more equitable distri-bution of wealth between North and South. On the extent of the increase of oil prices, Saudi Arabia was decidedly a dove. Indeed, one of the lesser-known facts about what is generically considered an "Arab" price hike, was that, at the fateful December 1973 meeting of the Organization of Petroleum Exporting Countries (OPEC) in Tehran, the two main hawks were Iran and Venezuela – both non-Arab countries and both at the time squarely within the US "sphere of influence."[12] The hawks saw no contradiction there, insofar as they considered the new prices consistent with the rules and logic of the free market. Perhaps a bit disingenuously, the Shah of Iran frequently reiterated his concern that the West was too dependent on oil, and that only significantly higher prices would lead to less waste and to a more resolute search for alternative sources of energy. Saudi Arabia had good reasons to lead the doves. It was sparsely populated and did not need all the additional income. Also, having the largest oil reserves in the world, it was worried that too steep a rise would encourage the development of alternative sources of energy which in time may altogether supplant oil. Perhaps most importantly, Saudi Arabia, along with other Gulf states, was also heavily invested in international markets and was economically and militarily dependent on the United States. Crippling the United States. and the world economy would be self-defeating. When in the following years the Shah of Iran pushed for further price increases, Saudi Arabia refused to go along, for a time creating a two-tiered price system within OPEC.[13]

Overall, the relations between Saudi Arabia and the United States had been very close, although they were marred by differences over America's staunch support of Israel. The strong bilateral ties were reinforced by the official visits of King Faisal to Washington in 1966 and 1971, as well as to President Nixon's visit to Riyadh in July 1974 at the height of the Watergate scandal and shortly before his resignation. In the context of the Cold War, and despite the events of 1973, Saudi Arabia was firmly in the American camp. In the words of George Lenczowski:

> The two countries had a long history of mutual cooperation based on common concerns and complementary interests. Both were anticommunist and opposed to radical revolutionary movements anywhere in the world; both looked for stability and security in the Arabian Peninsula and the Persian Gulf; and both were interested that Saudi petroleum should flow uninterruptedly to the consumers in the industrialized democracies for the mutual benefit of the buyers and the sellers. The fact that a purely American company, Aramco was the sole operator of oil fields on Saudi territory added to the closeness of this relationship.[14]

Edward Mortimer observed that, for King Faisal, as for his successors, "the interests of Islam are in the last resort identified with those of the 'free world' – which Faisal saw as the Christian world, ruled by 'people of the book' – against those of atheistic communism."[15]

So despite policy differences over Israel and an oil policy that provided, among other things, for a gradual nationalization of Aramco, cooperation between the two countries actually increased, especially in military and financial matters. From 1974, the Saudis significantly increased their purchases of American weapons and chose to invest a significant part of their new-found wealth in US Treasury Bonds, while maintaining most of their deposits in American banks.[16]

It is thus not surprising that despite the heated rhetoric, American leaders such as Secretary of State Henry Kissinger considered the oil crisis to be a benign development that would further the geopolitical position of the United States.[17] His view was that in relative terms, the United States was less dependent on oil than Europe and Japan, and that most of the oil windfall would find its way back into the United States in the form of military and civilian contracts or Treasury Bond purchases. In a geopolitical perspective, the Shah of Iran, the leading hawk on oil prices, was designated as the regional "policeman" and granted "blank check" privileges in his shopping sprees: Iran, then considered to be a rock of stability in a highly unstable area, became the only country allowed to purchase, on a cash basis, any weapons it wanted. In 1978–9 the second "oil shock" occurred, triggered by riots and strikes in Iranian oil fields, and later by the Iranian revolution. Fearing

a domino effect in the region, in January 1980 President Jimmy Carter formulated
what became known as the Carter Doctrine: "Let our position be absolutely clear.
An attempt by any outside force to gain control of the Persian Gulf region will
be regarded as an assault on the vital interests of the United States of America,
and such an assault will be repelled by any means necessary, including military
force."[18] The alliance between the United States and Saudi Arabia and other
Persian Gulf states was consolidated as these countries became more dependent
than ever on American protection.[19]

II Islamic Finance and the Global Economy

By the mid-1980s, the circumstances that had given rise to Islamic banking
had subsided. More specifically, oil revenues had fallen to such an extent that
most Islamic countries were experiencing serious fiscal and balance of payment
problems. In Saudi Arabia, for example, oil revenues declined from a high of
$120 billion in 1981 to $17 billion in 1985.[20] In most countries, the economic
downturn had dramatic political and economic consequences: budget cuts, tax
increases, cancellation of contracts, sharp drops in labor remittances, etc. Yet
Islamic banking kept growing.

This section considers the trends that help to explain the recent growth of
Islamic finance: the emergence of a global economy which limits the options of
national governments and is characterized by new norms and a new ideology;
the transformation of the financial sector, whereby the lines between commercial banking, on the one hand, and investment banking as well as other financial activities, on the other hand, are increasingly blurred; the rise of Islamism,
which has put pressure on governments throughout the Muslim world to allow
for religiously-inspired financial products and institutions; and the very preoccupations – ethical, political, economic, and social – resulting from the excesses of
globalization and the search for correctives.

1 The Global Economy and its Ideology

The 1970s were characterized by the emergence of a regional economy within
an international system still dominated by the confrontation between the United
States and the Soviet Union. The petrodollar windfall had reconfigured economic
relations within the Islamic world. A sharp increase in trade, aid, and labor remittances transformed the economies of the Muslim world. The poorer countries
could also count on financial aid from one of the superpowers, and sometimes
from both. In the wake of the Camp David Accord, Egypt became the second
largest recipient of US aid (after Israel), while countries such as Syria or Iraq
received significant aid from the Soviet Union. In the wake of the oil bonanza,
the abundant deposits in international bank were often "recycled" into loans to
governments, which in those years of statism played a central role in economic
development.

Throughout the 1980s, both the regional economy and the Cold War system slowly disintegrated. The debt crisis (starting in August of 1982) led banks to reconsider their commitment to sovereign lending.[21] With the accession to power of Mikhail Gorbachev in 1985, East–West relations were transformed. The fall of the Berlin Wall in November 1989 and the disintegration of the Soviet Union in December 1991 marked the end of the Cold War. Within the Islamic world, the Gulf War marked the end of the regional economy.[22]

The changes leading to a New World Order were accompanied by an ideological shift. Traditional views on development had already been under sharp attack.[23] Since 1979, the World Bank had changed its focus from financing individual projects to transforming entire economies. With the Philippines as its first guinea pig, it set out to transform economic (and hence political) "structures" in exchange for aid.[24] And since the debt crisis (starting in August 1982), the IMF has become a sort of "global bankruptcy judge," disbursing funds only on condition that countries adopt "structural adjustment" policies.[25] In the cases of both the IMF and World Bank plans, the typical package included addressing macroeconomic imbalances and implementing sound fiscal and monetary policies, reforming the public sector, modernizing the supervisory and legal infrastructure, liberalizing financial markets, eliminating subsidies, promoting the free flow of capital and investment, etc. It should, therefore, come as no surprise that some have called such "structural adjustment programs" the equivalent of "a foreign-controlled coup in slow motion."[26]

The new paradigm was strengthened by the collapse of Communism in Eastern Europe and the implosion of the Soviet Union, which were interpreted as the victory, in the battle of ideas, of capitalism and the market economy over socialism and central planning.[27] Old dogmas regarding the respective roles of states and markets were turned on their head: government leaders were now seen as neither able nor willing to promote the public good; state controls could only encourage inefficiency, stifle entrepreneurship and delay reform. What came to be known as the "Washington consensus" was shared by the United States and other industrialized countries and by international organizations. The state, once seen as the provider of solutions, was now perceived as the major obstacle to development. All attempts at central planning, and even milder forms of industrial policy, were doomed. State-led policies, protectionism, and import substitution had to be replaced by privatization, deregulation, and export orientation. Foreign "experts," some of whom such as Harvard's Jeffrey Sachs achieved celebrity status, advised governments, often with disastrous results, on the reform process and the transition to free market economies.[28]

Reform was the *sine qua non* of obtaining access to international financing and to global markets. In order to obtain financial help from international organizations, or to be allowed to join the World Trade Organization (WTO) governments had to embrace – perhaps more accurately claim to embrace – the new ideology of reform. Governments also came under the surveillance of markets. Embracing the new ideology was more a matter of necessity than choice. With the drying up of external aid and the virtual end to sovereign loans by banks, the only option for governments was to borrow on the international markets. An added incentive for reform was related to a new phenomenon – the grading of countries and their debt by rating agencies. Throughout the 1990s, Moody's and Standard & Poor's awarded ratings to emerging markets, based in large part on an evaluation of how well the reforms demanded by "the markets" and their proxies were implemented. The cost of a bad rating is very high: punishing interest rates, perhaps even the outright inability to tap international markets.[29] At a time when private and public borrowers are fiercely competing across the globe to attract capital, in what John Maynard Keynes used to refer to as a "beauty contest," poorly-rated countries are likely to be shunned.

In short, the after-effects of the debt crisis and the end of the Cold War, along with the impacts of deregulation and technological change have recast the choices available to national governments. Unless they prefer autarky, countries are forced to conform to the dictates of the global economy. Most Islamic countries are heavily indebted and increasingly dependent on the outside world for financing, and the political and economic clout of bankers and other financiers is on the rise.[30] In order to raise funds in the international markets, or to obtain aid from the IMF or the World Bank, governments must adopt policies that conform to the new international orthodoxy (economic austerity, liberalization of trade and capital flows, privatization, deregulation, and dismantling of the public sector).[31] Even so-called "rogue states" such as Iran or the Sudan, lest they be financially starved, have to deal with the IMF and the World Bank and thus comply with demands related to economic policy.

The tidal wave of liberalism was somewhat late in reaching the Islamic world, but it is now clearly there.[32] The "alliance" between Islamists and liberals is justified by the existence of a common target: the all-powerful (and secular) state. Two areas of convergence between the Islamist critique of statism and the Washington consensus should be emphasized. First, the Islamic commitment to private property, free enterprise, and to the importance of contracts, as opposed to state-led economic policy and the arbitrary decisions that go along with a strong state bureaucracy. In many countries, Islam has become the tool of entrepreneurs seeking to get around restrictive regulation and an instrumental factor in privatization and deregulation – and the best excuse to disengage the state from the economy. Insofar as financial liberalization is "the process of reducing government control over the allocation of credit,"[33] Islamic bankers were bound to make common cause with economic liberals. Second, the parallel between the "privatization of welfare" (through reliance on zakat and other religiously-based redistribution schemes) advocated by Islamists and the downsizing of the state that is central to the new ideological consensus. Private virtue thus meets efficiency: by helping the poor, the wealthy become better human beings; and the voluntary provision of charity reduces the need for public welfare organizations that are usually more costly to run.[34]

This is not a new phenomenon. In medieval Muslim society, the Shariah was often used as a shield for private property against arbitrary confiscation.[35] Today the merchant classes are using the Koranic emphasis on private property rights and Islam's positive view of commerce and profits to pursue policies of privatization and deregulation. Even Islamic republics have on occasion openly embraced neo-liberalism. Thus, in Sudan between 1992 and the end of 1993, economics minister, Abdul Rahim Hamdi – a disciple of Milton Friedman and incidentally a former Islamic banker in London – did not hesitate to implement the harshest free market remedies dictated by the IMF. He said he was committed to transforming the heretofore statist economy "according to free-market rules, because this is how an Islamic economy should function."[36]

2 The Transformation of Banking and Finance

For most of the past decades, the world of finance was neatly divided between commercial banking on the one hand, and investment banking and other forms of finance, on the other hand. In the United States, the 1933 Glass–Steagall Act, for example, prevented the two types of institutions from encroaching on each other's territory. Typically, commercial banks were regulated like utilities. They benefited from government-sanctioned oligopolies, as products, rates, and geographic expansion were tightly regulated, and deposits up to a certain level were covered by insurance. The main source of profit for commercial banks came from interest income (the difference between interest earned on loans and interest paid on deposits). Since the 1970s, the nature of banking has started to change, and virtually every country has embarked on a wholesale overhaul of its banking system.[37] "What is going on now is a revolution in the way finance is organized," wrote Adrian Hamilton, "a revolution in the structure of banks and financial institutions and a revolution in the speed and manner in which money flows around the world."[38] This revolution was made possible by the impact of technology on financial services. According to Peter Dicken, "information is both the process and the product of financial services. Their raw materials are information: about markets, risks, exchange rates, returns on investment, creditworthiness. Their products are also information: the result of adding value to these informational inputs."[39]

Five major trends capture change in international finance. First, the impact of the new dominant ideology on financial policy. In contrast to the previous belief that strict government controls were necessary, a new ideology stressing the importance of free markets asserted itself in the mid-1970s in the United States and soon became the new worldwide orthodoxy. Starting with the US decision to deregulate commissions on securities transactions on May 1, 1975, and then to phase out interest rate controls and credit restrictions in landmark pieces of legislation enacted in 1980 and 1982, an irreversible process of deregulation has been underway. European countries followed suit, most dramatically with the British "Big Bang" of 1986, and later with the creation of a single European financial market. Alone among industrialized countries, Japan engaged – at least until its

1997 announcement of a phased-in "Big Bang" – in a reluctant, incremental and tightly-controlled process of deregulation.[40] As for emerging markets, during the 1980s most underwent a conversion to free market economics. As we saw earlier, the liberal ideology spread to most of the world and a huge privatization effort has since been underway.[41] Latecomers had a tendency to embrace the new ideology with a vengeance.

Second, the globalization of finance brought about by technological change and the opening of national markets to foreign competition. Richard O'Brien has written about the "end of geography," whereby "financial market regulators no longer hold full sway over their regulatory territory,"[42] and firms rethink their strategy in function of a global market. With the lifting of restrictions on capital movements, financial markets are increasingly interconnected. While interest rates are still far from achieving full convergence,[43] they are now increasingly sensitive to market forces and global capital movements.[44] In addition, governments now find themselves under the constant surveillance of "the markets" via such proxies as rating agencies, securities analysts, and the like.[45] Not since the glory days of the Gold Standard (1870–1914) have countries been so subjected to the whims of international capital. It is estimated that $1.25 trillion change hands every day in the foreign exchange markets. In an era of quicksilver capital, foreign investors have the power to enter and exit a market as they please, and little can be done by governments to stem the flow of short-term and often speculative funds.[46]

Third, the changing dynamics of competition. Deregulation and liberalization have intensified competitive pressures and blurred the lines within the financial sector. The cozy world of national oligopolies started fading with the erosion of the near-monopoly of banks on the intermediation process (the conversion of savings into loans). Banks were squeezed on both sides of their balance sheets. On the asset side, they lost the core business of lending to large and even not-so-large corporations, to commercial paper and junk bonds. Indeed, major corporations discovered that commercial paper was a much cheaper source of short-term working capital – as well as a higher-yielding short-term investment for their own excess cash.[47] The amount of commercial paper outstanding increased fourfold in the 1970s to $124 billion, and then quadrupled again in the 1980s to $570 billion as of December 1990. By contrast, all money center banks' commercial and industrial loans at that time was only $322 billion.[48] Banks also lost high-margin borrowers when second-tier corporations started issuing junk bonds, mostly under the aegis of the ill-fated Drexel Burnham Lambert.[49] On the liability side, depositors left banks in droves for higher yields in mutual funds, money market funds, or even stocks and bonds.[50] All these developments put tremendous pressure on banks' margins. Having lost their core businesses, indeed their franchise, they had to venture, initially without much success, into new territories, for which they were singularly – whether because of their inherently conservative culture, or regulatory strictures to which they were still subjected – ill-prepared.[51]

With the commercial banks in competition with securities firms, insurance companies, mutual funds, pension funds, hedge funds, etc., investors faced a growing range of choice. Increasingly, loans and other financial assets were securitized: that is, converted into tradable securities that can be bought and sold on the market. Fierce competition brought forth industry consolidation. Unable to compete, a growing number of firms fell by the wayside as a few players grew bigger, typically evolving into conglomerates combining banking, securities, and insurance activities in a single group.[52] Most countries have been moving toward a German-style universal banking model, where a financial institution can be at once a commercial bank, an investment bank, and a shareholder in industry.

In the United States, while Glass–Steagall is still on the books – although since 1991 there have been annual Congressional attempts to formally abolish the 1933 legislation – barriers separating various types of finance have been slowly but surely disappearing. Commercial banks have acquired other types of financial institutions, and have reinvented themselves. Among the first to move away from traditional commercial banking were J. P. Morgan and Bankers Trust, the latter redefining itself as a "risk manager" and creating a variety of new "derivatives" designed to fulfill a variety of commercial and investment needs.[53] Similarly, John Reed, the chairman of Citicorp – usually considered to be the most innovative commercial bank – redefined money as "information on the move." Leading banking experts even argued that "the commercial bank – the institution that accepts deposits payable on demand and originates loans – has outlived its usefulness and is in terminal decline."[54] Such experts as consulting firm McKinsey's Lowell Bryan suggested that the wave of the future was the "securitization" of all loans. As a result banks would no longer be necessary, and could be "broken up."[55] To be sure, banks have not disappeared, but their share of the broad financial sector has steadily dwindled. For decades, commercial banks had somewhere in the order of magnitude of 70 per cent of the financial assets of the United States. That share has now fallen to about 30 per cent.[56]

By the same token, innovation in products and risk management techniques have taken center stage. Deregulation and technological change allowed the creation of a wide array of financial products. Hence, the explosion of derivatives – products such as swaps, options, and futures whose value is derived from an underlying asset. "Financial engineers" are now in a position to create an infinite variety of new financial products through a process of slicing and splicing. For example, the interest and principal components of a bond can be split and sold separately, or they can be combined with other instruments and packaged as a single product. Initially devised as hedging devices, many such products have in fact amplified the risk exposure of their users. With the proliferation of derivatives, risk management and control are now at the core of financial strategies. Increasingly, risk management is global, cutting across products, countries, and legal entities.[57]

Fourth, the new relation between finance and economics. Until recently, finance was a reflection of the underlying real economy. Increasingly, the relationship has been reversed. Economics now seems driven by finance.[58] In many respects there is even a disconnect between finance and the underlying economic reality, posing new risks to the economy and new challenges to governments who now ponder John Maynard Keynes' famous statement: "Speculators may do no harm as bubbles on a steady stream of enterprise. But the position is serious when enterprise becomes the bubble on a whirlpool of speculation."[59]

Fifth, the new power of central banks. Once relegated to a purely technical role and typically confined to being an appendage of the Ministry of Finance, central banking has become a locus of economic, and indeed political, power. The prototype of the new central banker is Paul Volcker, who chaired the Federal Reserve Bank between 1979 and 1987, and whose anti-inflation policy became legendary.[60] As price stability came to define the new orthodoxy of economic policy, the central banks were bound to became the guardians of the dogma. The underlying rationale was that vote-seeking politicians were spendthrift by nature, and that only "independent" experts could insulate monetary policy from political pressures. So despite occasional criticisms of the growing power of unelected technocrats, a number of countries have moved to grant independence to their central bankers, considerably increasing their power in the process.[61] Between 1989 and 1998, more than twenty-five countries have upgraded the legal independence of their central banks.[62]

Based on all of the above, we can see how the new world of finance has facilitated the growth of Islamic finance. Where interest income was once the cornerstone of banking, its relative importance has steadily declined in recent years. As a result of competitive pressures and thinning margins, most financial institutions have increasingly been relying on fee and commission, rather than on interest, income. On traditional banking operations – deposit-taking and lending – banks have discovered that tacking on fees was as inconspicuous as it was lucrative. But more significantly, banks are now engaged in financial operations – such as the creation and sales of derivatives and other new products – that do not directly involve interest. The downgrading of interest has to some extent allowed the sidestepping of the most controversial aspect of banking and move beyond sterile debates about riba.

Another striking development is the convergence between the profit-and-loss sharing logic of traditional Islamic finance and many modern financing techniques. Indeed, modern finance has seen a sharp increase in risk-sharing arrangements, along the lines of the merchant banking or the venture capital model, where the financier is no longer a lender but a partner.[63] As for the financial innovation made possible by deregulation, it allowed the creation of specially tailored Islamic products. A few years ago, financial institutions could sell only a narrow range of financial products. After deregulation started, there were fewer and fewer constraints on the products that "financial engineers" could devise,[64] and the dysfunctions of the system became clear after 2007. The logic of engineering (which in the case of Islamic finance occurred under the close surveillance of Shariah advisors) allowed the creation of financial products based on religious needs.

3 The Rise of Islamism

The Islamic revivalism phenomenon has challenged most of the assumptions of Western liberal secularism and development theory. In an influential study of the Middle East published in 1958, Daniel Lerner announced the "passing of traditional society."[65] An entire generation of scholars of the Middle East and the Islamic world viewed the march of secularization and Westernization as inexorable. As we saw, Islamic finance is the product of a new wave of political Islam launched in the years of the Arab Cold War. Since the early 1970s, even pro-Western, secular leaders, such as Anwar Sadat in Egypt or Zulficar Ali Bhutto in Pakistan, have actively courted Islamic leaders and made increasing use of religious symbols in politics. It took the Iranian revolution of 1978–9 for the scholarly community outside the Islamic world to take notice. Still, with the first rumblings against the Shah, most "experts," ignoring the happenings in the holy city of Qom and concentrating instead on the "viable alternatives" for Iran's future – the military, the Communists, secular nationalists – considered an Islamic revolution to be a logical impossibility. When the Ayatollah Khomeini rose to prominence during his brief exile in France, few imagined that he would be anything more than a figurehead or a unifying, but politically inconsequential, symbol.[66] Predictably, the Iranian revolution brought about a pendulum swing in outside perceptions of Islam. Once ignored, Islam now became a ubiquitous and monolithic threat.[67]

The brand of Islam best known outside the Islamic world is revolutionary or radical, and usually anti-Western. Since the Iranian revolution, a number of developments have highlighted the political dimension of Islam. Only a few months after an Islamic republic had been proclaimed in Iran, the Grand Mosque in Mecca was seized by religious extremists.[68] In 1981, Anwar Sadat was assassinated by an Islamist organization, which argued that it was its religious duty to do so since in its view jihad was the sixth pillar of Islam.[69] In Syria, increasing activity by the Muslim Brothers resulted in the Hama massacres of 1982.[70] Throughout the mid-1980s, "Islamic terrorism" took center stage. A number of terrorist incidents, inside and outside the Muslim world were traced to Islamic extremists or to one of the other "rogue states" (at various times, the list included Iran, Iraq, Libya, Syria, and the Sudan). The long-drawn-out hostage crisis in Lebanon, where Westerners were kidnapped by Hezbollah, a Shia party of Iranian obedience, was a daily reminder of the dangers of Islamic "fundamentalism." During the Gulf War of 1991, although most Islamic governments were part of the US-led coalition Islamic public opinion seemed to be deeply divided. The presence of foreign troops in Saudi Arabia, the birthplace of Islam, was especially controversial. Later that year in Algeria, the Algerian Islamic Salvation Front (FIS) was poised to sweep to power in the Algerian parliament in the first open elections in the history of the country when the electoral process was cut short, igniting a bloody civil war. Throughout the Islamic world, Islamic parties and organizations had burst upon the political scene. Some were part of the existing institutional and electoral system, others operated outside it. Even secular Turkey had a year-long experience with an Islamist prime minister.

Religious sentiment though ran deeper and went beyond politics, although private and religious manifestations of Islam seldom makes headlines. In reality, throughout the Muslim world there had been increased manifestations of religious sentiment that were quite diverse – ranging from demands for an Islamicization of political life to a rise in "pietism" – and different from the Iranian model. Thus, while Hamas, Hezbollah, the Muslim Brothers or the Taliban are household words, few people outside the Islamic world have ever heard of the Tablighi Jamaat, which in terms of numbers and impact far outstrips fundamentalist organizations. According to Yahya Sadowski:

> In part precisely because it is so apolitical, governments from Tunisia to Pakistan have not only tolerated but encouraged Tabligh's spread. After putting down strong roots in India, it grew rapidly across Pakistan, Afghanistan, Bangladesh, and Sri Lanka into southeast Asia. It is one of the three movements that led the Islamic revival in Malaysia and plays an important role in Indonesia as well. It is highly popular among Muslim minorities in the West, including America, England, and France. It has a firm foothold in parts of the Middle East as well, though it has not yet spread as widely there as in other parts of the Muslim world.[71]

Such aspects of the Islamic revival are reflected in increased emphasis upon religious observance (mosque attendance, fasting, etc.), religious programming on television, as well as dynamic *daawa* (missionary) movements aiming at converting non-Muslims, and also at bringing Muslims to deepen their religious knowledge and commitment. Islam is also playing a large role in civil society. It has penetrated deeply within associations, ranging from trades unions to civic organizations to student groups and is now part of the mainstream of society.[72]

As for the reasons for such reawakening, many have been suggested: the vacuum left by secular ideologies, socialism in particular, that were discredited both politically and economically, as well as the moral outrage at the extent of oppression and corruption; the attempts by certain groups, especially among the lower classes and those traditionally under-represented in government, to secure a place for themselves in the political arena; an identity crisis and the search for roots in a world dominated by commercialism and materialism and in settings where rapid demographic growth combined with poverty and unemployment produce a sense of hopelessness. All these factors were intensified by economic problems and political demands. The decline in oil prices led to significant job cutbacks in oil-producing countries, falling remittances and the return home of migrant workers to dire economic conditions. Most governments, strapped for cash, embarked on austerity policies, which had the dual consequences of increasing discontent and providing Islamic movements with the opportunity to fill a vacuum. Schools and hospitals, along with a host of welfare services were increasingly run by Islamic groups. Islam had also become, if not the language of protest, at the very least a means by which opposition could be expressed with minimal government interference.[73] Insofar as the phenomenon is multifaceted, every one of these explanations is to some degree plausible. Taken together, they explain why different groups and social classes found reasons to embrace, or return to, Islam.

Beyond the diversity found within Islam (pietist or political, modernist or revivalist, quietist or activist, moderate or radical, conservative or revolutionary, moderate or radical, pro-Western or anti-Western), there has been virtually everywhere some demand for enhancing the role of religion in political and economic life. A diverse group of countries – including secularly-oriented ones such as Egypt and Yemen – have responded by upgrading the role of the Shariah in the constitution. A standard, if usually vague, demand by Islamic groups everywhere is to Islamicize the financial system, or at the very least to allow for Islamic financial products. So typically, as banking laws are being overhauled, some provision is made to permit, if not promote, some form of Islamic finance. It is also common both for countries exposed to Islamic challenges and to newly-formed or newly-independent Muslim countries to announce financial Islamicization. Soon after the 1991 Gulf War, one of the first decisions of the returning Kuwaiti government was to form a committee to study changes to the constitution in order to make the Shariah "the sole source of legislation" (rather than simply a "a main source"). A key provision was to propose Islamic banking legislation (so politically contentious was the issue that the Islamic banking legislation was only passed in 2003).[74] And in the Philippines, barely six weeks after the government had signed the 1996 peace agreement with the Islamic rebels, five Islamic banks had requested permission to establish branches in the southern part of the country where a majority of the five million Muslims live.[75] Similarly, soon after Chechnya proclaimed its independence from the Russian Federation, one of the first announcements of the President of the breakaway republic was that the financial system would be Islamicized.[76]

In sum, at a time of Islamic reawakening, the toleration, if not the promotion, of Islamic finance is for most governments a low-cost, low-risk (insofar as the details of legislation are left for experts to work out) proposition.

4 The Concern with Ethics

Morality and ethics have always been the Achilles' heel of the market economy. Just as free market ideas and policies triumph, there is a renewed interest in ethical matters. So there is no real contradiction: the greater the triumph of the free market, the more vocal the challenge to the "entrenched utilitarian, rationalistic, individualistic, neo-classical paradigm which is applied not merely to the economy but also, increasingly to the full array of social relations, from crime to family."[77]

Until recently, the imperfections and the excesses of the market were addressed by law and public policy. In the US financial system the rigor of the marketplace was mitigated by strict regulation and by legislation such as the Community Reinvestment Act, the Fair Housing Act, or the Equal Credit Opportunity Act.[78] Such laws required, among other things, financial institutions to go beyond considerations of profit maximization to achieve other societal goals and ensure the provision of credit to under-served neighborhoods and groups. In recent years, many of these strictures have been relaxed. The trend toward deregulation (since 1980) was accompanied by a search for non-legislative and non-regulatory correctives, ranging from moral suasion to the promotion of personal ethical behavior.[79]

Examples of the renewed interest in the ethical dimension of business and finance in an era of unfettered capitalism are numerous.[80] Ethics is now a fixture on business school curricula. Companies play up their philanthropic efforts and their "social responsibility." "Socially responsible" funds are booming.[81] Individualism or materialism have come under attack, and ideas about "communitarianism," "civic virtues," "meaning," "corporate citizenship," and "stakeholding"[82] have been widely promoted by intellectuals and also by political figures, including the likes of Bill Clinton and Tony Blair. The underlying theme is that rights cannot exist in the absence of corresponding obligations, and that aggressive individualism is not a sustainable basis for any society. Individuals are called on to give their time and effort to their communities. Corporations are called on to acknowledge a wider range of responsibilities than the maximization of shareholder value.[83]

In 1997, the Philadelphia "Summit for the Future of America" was a major media event: under the chairmanship of General Colin Powell, and in the presence of Bill Clinton and former presidents Bush, Carter, and Ford, the summit emphasized the importance of volunteering, civic virtue, and community involvement as necessary to the proper functioning of a free market economy.[84] In such a context, religion can be an essential part of the "matrix of culture and the institutional structures that provide a context for personal behavior."[85] As illustrated by the slogan "doing well by doing good," ethical behavior can be compatible with a market economy. In the quest for a free enterprise system that is circumscribed by moral norms and codes, religion, and Islam in particular – a religion that holds positive view of economic activities while providing for a strict ethical framework – can play a central role.

III Current Debates on Islamic Finance

Opinions differ as to the political impact of Islamic finance. Some see in it a "democratizing" and a "moderating" factor, arguing that by legitimating certain forms of modern business, it may strengthen civil society against the arbitrary rule often found in Islamic countries.[86] In the words of Clement Henry:

> While Islamic bankers do not necessarily share any commitment to Western-style liberalism or democracy, their drive for markets and profits may indirectly contribute to a more competitive politics. Their economic success

sets the stage for greater democracy by encouraging popular participation in financial activities, by shifting the political weight within popular Islamist movements in favor of "responsible" business elements ready to coexist with the capitalist order, and by accumulating finance capital, helping to consolidate the structural power of the commercial banking system and the autonomy of the private business sector.[87]

Yet following September 11, 2001, there was a surge of Islamophobia in the West, which portrayed all things Islamic, and in particular Islamic banks, in the worst possible light.[88] The outrage provoked by the terrorist attacks gave credence to anti-Islamic views, which moved quite close to mainstream and policy-making circles. Thus, journalist Steven Emerson, whose primary claim to fame until then had been his assertion that the 1995 Oklahoma City bombing "could only have been perpetrated by Middle Eastern terrorists," said that the days following September 11, "he has fielded 1,000 calls, many from news organizations,"[89] thus becoming one of the most ubiquitous "terrorist experts."

More worrisome, many figures that are part of the political establishment have attacked Islam as a religion. In October 2001, the Reverend Franklin Graham, who officiated at President Bush's inaugural, and was the son and heir apparent of the Reverend Billy Graham, probably the most respected religious figure in America, proclaimed: "The God of Islam is not the same God [as that of Christianity]. It's a different God, and I believe it is a very evil and wicked religion." As for the Reverend Pat Robertson, one of the most prominent televangelist who heads a media empire and was once a presidential candidate, he said that Muslims "want to coexist until they can control, dominate and then if need be, destroy." Lieutenant General William G. Boykin, who as Deputy Undersecretary of Defense for Intelligence was one of Donald Rumsfeld's closest advisors, made similar attacks in churches about Islam's God being an "idol." Mainstream publications frequently carried anti-Islamic articles, and bookstores were full of books denigrating Islam and Muslims.[90]

In sum, there are sharply different views of the political-economic consequences of Islamic finance. Within Islamic countries, some have viewed it as encouraging political Islam, while others have seen it as a deflecting factor.[91] In Western countries, public attitudes to Islamic finance reflected the same ambivalence. Where some have seen Islamic finance as a means of "infiltrating" the system or breaking the separation of church and state, others have looked at it as a way of offering pious Muslims the opportunity to practice their religion within a secular environment. The British government has stressed the economic and political benefits of Islamic finance, in particular the role it could play in integrating Muslim communities within the broader society.[92] Yet at the same time, the growing presence of Islamic finance in the West has elicited more attacks, by a variety of political groups, in the media and in public opinion.[93]

Notes

1. Malcolm H. Kerr, *The Arab Cold War: Gamal 'Ab'd al-Nasir and his rivals 1958–1969* (Oxford: Oxford University Press, 1970). For a recent analysis of the impact of the Cold War on political Islam, see Robert Dreyfuss, *Devil's Game: How The United States Helped Unleash Fundamentalist Islam* (New York: Metropolitan Books, 2005).

2. Edward Mortimer, *Faith and Power: The Politics of Islam* (New York: Random House, 1982), pp. 177–80.

3. George Lenczowski, *The Middle East in World Affairs* (Ithaca, NY: Cornell University Press, 1980), p. 603.

4. Nazih N. M. Ayubi, "The Political Revival of Islam" in *International Journal of Middle East Studies* (December 1980), p. 489.

5. Mortimer, *Faith and Power*, p. 178.

6. Mortimer, *Faith and Power*, p. 217.

7. Mortimer, *Faith and Power*, p. 218.

8. Mortimer, *Faith and Power*, p. 218.

9. Daniel Yergin, *The Prize: The Epic Quest for Oil, Money and Power* (New York: Simon and Schuster, 1991), pp. 563–87.

10. Yergin, *The Prize*, p. 595.

11. Quoted in Jack Anderson, with James Boyd, *Fiasco: The Real Story Behind the Disastrous Worldwide Energy Crisis – Richard Nixon's "Oilgate"* (New York: Times Books, 1983), p. 256.

12. Lenczowski, *The Middle East in World Affairs*, p. 214.

13. Lenczowski, *The Middle East in World Affairs*, p. 607.

14. Lenczowski, *The Middle East in World Affairs*, p. 608.

15. Mortimer, *Faith and Power*, p. 180.

16. Lenczowski, *The Middle East in World Affairs*, p. 609.

17. David Calleo, *The Imperious Economy* (Cambridge, MA: Harvard University Press, 1982), pp. 120–1.

18. George Lenczowski, *American Presidents and the Middle East* (Durham, NC: Duke University Press, 1990), p. 206.

19. Yergin, *The Prize*, p. 702.

20. Kiren Aziz Chaudhry, *The Price of Wealth: Economies and Institutions in the Middle East* (Ithaca, NY: Cornell University Press, 1997), p. 7.

21. Paul Volcker and Toyoo Gyohten, *Changing Fortunes: The World's Money and the Threat to American Leadership* (New York: Times Books, 1992), pp. 193–4.

22. Chaudhry, *The Price of Wealth*, p. 2.

23. Deepak Lal, *The Poverty of 'Development Economics'* (Cambridge, MA: Harvard University Press, 1985). See also Richard E. Feinberg and Valeriana Kallab (eds.), *Adjustment Crisis in the Third World* (New Brunswick, NJ: Transaction Books, 1984).

24. Robin Broad and John Cavanaugh, "No More NICs," *Foreign Policy*, Spring 1988.

25. Jacques B. Gélinas, *Freedom from Debt: The Reappropriation of Development through Financial Self-reliance* (London: Zed Books, 1998), p. 13.

26. Gélinas, *Freedom from Debt*, p. 54.

27. Daniel Yergin and Joseph Stanislaw, *The Commanding Heights: The Battle Between Government and the Marketplace that is Remaking the Modern World* (New York: Simon and Schuster, 1998).

28. Ibrahim Warde, "Les faiseurs de révolution libérale," *Le Monde diplomatique*, May 1992.

29. Ibrahim Warde, "Ces officines qui notent les Etats," *Le Monde diplomatique*, February 1997. See also Richard Farnetti and Ibrahim Warde, *Le modèle anglo-saxon en question* (Paris: Economica, 1997), Ch. 4.

30. Clement M. Henry, *The Mediterranean Debt Crescent: Money and Power in Algeria, Egypt, Morocco, Tunisia and Turkey* (Gainesville, FL: University Press of Florida, 1996).

31. Iliya Harik and Denis J. Sullivan (eds.), *Privatization and Liberalization in the Middle East*

(Bloomington, IN: Indiana University Press, 1992).

32. Leonard Binder, *Islamic Liberalism: A Critique of Developmental Ideologies* (Chicago, IL: University of Chicago Press, 1988).

33. Stephan Haggard, Chung H. Lee, and Sylvia Maxfield (eds.), *The Politics of Finance in Developing Countries* (Ithaca, NY: Cornell University Press, 1993), p. 314.

34. In the same vein, some researchers in sociology and political science have detected the rise of "market Islam" at the individual level, see Patrick Haenni, *L'Islam de marché: L'autre revolution conservatrice* (Paris: Editions du Seuil, 2005).

35. Ellis Goldberg, "Private Goods, Public Wrongs and Civil Society in some Medieval Arab Theory and Practice," in Ellis Goldberg, Resat Kasaba and Joel S. Migdal (eds.), *Rules and Rights in the Middle East: Democracy, Law, and Society* (Seattle, WA: University of Washington Press, 1993), p. 251.

36. Judith Miller, *God Has Ninety-Nine Names: A Reporter's Journey through a Militant Middle East* (New York: Simon and Schuster, 1996), p. 144.

37. Martin Mayer, *The Bankers: The Next Generation* (New York: Truman Talley Books/ Dutton, 1997).

38. Adrian D. Hamilton, *The Financial Revolution* (Harmondsworth: Penguin Books, 1986), p. 13.

39. Peter Dicken, *Global Shift: Transforming the World Economy* (New York: Guilford Press, 1998), p. 401.

40. Michael Moran, *The Politics of the Financial Services Revolution, The USA, UK and Japan* (New York: St. Martin's Press, 1991).

41. Ingo Walter, "Global Competition and Market Access in the Securities Industry," in Claude E. Barfield (ed.), *International Financial Markets: Harmonization versus Competition*, Washington, DC: AEI Press, 1996), p. 84.

42. Richard O'Brien, *Global Financial Integration: The End of Geography* (New York: Council on Foreign Relations Press, 1992), p. 1.

43. Richard C. Marston, *International Financial Integration: A Study of Interest Differentials Between the Major Industrial Countries* (Cambridge: Cambridge University Press, 1995), p. 179.

44. J. Pierre V. Benoit, *United States Interest Rates and the Interest Rate Dilemma for the Developing World* (Westport, CT: Quorum Books, 1986).

45. Ibrahim Warde, "Ces officines qui notent les Etats," *Le Monde diplomatique*, February 1997.

46. William Greider, *One World, Ready or Not: The Manic Logic of Global Capitalism* (New York: Simon and Schuster, 1997).

47. Roy C. Smith, *Comeback: The Restoration of American Banking Power in the New Economy* (Cambridge, MA: Harvard Business School Press, 1993), p. 51.

48. Smith, *Comeback*, p. 52.

49. Connie Bruck, *The Predators' Ball: The Inside Story of Drexel Burnham and the Rise of the Junk Bond Raiders* (New York: Penguin, 1989).

50. James Grant, *Money of the Mind: Borrowing and Lending in America from the Civil War to Michael Milken* (New York: Farrar, Straus and Giroux, 1992), pp. 368–442.

51. Joseph Nocera, *A Piece of the Action: How the Middle Class Joined the Money Class* (New York: Simon and Schuster, 1994), pp. 231–410.

52. Mayer, *The Bankers*.

53. Smith, *Comeback*, p. 4.

54. *The Financial Times*, July 14, 1997.

55. Lowell Bryan, *Breaking Up the Bank: Rethinking an Industry Under Siege* (New York: Irwin Professional Publishing, 1988).

56. *American Banker*, July 15, 1996.

57. Keith Redhead, *Financial Derivatives: an Introduction to Futures, Forwards, Options and Swaps* (New York: Prentice Hall, 1997).

58. Olivier Piot, *Finance et économie: la fracture* (Paris: Le Monde-Editions, 1995).
59. Quoted in John Kenneth Galbraith, *A Short History of Financial Euphoria* (New York: Penguin, 1990), p. 26.
60. William Greider, *Secrets of the Temple: How the Federal Reserve Runs the Country* (New York: Simon and Schuster, 1987).
61. Steven Solomon, *The Confidence Game: How Unelected Central Bankers Are Governing the Changed Global Economy* (New York: Simon and Schuster, 1995). See also Marjorie Dean and Robert Pringle, *The Central Banks* (London: Hamish Hamilton, 1994).
62. *The Financial Times*, June 1, 1998.
63. John W. Wilson, *The New Venturers: Inside the High-Stakes World of Venture Capital* (Reading, MA: Addison-Wesley, 1985).
64. See Ibrahim Warde, "La dérive des nouveaux produits financiers," *Le Monde diplomatique*, July 1994.
65. Daniel Lerner, *The Passing of Traditional Society: Modernizing the Middle East* (New York: Free Press, 1958).
66. James A. Bill, *The Eagle and the Lion: The Tragedy of American-Iranian Relations* (New Haven, CT: Yale University Press, 1989).
67. See Chapter 11.
68. Yaroslav Trofimov, *The Siege of Mecca: The Forgotten Uprising in Islam's Holiest Shrine and the Birth of al-Qaeda* (New York: Doubleday, 2007).
69. Mohammed Hassanein Heikal, *Autumn of Fury: The Assassination of Sadat* (New York: Random House, 1983).
70. Thomas Friedman, *From Beirut to Jerusalem* (New York: Farrar, Straus and Giroux, 1989).
71. Yahya Sadowski "'Just' a Religion: For the Tablighi Jama'at, Islam is not totalitarian," *The Brookings Review*, 14:3 (Summer 1996), pp. 34–5.
72. John Esposito, *The Islamic Threat: Myth of Reality* (Oxford: Oxford University Press, 1991), p. 132.
73. Esposito, *The Islamic Threat*, pp. 132–6. See also Paul Salem, *Bitter Legacy: Ideology and Politics in the Arab World* (New York: Syracuse University Press, 1994), p. 260; Emmanuel Sivan, *Radical Islam* (New Haven, CT: Yale University Press, 1985); Gilles Kepel *Muslim Extremism in Egypt: The Prophet and Pharaoh* (Berkeley, CA: University of California Press, 1986); Olivier Carré, *L'Islam laïque ou le retour à la Grande Tradition* (Paris: Armand Colin, 1993); Gilles Kepel, *La revanche de Dieu: Chrétiens, juifs et musulmans à la reconquête du monde* (Paris: Editions du Seuil, 1991); Olivier Roy, *L'échec de l'Islam politique* (Paris: Editions du Seuil, 1992).
74. Agence France-Press, May 4, 1997.
75. *The Financial Times*, October 29, 1996.
76. *Dow Jones International News*, June 8, 1997.
77. Amitai Etzioni, *The Moral Dimension: Towards a New Economics* (New York: Macmillan, 1988), p. ix.
78. Ibrahim Warde, *Foreign Banking in the United States* (San Francisco, CA: IBPC, 1998).
79. Zuhayr Mikdashi, *Les banques à l'ère de la mondialisation* (Paris: Economica, 1998), pp. 332–40.
80. Daniel M. Hausman and Michael S. McPherson, 'Taking Ethics Seriously: Economics and Contemporary Moral Philosophy," *Journal of Economic Literature*, 31:2 (1993), pp. 671–731.
81. Ibrahim Warde, "Les riches entre philanthropie et repentance," *Le Monde diplomatique*, December 1997.
82. See, for example, Amitai Etzione, *The Spirit of Community: The Reinvention of American Society* (New York: Touchstone Books, 1994), Michael Sandel, *Democracy's Discontent: America in Search of a Public Philosophy* (Cambridge, MA: Harvard University Press, 1996).
83. Will Hutton, *The State We're In* (London: Jonathan Cape, 1995).

84. Maxime Rodinson, *Islam and Capitalism* (London: Penguin, 1974), p. 48.
85. John Adams, "Economy as Instituted Process: Change, Transformation and Progress," *Journal of Economic Issues*, 28:2 (1994), p. 332.
86. Alan Richards, "Economic Imperatives and Political Systems," *Middle East Journal* (Spring 1993), p. 225.
87. Henry, *The Mediterranean Debt Crescent*, p. 22.
88. See Chapter 11.
89. Felicity Barringer, "Terror Experts Use Lenses of Their Specialties," *The New York Times*, September 24, 2001.
90. See, for instance, Paul Sperry, *Infiltration: How Muslim Spies and Subversives have Penetrated Washington* (Nashville, TN: Nelson Current, 2005), Steven Emerson, *American Jihad: The Terrorists Living Among Us* (New York: Free Press, 2003), Daniel Pipes, *Militant Islam Reaches America* (New York: W. W. Norton, 2002).
91. See Chapter 11.
92. See Chapter 6.
93. See Chapter 11.

6

COUNTRY DIFFERENCES

There are major differences across countries in the role, the importance, the status, and the characteristics of Islamic financial institutions. Their role in national economies ranges from essential to insignificant. Their "special character" may or may not be recognized by regulators. In some countries, they are strongly encouraged by the authorities; in others they are barely tolerated. One of the themes running through this book is that of the diversity of Islamic finance. Even those countries that have fully Islamicized their financial systems – Pakistan, Iran, the Sudan – did so under different religious, political, economic, and cultural circumstances. In most cases, Islamicization did not occur in a carefully thought out application of Islamic principles and jurisprudence, but in an *ad hoc* manner and as a result of situational factors.

This chapter discusses the experience of countries that have undergone full Islamicization of their financial systems. It also examines the case of Malaysia, a country that has promoted Islamic finance alongside conventional banking, and looks at those countries and territories such as Bahrain, the United Kingdom, Singapore, and Hong Kong, that have announced their intention of becoming hubs of Islamic finance.

I Pioneers of Full Islamicization: Pakistan, Iran, and The Sudan

1 Pakistan

The Pakistani experiment in Islamic banking is nothing short of contradictory. A number of Pakistani scholars, starting with Abul Ala Mawdudi have pioneered the study of Islamic economics and finance. Pakistan was also the first country, in 1979, to embark on a program of full Islamicization of its economy and financial system. The Pakistani government went farther than most Islamic governments in recreating the concepts, language, and institutions of early Islam. This commitment has been constantly reaffirmed since, with countless measures designed to achieve that goal. Indeed, Islamic banking is on the platform of every major political party and for any politician not endorsing it amounts to political suicide.[1] Yet almost 20 years after the Islamicization had begun, a leading Pakistani economist could state: "I don't think in the next few years [Islamicization] is going to happen. The roots of the British banking system are very strong."[2]

The Pakistani case, pioneering as it is, is testament to the fact that situational factors can thwart the best intentions of governments. Turmoil, poverty, and indebtedness have imposed sharp constraints on policy options. The British legacy had also created commercial habits and a financial culture that could not be undone by reform. The heavy foreign debt – some $42 billion in 2008 – in addition to being interest-bearing meant that the IMF and other foreign creditors had a say in how the economy was managed.[3]

Pakistan is a young country. Even the idea of a separate state for Indian Muslims is relatively recent. For decades there had been a common Hindu–Muslim independence movement sparked by anti-British sentiment. But in 1930, Muhammad Iqbal (1875–1935), the poet and major figure of Islamic reform, started calling for a Muslim homeland. And from 1940, Muhammad Ali Jinnah (1876–1948), the thoroughly Westernized leader of Indian Muslims, and his Muslim League Party championed the cause of Muslim nationalism. In 1947, the British departed, India was partitioned, and the independent state of Pakistan was born. Pakistan thus constituted both a rejection of a multi-confessional, secular India and an attempt to recreate an Islamic order after a long period of Western colonial rule. The country's name was both an acronym of some of the regions that were carved out of India to create the new state, and a word in Urdu, Pakistan's principal language, which means "land of the pure." The founding fathers were secular, Westernized people who were nonetheless intent on creating an Islamic state.

The task was complicated by the huge problems facing the new state: the population transfers and civil strife that followed the partition, the consistently troubled relations with India, with whom Pakistan fought three wars, etc. In addition, there was still a well-entrenched British influence and a lack of consensus about the kind of Islam that should be adopted. For not only does Pakistan have a substantial Shia community (accounting for 20 per cent of the population), but even the Sunni majority (75 per cent) is divided among three major sects and dozens of amorphous groups, making a consensus on the interpretation of Islam nearly impossible.

Still, all the successive leaders of the country have reaffirmed the Islamic character of Pakistan, and their desire to harness Islam to the goals of economic growth and modernization. In 1949, the Constituent Assembly defined Pakistan as a state where "the Muslims shall be enabled to order their lives in the individual and collective spheres in accord with the teachings and requirements of Islam as set out in the Holy Quran and the Sunna." It declared that "sovereignty over the entire universe belongs to God Almighty alone" and that, therefore, authority would be exercised by the people of Pakistan only "within the limits prescribed by Him." The new country was an "Islamic Republic," that would build itself a capital city called Islamabad.

At times, leaders felt stifled by traditional religious interpretations. Thus, Mohammed Ayub Khan, who came to power in 1958, set out to "liberate the spirit of religion from the cobwebs of superstition and stagnation which surround it and move forward under the forces of modern science and knowledge." He once stated: "The miracle of Islam was that it destroyed idolatry, and the tragedy of Muslims has been that they rendered religion into the form of an idol."[4]

Throughout the 1970s Pakistan drew closer to the Islamic world, and particularly to Saudi Arabia.[5] Interestingly, most of these developments occurred under the rule of Prime Minister Zulficar Ali Bhutto, whose name is usually associated with socialism and secularism, but who nonetheless made increasing use of Islamic language and symbolism. The country received significant amounts of aid – in addition to growing labor remittances – from oil producing countries, and became one of the most active members of the OIC. In 1977, the military, led by Mohammed Zia ul-Haq, seized power with the support of Jamaat-i-Islami, the country's best organized and strongest religious party. In a televised address to the nation on the day of the coup, the new leader, who remained in power until his death in 1988 in a mysterious plane crash, praised the "spirit of Islam" that had inspired the opposition to the Bhutto regime, concluding: "It proves that Pakistan, which was created in the name of Islam, will continue to survive only if it sticks to Islam. That is why I consider the introduction of an Islamic system as an essential prerequisite for the country."[6]

In 1979, Zia appointed a twelve-member committee of "scholars, jurists, ulema, and prominent persons from other walks of life" to formulate recommendations for the structure of an Islamic government system.[7] The recommendations included the creation of a new Islamic economic order, the substitution of traditional Islamic laws and punishments for inherited Western codes, and the creation of a pure Islamic form of government designed to serve as a model for other Muslim states.

The first phase of economic reform (1979–85) had three significant components. The zakat, a 2.5 per cent per annum levy on savings accounts, various kinds of bank deposits, unit trusts, government securities, corporate shares and debentures, annuities, life insurance, and other comparable assets would be distributed through an elaborate voluntary system of zakat committees at federal, state, and village levels who in turn would channel the money collected to benefit the *mustahaqueen*, the deserving, or those living below the poverty line. The ushr (literally tithe), would be imposed at a rate of 5 per cent on all agricultural produce above a certain level. The hope at the time was that it would raise enough revenue to allow the abolition of income tax and reduce corporate tax, thereby releasing pent-up entrepreneurial energies to the benefit of the country's economic development. The third component was the partial Islamicization of the banking system through the introduction of PLS accounts.[8]

Such measures did not go without political controversy. The introduction of zakat caused an outcry among Pakistan's Shia minority, who objected to its being collected and distributed through the state, as opposed to through their own ulemas. Following riots in Islamabad, the government gave ground, allowing Shia groups to collect and distribute the zakat on their own. Overall, there was skepticism that the new Islamic taxes would truly alleviate poverty, or that the creation of PLS windows, opened in all 7,000 branches of domestic banks, would create a qualitatively different banking system (a "profit-and-loss sharing project" instead of a fixed pre-determined interest), or that it would draw the amounts hoarded by pious (or suspicious) peasants into the banking system.

Pakistan was also the first country to revive the old Islamic institution of hisbah, the office that supervised markets, provided municipal services, and settled petty disputes. But in its new incarnation, the office had the much more limited role of protecting ordinary citizens against administrative wrongs.[9]

In December 1984, the Pakistani government called on all five nationalized Pakistani banks and the seventeen foreign banks operating in the country to submit proposals of more "godly and brotherly" ways to generate profits. In the second phase of Islamicization, which was implemented through a series of measures imposed between January and July 1985, interest was outlawed. In reality, however, huge loopholes remained, and successive governments, despite their official commitment to interest-free banking, proved to be quite pragmatic in their actions. Foreign currency deposits, foreign loans, and government debt continued to function on the basis of interest. Overall, the Pakistani authorities took care to ensure that the new modes of financing did not upset the basic functioning and structure of the banking system. As a result, the exceptions proved more significant than the rule: the (interest-bearing) government debt was four times larger than the private sector's debt,[10] and about 80 per cent of domestic deposits were denominated in foreign currencies that allowed interest payments.[11]

The government was thus caught between two sets of conflicting forces. On the one hand, religious groups, as well as a large domestic constituency, had been calling for Islamicization. On the other hand, however, Pakistan had a long tradition of conventional, interest-based banking, and was under pressure from the IMF and other foreign creditors to privatize its banking sector and liberalize its economy. The alliance between the military, which was committed to a policy of neo-liberalism, and the main religious party had been fraught with ambiguity. In the words of one scholar:

> Aside from abstract notions about the shape and working of the ideal Islamic state, the party had little to offer in the way of suggestions for managing its machinery. Its notions about the working of Islamic dicta in economic and political operations provided Zia with no coherent plan of action. Just as the Jamaat became disappointed with the politics of Zia's regime, so the general became disillusioned with the practical relevance of the Jama'at's ideas."[12]

In 1992, the country's Federal Shariah Court ruled that interest paid or charged by banks and other financial institutions were un-Islamic. The government was given a few months to amend its financial laws accordingly, otherwise the existing laws "will cease to have effect." (The government, though still committed in theory to the elimination of riba, appealed the decision.[13]) In January 1998, it decided "in principle" to eliminate riba from the economic system of the country.[14] These conflicting pressures occurred at a time when a third of the four public banks' assets were non-performing and 30 per cent of their branches unprofitable. Most Pakistani banks were also seriously overstaffed: by some estimates, they had twice as many employees as they needed.[15]

One of the useful lessons of the Pakistani experiment concerns the ways in which banks, businesses, and individuals responded to Islamic finance. PLS was mostly shunned by banks, where 90 per cent of transactions consisted of mark-up schemes.[16] The new system also gave rise to questions of "Islamic moral hazard," with many Pakistani businessmen taking advantage of the new laws to reduce their outstanding debts.[17] More generally, risk aversion and preference for the short term accounted for the behavior and demands of bankers, businessmen, and depositors.[18] Typical criticisms of Pakistan's Islamic finance policy were about unrealistic expectations, overreach, and rhetorical excess. One specialist criticized the belief "that the simple statement by a Muslim government that its banking system is Islamic suffices to make it so."[19] Others have argued that the changes introduced in Pakistani banking "were nominal, not substantial," and that the process of Islamicization "had lost its sense of direction" or that it "was put in reverse gear."[20]

To all intents and purposes, there was a "reset" of the Islamic system, which essentially restarted on a sounder and more realistic basis. A dual financial system is now in place, where conventional and Islamic banking coexist. Compared with its early ambitions, the Islamic sector is now very small (3 per cent of the market), but is poised to grow significantly, especially since a number of foreign Islamic institutions have recently entered the market.[21] Between 2003 and 2004, the number of bank branches offering Islamic financial services rose from seventeen to forty-seven.[22] The government has worked with the Central Bank to introduce Islamic treasury bills, or Baitul Maal certificates. Other notable developments include the creation by the Pak-Kuwait group of Meezan Bank, an Islamic commercial bank, of the Pak-Kuwait Takaful Co. Ltd (PKTCL), the first Islamic general *takaful* (Islamic insurance – see Chapter 7) in the country, and Investment Management Ltd, an Islamic mutual fund.[23] Pakistan's Faysal Bank is also working to create new Islamic products such as credit cards and insurance.[24] In 2008, Dubai Islamic Bank (DIB) was given permission by the government to establish approximately fifty branches across Pakistan over the next three years.[25]

2 *Iran*

Iranian banks are nominally the largest Islamic banks in the world.[26] Yet for political reasons having to do with the Iranian revolution (1979); the Iran–Iraq War (1980–8), during which all Gulf countries sided with Iraq; and a harsh sanctions regime which has isolated Iran, as well as religious ones (Iran being a Shia country, while most of the Islamic world is Sunni), there are few contacts between Iranian and non-Iranian Islamic banks. Furthermore, little is known about the precise functioning of Iranian banks. Their existence and evolution can be understood only with reference to post-revolutionary Iranian history, which can be divided into two distinct phases.

In the early years (1979–88), three factors were decisive: first, the desire to achieve economic independence and mark a decisive break with the Shah's economic policies; second, the need to resolve the ideological struggle between conflicting strands – conservative–free market on one side and populist–socialist on the other – of the coalition that brought about the revolution; and, third, the need to consolidate the revolution at a time of war against Iraq. In recent years (roughly since 1989) the challenges have been different, and the economic debates centered around new issues: reconstruction and its financing; oil production and sales; and the integration of the country within the global economy. During both periods, banking issues were rather secondary, and seldom rose to the level of "high politics."

At the time of the Islamic revolution, it was inevitable, given Iran's history, that economic nationalism would take center stage. Since the late nineteenth century, foreigners (initially the British and to a lesser extent the Russians, later the Americans) have been perceived as having exploited the country to their own benefit (first tobacco and then oil concessions were the most visible examples) and of having exerted undue influence on Iranian politics. The circumstances of the removal of Mossadegh and the role played by the US Central Intelligence Agency (CIA) in re-installing the Shah in 1953 still loomed large in the Iranian psyche. The close military and economic ties between the Shah and the United States during the years of the oil boom were a major factor in the revolution. The hostage crisis (November 1979–January 1981) and the subsequent freezing of $10 billion in Iranian assets in the United States fed anti-West attitudes.

Another peculiar feature of the Iranian situation was the strong leftist leanings of one segment of the revolutionary coalition. The Communist Party (Tudeh) was a long-time opponent of the Shah, along with a myriad of other groups (most significantly the Mujahedeen-e Khalq), and embraced left-leaning, sometimes Marxist, ideologies. One of the main actors of the revolution was Abul-Hasan Bani-Sadr, a French-educated economist, who was an aide to Khomeini in his exile and later became the first elected president of the Islamic Republic (1980–1). Although associated during his short presidency with the moderate camp, his writings had a distinct Marxist flavor. Shortly before the revolution, he had written an analysis of the "economics of towhid" (*Eqtesad-e Towhidi*), which fused the theological concept of *towhid* (the oneness of God) with a populist political-economic interpretation. Except, of course, for its religious component, the analysis rejoined the "final Communist" stage predicted by some Marxist historians.[27] This was bound to provoke a clash with advocates of an Islamic Third Way, among clerics influenced by the writings of Mohammed Baqer es-Sadr,[28] and with the advocates of a more conventional *laissez-faire* or market economy, who were primarily Western-trained economists supported by economically-conservative segments of the coalition – primarily the high clergy and the Bazaar.[29] Yet given the circumstances of the revolution, it was clear that anything marking a break with the policies of the Shah's regime would prevail.

The early assertion of economic nationalism took many forms. The vast holdings of the Shah and his entourage were confiscated and taken over by Islamic foundations. Banks were nationalized. In the new Constitution, Article 77 provided that all international treaties, conventions, contracts, and agreements had to be approved by the Majlis (Parliament), and Article 81 stated that "granting of concessions to foreigners for the establishment of companies or organizations in the commercial, industrial, agricultural, mining and service fields" was strictly forbidden.[30] A reinforcing factor was the Iran–Iraq War, which justified the centralization of economic decision making and led to the consolidation of statist, command economy-style allocation mechanisms: price controls; rationing of goods; quantitative regulation of imports; etc.[31]

Two contentious economic issues took center stage and dominated the first decade of the revolution: the nationalization of foreign trade and the issue of land reform. In April 1980, the Revolutionary Council, which was captured early on by the radical clergy, introduced a land reform bill, designed to transfer ownership of "temporary cultivation agricultural land" (land seized by peasants and by revolutionary organizations in the immediate aftermath of the revolution) from the owners to the cultivators actually working the land.[32] It took over six years for the Majlis to approve the bill in a controversial and contested vote. The resolution of the issue was complicated by the power structure of Iranian politics. The Majlis was dominated by populists, but its decisions could be overridden by the Council of Guardians (a body of senior Islamic jurists and experts on Islamic law), who firmly believed in private property. Conflicts between the two bodies were typically arbitrated by the Ayatollah Khomeini in his capacity as supreme ruler. The policies were all the more inconsistent and contradictory as Khomeini's decisions tended to go back and forth between populism and liberalism.[33]

By the end of the first decade following the revolution, the Iran–Iraq War had ended and the Ayatollah Khomeini had died (1989). A number of constitutional and institutional changes occurred, which transformed power relations. For example, the velayet-e Faqih position, tailor-made for Khomeini, was weakened. Ending Iran's isolation, rebuilding the infrastructure, and resuming oil experts were the new priorities. The power struggle was now between the "ideologues," who sought to preserve the orientations of the early years of the revolution, and the "pragmatists," who sought to loosen the grip of the government and improve ties with the outside world, the United States in particular.

On economic matters, the pragmatists scored a few points at a time when foreign loans and foreign investment (especially in the oil sector) were sorely needed. Article 81, which stated that all forms of foreign loans, investment, and participation were forbidden, was reinterpreted by the Council of Guardians to mean that "contracts where one party is a ministry or a government agency or company and the other party is a private foreign company, are not considered international contracts and are not subject to Article 77 of the constitution."[34]

Another aspect of Iran's opening to the outside world was related to the implosion of the Soviet Union. A number of ethnic groups in newly independent states of central Asia had ethnic, linguistic, or historical ties to Persia, and Iran saw all the religious, political, and economic advantages that closer ties with these countries or some of their ethnic groups could bring, at a time when Russia, the United States, Turkey, and Saudi Arabia were all seeking to consolidate their own positions in the region.

Financial policy reflected the broader evolution of Iranian politics. Soon after the revolution, the banking industry had been nationalized and consolidated through a vast movement of mergers. The 1983 Usury-Free Banking Act phased out over a three-year period interest-based practices. But bank policy was strictly dirigiste. The amounts of credit and foreign exchange available to banks were rationed by the main regulatory authorities, the Central Bank as well as the Supreme Council of Banks (a body whose members include the governor of the Central Bank as well as other government officials). And since interest rates were eliminated, the profit rate became the main policy instrument: a ceiling on profit rates was imposed. But as was the case in other countries that had Islamicized their banking systems, interest-based finance was not completely eliminated. Overseas banking operations, for example, continued to operate on the basis of interest,[35] and as the next pages show, informal and semi-informal interest-based finance has thrived.

One of the lessons of the Iranian experiment is that certain religiously-motivated reforms can give rise to even worse religious transgressions. Riba may have been eliminated in theory, but a much higher interest rate appeared in disguised form in informal markets. The world of Iranian finance became more speculative than it had ever been before. Fraud is rampant and seldom sanctioned, and one of the more curious elements of the official banking system is the proliferation of lotteries and randomly offered gifts (thus raising religious issues related to maysir) as a means of encouraging savings accounts.

More specifically, the tight regulatory framework was conducive to the growth of the informal sector. Some 1,300 Islamic credit funds have become essentially "usury stores." Under the aegis of the Bazaar, they were federated into an "Organization of the Islamic economy," offering annual "profit participation" rates in the 25 to 50 per cent range.[36]

The powerful foundations, which now possess the Shah's assets, function outside of any substantive governmental control. By one account, "the ability of the Central Bank of Iran to tax the Bonyad-e Mostazafan (Foundation of the Oppressed), or to monitor its foreign-currency flows – let alone audit its activities – is close to nil."[37] An unregulated financial market, administered by Bazaaris, has filled the gaps opened by official banking restrictions. Abuses have been common, and a number of financial scandals have been discovered.[38] The most massive fraud occurred between 1992 and 1996. Some $4 billion disappeared and the primary suspect was Morteza Rafiqdoust, younger brother of the head of the Bonyad foundation.[39]

In the 1990s, the government moved toward greater financial liberalization. Many controls were loosened, especially in relation to foreign exchange.[40] The Supreme Council of Banks, which had previously set a uniform profit rate for all banks, now allowed banks a broader margin of profit and permitted them to increase their "fees" and the various forms of remuneration of deposits.[41] Another significant development was the establishment of "special economic zones" in the southeastern, northern and northeastern parts of the country. Free trade zones were set up on the islands of Kish and Qeshm, and in Chabahar in the Persian Gulf. Iran expected to attract $5 billion in foreign investment.[42]

Since September 11, 2001 Iran has been considered a major pariah regime by the United States and other countries. More sanctions were imposed by the United States and United Nations on Iran's banking sector. On March 3, 2008, the Security Council passed resolution 1803 that "calls on member states to exercise vigilance over the activities of financial institutions in their territories with all banks domiciled in Iran, and their branches and subsidiaries abroad."[43] The resolution specifically mentions Bank Melli and Bank Saderat from Iran. These banks, along with Bank Sepah, were also the subject of sanctions by the United States in 2007 for anti-proliferation and anti-terrorism reasons.[44] The sanctions, officially designed to stifle Iran's nuclear program and "moderate" its regime, have forced major international banks and financial institutions to either cut completely or scale back business in Iran.[45] Little is known, however, about how effective these sanctions will be in the long term due to the large informal economy and the porous nature of the sanctions regime.

President Mahmud Ahmedinejad has attempted to counter the souring economy by reiterating the official commitment to an interest-free banking system based on Islamic principles. He has repeatedly asserted that banks should not be engaged in profit-making activities.[46] Through recent bank privatization and greater promotion of Islamic banking, Iran hopes to establish itself as an important Shia alternative and model in banking and finance for the region.

3 The Sudan

As the largest country in Africa with 35 million inhabitants, the Sudan has been buffeted in the past three decades by political turmoil, famine, civil war, and international sanctions. When it gained independence in 1956 (it had previously been ruled as an Anglo-Egyptian condominium), the Sudan was deeply divided geographically, religiously, and politically. Straddling the Arab world and Africa, the country had a significant (estimated anywhere between 30 and 40 per cent) minority of Christians and animists, living mostly in the south. In its institutions and legal system, the British influence was pervasive. Culturally, and to a large extent politically, Egypt exerted a dominant influence. Both the Communist Party and the Muslim Brothers were well entrenched.

When they seized power in 1969, Jaafar al-Nimeiri and his "Free Officers" appeared to follow the model of the 1952 Egyptian revolution. Nimeiri looked up to Nasser and seemed poised to emulate his populist and socialist model of government. An attempted coup by the Communists in 1971 led to significant changes. Increasingly, and in a striking parallel with the evolution of neighboring Egypt, Nimeiri turned against his leftist allies, became an ally of the United States and Saudi Arabia and sought to improve relations with Islamic groups. Over the years, the once secular Nimeiri became increasingly religious. Some have claimed that his new-found religious zeal was genuine, and had started after he narrowly escaped death in an assassination attempt. Others have argued it was a tactical move designed to consolidate his hold on power. Regardless of the causes, his displays of piety were innumerable. He led prayers in mosques, and he seemed intent on Islamicizing all aspects of Sudanese life. The constitution of 1973 stated that "Islamic law and custom shall be the main sources of legislation." As part of this policy, Numeiri appointed a committee for the "Revision of Sudanese laws to bring them in conformity with Islamic teaching."

In 1978 Nimeiri signed the National Reconciliation Pact, which enabled the Islamic opposition to return to public life. Islamic political parties were able to compete successfully for parliamentary seats in national elections. The Muslim Brotherhood became closely associated with the new government. Hassan al-Turabi, the Sorbonne-educated leader of the Brotherhood and former dean of the University of Khartoum Law School, was appointed to the post of Attorney General in 1979. Since that time, Turabi seems to have built his power base, eventually becoming the dominant figure of Sudanese politics, in part thanks to his involvement in the Faisal Islamic Bank of Sudan, which had been created in the late 1970s, simultaneously with the Faisal Islamic Bank of Egypt.[47] Both countries had then extended significant exemptions and privileged to the Saudi financed institution.[48]

The process of Islamicization culminated with the proclamation, on September 8, 1983, of an "Islamic revolution" that would impact Sudanese politics, law, and society. These "September laws" caught everyone by surprise. Sadiq al-Mahdi, a former prime minister and the Oxford-educated great-grandson of the Sudanese Mahdi (the Islamic revivalist reformer who had driven out the British and established an Islamic state in the Sudan in the 1880s), dismissed Nimeiri's "Islamic" September laws as opportunism, arguing that the imposition of Islamic law was premature and unjust, since such laws first required the creation of a more socially just society.[49] The most dramatic and controversial aspect of the legislation was the imposition of *hudud* (punishments such as dismemberment and death by stoning). Even Turabi, who was then in charge of revising the Sudanese laws to ensure their conformity with the Shariah, was surprised by the legislation and found the penal code too harsh, though he later embraced it.[50]

In the following months, new guidelines were enacted for banking and taxation. In December 1983, the entire banking system, including foreign banks, was Islamicized, and interest was outlawed. By one account, "Nimeiri timed this to outflank the traditional religious and political leaders and cultivate the allegiance of the Muslim Brothers, the only political group still supporting him."[51] The

Zakat Tax Act of 1984 replaced much of the state's taxation system with Islam's alms tax: the government was empowered to levy, collect, and distribute what had been a voluntary alms tithe. Other Islamic banks were created, mostly specialized by region and by sector. The specifics of Islamic banking legislation were inconsistent, since the process of Islamicization was erratic, and in a poor, isolated, war-torn and heavily indebted country, careful ijtihad on banking matters was far from being a high priority.

In early 1985, a year and a half after the September laws, Nimeiri turned against the Muslim Brothers, accusing them of plotting to overthrow him, and arrested more than 200 of their leaders, including Turabi. But it wasn't long before he himself was overthrown. It happened in April 1985, while Nimeiri was on a visit to the United States. Elections were held in 1986, and a new government led by Sadiq al-Mahdi came to power. It suspended the application of Islamic law, and restored the criminal court system based on civil codes inspired by the British–Indian tradition. Another coup led by a coalition of military leaders and Islamists took place in June 1989. Hassan al-Bashir was the leader of the coup, but effective power was exercised by Hassan al-Turabi, now Speaker of Parliament. Once the voice of moderate Islam, Turabi grew more radical. He established close ties with Iran, leading some to speculate about the emergence of a Khartoum–Tehran axis. In 1991, the Shariah was reintroduced in all the northern provinces, where they would apply to Muslims and non-Muslims alike.

The ups and downs of Islamicization can be explained by the chaotic situation in the country, the presence of non-Muslims (who objected to the application of the Shariah and who had been in rebellion against the government since the early 1980s), by the divided nature of Sudanese Islam (with a strong Sufi tradition at odds with the more politicized and sometimes radical Islam of the National Islamic Front), and by outside influences (of Egypt, Libya, Saudi Arabia, the United States, the IMF, and the World Bank – all against a backdrop of economic disintegration.

The same erratic patterns prevailed in the country's relations with the West. For most of his years in power, Nimeiri enjoyed close relations with the United States. But the government's violations of human rights during the civil war resulted in suspension of US aid. In 1985, during a visit to the Sudan, the then Vice President, George Bush, reportedly obtained four conditions in exchange for the resumption of aid: discontinuation of the hudud; dismissal of Islamic activists from the government; the halting of contacts with Libya; and acceptance of reforms demanded by the IMF.[52] In the 1990s, the Sudan was added to the list of countries supporting terrorism, and was subjected to a US bombing in 1998 (on the grounds that the Sudanese regime had ties to Usama bin Laden).

The relations with the IMF were also marked by a familiar cycle: suspension of aid; promises of reform followed by partial reform; resumption of aid; unrest followed by a halt in the application of IMF policies; and suspension of aid again. In 1990, the IMF took the unusual step of declaring the Sudan non-cooperative because of its non-payment of arrears to the Fund. In 1992, the IMF threatened to expel the Sudan from the Fund. In response, the government administered shock therapy to the economy, devaluing the Sudanese pound, lifting price controls, and ending government subsidies, including those destined for the poorest regions of the country. The main architect of the policies, economics minister Abdul Rahim Hamdi, formerly an Islamic banker, justified the policies by saying: "The population accepts these hardships, because it supports Islam and us."[53]

Since 1983, Sudanese Islamic banking has relied on a select number of contracts. The most widespread of these contracts has been murabaha. In the words of one scholar, "murabaha is the most versatile contract, since it is used in every sector of the [Sudanese] economy; for import and export trade its share is 80 per cent and 100 per cent respectively."[54] Banks also offer common contracts such as musharaka and ijara.

Recently, PLS contracts have gained in importance.[55] In 2000, the Sudan also worked with the IMF to create Central Bank Mudaraba certificates (CMCs), "an equity-based paper traded between banks and with no maturity date." It also created Musharaka certificates (GMCs) "with a fixed maturity of one year and based on government equities in industrial, commercial and telecommunication companies."[56] CMCs and GMCs are expected to help the government with liquidity management.

In recent years, Sudan has partnered with major Islamic banking hubs like Bahrain and Qatar to help improve its banking sector. Bahrain and Sudan, for example, launched the first Takaful Re or Islamic reinsurance company in 2008.[57] The Bahraini Islamic investment firm, Liquidity Management Center, also teamed up with the government to help sell the first *sukuk eve* issued by the government, for a value of €68 million.[58] Further, Qatar Islamic Bank recently signed a memorandum of understanding with the government to set up a commercial and investment bank in Khartoum.[59]

The Islamicization of Sudan's banking sector was also complicated by the civil war and its aftermath. In 2007, for example, the South Sudan Cabinet rejected the establishment of an Islamic banking system in the south on the grounds that Islamic banking went against the recent Comprehensive Peace Agreement (CPA) that permitted the creation of a traditional interest-bearing capitalist system. More importantly, the south was reacting to the north's decision to oppose the establishment of any traditional banks in the north that charged interest.[60]

II The Special Case of Malaysia

Two features set Malaysia apart from other countries discussed in this chapter: first, the creation of an Islamic banking system functioning alongside the conventional one; and, second, the harnessing of Islam to the goal of economic growth through the embrace of high-technology and finance.

Malaysia, a multicultural country of 20 million people, with thirty ethnic groups and sub-groups in thirteen states, has three distinct ethnic-religious communities: 61 per cent of the population are bumiputras, 30 per cent Chinese. and 9 per cent

Indians. Malays are overwhelmingly Sunni Muslims, although there is also a small Shia community. For generations, the Malaysian economy had been controlled by minority communities (Chinese and to a lesser extent Indians). Except for a small Westernized elite, the Malays, or bumiputras (literally sons of the land), kept to their villages and were excluded from business life. At the time of the Malaysian independence in 1957, a deal was struck whereby in exchange for citizenship for the Indians and Chinese, the bumiputras were given political supremacy. Malay became the official language, and Islam the state religion. Ever since, politics and economics have largely been structured along religious and racial lines.

Following riots in 1969, the government adopted a New Economic Policy (NEP) in 1970, which provided a host of preferential policies for bumiputras: quotas in universities, housing, government jobs, government contracts, etc. This massive affirmative action was designed to increase the Malay share of corporate wealth from 2.4 per cent in 1970 to about 30 per cent in 1990.

By 1990, when the government undertook a review of the NEP, significant progress had occurred, although it fell short of the 30 per cent objective. According to government statistics, the country's accomplishments were many: the percentage of the population living under the poverty line dropped to around 8 per cent by 1995 from 60 per cent in 1970; literacy rates exceeded 85 per cent; and life expectancy became comparable to that of developed countries. The share of wealth of the bumiputras had increased to 20 per cent and the country had achieved a remarkable economic transformation. The main architect of the transformation of Malaysia from agricultural backwater to Asian "tiger" was Mahathir Mohammed, a physician who was Prime Minister between 1982 and 2003. In addition to persevering with the giant "affirmative action" program designed to benefit the Malays, his grand ambition was to turn Malaysia into a rich country by the year 2020. Throughout his rule, there was no shortage of grandiose projects, such as the Multimedia Super Corridor outside the capital Kuala Lumpur where the Petronas Twin Towers, until 2004 the world's tallest building, came to symbolize the country's ambitions.[61] Until the 1997 Asian economic crisis, Malaysia was a "model" economy, with a thriving middle class and growth rates approaching double digits.

Islam was to be a key part of the government's ambitions. In that respect, the Malaysian brand of Islam does not fit typical Western perceptions and stereotypes. It is fused with other influences (nationalism, capitalism, "Asian values") to produce a unique ideology of development.[62] Rather than being an obstacle to change, religion was to be an engine of growth and modernization and a tool to promote financial innovation. An Islamic financial system that could offer a growing array of sophisticated financial services was part and parcel of the effort to turn Kuala Lumpur into a leading regional, if not international, financial center.[63]

The role of religion in Malaysia is a study in paradox: the system of government is secular, yet Islam is ever-present; the constitution recognizes the primary position of Islam, but it also guarantees freedom of worship to other religious groups. The dominant political party is wholly Malay and, therefore, Muslim. The justice system consists of civilian courts which are administered centrally, and separate Islamic courts answerable to local state authorities. The Malaysian brand of Islam is pragmatic and tolerant, yet strict traditionalists are a political force. The northeastern state of Kelantan, for example, is controlled by the Parti Islam Se Malaysia, an opposition party whose ideology is traditional if not reactionary. On a number of occasions, Shia militants have been imprisoned on the grounds that their teachings could divide society and trigger violence between sects. By most standards, the brand of Islam promoted by the government is a modernist one, although some of the most prominent political figures (such as one-time Deputy Prime Minister Anwar Ibrahim[64]) were at one time considered fundamentalists.[65]

Malaysia is a nation in a hurry, and on numerous occasions, Mahathir has shown impatience with ulemas arguing over the finer points of religion rather than putting religion at the service of developmental goals. He has accused them of being dilatory, inconsistent, or too harsh. According to Mahathir: "Only when Islam is interpreted so as to be relevant in a world which is different from what it was 1,400 years ago can Islam be regarded as a religion for all ages." More specifically, he objected to those who wanted to interpret the Koran too literally. For him, the tolerant, forgiving spirit of religion should be the starting point.[66] Or in the words of Anwar Ibrahim, "In implementing Islamic principles in banking and finance, we must address substantive issues rather than be always preoccupied with terminology and semantics."[67] A recurring theme in speeches and publications was that hard work was a form of "jihad."[68]

The ulemas were challenged to a new "ijtihad": rather than be content with the imitation of existing models, they were asked to adopt a more innovative approach, exploring the wide array of Shariah concepts that had not even been tested. They were also encouraged to look at the state-of-the-art in global finance, and create corresponding Islamic products.[69] The only products to be excluded were those that went explicitly against Islamic beliefs.

A number of Islamic research centers and universities engaged in a vast effort to legitimate modern finance, and in particular to create an "Islamic capital market" that would use specially designed interest-free bonds and other securities. The International Islamic University opened a management school. The Malaysian Institute of Islamic Understanding (IKIM) held seminars on all aspects of religion and finance. The message was that industrialization and productivity were fully compatible with piety, and that welfare in this world was fully compatible with salvation in the next.

In order to avoid bickering among rival schools of Islamic thought, in 1997 Mahathir established a National Syariah (Shariah) Board designed to harmonize financial practices and review the compatibility of new financial products with religion. In a statement, Bank Negara Malaysia (BNM), the country's central bank, said that it would be "the sole authoritative body to advise BNM on Syariah issues pertaining to Islamic banking and takaful [insurance] operations."[70] Such a Board was also to play a key role in establishing Malaysia's credibility as a hub for Islamic products.

The contrast with other countries is clear. Malaysia has not sought full Islamicization but has implemented a parallel system, with Islamic banks operating alongside conventional ones. It was a two-pronged policy designed to promote Islamic finance, and turn Kuala Lumpur into both an international Islamic finance center and a key conventional regional finance center that could compete with Hong Kong or Singapore. In addition, Labuan would become an international offshore financial center with a focus on Islamic products. Importantly, Islamic banking was not limited to providing special or exceptional treatment to certain banks in order to placate or co-opt certain groups. Rather it was a principal tool in the country's developmental policy, and was designed to form the vanguard of financial modernization. A number of privileges, for example, greater flexibility with respect to their liquid asset holdings, were given to Islamic banks.[71]

Islamic finance cannot be separated from Malaysia's NEP, from the promotion of Kuala Lumpur as a financial center, or from the effort to enhance the role of bumiputras in the economy. The first experiment in Islamic finance can be traced back to the Muslim Pilgrims Savings Corporation, which was set up in 1963 to help people save toward performing hajj. In 1969, it evolved into the Pilgrims Management and Fund Board, or the Tabung Haji as it is now popularly known. In 1983, Parliament passed the Islamic Banking Act, which created Bank Islam Malaysia Berhad (BIMB), a full-fledged commercial bank, controlled by the government and in which the Tabung Haji had a 12.5 per cent participation. The bank's memorandum of association stated that "all businesses of the company will be transacted in accordance with Islamic principles, rules and practices." The bank has been at the forefront of financial innovation. In 1985, it set up Syarikat Takaful Malaysia, which it touted as the world's first Islamic insurance company. (In reality, other Islamic insurance companies have claimed precedence.[72]) In 1990, it issued Islamic corporate bonds. The bank also introduced Islamic acceptance bills and an Islamic export credit refinancing facility. In 1993, Malaysia took a further pioneering step when it introduced its dual banking system. Conventional banks were allowed to offer Islamic banking services. A bank could thus have under the same roof two windows, one for conventional banking operations, the other for interest-free transactions.[73] Throughout the 1990s, the government was also very active in encouraging the creation of Islamic products, ranging from insurance to bonds, introducing a secondary market for banking products, and promoting an Islamic capital market in Kuala Lumpur whose products and practices mirrored conventional capital markets. In January 1994, the Islamic Interbank Money Market (IIMM) was introduced. Islamic unit trusts (IUT), Islamic debt securities (IDS), and Islamic commercial paper, were created alongside an Islamic interbank and check-clearing system. The introduction of indices and benchmarks – such as the RHB Islamic Index which tracks the performance of listed companies that do not contravene Islamic principles, or the minimum benchmark for mudaraba interbank investments by which a bank obtains an investment from another on a trustee profit-sharing basis – were other steps taken by Malaysia to promote credible capital markets. Credible capital markets have been perceived in recent years as being Malaysia's primary competitive advantage in relation to other Islamic financial centers.[74]

Malaysia encouraged its Islamic bankers to become global leaders by offering home mortgages and a wide array of financial services to consumers. It was the first country to introduce Islamic mortgage bonds. Since 1994, it has been possible to use mudaraba bonds to purchase housing loans from BIMB. The bonds are based on the profit-sharing principle with the profits generated shared according to an agreed ratio.[75] One institution, Arab-Malaysian Bank, engaged in aggressive marketing of the country's first Islamic credit card – an interest-free Visa card on which users can charge an amount equal to their deposits in the bank for a fee that is a percentage of their annual spending. The bank said it would reject payments for night clubs, massage parlors, and other religiously forbidden activities.[76] Another singular characteristic of the Malaysian system is that Islamic products were geared to non-Muslims as well as to Muslims. Muslims would have the opportunity to invest according to their religious beliefs, while non-Muslims, especially the Chinese minority which controls most of the country's wealth, would have an extension of choice in money management.[77]

Constant financial innovation was justified by the need to remain ahead of the pack. Financial products are easy to imitate, and Malaysian leaders felt that other Islamic financial centers were closing in on them.[78] But conservative scholars, mostly outside Malaysia, considered that it was going too fast, and that in its rush to grow, Malaysian finance was cutting too many corners. One of the most controversial issues was that of the dual-window strategy. Even in the definition of acceptable products, Malaysia was considered to be too lax.[79] For example, call warrants were deemed acceptable as long as the underlying shares were halal.[80] In other words, complex new financial instruments are often given the benefit of the doubt.

Significantly, in addition to catering to non-Muslims, many Islamic institutions were also managed by non-Muslims. And among the pioneers of Islamic finance were foreign institutions such as UK-based Standard Chartered Bank. In mid-1997, at the time of the Asian financial crisis, Malaysia had twenty-five commercial banks, twenty-two finance companies and five merchant banks that offered Islamic banking services. But Islamic assets still represented only 2 per cent of total financial assets. By 2005, the Central Bank stated that Islamic investments represented 11 per cent of total banking assets in Malaysia.[81]

Earlier misgivings about diverging interpretations of Shariah law between Malaysia and Arab countries gave way to a search for common ground. The most dramatic example was the 2002 sovereign Malaysian sukuk, which explicitly targeted Gulf investors (for that issue, Malaysian as well as Arab Shariah scholars gave their endorsement). Soon afterwards, those ijara sukuk formed the template for a number of Arab sukuk issues. The Malaysian Central Bank alongside its Arab counterparts played a key role in finding a common understanding. As a way of promoting its own viewpoint, Bank Negara Malaysia is spending $57 million to invite Islamic scholars from around the world to Kuala Lumpur for a "Shariah dialogue" program.[82]

Malaysia also started working closely with Arab regulators, especially those of Bahrain and the United Arab Emirates. The Dubai Financial Services Authority (DFSA) recently entered into a memorandum of understanding with Bank Negara Malaysia, committing both parties to the further development of international Islamic finance markets. As a result of the joint initiative, Dubai International Financial Center (DIFC) domestic funds will be the first foreign funds permitted for resale in Malaysia.

Especially worthy of mention is the 2002 creation of the Islamic Financial Services Board (IFSB) in Malaysia. This organization has sought to coordinate bank supervision, promote Islamic finance, and facilitate the integration of the Islamic sector in mainstream finance. Working closely with the IMF, the Islamic Development Bank and the Basel Committee, the IFSB issued a draft in 2005 on the Basel 2 rules for Islamic institutions.

The relatively closed Malaysian market, as part of its liberalization, also opened its doors to outside institutions and in particular to Arab Islamic banks. At the end of 2001, the Malaysian government established the first IIFM at its Labuan IOFC, where foreign Islamic institutions were encouraged to establish branches. The Malaysian Central Bank introduced tax incentives to encourage overseas institutions to enter or expand in Islamic banking, insurance, and fund management.[83] Foreign institutions can now hold up to 49 per cent of Malaysian Islamic banking units.[84]

Most significantly, since 2006, three Arab Islamic banks have been authorized to operate in Malaysia: Kuwait Finance House; Saudi Arabia's al-Rajhi; and the Asian Finance House. The first two powerhouses of Islamic finance had initially been major players confined to their home markets, while the third is a joint venture of Qatar Islamic Bank and other Middle Eastern investors. Saudi-based al-Rajhi, whose Malaysian operations have a four-member Shariah Board consisting of two Saudis and two Malays, has experimented with products inspired by Malaysian practices before trying to re-export them to its home market. One example is a PLS account whose remuneration, like those of a conventional savings account, is fixed and pre-determined (thanks to a profit reserve account which allows the bank to cover fluctuations in its profits and losses).[85] Another interesting development is the new permission to include Arab scholars on Malaysian bank Shariah Boards.[86]

Today, Malaysia maintains twelve Islamic banks, six Islamic units of conventional banks and three foreign Islamic banks. The Islamic sector controls 12 per cent of banking assets and seems on track to reach the government goal of 20 per cent of assets by 2010. In addition, some 80 per cent of shares traded on Bursa Malaysia, the country's stock exchange, are Shariah compliant.[87]

III New and Rising Islamic Financial Hubs: Bahrain, Singapore, the United Kingdom, and Hong Kong

1 Bahrain

At the outset a distinction should be established between such offshore banking centers as the Cayman Islands that are welcoming of any and all foreign banking institutions, and those financial centers within Islamic countries that aim to compete regionally by playing the Islamic banking card. In Malaysia, the Labuan IOFC has been created to play such a role. In the Persian Gulf, the United Arab Emirates (in particular Dubai and Abu Dhabi) have stepped up their involvement in Islamic finance. Qatar under its new, modernizing ruler has attempted to step out of its financial isolation by promoting a policy of greater integration in the regional economy and by authorizing the establishment of an offshore banking center. But it is Bahrain that is today by far the leader in offshore Islamic banking.

Bahrain is the smallest country of the Gulf Cooperation Council, the first where oil was discovered (in 1932), and the first to be preoccupied about the prospect of running out of oil. As part of its policy of diversification away from oil, the country rulers have focused on financial services. Since its establishment in 1973, the Bahrain Monetary Agency (the successor of the Bahrain Currency Board) has been promoting the country as an international financial center. It has been encouraging major international financial institutions to use Bahrain as their regional base, by touting a number of competitive advantages: a strategic geographic location; a tax-free environment; a skilled workforce; a pragmatic economic policy; a clearly defined legal and administrative framework; a well-developed infrastructure; state-of-the-art telecommunications; a convertible currency; a liberal trade regime; and the absence of restrictions on foreign exchange.

Among Bahrain's selling points to the international financial community are its financial focus and the quality of its regulatory system. Bahrain was one of the first countries outside the G10 to impose the Basel capital ratios, and Bahraini banks have maintained an average capital asset ratio in excess of 10 per cent, above the mandatory 8 per cent ratio. In 1997, best practice guidelines were issued, modeled after those of the United Kingdom, and all Bahraini banks are expected to comply with the International Accounting Standards (IAS). Locally incorporated banks were required to publish their financial statements on a quarterly basis.

The Bahrain Stock Exchange (BSE) is heavily weighted (about 75 per cent) toward financial stocks. It is open to cross-border listing of regional and international stocks, bonds, and mutual funds and financial derivatives. It has cross-listing accords with most surrounding countries. Bahrain intends to become the primary offshore center for Islamic banking. It already has the highest concentration of offshore Islamic financial institutions. In 1996, Citibank, soon followed by other Western banks, opened a wholly-owned Islamic bank. In 1998, Saleh Kamel, head of the al-Baraka group, one of the two major transnational Islamic banking groups, established an offshore banking unit in Bahrain to bring together his group's diverse global banking interests.[88]

The Bahrain Monetary Authority (BMA) has Shariah advisors to help with the auditing of the banks, and a new regulatory system is being worked out to take into account the special characteristics of Islamic financial products. The BMA is also developing short-term financial instruments that would provide liquidity for Islamic banks.[89]

Since 2001, the BMA has viewed sukuk issuance as an essential part of developing its Islamic financial sector. In 2001, it issued *Sukuk al-Salam*, the first of its type in the world.[90] Moreover, it seeks to make the BSE the key trading outpost for global sukuk.[91]

Bahrain is also home to the IIRA, which was established as the first of its kind in 2002.[92] The IIRA will help to expand the role of Islamic banks and financial institutions in the global market, in addition to creating greater transparency across the sector.[93] Shortly afterwards, the IIFM was created to assist in increasing cross-border investment of Islamic financial instruments.[94]

Today, Bahrain has transformed itself into one of the world's leading Islamic banking hubs with more than twenty-five banks, ten insurance companies, and thirty-four Islamic mutual funds.[95] The only weaknesses that remain, however, are Bahrain's political instability and reliance on oil money and large wholesale deposits. Although the Shia make up a slight majority of Bahrain's 500,000 citizens, the ruling al Khalifa family is Sunni. Parliament was dissolved over two decades ago.

2 *Singapore*

Since the 1960s, Singapore has been a major international financial hub due to its strong economic and financial fundamentals, sound investment policies and laws, favorable business environment, and educated working class.[96] Today, Singapore aims to maintain its reputation as a major international financial center – a new Switzerland – by tapping into the lucrative Islamic financial sector. More importantly, it aims to take advantage of having easy access to one-third of the world's Muslim population to promote Islamic banking and finance. Singapore must also compete with Malaysia and Hong Kong for a share of the market.

To assert itself as an important regional player in Islamic banking and finance, Singapore has aligned the tax laws of numerous Islamic financial products with similar conventional financing products. For example, it eliminated double stamp duties on Islamic transactions concerning real estate and decided to grant concessionary tax treatment on income from Islamic bonds, making them akin to conventional bonds.[97] According to the Monetary Authority of Singapore, banks will also be able to offer a line of financial products under murabaha.[98] In general, Singapore is using Bahrain and the United Kingdom as Islamic banking models to help in the development of its Islamic financial sector. The United Kingdom and Bahrain models accommodate both Islamic and conventional banking within a common regulatory structure.[99]

In 2005, the International Shariah Board for Economic Development (Isbed) opened offices in Singapore. At the same time, it disclosed plans for a new Islamic financial index composed of stocks listed on the Singapore Exchange.[100] The stock index, the FTSE SGX Asia Shariah 100, lists companies that are Shariah-compliant.[101]

In 2007, DBS Group Holdings and a group of twenty-two Middle Eastern investors established Singapore's first Islamic bank, Islamic Bank of Asia. DBS will possess 60 per cent of the bank and supply $250 million for the start-up capital of the joint-venture.[102] Currently, Singapore boasts an estimated $1.32 billion of Shariah-compliant property funds and $500 million in Islamic insurance funds.[103]

International Islamic financial institutions have also commenced operations in Singapore. Malaysia's RHB group was the first commercial bank to receive an operations license from the government to run an Islamic bank. It also established its own branch, RHB Islamic Bank.[104] Additionally, Kuwait Finance House (Malaysia) Bhd (KFHM) launched its Singapore fund management operations in 2008.[105]

3 Hong Kong

Hong Kong's prominent position as a major international financial center and its proximity to China make it attractive for Shariah-compliant financial houses. More importantly, China offers a relatively untapped market with an estimated 20 million Muslims.[106] "Hong Kong is late in coming into the game, but it's just a matter of the legal system being put in place to accommodate the Islamic product," said Edwin Hitti, president of Hong Kong's Arab Chamber of Commerce and Industry, and founding member of Hong Kong's Islamic Stock Exchange.[107] Currently, Hong Kong is engaged in assessing its tax laws to guarantee that Islamic financial transactions will not be disadvantaged due to their unique configuration.[108] Most importantly, it needs to remove double taxation on Islamic finance products that must comply with Shariah law.[109]

The Hong Kong Monetary Authority (HKMA) has recently named a working group to study the feasibility of creating an Islamic bond market in Hong Kong. In addition to studying taxation, it will also study such vital issues as legal and regulatory frameworks. It will also make recommendations for the immediate introduction of Islamic debt offerings in Hong Kong.[110] At the same time, the Arab Chamber of Commerce and Industry created a five-member Shariah advisory council, the Hong Kong Shariah Advisory Council (HKSAC), consisting of Islamic scholars and professionals.[111] The HKSAC is chaired by Muhammad Arshad, chief Imam of the Incorporated Trustees of the Islamic Community Fund of Hong Kong, a governing body dedicated to local Islamic affairs.[112]

Hong Kong still has much to accomplish before setting up a proper support system for its Islamic banking and finance sector. Such a system will be essential for long-term investment in the sector. Islamic investors must feel comfortable and confident that their investments will abide by Shariah law. Investors will feel more confident once Hong Kong has created Shariah compliance certification, a legal arena in which to resolve disputes concerning Islamic investments or financial products, and Islamic financial reporting standards.[113]

As in Singapore, international financial institutions are opening up Islamic windows or branches in Hong Kong. HSBC's local unit, Hang Seng Bank, for example, established Hong Kong's first Islamic fund, the Islamic China Index Fund, after being asked by a Middle East financial institution in 2006 to help oversee its investments in Hong Kong and China.[114] In 2008, Hang Seng listed a $550 million exchangeable sukuk on the Hong Kong Stock Exchange.[115]

4 The United Kingdom

In the last few years, the United Kingdom, home to more than 2 million Muslims, has been trying to establish itself as a major Islamic finance center. Gordon Brown, since his days as Chancellor of the Exchequer, as well as the successive Mayors of London, have been for economic as well as political reasons (the integration of an often disenfranchised community) committed to the goal of turning London into a global hub.[116]

A number of tax and regulatory changes have been undertaken to fulfill that goal. Especially notable is the introduction of a new sukuk regime similar to that for conventional securitizations,[117] adding sukuk to the London Stock Exchange,[118] and the announcement that the British government would in the near future be issuing sovereign sukuk. "These changes," the Treasury said, "will ensure that British Muslims can get competitive financial services and the city remains at the forefront of developments in financial markets around the world."[119]

Recently, five British Islamic banks have been created: one retail bank, the Islamic Bank of Britain, launched in 2004; the European Islamic Investment Bank, created in 2005; the Bank of London and Middle East, established in 2007; Gatehouse Bank, set up in 2007; and the European Finance House, launched in January 2008.[120] In addition, the big financial institutions such as HSBC and Lloyds TSB routinely offer Islamic financial products and services.[121] Altogether there are now some $30 billion in Shariah-compliant assets in the United Kingdom.

Notes

1. Ibrahim A. Karawan, "Monarchs, Mullas, and Marshals: Islamic Regimes?," in Charles E. Butterworth and I. William Zartman (eds.), *Political Islam, The Annals of the American Academy of Political and Social Science* (November 1992), p. 116.
2. *The Financial Times*, August 12, 1997.
3. *The New York Times*, July 22, 1998. See also Syed Fazl-e-Haider, "Economic mess for Pakistan's government," *Asia Times*, February 21, 2008.
4. Edward Mortimer, *Faith and Power: The Politics of Islam* (New York: Random House, 1982), p. 211.
5. See Chapter 5.
6. Mortimer, *Faith and Power*, p. 221

7. Mortimer, *Faith and Power*, p. 222.
8. See Chapter 7.
9. Muhammad Akram Khan, *An Introduction to Islamic Economics* (Islamabad: International Institute of Islamic Thought and Institute for Policy Studies, 1994), p. 83.
10. Fuad al-Omar and Mohammed Abdel-Haq, *Islamic Banking: Theory, Practice and Challenges* (London: Zed Books, 1996), p. 99.
11. *The Financial Times*, August 12, 1997.
12. Seyyed Vali Reza Nasr, *The Vanguard of the Islamic Revolution: The Jama'at-i Islami of Pakistan* (Berkeley, CA: University of California Press, 1994), p. 194.
13. *The Financial Times*, November 28, 1995.
14. *Business Recorder*, January 22, 1998.
15. *The Financial Times*, August 27, 1997.
16. Al-Omar and Abdel-Haq, *Islamic Banking*, p. 99.
17. See Chapter 8.
18. See Chapter 8.
19. Nicholas Dylan Ray, *Arab Islamic Banking and the Renewal of Islamic Law* (London: Graham and Trotman, 1995), p. 81.
20. Al-Omar and Abdel-Haq, *Islamic Banking*, pp. 99–100.
21. Farhan Bokhari, "Islamic Finance – Promise in Pakistan – If Pakistan successfully launches an Islamic-compliant treasury bond, it will lift the growth potential of the country's embryonic Islamic banking sector," *The Banker*, April 2007.
22. Haris Zamir and Shanthy Nambiar, "Pakistan pushes Islamic Banking," *International Herald Tribune*, September 6, 2005.
23. "Islamic Insurance Company Launched in Pakistan," *BBC Worldwide Monitoring*, April 22, 2006.
24. Naween A. Mangi, "Pakistan's Faysal Bank to Expand, Open Islamic Unit," *Bloomberg News*, June 5, 2008.
25. Farhan Bokhari, "Islamic Finance – Promise in Pakistan," *The Banker*, April 2007.
26. *Directory of Islamic Banks and Financial Institutions* (Boston, MA: AIU Financial Consulting, 2010).
27. Sohrab Behdad, "The Political Economy of Islamic Planning in Iran," in Amirahmadi Hoeshang and Manouchehr Parvin (eds.), *Post-Revolutionary Iran* (Boulder, CO: Westview Press, 1988), p. 116.
28. Chibli Mallat, *The Renewal of Islamic law: Muhammad Baqer as-Sadr: Najaf and the Shi'i International* (Cambridge: Cambridge University Press, 1993).
29. Jahangir Amuzegar, *Iran's Economy under the Islamic Republic* (London I. B. Tauris, 1993), p. 32.
30. Mehrdad Valibeigi, "Islamic Economics and Economic Policy Formation in Post-Revolutionary Iran: A critique," *Journal of Economic Issues*, 27 (September 1993).
31. Patrick Clawson, "Islamic Iran's Economic Politics and Prospects," *Middle East Journal*, 42:3 (Summer 1988).
32. Shaul Bakhash, "The Politics of Land, Law, and Social Justice in Iran," *Middle East Journal*, 43:2 (Spring 1989).
33. Ali Rahnema and Farhad Nomani, *The Secular Miracle: Religion, Politics and Economic Policy in Iran* (London: Zed Books, 1990).
34. Valibeigi, "Islamic Economics and Economic Policy Formation in Post-Revolutionary Iran: A critique."
35. Valibeigi, "Banking and Credit Rationing in Post-Revolutionary Iran," *Journal of Iranian Studies* (Spring 1993).
36. Olivier Roy, *L'échec de l'Islam politique* (Paris: Editions du Seuil, 1992), p. 76.
37. *The Atlantic Monthly*, March 1996.
38. Sami Zubeida, "Is Iran an Islamic State?," in Joel Beinin and Joe Stork (eds.), *Political Islam: Essays from Middle East Report* (Berkeley, CA: University of California Press, 1997), p. 113.

39. Ibrahim Warde, "Comparing the Profitability of Islamic and Conventional Banks" (San Francisco, CA: IBPC Working Papers, 1997).
40. Alan Richards and John Waterbury, *A Political Economy of the Middle East* (Boulder, CO: Westview Press, 1996), p. 243.
41. *The Financial Times*, February 8, 1993.
42. Agence France-Presse, May 27, 1998.
43. John McGlynn, "The Day the US Declared War on Iran," *Asia Times*, April 1, 2008.
44. John McGlynn, "The Day the US Declared War on Iran."
45. Robin Wright, "Iran Feels Pinch as Major Banks Curtail Business; US Campaign Urges Firms to Cut Ties," *Washington Post*, March 26, 2007.
46. "Iran President Calls for Interest-Free Banking," *BBC Monitoring Middle East*, September 5, 2007.
47. See Chapter 11.
48. See Chapter 4.
49. John L. Esposito, *The Islamic Threat: Myth or Reality?* (Oxford: Oxford University Press, 1992) p. 90.
50. Esposito, *The Islamic Threat*, p. 90.
51. Khalid Medani, "Funding Fundamentalism: The Political Economy of an Islamist State," in Beinin and Stork (eds.), *Political Islam*, p. 168.
52. Esposito, *The Islamic Threat*, p. 91.
53. Judith Miller, *God has Ninety-Nine Names: A Reporter's Journey through a Militant Middle East* (New York: Simon and Schuster, 1996), pp. 144–5.
54. Endre Stiansen, "Interest Politics: Islamic Finance in the Sudan, 1977–2001," in *The Politics of Islamic Finance* eds. Clement M. Henry and Rodney Wilson (Edinburgh: Edinburgh University Press, 2004), p. 161.
55. Endre Stiansen, "Interest Politics: Islamic Finance in the Sudan, 1977–2001," p. 159.
56. Indira Chand, "Reforms Aim to Keep Pace," *The Banker*, August 2000.
57. "Bahrain, Sudan Plan First Islamic Reinsurance Firm," *Bahrain Tribune*, June 1, 2004.
58. Dominic O'Neill, "Sudan: Middle East turns Bullish on Sudan," *Euromoney*, February 2008.
59. Pratap John Ali, "Best Options for Qatari banks," *Gulf Times*, April 30, 2007.
60. Abdalla Ali, "Islamic and Traditional Banking in southern Sudan," *Sudan Tribune*, August 14, 2007.
61. *Far Eastern Economic Review*, September 4, 1997.
62. Khoo Boo Teik, *Paradoxes of Mahathirism: An Intellectual Biography of Mahathir Mohammed* (Oxford: Oxford University Press, 1995).
63. *Asian Business Review*, April 1, 1996.
64. The one-time heir apparent was later disgraced and served a prison sentence.
65. Chandra Muzaffar and Farish A. Noor, "Malaysia in turmoil, Anwar Ibrahim and Mahathir Muhammad," *Middle East Affairs Journal*, 4:3–4 (Summer–Fall 1998), pp. 157–70.
66. *The Financial Times*, April 26, 1997.
67. *The Financial Times*, November 28, 1995.
68. *The Economist*, August 7, 1993.
69. *Business Times*, July 17, 1997.
70. *Business Times*, July 10, 1997.
71. Rodney Wilson, "Islamic Development Finance in Malaysia," in Saad al-Harran (ed.), *Leading Issues in Islamic Banking and Finance* (Selangor, Malaysia: Pelanduk Publications, 1995), p. 65.
72. See Chapter 7.
73. *The Financial Times*, November 28, 1995.
74. *Business Times*, July 17, 1997.
75. Al-Omar and Abdel-Haq, *Islamic Banking*, p. 85.

76. *The Financial Times*, April 26, 1997.
77. *The Financial Times*, October 3, 1996.
78. *Business Times*, July 17, 1997.
79. *The Financial Times*, November 28, 1995.
80. *Business Times*, August 5, 1997.
81. Assif Shameen, "Islamic Banks: A Novelty No Longer," *Business Week*, August 8, 2005.
82. Yaroslav Trofimov, "Borrowed Ideas: Malaysia Transforms Rules For Finance Under Islam; In a Lesson to Arabs, Asian Bankers Mix Religion, Modernity," *The Wall Street Journal*, April 4, 2007.
83. Roula Khalaf, Gillian Tett, and David Oakley, "Eastern Promise turns to Western Delight," *The Financial Times*, January 18, 2007.
84. Ibrahim Warde, "Islamic Finance After September 11: Toward Arab–Malaysian Integration," in Mercy Kuo and Eric Altbach (eds.), *Islamic Finance in Southeast Asia: Local Practice, Global Impact* (Seattle, WA: National Bureau of Asian Research, 2008).
85. Trofimov, "Borrowed Ideas."
86. "CIMB appoints Sheikh Nizam Yaqubi to Syariah body," *The Edge*, July 11, 2006.
87. Ibrahim Warde, "Islamic Finance After September 11."
88. *The Banker*, June 1998.
89. *Dow Jones International News*, December 5, 1998.
90. Indira Chand, "$25 million Bahrain Islamic Bills Issue is a Huge Success," *Gulf Daily News*, June 13, 2001.
91. "Bahrain – Bahrain Bolsters the Islamic Finance Industry – The Burgeoning Sukuk Bond Market is just one Sign of the Global Islamic Financial Services Industry's Spectacular Growth, which Bahrain is Promoting by Providing a Sound Investment," *The Banker*, October 2004.
92. "Islamic Rating Agency set up Bahrain Banking Facilities Ideal," *Bahrain Tribune*, October 30, 2002.
93. "Islamic Rating Agency set up Bahrain Banking Facilities Ideal," *Bahrain Tribune*, October 30, 2002.
94. "GCC–Bahrain–Fertile Ground–Islamic Banks are flourishing in Bahrain," *The Banker*, August 2002.
95. "Bahrain – Hub of Sharia Finance," *The Banker*, March 2006.
96. Angelo M. Venardos, *Islamic Banking and Finance in Southeast Asia*, 2nd edn. (Singapore: World Scientific Publishing Company, 2006), 206.
97. Wong Wei Kong, "An Exciting Future in Finance," *Business Times Singapore*, August 9, 2006.
98. Linus Chua, "Singapore opens Sharia-based Financing; As Oil Money Flows, Demand for Investment Products Hitches a Ride," *International Herald Tribune*, June 13, 2006.
99. Pauline Ng, "PHB keen on Islamic Banking in Singapore," *The Business Times Singapore*, June 3, 2005. See also "Singapore Keen to Replicate Bahrain model," *Bahrain Tribune*, December 13, 2004.
100. Grace Ng, "Singapore Chosen as Base for New Global Islamic Banking Body," *BBC Monitoring Asia Pacific*, August 31, 2005.
101. "Islamic Investors get Index in Singapore," *International Herald Tribune*, February 22, 2006.
102 Shamim Adam, "Singapore Encouraging Islamic Finance Sector," *International Herald Tribune*, May 18, 2007. See also Patricia Kowsmann, "Islamic Banking Moves into Singapore," *Wall Street Journal*, May 8, 2007.
103. Shamim Adam, "Singapore Encouraging Islamic Finance Sector," *International Herald Tribune*, May 18, 2007.
104. Pauline Ng, "PHB Keen on Islamic Banking in Singapore," *Business Times Singapore*, June 3, 2005.

105. "Kuwait Finance Launches Singapore Fund Ops," *New Straits Times*, May 6, 2008.
106. "Hong Kong Seeks to Become a Sukuk Hub," *Gulf Times*, December 30, 2007.
107. "Hong Kong Seeks to Become a Sukuk Hub," *Gulf Times*, December 30, 2007. See also Heda Bayron, "Hong Kong's Islamic New Year," *Arabian Business*, January 13, 2008.
108. Saeed Azhar and Umesh Desai, "Singapore, HK covet Malaysia's Islamic finance crown," *Reuters*, June 22, 2008.
109. Saeed Azhar and Umesh Desai, "Singapore, HK covet Malaysia's Islamic Finance Crown," *Reuters*, June 22, 2008.
110. "Hong Kong Chief Vows to Tap Islamic finance," *BBC Monitoring Asia Pacific*, November 1, 2007.
111. "Hong Kong Seeks to Become a Sukuk Hub," *Gulf Times*, December 30, 2007.
112. "Hong Kong Shari'ah Council Formed," *BBC Monitoring Asia Pacific*, October 15, 2007.
113. Heda Bayron, "Hong Kong's Islamic New Year," *Arabian Business*, January 13, 2008.
114. Heda Bayron, "Hong Kong's Islamic New Year," *Arabian Business*, January 13, 2008.
115. "Singapore, HK covet Malaysia's Islamic Finance Crown," *Reuters*, June 22, 2008.
116. David Oakley and Gillian Tett, "Britain leads Secondary Market for Islamic Bonds," *The Financial Times*, February 5, 2007.
117. "UK Sukuk Policies Welcomed," *Arab News*, April 4, 2007.
118. "UK Government Serious About Sukuk," *Arab News*, April 27, 2007.
119. "UK Sukuk Policies Welcomed," *Arab News*, April 4, 2007.
120. David Oakley, "UK's Fifth Islamic Bank to Tap Demand Growth," *The Financial Times*, April 21, 2008.
121. Nick Jackson, "As Islamic Banking Takes Off, New Courses are Being Set up in the Universities," *Independent*, January 17, 2008.

7

FINANCIAL PRODUCTS AND INSTRUMENTS

As discussed in previous chapters, most of the products offered by conventional financial institutions have some Islamic counterpart. Importantly, however, the underlying contracts are often fundamentally different. Consider the case of sukuk, or "Islamic bonds." From an investor's standpoint, the two are quite similar: they offer a fixed return at periodic intervals, they can be traded on the secondary market, and they will be redeemed at a certain date. Yet the underlying financial transactions are not the same: the conventional bond is an interest-bearing debt, whereas the typical *sakk* (plural sukuk) represents a share in an underlying asset (typically, real estate), and the periodic return usually represents a lease payment. Thus, although Islamic products were often created to mirror conventional ones, their implications (for example, in the case of default or liquidation) are by no means identical. The contractual documentation is also usually significantly different. For example, a conventional leasing contract is typically a short one, incorporating all the elements of the lease, whereas the Islamic documentation for a comparable transaction is likely to include several contracts, in line with the Shariah principles of simplicity and clarity: a contract for the lease proper; another for the option[1] to purchase the equipment; another for the agency agreement between lessor and lessee;[2] etc. Furthermore, the "fine print" in an Islamic contract is likely to include specific ethical and PLS features designed to prevent predatory practices.

This chapter starts with a discussion of the main building blocks of Islamic finance. The second part considers new horizons in Islamic finance – the ways in which building blocks have been combined to create new Islamic products.

I Building Blocks

In the classical Islamic tradition theory, the only straightforward loan is the *qard hasan* (literally good loan) or interest-free loan, and the only common form of deposit was *al-wadiah* (safekeeping). Typically, the qard hasan was given for benevolent non-business-related purposes, although it could be given to distressed merchants, while al-wadiah was akin to the contemporary practice of renting a safe-deposit box at a bank to store one's valuables. As the next pages show, a significant update of traditional Islamic practices was necessary to replicate the offerings of modern banks.

Islamic bankers have devised new products and instruments by updating or combining contracts that go back to classical Islam, by creating products that pose no religious objections, or by invoking custom (urf), overriding necessity (darura) or the general interest (maslaha) to justify the creation of sometimes controversial, if not outright dubious, instruments.

Considering the blurred boundaries of Islamic finance and the religious controversies surrounding financial instruments, a typology is useful. This chapter classifies financial products on the basis of the issues they raise – primarily legal, religious, and financial, but also strategic, regulatory, economic, and political – in the context of the global economy.

1 Sale-based Products

Sale has been called the "paragon transaction" in Islamic law, and the sale contract has been referred to as "the model contract, along the lines of which other contracts are constructed."[3] We have already seen that Islam was born in the trading city of Mecca, that the Prophet Muhammed was a merchant (as were the four "rightly-guided Caliphs" who later led the Islamic community after his death), that merchants played a central role in the expansion of Islam, and that major trading routes were for centuries under Islamic control.

A cornerstone of Islamic finance is the Koranic verse which states: "Allah has allowed trading and forbidden riba" (2:275). It is, therefore, not surprising that the overwhelming majority of transactions of Islamic financial institutions are sale-based.[4]

(a) Murabaha and Other Mark-up Schemes

The best-known sale-based instrument is the murabaha, a cost-plus contract in which a client wishing to purchase any type of good asks the bank to purchase the item and sell it to him at cost plus a declared profit. In traditional fiqh, murabaha was a form of sale where a buyer would ask a seller to buy a good on his behalf and resell it to him after adding a pre-determined mark-up. The rationale was that merchants new to a market would prefer to negotiate the profit margin of the intermediary rather than the final price. Importantly, however, traditional murabaha was a spot transaction. The innovation of modern Islamic finance lies in the addition of an element of financing, since the bank will purchase the required goods directly from a supplier and sell them to the "borrower" for future payment. Proponents of murabaha stress its transparency, since the buyer is in a position to know exactly the cost of the goods (and associated expenses) as well as the profit made by the bank, which may be a lump sum or a percentage.

In the early years of modern Islamic finance, murabaha and other mark-up transactions were regarded as temporary modes of finance, used for reasons of ease and convenience when mudaraba and musharaka were not possible, and generating income while banks devised authentic risk-sharing instruments.[5]

But over time, rather than disappearing, murabaha and comparable sale-based contracts grew significantly and today they constitute the bulk of the activity of most Islamic banks.

The popularity of murabaha as a sale-cum-financing transaction could be attributed to its ability to replicate, in economic though not in religious, legal or regulatory terms, conventional loans. If a business needs $100 million to buy machinery, it could borrow money at 8 per cent a year to purchase it, or it could have the bank buy the machinery on its behalf, and pay the bank $108 million a year later. Beyond the bottom line, parallels abound: in both cases, the prior due diligence consists in examining the client's creditworthiness; the purchased asset serves as collateral, and the bank can also require other guarantees from the client; after the deal is completed, the relationship of the client to the bank is that of debtor; and in case of non-repayment, comparable recourses are available.[6] Regulators as well as conventional bankers are thus usually comfortable with such transactions. But this is also precisely why murabaha and other mark-up schemes are criticized – on the ground that such contracts may disguise the interest through semantic games to the point that some have characterized them as "hiyal".

From a religious standpoint, structuring a transaction as murabaha does sidestep riba, but it is far from the Islamic ideal of partnership finance. Most scholars would consider murabaha permissible. Indeed, if we go back to the notion of a continuum of injunctions (obligatory, meritorious, morally neutral, reprehensible, and forbidden), murabaha would be positioned, depending on the specifics, somewhere around the middle of the spectrum. By being low risk and short term, murabaha transactions do not fulfill the stated objectives of Islamic banking – to share risk with the customer and achieve social and developmental goals. Yet at the same time, riba is circumvented, real assets are being acquired, and the specifics of the Islamic transaction contain enough ethical safeguards to reassure religious scholars.[7]

Theological debates about murabaha revolve primarily around the justification for, and the extent of, the bank's remuneration. In Islam, the justification for profit is risk-taking, and thus the amount of the profit is directly related to the risk incurred: the greater the risk, the greater the profit. Since the deal involves two sales transactions (one consisting in buying the goods from the manufacturer; the other in selling the goods to the "borrower"), the main difference with a conventional banking loan is that there is a period during which the financial institution owns the goods. During that time the bank bears the risks of ownership: the goods may be damaged or destroyed; the seller may go bankrupt, etc. The longer the period of ownership, the greater the risk. For Shariah scholars, the best murabaha is the one where the financier purchases the commodity directly or through an agent, and then truly assumes ownership risk before selling it to the customer.

Yet from a prudential standpoint, neither the banks nor their regulators want to be subjected to ownership or inventory risk. The period of ownership will, therefore, be more symbolic than real (since the duration can theoretically be of just a few minutes or even just one second), and the profit of the bank, as murabaha is generally practiced, will likely correspond to the prevailing rate of interest for the period involved.

Importantly, however, the fact that the transaction is structured as a sale has significant legal implications. Islamic jurisprudence has laid down an elaborate set of rules governing sales. A sale is the exchange of a thing of value by another thing of value by mutual consent. The subject of sale must be in existence at the time of sale, and it must be in the physical or constructive[8] possession of the seller. Needless to say, the products sold cannot be among those forbidden by the Shariah. The delivery of the products must be certain and should not depend on a contingency or chance.[9] Unlike a loan, the total amount due does not consist of a principal and an interest component, but only of a principal. There are consequences both in terms of conditions of validity of the sale, in case of prepayment or default, or whenever the terms of the loan need to be renegotiated.[10]

A murabaha transaction can be broken up into different steps. First, is the agreement whereby the bank promises to sell and the client promises the buy the good. Second, is the actual purchase of the commodity. Often, the bank appoints the client as its agent for purchasing the commodity on its behalf, and an agreement of agency is signed by both parties. The bank is then the owner of the commodity. Third, is the sale of that commodity by the bank to the buyer, to whom the ownership and risk of possession are actually transferred. The first step is not an actual sale, but a promise (*waad*), while the next two steps are sales. At the end of the process, the relation between the bank and the client will be that of creditor and debtor.

There have been numerous attempts to establish common norms and standard contracts for murabaha transactions. Organizations such as the IFSB and the AAOIFI have made great strides in recent years in bringing greater coherence and harmonization, if not uniformity, to murabaha contracts. This has contributed to a noticeable increase in cross-national transactions, though country-specific and product-specific murabaha contracts persist. In certain countries, murabaha transactions are better known by other names, such as the Bai' Bithaman Ajil (BBA), literally "deferred payment sale," common in Malaysia.

(b) Musawama

Musawama (bargaining) is sale in which the price of the commodity to be traded is stipulated without any reference to the price paid or cost incurred by the bank. It lacks the transparency of murabaha (where the bank must disclose its cost), but the logic behind it is that it is closer in spirit to the idea of the bank as merchant. Indeed, the bank will earn its profit by seeking the best possible deal and this (at least in a truly competitive market) should put pressure on the banks to lower prices. Of course, it is not excluded that banks could collude to keep prices high.

(c) Istisnaa and Salam

There are only two exceptions to the rule that a sales contract is invalid if the item being sold is not in existence at the time of the sale. They are *istisnaa* (commissioned manufacturing) and *salam* (forward sale).

Istisnaa is a contractual agreement used to finance manufacturing items or construction projects. Under such a contract, the bank enters into an agreement with the manufacturer (or contractor) to manufacture and deliver the goods (or build a house) at an agreed future date. The manufacturer bills the bank periodically, and delivers the goods (or completes the project) at the end of the contract. The subject matter, price, and delivery date must be known and specified to eliminate the element of gharar. Changes are allowed if the specifications are modified by the contracting parties subject to mutual agreement or due to unforeseen contingencies.

Salam is a contract that has existed since the early days of Islam to finance the production of agricultural goods and basic commodities. Under a salam contract, a buyer pays money up front for goods to be delivered at a future date. Goods must be fungible and clearly defined. Scholars are now debating whether the logic of salam could be extended beyond agricultural products and commodities; that is, whether a salam logic could apply to financial paper – in which case salam sales could become a substitute for short sales, and an essential building block for Islamic derivatives and hedge funds.

(d) Controversial Sales: Tawarroq and 'Ina

Unlike murabaha, where bank credit is extended to purchase a real asset, in *tawarroq* and *'ina*, what the customer needs is not a specific asset, but cash. Buying and selling an asset is simply contrived to justify obtaining cash. Not surprisingly, both transactions are highly controversial from a religious standpoint, though tawarroq is widely practiced in the Gulf region (sometimes to justify issuing credit cards or lines of credit), and *bay' al 'ina* is accepted practice in Malaysia.

Tawarroq (literally, turning a commodity into silver, or monetizing it) consists of buying a commodity on credit and then selling it immediately for cash to a third person. It was a traditional means of obtaining cash in the Arabian Peninsula, where it was not uncommon for an individual to buy a commodity on credit and then soon afterwards turn around and sell it for cash. In such "classical" tawarroq, which was considered licit by scholars, the client in need of cash, after purchasing and taking possession of the commodity from the seller, would sell it in the marketplace to a third party without the initial seller's assistance or even knowledge.

The modern twist in the "organized tawarroq" or "bank tawarroq" lies in the direct involvement of the financial institution in all phases of the transaction. The bank purchases some commodity from the market, say aluminum, from the London Metal Exchange (LME), then sell the aluminum to the customer on a murabaha basis for deferred payment. Subsequently, the bank (as the customer's agent) sells the metal on the LME for immediate cash. As a result, the bank will gain murabaha profit and agency fees, and the customer will obtain cash. The aluminum will not change hands.

There are serious disagreements among scholars on the matter of organized or bank tawarroq. Most, while not necessarily calling it illicit, discourage its use because the link to the asset is spurious and it can lead to a proliferation of debt. In other words, the main problem is one of advisability rather than permissibility. Typically, scholars will want to look at the specifics of the transaction and at the particular circumstances of the customer. Thus, the AAOIFI has stated that tawarroq is acceptable if it involves four parties (a buyer, a seller, the buyer's commodity broker, and the seller's commodity broker).[11] Also scholars can be more lenient if it is being practiced for production as opposed to consumption, and in case of dire necessity: that is, if the client needs the cash and cannot obtain it in any other manner. Most scholars have called on banks to phase out the use of tawarroq.

Bay' al 'ina involves only two parties: the bank sells a product to a customer on credit and then buys it back from the same customer at a lower price for cash. Three of the four Sunni schools of fiqh consider it a hila and forbid its use. The fourth, the Shafii School, allows it on technical grounds (because it does not want to judge a person's intentions or disallow trade) but finds it reprehensible.[12]

2 Leasing-based Products

Ijara or leasing is also technically a sale contract, since it is understood from the standpoint of classical Islamic fiqh as the sale of *usufruct* (*manfaa*) and as such its rules closely follow those of ordinary sales. Yet as one of the fastest growing activities of Islamic financial institutions, it also presents enough distinctive characteristics to warrant being discussed separately.

The principle of ijara is well known and virtually identical to conventional leasing: the bank leases an asset to a third party in exchange for a specified rent.[13] The amounts of payments are known in advance and the asset remains the property of the lessor. Although initially directed primarily at businesses, ijara is increasingly used in retail finance, primarily for home mortgages, cars, and household needs. In recent years, leasing contracts have also been commonly used for big ticket items such as aircraft or ships, and have become essential building blocks in project finance.

In order to avoid the elements of riba and gharar, there are a few differences between ijara and conventional leasing. The law views some benefits and burdens of the property as belonging naturally and unchangeably to the lessee, others to the lessor. For example, the law provides that the duty to repair the goods always falls on the lessor, since the repair benefits him as the owner. Also, the usufruct is not something existent and tangible, but a stream of use extending into the future, which is risky and unstable. Islamic law thus gives broad scope to the lessee to cancel the lease if the usufruct proves to be less valuable than expected.[14] Finally, the price at which the asset may be sold to the lessee at the expiration of the contract cannot be pre-determined.[15] In practice, however, numerous compromises have been arrived at, often because national regulation does not allow sufficient flexibility to accommodate Shariah-compliant leases.

A number of reasons account for the rapid growth of leasing: it is an acceptable instrument in the eyes of most scholars; it is an efficient means of financial intermediation; by financing assets, it is a useful tool in the promotion of economic development; it is a well-established instrument that lends itself to standardized mechanisms and procedures; and most importantly, and unlike sales contracts such as murabaha, an ijara contract can be sold at any price on the secondary market. It is thus a flexible mode of financing that lends itself to securitization and secondary trading and to collaboration with conventional institutions. This explains why ijara sukuk are by far the most popular form of sukuk.

3 Equity-based and PLS Products

When it first came into existence, Islamic finance purported to offer an alternative model based on partnership finance. The basic idea was that instead of lending money at fixed rate of return, the banker would form a partnership with the entrepreneur, sharing in a venture's profits and losses. Under such an equity-based model, the bank provides finance, while the entrepreneur carries out the business venture whether trade, industry, or service, with the objective of earning profits. Profits are shared in a pre-determined ratio; losses are borne by the bank.

The partnership could be of one of two types: mudaraba (commenda partnership or finance trusteeship) and musharaka (longer-term equity-like arrangements). The mudaraba is an association between the *rabb al maal* (financier) and the *mudarib* (entrepreneur), where profits and losses are shared based on an agreed-upon ratio. The mudaraba can be restricted (if the contract specifies a particular line or place of business for the mudarib) or unrestricted. Musharaka is similar in its principle to mudaraba, except for the fact that the financier takes an equity stake in the venture. It is in effect a joint-venture agreement, whereby the bank enters into a partnership with a client in which both share the equity capital, and sometimes the management, of a project or deal. In both the mudaraba and the musharaka cases, the bank would receive a contractual share of the profits generated by business ventures.

Early pioneers of Islamic finance envisioned banks as functioning on the basis of the "double mudaraba" principle. On the liabilities side of the balance sheet, the depositor is the rabb al maal and the bank is the mudarib. On the asset side of the balance sheet, the bank is the rabb al maal and the client is the mudarib.

The principle of partnership finance is certainly seductive since in theory there would be a harmony of interests among depositors, financial institutions, and entrepreneurs. The bank would essentially be a venture capitalist financing promising entrepreneurs. Partnership finance was supposed to bring a wide range of economic benefits to society, through mobilization of savings, productive investment, and, more generally, economic development. It was regarded as vastly superior to the classical interest-based banking model. In addition to objections about riba, there are economic and financial misgivings to interest-based lending: it is unjust because the risk is borne primarily by the borrower; it favors already established businesses and those who can provide collateral; and it offers no assurance of a direct link to the real economy.

Partnership finance was at once the most "authentic" form of Islamic finance since it replicated transactions that were common in the early days of Islam,[16] the one that is most consistent with the value system and the moral economy of Islam, and the most "modern" one. Indeed, venture capital and private equity – both among the fastest growing segments of contemporary finance – would be the conventional equivalents of PLS arrangements. Conventional, interest-based banking is only marginally concerned with the success of the ventures it finances. In contrast, under PLS, Islamic institutions, as well as their depositors, link their own fate to the success of the projects they finance. The system allows a capital-poor, but promising entrepreneur, to obtain financing. The bank, being an investor, as opposed to a lender, has a stake in the long-term success of the venture. The entrepreneur, rather than being concerned with debt-servicing, can concentrate on a long-term endeavor that in turn could provide economic and social benefits to the community.[17]

The specifics of the mudaraba are straightforward: the rabb al maal, in the role of the silent or sleeping partner, entrusts money to the mudarib who, as managing trustee, is to utilize it in an agreed manner. After the operation is concluded, the rabb al maal receives the principal and the pre-agreed share of the profit. The mudarib keeps for himself the remaining profits. The rabb al maal also shares in the losses, and may be in a position of losing all his principal.[18] His liability is exclusively limited to the provided capital, just as that of the entrepreneur is restricted solely to his labor. In other words, the mudarib does not share in the losses except for the loss of his time and efforts., however, if negligence, mismanagement, or fraud can be proven, the entrepreneur may be financially liable. Under certain circumstances, for example, if the mudarib has engaged in religiously illicit activities (speculation or the production of forbidden goods or services), or if the bank has imposed a collateral for its investment, the mudaraba or musharaka contracts can be considered null and void. Recent variations on mudaraba and musharaka, are the diminishing mudaraba (*mudaraba mutanaqisa*) and the diminishing musharaka (*musharaka mutanaqisa*), where the bank's share is progressively reimbursed, allowing the entrepreneur to gradually increase his share in the project. Such a financing system was common in medieval Arabia where wealthy merchants financed the caravan trade. They would share in the profits of a successful operation, but could also lose all or part of their investment if, for example, the merchandise was stolen, lost, or sold for less than its cost.

Specific mudaraba contracts were codified by medieval jurists and could take on extreme complexity. Different fiqh traditions explain variations. Hanafis and Hanbalis argue, for example, that the profit can be shared only when the activity is completed and the financier has been reimbursed his principal; while Malikis and Shafiis permit the distribution of the profit even before the operation is completed and the principal been reimbursed. The mudaraba contracts also influenced other cultures. The commonly used "commandite" in French law grew out of the mudaraba contracts. It is also said that when Christopher Columbus undertook his voyage of discovery, his partnership contract was drawn by Islamic scholars.[19]

The musharaka form is more flexible. It makes it possible, for example, for the entrepreneur to contribute capital in addition to labor. Profits are divided on a pre-determined basis, and any losses shared in proportion to the respective capital contributions (whereas in a mudaraba, the mudarib does not suffer financial losses). The two methods can be combined. For example, the initial capital of a project can be financed by musharaka, while later working capital may be provided according to murabaha.

Pioneers of Islamic finance have also noted possible drawbacks: the mudaraba is a medieval contract that is not necessarily adapted to contemporary economic realities; and it may contravene the original meaning of riba (in the sense of lack of equivalency of counterparties), and may lead to one party taking advantage of the other, which happens if one of the participants has incomplete knowledge or a weak bargaining position. In addition, PLS arrangements create managerial and regulatory problems that have yet to be fully mastered. For example, the mudarib can ask for more money than he needs, or he can engage in high-risk endeavors, knowing that he will not be committing his own money. The bank can also take advantage of a mudarib who is pressed for cash, or of depositors who know little about the deal. It can also structure the transaction so as to transfer the risk to the other participants.[20] To avoid such abuses, all parties are expected to exert due diligence, and all operations must be characterized by transparency. The mudarib must prove that he is reputable and experienced, and that he enjoys high moral standing within the business community. The project must be viable and assessed independently by the bank or by external consultants. The bank must ensure that its funds are properly spent, and that the venture being financed is properly monitored.[21]

The first Islamic banks plunged into mudaraba with great enthusiasm (and virtually no experience). The result was, to put it mildly, disappointing, and as a result, virtually all institutions (except perhaps in the Sudan, Pakistan, and Iran, the three countries which at least in theory have Islamicized their entire banking system)[22] decided to steer clear of PLS, and focus instead on sale-based, or mark-up transactions.

The ideal of partnership finance has not really materialized. Maybe banks simply cannot be good venture capitalists. Indeed, banking and venture capitalism are completely different businesses; a good banker is not necessarily a good venture capitalist and vice versa. Most venture capitalists are entrepreneurs by background, concerned with the growth of a business rather than the repayment of loans. It is also questionable whether it is a good idea to use the money of small depositors to invest in new business ventures, which are risky by definition. In a free enterprise system, most new businesses fail, and most new products never find a market. Another difficulty of Islamic institutions is that in their early years they operated in an environment where the necessary "infrastructure" of venture capitalism (especially in terms of an appropriate bankruptcy system which would provide an exit strategy for failed ventures) was lacking.

Despite all this, the PLS and risk-sharing logics of Islamic finance have not disappeared entirely. On the liabilities side of the balance sheet, the mudaraba logic still prevails, since all investment accounts, usually referred to as profit-sharing investment accounts (PSIA) are mudaraba contracts, where the depositor is the rabb al maal and the bank the mudarib. Investment accounts come in two forms. They can be general accounts which are based on the overall performance of the bank: investors do well if the bank does well overall, and vice versa. The return paid is determined by the yield obtained from all the activities of the bank. After deducting such administration costs as wages, provisions, and capital depreciation, the bank pools the yields obtained from all ventures, and the depositors, as a group, share the net profits with the bank according to a pre-determined ratio that cannot be modified for the duration of the contract. Different banks have different policies concerning the calculation and disbursement of profits. Increasingly, as a way of "smoothing" the returns (to avoid wide fluctuations, which can have negative consequences as extremely high returns can attract deposits but also create expectations that cannot be met, while very low returns can result in depositors leaving the bank in droves), banks have been creating a profit equalization reserve. So the sharing of the profit could take the form of 50 per cent for the bank, 30 per cent for profit equalization reserves, and 20 per cent for the depositor. (In a few instances, the remuneration can as a result of such smoothing parallel that of conventional savings accounts.[23]) Some banks do the calculation and disbursement monthly, others quarterly, others still semi-annually or even annually.

The other type of mudaraba account is the special investment account, where the same logic applies, except that the partnership between the account holder and the bank will be limited to a specified asset or group of assets. Depositors can reap profits from a venture's success, but risk losing money if investments perform poorly.[24]

On the asset side of the balance sheet, the most common PLS product is the diminishing musharaka which is increasingly used to finance Islamic mortgages. This is, for example, how a diminishing musharaka mortgage (which also includes an element of ijara) would work: the client forms a partnership with the bank, with the bank providing 80 per cent of the purchase price, and the client 20 per cent. Over a period of 10 years, the client will make periodic payments to the bank, progressively increasing his ownership share, while the bank will make its profit from the rent paid by the client for the share the bank owns.

Just as an element of ijara can be incorporated in a musharaka, a risk-sharing logic is often part of Islamic contracts of sale and ijara, especially when the debtor is unable to pay through no fault of his own. In contrast to conventional finance, where banks are likely to take advantage of distressed borrowers, the attitude of Islamic institutions is that they should forsake some of their profits by, for example, extending a qard hasan (interest-free loan) to help the distressed borrower.[25]

It should also be said that Islamic finance balance sheets tend to overstate the volume of mudaraba transactions because they sometimes include fund management activities that have little to do with the financing of new enterprises that pioneers of Islamic finance had in mind. Indeed, there is something of a mudaraba logic to the fund management industry, since it is generally accepted that allowing managers of certain types of funds to keep a chunk of their winnings gives them an incentive to improve their performance. Thus, a fund manager paid on a "2 and 20" base, will get 2 per cent of total assets as a management fee, and keep 20 per cent of investment gains (above some agreed-upon benchmark).

II New Frontiers in Islamic Finance

1 Financial Innovation

On the matter of investments in international markets, important changes have taken place since the emergence of modern Islamic finance in the mid-1970s. In those days, the financial world at large had yet to undergo its revolution. Deregulation was still an abstract concept, and there was little financial innovation. Equity markets, as illustrated by the sharp drop in the Dow Jones Industrial Average in 1974–5, were bearish. Commodity markets, led by oil, were in contrast bullish. Generalized floating currencies also offered new opportunities for foreign exchange operations.

The early doctrine could be summarized as follows: trading in commodities markets was encouraged, since the buying and selling of "real goods" was involved; foreign exchange trading, by analogy with early Islamic dealings in precious metals, was permitted; bonds, whether corporate or governmental, were frowned upon since they involved interest. As for equities, legal scholars were divided. For some, equity investment was based on the principle of PLS, since investors linked their financial future to that of the companies in which they invested. For others, equities were not acceptable because many companies earned all or part of their income from illicit activities (banks rely on interest income; hotels, restaurants, or airlines usually sell liqor, etc.). Even more significantly, most Western companies pay interest on borrowings and earn interest on their cash deposits.

Another principle of the early days of modern Islamic finance was that investments, whether in equities or commodities, could not be bought for short periods solely to make a profit. Placements had to be for the long term and for the purpose of promoting investment.[26] By the 1980s and especially by the 1990s, Islamic financial institutions had changed their outlook as a result of the dramatic changes in the international environment, and of their own experiences. Many leading Islamic banks had lost considerable amounts on foreign exchange and commodities markets. Most of these investments were all the more controversial since they often violated the spirit, while conforming with the letter, of Islamic finance. Indeed, they were essentially short term and speculative, and had no developmental or community-related purpose. At the same time, financial deregulation offered more opportunities and more pitfalls. Deregulation made it possible to slice-and-dice financial products to satisfy investor preferences – including religious preferences. The appearance of religious screens also had a reassuring effect.

The question of financial derivatives remains fraught with controversy. Those who stress the economic benefits of derivatives (on matters ranging from hedging and risk control) are pitting against those raise theological objections (such as gharar) and note the distance, if not the outright disconnect, between derivatives and underlying assets. The first typically invoke the *maqasid al-Shariah* (the objectives of the Shariah, which include prosperity), whereas the second stress the fiqh tradition and well-established positions against speculation or the selling of promises (inherent to forwards, futures, or credit derivatives). Until the financial crisis of 2008, partisans of the economic approach seemed to be gaining ground, as more Islamic derivatives were being created, albeit through Islamic contracts. Thus, a range of options were created based on the Islamic tradition of *'arbun* (non-refundable downpayment) and *waad* (buyer's promise to purchase). Even Islamic hedge funds were devised that made extensive use of salam contracts.

The collapse of credit default swaps (CDS) market was seen by critics as a vindication of their position. The current situation can be summarized as follows: plain vanilla derivatives that are well understood and whose economic benefits are demonstrated will increasingly find Islamic counterparts, whereas the more exotic derivatives will not.

2 Sukuk

Sukuk are certificates that represent ownership of an underlying pool of assets, or the usufruct (manfaa) of such assets, and, therefore, entitle their holders to returns resulting from the sale or lease of the assets.[27]

There have been many attempts to create Shariah-compliant instruments resembling bonds that were given the name of an early Islamic financial instrument known as sakk (plural sukuk). It is only in the early years of the twenty-first century that such attempts finally came to fruition, and became a means for governments and companies to raise money through Islamic capital markets.

An ijara sukuk issued in 2002 by the Malaysian government and approved by both Arab and Malaysian scholars was especially influential as it provided a template for what became a popular form of tradable sukuk. Under such a template, a special purpose vehicle buys assets such as real estate from an issuing entity or other sellers, and then leases it back to the issuing entity – a special purpose vehicle (or SPV) for a period equal to the maturity of the bond. Sukuk buyers receive periodic rental payments depending on the terms of the lease. At the end of the lease (typically five years), the property is sold, the SPV is liquidated and the sukuk holders receive their share of the sale.[28]

The other major type of sukuk is the mudaraba sukuk, whose goal is to provide an opportunity for public shareholding in big investment projects. The sukuk represent a share of ownership in a given project in which the sukuk holders are collectively the rabb al maal. Returns are based on the performance of the project.

In addition to the ijara sukuk and mudaraba sukuk, the AAOIFI has identified twelve other types of sukuk. As explained by Rodney Wilson:

> Sukuk have different structures and different risk and return characteristics, with salam sukuk corresponding to bills, ijara sukuk, the most popular, to floating rate notes and mudaraba sukuk to fixed return bonds. As with the latter, modest capital gains and losses are possible on mudaraba sukuk if the security has years to its maturity, but as maturity approaches the market value will converge with the face value. With ijara sukuk the market value will not vary from the face value unless expectations of a possible default change. Investors, therefore, are very concerned with rating issues, as with comparable conventional securities. In summary sukuk must conform to the principles of Islamic law, but their behaviour in terms of pricing and returns will be determined by the market.[29]

From the investors' standpoint, these instruments do resemble conventional bonds, although the underlying structures are fundamentally different. A bond is a contractual debt obligation whereby the issuer is contractually obliged to pay to bondholders, on certain specified dates, interest and principal. In contrast, sukuk holders are the owners of a specific asset and are entitled to receive the profit or usufructs generated by such assets, as well as the proceeds from the sale of the asset. Like bonds, such sukuk are fully tradable (except if the underlying asset is a debt), they provide periodic revenues, and hold the possibility of capital appreciation.

In the last few years, dozens of sukuk have been issued (mostly ijara and mudaraba) by issuers as diverse as the governments of Qatar and Bahrain, the Islamic Development Bank, DP World, Nakheel, Aston Martin, and the German state of Saxony-Anhalt. Most of the issues proved very popular with Islamic investors and many non-Islamic banks and institutional investors,[30] although given the abundance of liquidity and the paucity of similar instruments, many investors adopted an own-to-hold strategy, and secondary trading was generally thin. In a number of countries (most prominently the United Kingdom, but also France, Japan, and South Korea), governments have changed their laws and tax codes to make possible the issuance of sukuk that would be held and traded in the same way as conventional bonds.

The market for sukuk went from almost zero in 2000 to about $100 billion in 2008. That year, however, saw a decline in sukuk issuance due to a combination of two factors – the credit crunch and religious uncertainties. Indeed, in November 2007, Sheikh Taki Usmani, one of the most respected Shariah advisors and the chair of AAOIFI's Shariah Board called for a course correction when he stated that perhaps as much as 85 per cent of the sukuk in existence had religiously questionable features. He objected primarily to the repurchase guarantee – that promised to pay back the face value of the bond at maturity or in case of default

– which he deemed contrary to the PLS concept. In later months, clarifications were issued on the exact nature of the rights and obligations of sukuk holders.

What is still unclear is what happens to sukuk when they fail – an issue that has not been tested in court. In Malaysia, some sukuk issues have junk status, and two other sukuk are already in default: the East Cameron Gas Company in the United States and Investment Dar of Kuwait. One of the unresolved questions is whether sukuk holders should stand in the line of creditors or in the line of owners of underlying assets.

3 Religious Screens

One of the most significant innovations in Islamic finance was the introduction of standardized investment screens. Investment screens were pioneered by the Dow Jones company when it established in 1999 Dow Jones Islamic Market (DJIM) index. Other companies have followed suit, among them Standard & Poor's (since 2007) and FTSE (since 2008). Although every screening company has its own standards and methodologies, the underlying logic of screening stocks for Shariah compliance is the same.

Drawing on classical Islamic jurisprudence on the mixture of permissible and impermissible, the halal and the non-halal, and a Hadith on resolving the "how much is too much question," a number of criteria and ceilings were devised. The Hadith in question states that "The dividing line between a majority and a minority is one third, and the third as a portion is considered to be much."[31] The Dow Jones methodology was established by its own Shariah Board. There are now more than 100 Dow Jones Islamic indexes, applying the same filters to different sectors, regions, and asset classes.

There are typically three levels of screening to determine Shariah-compliance. The first is the primary sector of activity of the company. Always excluded are companies involved in gambling, pornography, alcohol, pork, and conventional finance. Beyond such sectors, different screening companies differ in their methodology. The hospitality industry (hotels and restaurants) is often screened out because of its reliance on alcohol sales, and so are controversial or "sinful" sectors such as weapon or tobacco manufacturers.

After a firm's activities are deemed acceptable, more specific financial filters (primarily based on debt and interest income) typically based on the "one-third rule" are applied. The first criterion is the level of debt: companies whose total debt divided by twelve-month average market capitalization is 33 per cent or more are screened out. Companies can also be screened out for ethical lapses.

Another aspect of the screening is the recommended purification. The logic is that dividends from companies that pass the sectoral and financial screens, but still receive interest payments or have a small (less than 5 per cent) involvement in illicit activities, must be purified. What it means in practice is that the investors are made aware of the percentage of company income that is tainted, the recommendation being that they donate such amounts to charity.

Screens were initially used for the benefit of mutual fund investors, by following the logic of socially-responsible funds, who select funds on the basis of criteria other than performance (for example the environment, labor, or political preference). Islamic screens are now used beyond mutual funds for all sorts of investments, such as private equity and other funds, even to decide whether an Islamic institution should be doing business with a certain company. The indices are heavily weighted towards technology, energy, resources, infrastructure, pharmaceuticals, telecommunications, and consumer goods.

It should be noted that ethical business is also high on the agenda of other religions and interfaith groups.[32] Shariah-compliant mutual funds have generally done quite well despite the fact that screening mechanisms can hinder performance (since they rule out well-performing stocks) and add to the cost of managing the fund.[33] They have done especially well during the turmoil of 2007–8, helped in part by their systematic exclusion of financial stocks that were battered by the crisis.[34]

4 The Case of Takaful

The case of takaful is testament to the ability of Islamic finance to evolve in its interpretations and practices. For years, it had been an article of faith that insurance was not compatible with Islam, because it contained elements of gharar, maysir, and riba. Some religious scholars even saw the practice as an attempt to interfere with God's will. Since it was all about uncertainty and chance occurrences, insurance looked like a catalog of prohibited practices: inequality between premiums paid and benefits collected (or not collected) from the insurance company; premiums placed in interest-bearing instruments; late payment of premiums resulting in interest and late fees; uncertainty over subject matter and duration of contracts, etc. In the early days of Islamic finance, it was also commonly asserted that no Islamic precedent could be found.

In one of the official publications of the IAIB from 1980, one could find a damning indictment of an industry pervaded by "usury, deceit, misrewarding, gambling, and betting."[35] Especially troublesome in the eyes of many Muslims was life insurance, perceived as gambling on matters of fate and divine will.

But over time, and after much debate,[36] Islamic doctrine has come to terms with most forms of insurance – including life insurance. First came the recognition that the logic of insurance fits within the Islamic tradition. On the theological front, a new consensus formed around the view that taking precautionary measures against possible danger and its consequences was not incompatible with trust in God. A famous Hadith was quoted to that effect: when a Bedouin asked the Prophet whether, since he trusted in God and His protection, he could let his camel roam loose, the Prophet answered, "First tether, then trust in God."[37] In addition, many Islamic tribal practices were interpreted as solidarity mechanisms. Thus, if the member of a tribe was killed by a member of different tribe, the heir of the victim could be paid blood money (*diyya*) as a compensation by close relatives of the killer as a means of avoiding eye-for-an-eye retaliation. Similarly, when members of a tribe were taken prisoner, the ransom (*fidya*) was often paid by having other members of the tribe pitch in.

This is how the concept of "takaful," which literally means solidarity, and is nearly identical to Western-style mutual insurance, came to be accepted as a Shariah-compliant substitute to insurance. Virtually all forms of insurance now have a takaful equivalent. Even life insurance has lost the stigma that was long attached to it. Planning on receiving money upon someone's death is no longer seen as an illicit gamble on misfortune, if not as a God-defying act, but rather as a positive step designed to ease the lives of survivors. Significantly, life insurance is usually known as family takaful.

The functioning of takaful companies is, however, different in many ways to that of conventional insurance companies. In order to side-step the question of gharar, the participants do not pay a premium, but a *tabarru'* which means donation, gift, or contribution (the somewhat contrived justification being that the donation would be available to participants faced with difficulties). Each participant contributes into a pool that has sufficient amounts to cover expected claims. The funds are then invested in halal instruments. If the pool is overfunded, the surpluses are redistributed to the participants, either directly or in the form of discounts on their next contributions.

As for the professional management of takaful operations, it typically takes the form of either mudaraba or *wakala* (agency). In the first case, the remuneration is performance-based (the contributors are the rabb al maal and the operator is the mudarib), whereas in the second, the agent is remunerated on the basis of a set fee.

Notes

1. More likely to be a "promise" or *waad*.
2. In Islamic finance, the equipment owner must perform specific responsibilities, yet in practice he appoints the lessee as his agent to perform such tasks as maintaining or repairing the equipment.
3. Chibli Mallat, *Introduction to Middle Eastern Law* (Oxford: Oxford University Press, 2007), p. 311.
4. Saad al-Harran (ed.), *Leading Issues in Islamic Banking and Finance* (Selangor, Malaysia: Pelanduk Publications, 1995), p. xi, and Frank E. Vogel and Samuel L. Hayes, III, *Islamic Law and Finance: Religion, Risk, and Return* (The Hague: Kluwer Law International, 1998), p. 135.
5. Vogel and Hayes, *Islamic Law and Finance*, p. 143.
6. An important difference, however, is that if the bank's customer has acted in good faith, and that his financial distress is attributable to factors beyond his control, the bank has to show forbearance.
7. See Chapter 8.
8. Constructive possession means that, although the possessor has not taken physical delivery of the good, the good is legally under his control, with all the rights and liabilities involved (for example, in the case of the destruction of the good).
9. A conditional sale is invalid, unless the condition is recognized as a part of the transaction according to the usage of trade.
10. Once the sale is concluded, the agreed-upon selling price cannot be changed, so it

can neither be reduced in the case of early repayment, nor increased in the case of default. In the case of early repayment, the banker would usually offer a discount at his discretion, which would be regarded as a hiba or gift, and thus discretionary and non-negotiable. In the case of default, real costs incurred by banker would be added to the debtor's liability.

11. Datuk Zukri Samat, "Debate over Commodity Murabahah," Reuters, January 21, 2009.
12. See Chapter 2.
13. Fuad al-Omar and Mohammed Abdel-Haq, *Islamic Banking: Theory, Practice and Challenges* (London: Zen Books, 1996), pp. 11–19.
14. Vogel and Hayes, *Islamic Law and Finance*, pp. 143–5.
15. Al-Omar and Abdel-Haq, *Islamic Banking*, p. 66.
16. Abraham L. Udovitch, *Partnership and Profit in Medieval Islam* (New Haven, CT: Princeton University Press, 1970), pp. 170–248.
17. Mohammad Hashim Kamali, *Equity and Fairness in Islam* (Cambridge: The Islamic Texts Society, 2005), p. 104.
18. Murat Cizakça, *A Comparative Evolution of Business Partnerships: The Islamic World & Europe, with Specific Reference to the Ottoman Archives* (Leiden: E. J. Brill, 1996), pp. 4–6.
19. Drake Bennett, "The Zero Percent Solution," *Boston Globe*, November 4, 2007.
20. See, for example, Ziaul Haque, *Riba: The Moral Economy of Usury, Interest, and Profit* (Lahore: Vanguard, 1985), pp. 190–214.
21. Stéphanie Parigi, *Des Banques Islamiques* (Paris: Ramsay, 1989), p. 137.
22. See Chapter 6.
23. Yaroslav Trofimov, "Borrowed Ideas: Malaysia Transforms Rules For Finance Under Islam; In a Lesson to Arabs, Asian Bankers Mix Religion, Modernity," *The Wall Street Journal*, April 4, 2007.
24. Shahrukh Rafi Khan, *Profit and Loss Sharing: An Islamic Experiment in Finance and Banking* (Karachi: Oxford University Press, 1988).
25. Rodney Wilson, "Why Islamic Banking Is Successful? Islamic Banks Are Unscathed Despite of Financial Crisis," February 15, 2009, available at: IslamOnline.net.
26. *Al Mausua al Ilmiya wa al Ammaliya lil Bunuk al Islamiya (The Handbook of Islamic Banking)* (Cairo: International Association of Islamic Banks, 1977), vol. 5, pp. 427–37.
27. According to the definition of the AAOIFI, sukuk are "certificates of equal value representing after closing subscription, receipt of the value of the certificates and putting it to use as planned, common title to shares and rights in tangible assets, usufructs and services, or equity of a given project or equity of a special investment activity."
28. The Government of Malaysia raised $600 million through Ijara sukuk Trust Certificates (TCs). Under this arrangement, the beneficiary right to the real estate was been sold by the government of Malaysia to an SPV, which was then re-sold to investors for five years. The SPV kept the beneficiary rights of the properties in trust and issued floating rate sukuk to investors.
29. "Characteristics and Implications of Sukuk," Professor Rodney Wilson, Durham University, Harvard–LSE Workshop on Sukuks, London, February 7, 2008.
30. "Calling the Faithful," *The Economist*, December 7, 2006.
31. Mohamed A Elgari, "Islamic Equity Investment," in Simon Archer and Rifaat Abdel Karim (eds.), *Islamic Finance: Innovation and Growth* (London: Euromoney, 2002), pp. 153–4.
32. Rich Barlow "They Base Money Advice on the Bible," *The Boston Globe*, November 1, 2008.
33. Carolyn Cui, "Why a Fund's Piety is now Paying Off; Islamic Principles Help Amana Income Avoid Banks, Other Risky Bets," *The Wall Street Journal*, November 19, 2007.
34. Matthai Kuruvila, "Muslim Investors Profit by Adhering to Faith," *The San Francisco Chronicle*, February 9, 2009.
35. Ahmed Abdel Aziz al-Nagar *et al.*, *One Hundred Questions & One Hundred Answers Concerning*

Islamic Banks (Cairo: International Association of Islamic Banks, 1980), pp. 131–4.
36. Muhammad Nejatullah Siddiqi, *Muslim Economic Thinking: A Survey of Contemporary Literature* (Leicester: The Islamic Foundation, 1981), pp. 26–8.
37. Annemarie Schimmel, *And Muhammad is His Messenger: The Veneration of the Prophet in Islamic Piety* (Durham, NC: The University of North Carolina Press, 1985), p. 47.

8

STRATEGIC, MANAGERIAL, AND CULTURAL ISSUES

The rapid growth experienced by Islamic finance is likely to last for at least a few more years, driven by the opportunities presented by a huge Islamic market that is only partially tapped. But the picture is not all rosy. The Islamic financial market is increasingly competitive, and growing pains accompany rapid growth. This chapter focuses on the strategic, managerial, and cultural challenges facing Islamic banks. Some of the issues discussed here are common to emerging markets in general and are not exclusive to Islamic banks or even Islamic countries. Indeed, even the most "advanced" markets are not, as the recent financial meltdown has shown, immune to strategic, managerial, and cultural challenges. The world of finance is inherently prone to "manias, panics, crises, and crashes."[1] The religious dimension nonetheless adds an extra layer of problems.

I Competitive Challenges

When modern Islamic finance came into existence, the oil bonanza as well as the novelty of the concept allowed wide latitude for experimentation and error. Funds were plentiful for the handful of Islamic institutions that were in a position to share a monopoly on the small but growing niche of clients looking for Shariah-compliant investments. Many depositors did not even seek any remuneration, placing their money in al-wadiah accounts, thus providing banks with the cheapest possible funding.

In those years, Islamic financial institutions could flaunt their religious character by offering unique financial products. Indeed, prior to deregulation, conventional banks were still stifled by strict controls on product innovation. Strategic and managerial weaknesses could thus be hidden "behind a curtain of self-righteous platitudes about spiritual ideals."[2] Such weaknesses have become more glaring with the transformation of the world of finance, and in particular with the inroads made by conventional banks in Islamic finance. Competitive pressures are now appearing from all sides. This section focuses on two related issues: the Islamic banking franchise, and profitability and social goals.

1 The Islamic Banking Franchise

A bank's franchise, which can be defined as its "natural market" (or the reason why customers will normally choose it in preference to other banks), is a key competitive advantage. It is true that the Islamic market has greatly expanded, but it has also become increasingly competitive. Nowadays, every major international financial institution has Islamic operations, with most conventional banks in the Islamic world providing Islamic products, and increasingly, separate Islamic "windows." In interviews with conventional and Islamic bankers, one can hear on both sides hints of unfair competition. Conventional bankers say that the Islamic institutions tend to "own the Islamic franchise" and are perceived as "more truly Islamic." Among Islamic institutions, one could often hear the following sentence: "Conventional banks can do anything we do, whereas we cannot do anything they do."[3] In other words, conventional banks can now have the best of both worlds, offering jointly and to different clienteles both conventional and Islamic products.

A recent survey suggests that the perception by non-Islamic banks may not be warranted. It should be remembered that to create Islamic windows or Islamic subsidiaries, three conditions are required: that the funds be segregated (that is, that there be no co-mingling of Islamic and non-Islamic funds, and that Islamic assets be funded by Islamic liabilities); that Islamic activities be supervised by a Shariah Board; and that there be an understanding by top management of what Islamic finance entails and a commitment to maintaining the Islamic window or unit.[4] The survey asked 110 customers of Islamic banks about the religious criteria determining their choice of institutions, and over 60 per cent said that the presence of a reputable Shariah Board was the primary criterion (as opposed to the institution's nationality or the fact that it is primarily a conventional institution) for doing business with a given institution.[5]

Undoubtedly, competitive pressures are increasing. As the market expands and newcomers multiply, the options available to customers widen and both depositors and borrowers are likely to demand more innovative products. At the same time, the new norms of global finance are imposing new constraints on Islamic financial institutions. They are increasingly pressured to adopt – at the very least if they have international ambitions – new regulatory, accounting, and managerial rules.[6] The transformation and globalization of finance – new delivery systems, securitization, 24-hour trading – have brought with them new rules and norms that are rapidly spreading. Some are being imposed, often as a component of "structural adjustment" packages imposed on national economies by international organizations. Others are chosen willingly as a way of gaining credibility and acceptance in the international marketplace. One example would be the attempt to gain the international accreditation standard, ISO 9000, which recognizes organizational efficiency, from management style to training to customer needs. Another is the pressure to commit to better governance, though the concept remains ill-defined and often ill-understood.[7]

Whereas they were once at the forefront of innovation in their specific market niche, Islamic banks are now lagging behind, both in the creation and in the marketing of Islamic products. The predicament of Islamic banks is illustrated by the fact that conventional, and usually foreign, institutions are now often in a better position to introduce new financial products.[8] Examples abound of conventional banks being faster to introduce new Islamic products. In Pakistan, for example, Grindlays offered musharaka agreements to its clients before any of the Pakistani banks.[9] In the Islamic derivatives arena, virtually all innovation has come from institutions such as Deutsche Bank, BNP-Paribas, Standard Chartered, Citi Islamic, and HSBC Amanah. Non-Islamic involvement in Islamic banking has become one of the defining features of the second and third phases in the development of Islamic finance.[10] Not only are many Islamic products aimed at non-Muslims, but on occasion, non-Muslims have shared in the ownership of Islamic banks. In 1998, three of the largest foreign portfolio investors in Turkey – Alliance Capital Management's Turkish Growth Fund, international financier George Soros' Quantum Emerging Growth Partners, and the Bahamas-based New Frontier Emerging Opportunities Fund – acquired a 10 per cent stake in Ihlas Finans Kurumu, one of the Special Finance Houses.[11]

The mechanisms by which conventional and Islamic banks make their strategic decisions differ. Conventional institutions proceed through trial and error: countless ideas are considered and new products are launched in short order; a few succeed, most do not. Islamic financial institutions, however, cannot proceed in the same way, as they are hampered by the religious constraint: new products and new practices must first be cleared by Shariah Boards for religious rectitude. Yet in a harsh competitive environment, it is crucial to be swift and innovative: the product cycle is such that in the early stages, profit margins are high but later, as competition intensifies and as the product is commodified, fat margins disappear.

The easy solution is, of course, to try and compete on the basis of the leniency of Shariah Boards, in order to pursue whatever lucrative activities conventional banks are engaged in. The difficult solution is to improve management and lending policies, and in particular concentrate on what may constitute the Islamic bank's truly differentiating products, those based on PLS, a segment now neglected, if not completely abandoned, by a majority of Islamic institutions.[12]

As discussed later in the chapter and elsewhere in the book,[13] what from a conventional perspective may be looked at as interference from non-executives may not be such a bad thing after all. Indeed, another way of looking at Shariah Boards is from the standpoint of necessary checks and balances. By looking at criteria other than sheer profitability, Shariah advisors played a salutary role that may have saved most Islamic banks from many of the consequences of the 2007–8 meltdown.[14]

2 Profitability and Social Goals

Since the deregulation movement started in the 1980s, profitability has displaced size as the principal criterion by which conventional banks are compared and evaluated.[15] Relationship banking is also being replaced by price-based banking,[16] and bank analysts as well as the financial press consider purely financial criteria to be paramount. Islamic banks are a part of the global economy, and they are thus subjected to strong pressures to conform to such expectations. Yet by their very nature, they should not be judged solely on the profit criterion. Since the earliest days, it has been clear that Islamic banks should not be driven by profit maximization, but by the provision of socioeconomic benefits to their communities. According to the IAIB;

> The Islamic bank takes into prime consideration the social implications that may be brought about by any decision or action taken by the bank. Profitability – despite its importance and priority – is not, therefore, the sole criterion or the prime element in evaluating the performance of Islamic banks, since they have to match both between the material and the social objectives that would serve the interests of the community as a whole and help achieve their role in the sphere of social mutual guarantee. Social goals are understood to form an inseparable element of the Islamic banking system that cannot be dispensed with or neglected.[17]

Islamic banks are quick to point out that they are not charitable organizations, and that they must turn a profit, which is a pre-requisite to economic survival. But this should not be their sole, or even their primary, goal. Banks are expected to achieve a "reasonable" rate of return ("*arbah maakula*"), though such a definition has remained imprecise. Some have suggested it should be related to the average return in the economy.[18] In Iran, a maximum rate of profit is determined by the Central Bank. In the harsh environment of the global economy, Islamic banks must compete with conventional banks that usually focus exclusively on profit maximization. This allows them to offer better remuneration to their depositors and to their shareholders. It also allows them to generate the funds necessary to invest in innovation and technology.

Most strategic decisions involve socioeconomic and moral considerations. Where conventional banks can adopt a hard-nosed attitude, engaging, for example, in ruthless cost cutting, deciding to get rid of large numbers of employees and of unprofitable lines of business,[19] Islamic banks should consider other, non-financial factors first. At a time of profit-driven consolidations, mergers, acquisitions, and layoffs, Islamic banks face a dilemma: how can they compete with conventional banks if they do not play by the same rules? The compromise that Islamic banks have arrived at consists in recognizing, first, that the pursuit of profits should not be all consuming, and, second, that certain policies that reduce profitability are essential to their Islamic character: zakat and other charitable contributions made by the bank; qard hasan; micro-lending; in addition to ethical albeit costly practices such as sharing the risk of their clients' endeavors or avoiding taking advantage of distressed borrowers.

II Management, Control, and the "Islamic Moral Hazard"

The notion of moral hazard is commonly used in connection with financial regulation. It refers to policies, contracts, or transactions that may encourage reckless behavior.[20] In the insurance business, for example, insuring one's car can be a disincentive to taking good care of it. A dishonest person may go as far as wrecking the car to file a claim with the insurance company and receive enough money to buy a new one. To discourage such situations, insurance companies impose high deductibles, escalating premiums and other disincentives to reckless behavior.

Introducing religion into business transaction can provide a cover for fraud, precisely because of the trust generated by religious affinity. It is useful to remember that the words creed, credit, and credulity all have a common Latin source; that is, *credere*: to believe. Elie Wiesel, who was one of the victims of Bernard Madoff, the financier widely believed to have perpetrated "the largest fraud in history" said: "We gave him everything, we thought he was God, we trusted everything in his hands." Presenting himself as a pious man and a philanthropist, the confidence man exuded confidence. Appearing, to quote Wiesel, as "a savior," he swindled dozens of Jewish charities of over a billion dollars.[21]

By the same token, one could identify an "Islamic moral hazard" in that certain features of Islamic finance can encourage unscrupulous behavior. The presence of religion can give a false sense of reassurance, and blind trust that somehow "disables" controls and safeguards. For understandable reasons, most scholars steer away from that issue. For many, it is axiomatic that banks and their customers are people of virtue, who act at all times in a righteous manner. While it is undeniable that religious fervor is for many people a reason to work for an Islamic bank, or conduct business with it, it was soon discovered that religion could be a double-edged sword. In the Koran there are numerous references to hypocrisy (9:43–110). Since time immemorial, con artists have used the cover of religion as a means of rapid enrichment. Countless financial scandals have involved religious figures.[22] (One cannot help but think of a saying attributed to L. Ron Hubbard, founder of the Church of Scientology: "If you want to get rich, start a religion.") Even when the overwhelming majority of people are honest, all it takes is a few bad apples – a few dishonest customers or employees – for banks to incur serious difficulties. Indeed, one big swindle can bring a financial institution down.

Four factors are of special importance in that regard. One is the assumption of righteous behavior on the part of employees and customers, which sometimes turns certain institutions into a magnet for dubious characters. The second is the use of religion as a shield against scrutiny. The third is the religious and legal ambiguity that often allows borrowers to escape their obligations with impunity. The fourth involves conflicts of interest involving the bank and its clients.

In the early years, Islamic bankers failed to act prudently and exercise the kind of due diligence expected of bankers, because of implicit assumptions about the virtue of their employees and customers. In particular, forays into PLS activities proved to be disastrous. Bank executives acknowledged that they had trusted people who did not deserve their trust.[23] Hassan Kamel, chief executive of the (now-defunct) London branch of al-Baraka, explained why his bank was not involved in PLS operations: "The depositors wanted an Islamic deal without risk. They liked, at least, to guarantee their capital. The problem with PLS is that (the Islamic economists) assume the scenario of the entrepreneur being a good Muslim."[24] Hamid Algabid noted that the same problem was encountered by most Islamic institutions:

> At the beginning, confidence was the rule. The good faith of the participants could not be questioned since it was identified with religious faith. Since spiritual and temporal matters could not be dissociated, a pious man could only act in good faith. Experience has since shown that banking operations could not be based on that assumption, and particularly that guarantees could not be limited to the affirmation of one's Islamic faith.[25]

Internal control has also been a problem for the same reasons. In 1998 alone, the Dubai Islamic Bank (DIB), the oldest and one of the largest Islamic commercial banks, was hit by two scandals involving its employees. It incurred losses of $50 million when, according to a bank spokesman, "a bank official extended business loans without conforming to the bank's credit terms."[26] News of the losses caused a run on deposits: in one day, DIB clients are said to have withdrawn $138 million (or 7 per cent) of the bank's total deposits, forcing the Dubai Central Bank and the United Arab Emirates authorities to ride to the rescue, and provide the liquidity and the guarantees necessary to reassure depositors.[27] Another, more bizarre, swindle also involved a large, unauthorized loan. In a lawsuit filed in Miami, Florida, the DIB charged West African tycoon, Foutanga Dit Babani Sissoko, of bilking it of $242 million. A branch manager, who claimed that he gave the funds to Sissoko because he was under his "black magic" spell, was arrested.[28] A decade later, another scandal rocked DIB, as seven bank employees were accused of defrauding the bank of more than $500 million via CCH, its trade finance subsidiary.[29]

A second type of Islamic moral hazard occurs when the financial activities of certain Islamic institutions or groups become, on religious grounds, immune to scrutiny or criticism. In Iran, for example, a whole sector of the economy has been able to operate outside any regulatory framework, allowing abuses to persist and go largely unpunished:

> Mullahs in control of [foundations], and their appointed managers are hardly accountable, and run them as personal fiefs. Widely publicized corruption scandals and investigation by the Majlis led to the resignation of certain clerics in charge in late 1994 and 1995. But the foundations are still widely believed to foster nepotism and patronage, which adds to their political clout.[30]

A more subtle, but equally pervasive, form of Islamic moral hazard is the advantage that can be taken from ambiguity. Unlike secular systems, the legal system of Islam incorporates both an economic and a religious logic. In the words of Noel Coulson:

> Commercial law ... in the West is orientated towards the intrinsic needs of sound economics, such as stability of obligation and certitude of promised performance. In the religious law of Islam, on the other hand, equitable considerations of the individual conscience in matters of profit and loss override the technicalities of commercial dealings. It is the harmonization of these two very different approaches which poses the real challenge for developing Islamic law today.[31]

Islamic banks face a serious problem with late payments, not to speak of outright defaults, since some people take advantage of every dilatory legal and religious device. Indeed, like other religions, Islam recommends forbearance and even loan forgiveness to borrowers in difficulty (Koran 2:280-1). In a secular system, such prescriptions can be ignored, but in a religious or hybrid system they cannot. Secular bankers can use a whole array of tools – such as late fees, lawsuits, forcing bankruptcy, etc. – to protect their interests as lenders. Islamic bankers are hampered by the lack of clear-cut norms and remedies. In most Islamic countries, various forms of penalties and late fees have been established, only to be outlawed or considered unenforceable.[32] Late fees in particular have been assimilated to riba. As a result, "debtors know that they can pay Islamic banks last since doing so involves no cost."[33] In Pakistan, special banking tribunals were created, but they were in competition with other tribunals and lacked enforcement power. Attempts to expedite court processes would typically be bogged down by religious objections. Many borrowers took advantage of the ambiguity of a multi-layered legal system to avoid repaying much of their debt. Many businessmen who had borrowed large amounts of money over long periods of time seized the opportunity of Islamicization to do away with the accumulated interest of their debt, by repaying only the principal – usually a puny sum when years of double-digit inflation was taken into consideration.[34]

It should be noted that the same problems often hurt conventional banks in Islamic countries.[35] In Saudi Arabia, problems of late payment are endemic, and banks receive little help from the judicial system. Peter Wilson observed that "Saudi Arabia's bad loan problem is as old as the country's banking system, given the doctrinal dilemma of having an interest-based financial system in a country that officially prohibits interest."[36] More specifically:

> The Kingdom's law courts reflect the uneasy balance in the country. There are Islamic or Shariah courts that fall under the jurisdiction of cleric-dominated Ministry of Justice and special commercial committees under the sway of the more progressive finance and commerce ministries. Enforcement, however, remains the domain of the Interior Ministry and each province's governor. The result is a legal quagmire, as the country's

economic development has overwhelmed the abilities of the existing courts. Besides having to cope with an inadequate legal code, courts also have to contend with another force as well: the more than 7,000 princes who comprise the House of Saud and who in practice are beyond the jurisdiction of any court.[37]

This also explains why on many banking and financial matters, procedures are increasingly handled through specially created administrations.

The fourth type of Islamic moral hazard is related to possible conflicts of interest in the relations between the bank and its customers. We have already discussed the potential pitfalls of mudaraba or musharaka, whereby the mudarib may be tempted to "privatize the profits and socialize the losses."[38] Similar issues arise in the bank's relation with its depositors, when the roles are reversed and the bank is the mudarib. The logic of an investment account requires the bank to share its net profits with the account holder, on the basis of a certain ratio, say 70 per cent for the depositor and 30 per cent for the bank.[39] Empirical surveys have shown that banks often arbitrarily change distribution ratios, or take advantage of the latitude afforded by accounting rules either to cheat their customers or to achieve short-term gains at the expense of long-term competitiveness or even survival. Thus, when profits of a given institution decline, depositors may still expect a competitive rate of return, or else they may take their savings to a competing bank. Thus, in Egypt, from the mid- to the late 1980s, the IIBID distributed all its profits to investment account depositors, while the shareholders received nothing. In 1988, the bank even had to distribute to its depositors an amount exceeding its total net profit. The difference appeared in the bank's account as "loss carried forward."[40] Clearly such practices fly in the face of sound banking management practices, and cannot be sustained for long, yet they are likely to happen in the absence of strict regulatory controls.

III Marketing Issues and Challenges

Researchers asked ten customers of a now-defunct Islamic bank in London why they had deposited their money with that bank: "Eight of them said they had done so because it was Islamic. All of them said they were disappointed with the services and the treatment they got from the bank."[41] Today, given the intense competition in Islamic finance, few banks could retain such customers, and many banks are actually attempting to sharpen their marketing skills to attract and retain customers.[42] At the heart of the marketing effort lie a few basic questions: who are the actual and potential customers of Islamic financial institutions?; what are their motivations and behavioral characteristics?; what should banks do to reach them?; should the institution compete on the basis of religious credentials or on the basis of products and service?

There are two sets of reasons why people choose to deal with an Islamic financial institution. One is religious or ethical, the other is financial or pragmatic.[43] In the early years, there was an implicit tradeoff between the two since there was often a financial or commercial penalty to dealing with an Islamic institution. Remuneration on deposits, when it existed, was often lower, and lacked the element of certainty, since it depended on the bank's financial performance. The early Islamic institutions were often perceived as lacking experience and expertise. To be sure, there was the possibility that returns on PLS accounts would be higher than conventional interest, but such accounts also carried (in theory) the risk of loss of all or part of the principal.

The early assumption of Islamic finance was that the devout would be willing to sacrifice a share of their wealth as an act of faith, or to express solidarity with their community. In other words, there would be a "piety premium" (in the form of lower remuneration or higher cost) paid by Muslims to satisfy their religious preference. At least, such were the expectations of the first Islamic bankers.[44]

To this day, it is hard to truly measure the relative importance of the two sets of factors (religious–ethical versus financial–pragmatic). For one thing, as in any human endeavor, motives are complex. For another, surveys can be misleading since respondents are always likely to exaggerate the role of the religious motive. In addition, the sheer diversity of the 1.3-billion strong Muslim community worldwide makes any generalization based on a small sample hazardous.[45] This is frustrating from the standpoint of bank marketing. Indeed, while there are countless marketing tools available to segment markets and analyze customers' needs and characteristics,[46] the religious dimension remains elusive.

Perhaps the best way of approaching an answer is to state an axiom: given a choice between two identical products (or two identical banks) one conventional and one Islamic, the devout Muslim will choose the Islamic one. This, of course, may not answer the question, since products or banks are seldom identical, yet it helps to explain the growing convergence between Islamic and conventional banks (conventional banks creating Islamic products, windows, or subsidiaries; Islamic financial institutions broadening their product range, adapting to conventional benchmarks, and reaching to non-Muslims).[47] This in turn poses another marketing question: are all Islamic banks and products equally Islamic?

Surveys show that the two decisive factors in deciding whether an institution is truly Islamic are, first, the existence of a Shariah Board, and, second (in the case of establishments that offer both conventional and religious products), whether there is a clear segregation of funds and operations.[48] Other issues, such as the ownership of the institution (whether it belongs to a Western bank, for example), or whether they may cater to non-Muslims, seem to matter little.[49]

Not surprisingly, the religious dimension is the central part of the marketing effort of financial institutions. With various degrees of subtlety, marketing campaigns have warned against the ills of "usurious interest," denigrated their "usurious" competitors,[50] and associated success with religion. For example, one of the advertising slogans of the Egyptian IMMC, al-Rayyan, was "*al-baraka wara al najah*" or "the blessings behind success."[51] Marketing campaigns are usually stepped up during the holy month of Ramadan.[52]

Religious symbolism is visible in most Islamic financial institutions. The building and decor often reflect Islamic architecture. Koranic sayings often adorn the walls. Banks usually have a prayer room on the premises to help employees and customers fulfill *salat*, the Islamic obligation to pray five times a day. Beyond the traditional savings and checking accounts, banks often offer a Haj fund, designed to help customers save for a pilgrimage to Mecca. Those institutions located outside the Islamic world (where Friday is, therefore, a working day) usually close from 11 a.m. to 3 p.m. on Fridays. Some even close during the day to allow their employees and customers to perform their prayer obligations.

IV Asset-Liability Management

On the surface, income statements and balance sheets of Islamic banks are not fundamentally different from those of conventional banks (see, for example, the financial statements of Kuwait Finance House, below).

Table 8.1 Kuwait Finance House

Consolidated Income Statement
Year ended December 31, 2007

	2007	2006
	(in thousands of KD)*	
Income		
Murabaha, wakala, istisnaa and leasing income	466,893	327,523
Investment income	266,397	183,249
Fee and commission income	56,125	44,008
Net gain from dealing in foreign currencies	14,696	3,332
Other income	27,037	20,875
	831,148	578,987
Expenses		
Staff costs	73,783	72,269
General and administrative expenses	48,134	38,863
Murabaha and ijara costs	65,712	32,041
Depreciation	27,939	33,754
Provision for impairment	38,179	27,180
	253,747	204,107
Profit before Distribution to Depositors	577,401	374,880
Distribution to depositors	242,528	176,362
Profit after Distribution	334,873	198,518
Contribution to Kuwait Foundation		
for the Advancement of Sciences	2,847	1,673
National Labor Support tax	6,257	3,465
Directors' fees	200	150
Zakat (based on Zakat Law No. 46/2006)	174	

Profit for the Year	**325,395**	193,230
Attributable to:		
Equity holders of the bank	**275,266**	162,004
Minority interest	**50,129**	31,226
	325,395	193,230

Basic and Diluted Earnings per Share Attributable to the		
Equity Holders of the Bank	**166 fils**	102 fils

Consolidated Balance Sheet
Year ended December 31, 2007

	2007	2006
	(in thousands of KD)*	
Assets		
Cash and balances with banks and financial institutions	**553,565**	231,996
Short-term international murabaha	**1,067,291**	1,050,599
Receivables	**3,988,131**	2,778,166
Trading properties	**126,413**	90,463
Leased assets	**930,657**	647,939
Available for sale investments	**896,098**	583,351
Investment in associates	**341,279**	210,538
Investment properties	**247,300**	191,407
Other assets	**239,694**	128,327
Property and equipment	**407,488**	401,005
Total Assets	**8,797,916**	6,313,791
Liabilities, Deferred Revenue, Fair Value Reserve, Foreign		
Exchange Translation Reserve and Total Equity Liabilities		
Due to banks and financial institutions	**1,186,391**	1,080,004
Depositors' accounts	**5,361,155**	3,729,930
Other liabilities	**380,853**	289,325
Total Liabilities	**6,928,399**	5,099,259
Deferred Revenue	**374,608**	299,263
Fair Value Reserve	**86,843**	66,654
Foreign Exchange Translation Reserve	**1,972**	8,683
Equity Attributable to the Equity Holders of the Bank		
Share capital	**171,535**	122,525
Share premium	**464,735**	188,788
Proposed issue of bonus shares	**34,307**	18,379
Reserves	**427,925**	302,958
	1,098,502	632,650
Proposed cash dividend	**111,498**	69,839

Total Equity Attributable to the Equity Holders of the Bank	**1,210,000**	702,489
Minority interest	**196,094**	137,443
Total Equity	**1,406,094**	839,932
Total Liabilities, Deferred Revenue, Fair Value Reserve, Foreign Exchange Translation Reserve and Total Equity	**8,797,916**	6,313,791

* KD = US Dollars

The most important difference between Islamic and conventional banks is, on the assets side, that banks engage in a great deal of sale and leasing transactions,[53] and on the liabilities side, that most remunerated Islamic deposits take the form of Profit Sharing Investments Accounts (PSIA), which are essentially mudaraba accounts, where the depositor is the rabb al maal and the bank is the mudarib. Both parties enter into a partnership on the basis of an agreed ratio.[54] As for demand or checking-accounts deposits, they are considered to be the modern-day equivalent of the old Islamic practice of al-Wadiah, or safekeeping.[55]

Beyond those broad principles, specifics vary greatly. In the final analysis, what is allowed in a given country depends on what national regulators (influenced by global as well as Islamic norms) allow. One would readily recognize compromises made by Shariah advisors and bank regulators. For example, for obvious competitive reasons (the need to prevent potential massive withdrawal of funds), the loss component of PLS is actually borne by the Islamic bank alone. In other words, the bank customer will not in practice see any loss of principal. By the same token, although there is some contradiction between deposit insurance and the mudaraba logic, which mandates the sharing of profit as well as loss, regulators increasingly shield depositors from the potential of loss by forcing Islamic banks to become part of their national deposit insurance scheme. Similar compromises can be seen in the treatment of demand or checking deposits. In the early years of Islamic finance, such accounts were to be subjected to 100 per cent reserve requirement, based on the al-Wadiah logic that did not allow banks to put the original deposits to work. Increasingly, however, banks are not held to such strictures; they are simply expected by their regulators to invest such deposits in a conservative manner.

Despite such pragmatic evolution, the logic of asset-liability management (matching maturities of liabilities and assets; anticipating withdrawals; managing risk, etc.) in Islamic banks can be quite different from that of conventional banks. Yet, given the youth of the Islamic finance industry, there is a paucity of historical data that would allow us to determine with precision the risk profile of Islamic banks. A few broad principles can nevertheless be stated. The most fundamental, though often forgotten, one is that although Islamic products have often set out to mimic or recreate conventional products, they remain, from a legal, prudential, or regulatory perspective, different from conventional ones.[56] Another is that the asset-liability management function is complicated by the fact that Islamic banks are hampered by the paucity of hedging, risk management, and liquidity management tools.

The concentration of Islamic banks in politically volatile countries makes them more vulnerable to political risk. During the Gulf War in 1991, the Islamic banks in the Gulf region lost about 40 per cent of their deposits.[57] In those days, they were generally not part of deposit insurance programs that could reassure depositors and prevent massive withdrawals. Neither could they depend on the flexibility afforded either by a secondary market, or by a ready discount window. Securitization was generally not an option, nor was there a true Islamic inter-bank market to help fund daily liquidity. Conventional banks in contrast can reassure their depositors by providing deposit insurance, and they have flexibility in managing their assets and liabilities by reselling their loans to other finan-cial institutions, by transforming those loans into tradable securities, by using the discount facilities of their central bank, or by borrowing on the interbank market.

When it comes to risk management, Islamic banks face, in addition to those risks that are common to all banks, certain risks that are specific to them. They may, for example, face a commodities and inventory risk that stems from holding items in inventory either for resale in a murabaha or for leasing. Islamic institutions may also face specific risks related to PSIA: fiduciary risk (as bank mismanagement can give rise to litigation); displaced commercial risk (due to return-smoothing); and profit distribution risk. Islamic banks may also be confronted by a Shariah risk, related to possible changes in religious interpretation (where, as happened recently in connection with sukuk, existing practices can be deemed illicit). Though asset-liability management tools have improved in recent years, in part thanks to initiatives undertaken by the IFSB, they still have a long way to go.[58]

V Cultural Issues and Challenges

Many of the challenges faced by Islamic banks, especially when it comes to the gap between the promise and the performance of Islamic finance, are cultural and related to matters of risk and trust. Understanding culture is tricky since, in addition to its specifically religious component, it is the product of complex historical processes and is embedded within a political-economic order. Islamic institutions also evolve within, and interact with, a global financial system that has a culture of its own.

Every community or institution has, in the anthropological sense, a culture. Culture has been defined as "everything that people have, think, and do as members of their community."[59] It is principally about ideas, values, and attitudes as well as normative or expected patterns of behavior. By the same token, every bank can be said to have its own culture: "A bank's shared values constitute its culture. Such cultural values may relate to how communications take place, how decisions are made, or how people get ahead in the organization. They are the signature, the 'what makes us different,' of a bank."[60]

Given the diversity of the Islamic world, a common cultural denominator is elusive. Many authors hesitate to tread on that ground for fear of appearing unscientific or politically incorrect. Yet the reality of the cultural element is inescapable.[61] Luckily, a number of anthropologists have taken an interest in Islamic finance,[62] which raises the hope that this aspect of Islamic finance will be better understood in the future. Although a lot in this section is anecdotal and country-specific, broader patterns are emerging which account for the difficulties in developing PLS arrangements that are at the core of the Islamic banking philosophy.

Culture is notoriously tricky to analyze. It is multifaceted, somewhat amorphous and hard to pin down; it is closely intertwined with history and institutions. Culture does not emerge in a vacuum. It is the product of historical processes and socioeconomic variables. It is significant from our standpoint because it influences investors' preferences: in an uncertain political and economic environment people like to hold gold or cash and are wary of long-term risk; people accustomed to high inflation favor real estate and tangible assets; minorities who fear confiscation and expulsion feel safer owning jewelry and valuables that can be transported.

Different Islamic communities have had different histories, and thus different relations to money. Historical and anthropological observations capture some of these differences. Maxime Rodinson has noted, for example, "the traditions of generosity for the sake of prestige, familiar to the leaders of the desert communities."[63] Such a trait has undeniable political, economic, and financial implications in today's patrimonial Gulf states. In contrast, the image of financiers and businessmen as entrepreneurs à la Schumpeter, who thrive on risk and creative destruction, does not quite fit much of the contemporary Islamic context. Conservatism and risk avoidance are the rule. Consider, for example, this description of the typical Egyptian businessman:

> A Cairene entrepreneur, even one who faces no serious competition, still has to cope with unpredictable changes in inflation, vacillating exchange rates, and capricious government policies. The country lacks genuine capital markets, so the odds are that the entrepreneur's capital represents the sum of his family resources, either saved over long years or inherited from some glorious ancestor. One of the reasons that rent seeking is such a popular technique among businessmen is that it holds risk to a minimum. It is a way of getting the government to guarantee against the risks of certain ventures. As a result, Egyptian businessmen are not unimaginative, but they are justifiably cautious.[64]

Risk avoidance, given their experience and the environment within which they operate, is a perfectly rational behavior for many entrepreneurs. Long-term investment requires a culture and institutions that are predictable and foster trust.[65] In order to take a calculated risk, the entrepreneur will expect political and economic stability in his environment, and consistency in the enforcement of the law. In much of the Islamic world, people still have memories of expropriation and arbitrary decisions by governments that have adversely affected their business ventures.[66] Rampant inflation also discourages long-term investment, and so do currency fluctuations which can wipe out savings overnight.[67]

Another factor is that the worlds of business and finance are likely to be politicized and embedded within social institutions (family, tribe, ethnic or religious group). "Connected lending" (lending to entities otherwise related to the financial institutions) tends to be very high, and when loans go bad, custom and social mores prevent the use of modern enforcement techniques (foreclosures, forced bankruptcies, etc.). The protection of the law is not always assured, and the Islamic moral hazard discussed earlier is likely to make things worse. In many countries, delaying payment is a common practice, and defaulting borrowers – provided that they are well connected – are beyond the reach of the law.[68]

In that environment, successful financial institutions are often the most risk-averse. They are, therefore, unlikely to engage in risky entrepreneurial finance. Edmond Safra (1932–99), scion of a Syrian Jewish family that had been involved in banking for generations, who later went on to create a financial empire in Switzerland, Brazil, and the United States, and was long the preferred banker of many Middle Eastern potentates, stated his philosophy of banking as follows: "The book on banking was written 6,000 years ago. Banking is a simple, stupid business. First and foremost, you safeguard depositors' money – you, the banker, not the Federal Deposit Insurance Corporation. You invest it safely and pay your depositors a little less than the interest you receive. You keep your expenses low."[69] His banking precepts were inherited from a long tradition.[70] One precept he learned from his father was that "if you loan a man too much money, you turn a good man into a bad man."[71] This may be an apt, if forgotten, piece of advice.

The oil windfall has to some extent corrupted many elements of Middle Eastern business and finance, creating get-rich-quick mind-sets and favoring greed. The propensity to speculate in international financial markets and sometimes in domestic ones, may seem paradoxical, given the conservatism noted earlier (and, of course, in the light of the religious teachings of Islam), but it is easy to explain. Empirical studies show that investors in a bullish market, especially when they think that they are (by virtue of their "connections") insiders, often feel that speculative risk is preferable to productive risk.[72] Safra's general comments hint at the cultural and institutional difficulties associated with a more complex, participatory form of finance such as PLS.

Many observers have noted the correlation between Islamic views on risk and contemporary practices, especially in the Arab Middle East.[73] As other parts of the book show (in particular, Chapter 3), the injunctions against gharar are not injunctions against risk *per se*, but against dubious practices which include speculation, deceptive ambiguity, and risk shifting. Also, the prohibition of riba has made finance as a whole suspicious in the eyes of many Muslims. Perhaps the major remaining obstacle is in achieving coherence and consistency in laws and institutions, hoping that in due course it will transform the culture and reduce the Islamic moral hazard.

In justifying the paucity of long-term investment, there is a lot of blame to go around. Governments do not offer sufficient incentives: "individuals and enterprises are at the mercy of administrative interpretations and applications, and can only succeed through the informal facilitation and evasions of bureaucratic functionaries."[74] Banks, reluctant to develop PLS products, set the bar so high that few investments qualify. Many borrowers have manipulated the system to their advantage. Only a concerted effort can resolve the problem. The challenges ahead are twofold: banks themselves need to work at transforming their cultures; they also need to work at changing their surrounding political and business culture. Indeed, the necessity for change may be expressed in economic terms, but strong political impediments stand in the way.[75]

As a first step, Islamic banks must work to change their own operations, procedures, and culture. A prerequisite to instilling a culture fostering the development of PLS products is a better understanding on the part of bank managers and executives of the logic of venture capital.[76] This will result in the creation of successful, long-term products and in turn, by building a track record, instill the necessary confidence in the public.

The challenge of cultural change is all the greater since it should not simply consist in adopting the culture of global finance, with its often predatory and amoral features, but temper it with the moral values of Islam. Nabil Saleh wrote:

> It is not uncommon, in secular transactions, for one of the parties to be stronger than the other, or perhaps cleverer or more experienced; so the disadvantaged party is in need of some kind of protection and guidance before an agreement is concluded or a bargain struck. This was even more the case during the Prophet's time, when substantial difference in terms of enlightenment and development existed between bedouins and townsmen, and even between townsmen belonging to different settlements. One established hadith tells that Muhammad forbade a transaction known as talaqi al-rukban, which is a sale whereby a townsman meets a tribesman outside the market place and buys the tribesman's goods at a price cheaper than the price prevailing in the market, thus taking advantage of the seller's ignorance of the market price.[77]

One cannot help but relate this quote to contemporary accounts of the brave new world of finance. In his account of his experience as a mortgage bond salesman at Salomon Brothers, Michael Lewis describes the ways in which today's "townsmen" (New York traders) fleeced the "tribesmen" (regional savings and loans managers). He writes:

> The men on the trading floor may not have been to school, but they have Ph.D.'s in man's ignorance. In any market, as in any poker game, there is a fool. The astute investor Warren Buffett is fond of saying that any player unaware of the fool in the market probably *is* the fool in the market.

… Salomon bond traders knew about fools because that was their job. Knowing about markets is knowing about other people's weaknesses. And a fool, they would say was a person who was willing to sell a bond for less or buy a bond for more than it was worth. A bond was worth only as much as the person who valued it properly was willing to pay. And Salomon, to complete the circle, was the firm that valued the bonds properly.[78]

Similarly, Lewis identifies the inevitable conflicts of interest that accompany financial innovation: "If it was a good deal, the bankers kept it for themselves; if it was a bad deal, they'd sell it to their customers."[79]

Or consider Frank Partnoy's account of his experience selling complicated derivatives such as repackaged asset vehicles (RAVs), and principal exchange rate linked securities (PERLS) for Morgan Stanley. Such risky vehicles – "complex foreign exchange bets packaged to look like simple and safe bonds" – were sold to unsuspecting clients. The following quotes encapsulate the culture of the derivatives business: "Morgan Stanley carefully cultivated this urge to blast a client to smithereens." "No one seemed to care about whether clients actually understood what they were buying." "A salesman cared only about making the sale, not about the damage it might cause later. All derivatives salesmen knew that eventually some of their trades would blow up, and some of their clients would then go up in flames." "Wall Street has made, and continues to make, a huge amount of money on derivatives by trickery or deceit." "Derivatives are the most recent example of a basic theme in the history of finance: Wall Street bilks Main Street."[80]

VI Islamic Finance and Financial Bubbles

Like other financial institutions, Islamic institutions are subject to cycles of boom and bust, and despite their inherent conservatism, they are not immune to bubbles. It is true that Islamic finance emerged relatively unscathed from the first stages of the 2007–8 financial crisis, namely the sub-prime phase and the credit default swaps debacle.[81] But as soon as the effects of the crisis went beyond the financial sector and hit the real economy, the Islamic sector, being primarily asset-based, was negatively affected by the ensuing recession.

The economic downturn has exposed problems that were hidden by years of rapid growth. Indeed, as Warren Buffett once observed: "You only learn who has been swimming naked when the tide goes out – and what we are witnessing at some of our largest financial institutions is an ugly sight."[82] The religious factor makes it easy to forget that what is religiously permissible is not necessarily advisable from a business standpoint. And Islamic banks are also not immune to incompetence, greed, or outright fraud.

Yet the effects of the bursting bubble are likely to be different. First, because of their link to the real economy, Islamic institutions are not likely to be as exposed as institutions that gobbled up toxic assets.[83] Second, the aftermath of the bubble is likely to be different. After the failure of a certain asset class, investors usually tend to leave it in droves. Yet experience suggests that investors will not necessary leave the Islamic sector; rather, as happened before, Islamic institutions will adjust their practices and instruments, and Islamic products will remain in high demand.

Notes

1. Charles Kindleberger, *Manias, Panics, and Crashes: A History of Financial Crises* (New York: Basic Books, 1979).
2. Robin Allen, *The Financial Times*, November 28, 1995.
3. Ibrahim Warde, "Comparing the Profitability of Islamic and Conventional Banks," San Francisco, IBPC Working Papers, 1997.
4. This is obviously subjective, but the rationale is that the choice to engage in Islamic finance should not be simply opportunistic and not easily reversible.
5. Ibrahim Warde, "How Islamic is Islamic?," AIU Financial Consulting Working Paper, Boston 2009.
6. See Chapter 10.
7. Ibrahim A. Warde, "Sovereign Wealth Funds and the Politics of Boom and Bust," in Sven Behrendt and Bassma Kodmani (eds.), *Managing Arab Sovereign Wealth in Turbulent Times – and Beyond*, Carnegie Middle East Center: 16, April 2009.
8. Hamid Algabid, *Les banques islamiques* (Paris: Economics, 1990), p. 193.
9. *The Christian Science Monitor*, March 13, 1986.
10. See Chapter 4.
11. *The Wall Street Journal Europe*, June 16, 1998.
12. See Chapter 7.
13. See Chapters 4, 12, and Conclusion.
14. See Conclusion.
15. Zuhayr Mikdashi, *Les banques à l'ère de la mondialisation* (Paris: Economica, 1998), pp. 38–9.
16. Ibrahim Warde, "Les assises du système bancaire détruites par la déréglementation," *Le Monde diplomatique*, January 1991.
17. Quoted in Fuad al-Omar and Mohammed Abdel-Haq, *Islamic Banking: Theory, Practice and Challenges* (London: Zed Books, 1996).
18. Elias Kazarian, *Islamic versus Traditional Banking: Financial Innovation in Egypt* (Boulder, CO: Westview Press, 1993), p. 59.
19. Herve de Carmoy, *Strategie Bancaire: Le Refus de la Derive* (Paris: Presses Universitaires de France, 1988) p. 35.
20. See Ibrahim Warde, "Corporate Governance and the Islamic Moral Hazard," in S. Nazim Ali (ed.), *Islamic Finance: Current Legal and Regulatory Issues* (Cambridge, MA: Islamic Finance Project Islamic Legal Studies Program, Harvard Law School, 2005).
21. Ibrahim Warde, "Bernard Madoff, à la barbe des régulateurs de la finance," *Le Monde diplomatique*, August 2009.
22. Luigi DiFonzo, *St. Peter's Banker: Michele Sindona* (New York: Franklin Watts, 1983).
23. Algabid, *Les banques islamiques*, p. 182.
24. Al-Omar and Abdel-Haq, *Islamic Banking*, p. 43.
25. Al-Omar and Abdel-Haq, *Islamic Banking*, p. 43.
26. *Saudi Gazette*, April 1, 1998.
27. Agence France-Presse, April 1, 1998.
28. *The Atlanta Journal-Constitution*, August 30, 1998.
29. See Roula Khalaf, "Dubai's Islamic Bank Mystery," *The Financial Times*, June 23, 2008 and Simeon Kerr, "Seven Charged over Alleged $501m Dubai Fraud," *The Financial Times*, March 9, 2009.
30. Sami Zubeida, "Is Iran an Islamic State?," in Joel Beinin and Joe Stork (eds.), *Political Islam: Essays from Middle East Report* (Berkeley, CA: University of California Press, 1997), p. 113.

31. Preface to Nabil Saleh, *Unlawful Gain and Legitimate Profit in Islamic Law* (Cambridge: Cambridge University Press, 1986).

32. Frank E. Vogel and Samuel L. Hayes, III, *Islamic Law and Finance: Religion, Risk and Return* (Cambridge, MA: Kluwer Law International, 1998).

33. Vogel and Hayes, *Islamic Law and Finance*, p. 139.

34. Al-Omar and Abdel-Haq, *Islamic Banking*, p. 101.

35. Ibrahim Warde, "Bankruptcy, Financial Distress and Debt Restructuring," paper presented at the 2nd Annual Islamic Finance Symposium, "Islamic Finance: Resilience in a Time of Financial Crisis?," Boalt Hall, UC Berkeley School of Law, February 28, 2009.

36. Peter W. Wilson, *A Question of Interest: The Paralysis of Saudi Banking* (Boulder, CO: Westview Press, 1991), p. 109.

37. Wilson, *A Question of Interest*, p. 8.

38. See Chapter 7.

39. Increasingly, a share of the profits also goes to a smoothing reserve.

40. Kazarian, *Islamic versus Traditional Banking*, p. 179.

41. Al-Omar and Abdel-Haq, *Islamic Banking*, p. 45.

42. Ibrahim Warde, "Comparing the Profitability of Islamic and Conventional Banks."

43. In most cases, it means attractive remuneration of accounts or low cost of transactions. Pragmatic factors can also relate to convenience (say, for example, a convenient location) and other factors unrelated to religion or ethical preferences.

44. *Al Mausua al Ilmiya wa al Amaliya lil Bunuk al Islamiya* (*Handbook of Islamic Banking*) (Cairo: International Association of Islamic Banks, 1977), vol. 1, p. 10.

45. See Chapter 1.

46. See, for example, Jeffrey Westergren, "Customer Profiling Resource," *Bank Marketing*, vol. 28, March 1996, and Katherine Morrall, "Technology Updates Market Research Methods," *Bank Marketing*, vol. 26, April 1994.

47. See Chapter 4.

48. The third factor usually mentioned in fatwas on Islamic windows of non-Islamic banks – the commitment to the idea of Islamic finance, or more concretely, the commitment to maintaining the Islamic window, is seldom mentioned by customers of Islamic banks.

49. Ibrahim Warde "How Islamic is Islamic?."

50. Clement M. Henry, *The Mediterranean Debt Crescent: Money and Power in Algeria, Egypt, Morocco, Tunisia and Turkey* (Gainsville, FL: University Press of Florida, 1996), p. 263.

51. *Al-Ahram al-Iqtisadi*, July 18, 1985.

52. Michel Galloux, *Finance islamique et pouvoir politique: le cas de l'Egypte moderne* (Paris: Presses Universitaires de France, 1997), p. 66.

53. See Chapter 7.

54. Often there is a three-way division, for example, 40 per cent for the bank, 40 per cent for the customer, and 20 per cent for smoothing reserves (which help mitigate profit fluctuations over the years).

55. In a nomadic society it was common for merchants to entrust their money and valuables to other merchants on the basis of al-Wadiah. They would typically pay a fee for such safekeeping, and (unlike later Italian bankers) were not authorized to put such money to use in the meantime.

56. See Chapter 7.

57. Vogel and Hayes, *Islamic Law and Finance*, p. 8.

58. See Chapter 4.

59. Gary P. Ferraro, *The Cultural Dimension of International Business* (Englewood Cliffs, NJ: Prentice Hall, 1990), p. 18.

60. Steven I. Davis, *Excellence in Banking* (London: Macmillan, 1985), p. 14.

61. Ibrahim Warde, "The Analysis of Culture: Navigating between Economic Correctness

and Political Correctness," Unpublished paper.

62. Bill Maurer, *Mutual Life, Limited: Islamic Banking, Alternative Currencies, Lateral Reason* (New Haven, CT: Princeton University Press, 2005), and Bill Maurer, *Pious Property: Islamic Mortgages in the United States* (New York: Russell Sage Foundation Publications, 2006).

63. Maxime Rodinson, *Islam and Capitalism* (London: Penguin, 1978), p. 28.

64. Yahya M. Sadowski, *Political Vegetables? Businessman and Bureaucrat in the Development of Egyptian Agriculture* (Washington, DC: The Brookings Institution, 1991), p. 199.

65. Alain Peyrefitte, *La société de confiance* (Paris: Editions Odile Jacob, 1995).

66. Alan Richards, "Economic Imperatives and Political Systems," *Middle East Journal* (Spring 1993), p. 225.

67. Ibrahim Warde, "Les remèdes absurdes du Fonds monétaire international," *Le Monde diplomatique*, February 1998.

68. Peter W. Wilson, *A Question of Interest: The Paralysis of Saudi Banking* (Boulder, CO: Westview Press, 1991), pp. 4–8.

69. *Business Week*, March 7, 1994.

70. Bryan Burrough, *Vendetta: American Express and the Smearing of Edmond Safra* (New York: HarperCollins, 1992), p. 43.

71. *Business Week*, March 7, 1994.

72. Ibrahim Warde, "Middle Eastern Investment in the US," paper presented at the Middle Eastern Studies Association Annual Meeting, San Francisco, 1984.

73. Rodinson, *Islam and Capitalism*, pp. 161–2.

74. Sami Zubaida, "Religion, the State, and Democracy: Contrasting Conceptions of Society in Egypt," in Joel Beinin and Joe Stork (eds.), *Political Islam: Essays from Middle East Report* (Berkeley, CA: University of California Press, 1997), p. 51.

75. Sadowski, *Political Vegetables?*

76. Ibrahim Warde, "Islamic Profit-and-Loss Sharing: Lessons from the Venture Capital Experience," IBPC Working Papers, 1999.

77. Nabil Saleh, *Unlawful Gain and Legitimate Profit in Islamic Law* (Cambridge: Cambridge University Press, 1986), p. 49.

78. Michael Lewis, *Liar's Poker: Rising Through the Wreckage on Wall Street* (New York: W. W. Norton, 1989), p. 35.

79. Lewis, *Liar's Poker*, p. 222.

80. Frank Partnoy, *FIASCO: Blood in the Water on Wall Street* (New York: W. W. Norton, 1997).

81. See Chapter 4.

82. Francesco Guerrera and Justin Baer, "Buffett Defends Sovereign Wealth Funds," *The Financial Times*, February 29, 2008.

83. As already explained, there are a few exceptions, since in the case of tawarroq or bay' al 'ina, the link to real assets is spurious. See Chapter 7.

9

ECONOMIC ISSUES:
ISLAMIC FINANCE AND DEVELOPMENT

Insofar as "money is the only good that trades against all other goods," the financial sector "is unique in the degree to which its markets, prices, institutions, and policies impinge upon all others."[1] More specifically, in any modern economy, financial systems are central to long-term economic development in that:

(1) they facilitate trade: at the most rudimentary level, money minimizes the need for barter and thereby encourages commerce and specialization;

(2) they facilitate risk management, by pricing risk and providing mechanisms for pooling, ameliorating, and trading risk;

(3) financial intermediaries mobilize resources from disparate savers to investment in worthwhile investment projects;

(4) financial systems obtain information and evaluate firms, projects, and managers; and

(5) financial systems provide corporate governance. It is difficult if not impossible for individual investors to evaluate and monitor the performance of firm managers. Consequently, financial intermediaries are often charged with compelling managers to act in the best interests of firm claim holders (stockholders or creditors).[2]

Promoters of Islamic finance have argued that Islamic finance is not only consistent with capitalism (that is, with a market-driven allocation of resources), but that it is in many ways better suited to a dynamic economy. More specifically, Islamic finance could bring about more efficient mobilization of savings, more equitable and just distribution of resources, more responsible and profitable lending, as well as less volatile business cycles and more stable banking systems.[3]

This, of course, is the theory. The difficult part has been to translate the broad principles of Islamic finance into concrete reality. More specifically, in order to contribute to the process of economic growth and development, banks must learn how to transform savings into real investments, and how to do it efficiently – transforming small deposits into larger loans, acting as risk arbitrageurs among investments with different rates of return and risk levels, devising an attractive mix of financial instruments, etc. Following some comments on Islam and economic liberalism, this chapter considers four sets of economic issues and challenges: the mobilization of savings; economic development and fund allocation; Islamic capital markets; and macro-economic policies. The final part of the chapter discusses the respective roles of Islamic finance in project finance and poverty reduction.

I Islam and Economic Liberalism

Dominant approaches to development have changed dramatically since the 1980s.[4] Until then, development theorists emphasized "top-down" industrialization, with the state playing the main role in the economy. Economies were supposed to grow through centrally-planned development and import substitution policies.[5] Even in those countries committed to free enterprise, government agencies in charge of economic development established broad policy guidelines, and the role of the state kept increasing. The nationalization of oil and banking in Saudi Arabia and other Gulf states in the 1970s is a case in point. In most countries, the financial sector was used as a tool to implement the developmental goals of governments.[6]

Since the 1980s these policy dogmas have been reversed: export-led industrialization; privatization; and disengagement of the state have become the order of the day. The growing interest in Islamic economics and finance is not unrelated to these policy developments.[7] In the words of Karen Pfeifer:

> Far from being a throwback to the social system of the Middle Ages, Islamic economics is … a set of ideas evolving in the last decades of the twentieth century to explain and address the economic problems faced by the citizens of predominantly Islamic countries. Islamic economics responds to the achievements and failures of, first, state capitalism, and, second, the international capitalist system's antidote to state capitalism – economic liberalization.[8]

One should, however, be wary of drawing broad conclusions with regard to state-market or public–private relations. In assessing Egypt's infitah policy, Robert Springborg observed:

> Instead of undertaking basic structural reforms which would create an environment truly conducive to private investment, the government of Egypt has been preoccupied with tinkering with the legal superstructure. The tinkering has produced some more liberal conditions governing investment, but the gain is partially offset by uncertainty resulting from the tinkering itself. Moreover, even while seeking to entice private investment through special incentives, the Egyptian authorities have presided simultaneously over the further expansion of the state's role in the economy. Public revenue as a percentage of GDP climbed steadily during the infitah, rising from 34.4 per cent in 1975 to 43 per cent in 1984. The state, far from withdrawing from this arena in favor of private enterprise has occupied a greater share of it.[9]

In the twenty-first century, the coexistence of a commitment to economic liberalism, as evidenced by the entry of a number of Islamic states in the WTO, and a

resurgence of government power, fueled by a combination of economic and political factors (respectively, the oil boom of 2003–8, which replenished government
coffers in energy-rich countries, and the requirements of the "war on terror,"
which justified greater government intrusiveness) was further institutionalized.[10]

II Economic Development Issues

1 The Mobilization of Savings

(a) The Special Role of Banks

In most Islamic countries, banks are by far the main source of finance because
alternatives, such as capital markets, are, despite recent gains, still under-devel-
oped. They operate the payments systems, purchase most government bonds,
and are essential to the operation of all parts of the economic system. In such
an environment, banking assets tend to grow much faster than the economy as
a whole. Conversely, since banks hold the lion's share of financial assets and
are the dominant financial intermediaries, banking crises tend to hit developing
economies particularly hard.[11]

The Bank for International Settlements (BIS) has noted that rapid economic
growth in the 1990s "has led to an extraordinary expansion in the ratio of bank
credit to GDP that has no recent parallel in the industrial countries." The ratio in
Indonesia rocketed from 8.1 per cent in 1980 to 49.1 per cent in 1995. In Malaysia
the figures are 33.1 per cent and 76.9 per cent. (In the United States in the same
period the ratio rose from 62.1 per cent to just 63.3 per cent.)[12] Such rapid growth
is likely to create "lending bubbles" as abundant funds chase a limited number of
truly creditworthy ventures and tend to concentrate in short-term and speculative areas such as real estate and stock market investment. As soon as a downturn
occurs, many of these loans are likely to become irrecoverable and the cost of
supporting, recapitalizing, or restructuring the banking sector is likely to amount
to a large percentage of the GDP.

Banking in much of the Islamic world also tends to epitomize "crony capitalism."
To an even greater extent than industrial countries, banks in emerging markets
have very close ties with governments, and bankers are likely to belong to closed
elite circles.[13] In its survey of Middle Eastern billionaires, *Forbes* notes that banking
is a "proven route to riches": "All of the 11 billionaires and 2 of the heavy hitters
from the region are bankers or own stakes in banks."[14] One of the consequences
is that regulators often come under pressures to turn a blind eye to the impru-
dent practices of some bankers. "'What do you do if the president's brother
owns a bank,' asks one Southeast Asian supervisor. 'The answer is you leave him
alone.'"[15]

Within such an environment, the role of finance is skewed. Rather than going
to worthwhile investment projects, financing goes primarily to "well-connected"
borrowers or "politically-exposed persons" (PEP). Other functions mentioned
above – obtaining information, evaluating firms, projects and managers, and

providing corporate governance – are similarly distorted. Also, banks are often considered to be "trophies" that inexperienced businesspeople pay a high price to acquire, and sometimes mismanage or treat like a piggybank, at a high cost for the economy as a whole.[16]

(b) Informal Finance

In most developing countries there is an informal or parallel financial sector that is unregulated and does not appear in official accounts.[17] Prior to September 11, the goal of governments was one of double integration – of underground economies into legal national economies, and of national economy into the global system. Peruvian economis, Hernando de Soto, has been a strong advocate of ending the system of "legal apartheid" by bringing the poor, heretofore confined to the informal sector, into the legal economy. The influential economist also argued that this would offer a chance to resolve the problem of terrorism.[18] Yet, on the other hand, pressures to remain, or go further, underground have greatly increased especially in the context of the "war on terror."[19] It is not clear that the raft of laws and regulations, especially in developing countries, where people are accustomed to breaking cumbersome and "absurdly impractical" regulations,[20] had the intended effect. Many felt threatened and unduly singled out by national and international authorities, recreating a justification for going underground. In de Soto's words, many people "do not so much break the law as the law breaks them – and they opt out of the system."[21] Since its inception, one of the ambitions of Islamic finance has been to contribute to bringing the underground sector into the legal economy, but the results remain inconclusive.

The informal market includes not only black-market money changers and traders, but also deposits and savings accounts as well as loans. One mechanism, known as rotating savings and credit associations (ROSCAs), is described as follows by the World Bank: "ROSCAs intermediate in the most basic way. A small number of individuals, typically six to forty, form a group and select a leader who periodically collects a given amount [a share] from each member. The money collected [the fund] is then given in rotation to each member of the group."[22]

Historically, informal markets have emerged either out of the inability of the official sector to accommodate certain types of transactions, or out of a refusal by certain groups – for a variety of reasons including religious misgivings, lack of trust, fear of confiscation, avoidance of currency reporting requirements, and tax evasion – to integrate into the official government system. Within informal networks, religion, ethnicity, kinship, or neighborhood affiliations provide a sense of trust and act as substitutes for legally enforceable obligations.[23] The risk of social ostracism is indeed an effective enforcement mechanism.[24]

Economists disagree as to the merits of informal sectors. For hardcore free-marketeers, such sectors – insofar as they emerge spontaneously and are not "distorted" by government intervention or hamstrung by "financial repression" – represent true markets.[25] According to this view, a combination of excessive regulation, artificially low interest rates – which act as a disincentive to savings –

and directed credit – which in effect subsidizes certain sectors, certain groups, and certain regions at the expense of others – is harmful to economic development.[26] In countries such as Yemen or Somalia, the informal banking sector has for a long time been a factor of economic stability.[27] Critics, however, see inherent limits in informal markets. They are likely to remain small scale, and thus exclude significant segments of the population. And conversely, if they expand too fast, they are even more prone to fraud and abuse than the official sector under comparable circumstances. They also deprive the government of much needed revenues and prevent the conduct of a coherent macro-economic policy.

This is where Islamic finance can be seen as an attractive middle ground. One of the strong selling points of Islamic finance is that it attracts funds that would otherwise have remained outside the national financial system – sent abroad, kept "under mattresses," or otherwise hoarded, or at best confined to the informal sector. In the Islamic world, two main reasons are said to account for the refusal of some people to deposit their money in banking institutions: religious factors relating to interest payments; and the lack of trust in domestic financial institutions – the fear that they will collapse or that deposits will be confiscated by the government.[28]

Estimates as to the amounts left out of traditional banking circuits are hard to come by. Hikmet Guler, general manager of Turkey's Faisal Finance Institution, estimated in the late 1990s that in Turkey alone, some $50 billion were held outside the banking system.[29] Assuming that the estimate is realistic, the implication – in a country with a parallel Islamic sector that has only $1.5 billion in deposits – is that were Islamic banks allowed to expand and operate with fewer constraints, most of these funds would find their way into the official banking sector.

Yet it is not enough to create Islamic financial institutions. Such institutions must provide the necessary facilities, inspire confidence, and provide attractive investment options. Insofar as conventional banking is usually concentrated in prosperous enclaves and barely penetrates poor, rural, and remote areas,[30] the task of Islamic institutions is to fill that gap. But expanding a network to rural areas and servicing small accounts are not the best ways of building profitable operations.

Perhaps even more difficult than the logistical aspects are the psychological ones. In areas where people are used to keeping their (usually meager) savings under the proverbial mattresses, the language and symbolism of religion may help, but it is likely to be insufficient, at least from a developmental perspective. Indeed, a further challenge to Islamic banks is to promote investment accounts: that is, accounts that will serve to finance PLS operations. In contrast to conventional savings accounts which are usually short term (and often insured), these accounts are oriented toward the long term, and their fate depends on the success (or failure) of the corresponding investments. The possibility of losing one's savings does little to reassure the suspicious. Hence, the need to engage in a serious education and marketing effort and most importantly by a sustained effort at building confidence and a track record. Financial institutions must develop instruments that are convenient to small savers, intelligible to people unaccustomed to modern banking, and remunerative enough to be appealing.[31]

2 Islamic Banks and Economic Development

In the process of transforming savings into investments, Islamic financial institutions are different from conventional lenders insofar as they must take into account social and developmental factors. In that respect, Islamic banks are expected to play the role once played by state banks and development agencies. Those functions, as described by the *Handbook of Islamic Banking*, can be summarized as follows:[32]

- Broad social–economic benefits: investment policies must reflect the needs and the aspirations of the majority of the population, which must be included in the development process. Banks must favor projects in the food, housing, and health services sectors, in order to ensure their adequate supply and affordability.

- Job creation and focus on promising economic sectors: the emphasis should be on value-added sectors, as well as those sectors favored by national plans and objectives. Such sectors include agriculture, industry, and technology-intensive activities because of their potential for job creation, improvement of the balance of payments, and the promotion of technology and education.

- The promotion and stimulation of entrepreneurship: through PLS mechanisms such as mudaraba and musharaka, banks must give priority to small enterprises. Financing must be specific to each firm's economic and financial conditions. Banks must provide technical advice in order to improve the process of production. After a venture becomes self-sustaining, the bank should sell its share to the entrepreneur or other beneficiaries in order to free up funds that can be used to finance new ventures.

- The promotion of social justice and equality and the alleviation of poverty, through the establishment of a zakat fund, for the collection and distribution of funds to the poor, and the provision of interest-free loans (qard hassan) to deserving individuals.

- The regional distribution of investments must follow two sometimes contradictory principles: the promotion of regional balance, that is, channeling money to under-invested areas thus forestalling the need to migrate to more prosperous areas, along with the principle of investing savings mostly in the area where they have been mobilized, thus ensuring that people benefit from their savings.

These ideals reflect the mood and values of the period of the aggiornamento of Islamic finance. For one thing, state planning and top-down industrialization were still the norm in the 1970s. There was also a heady sense of solidarity and new beginnings, mixed with populism. For example, Islamic banks were not allowed to take part in the production and marketing of luxury activities (*israf wa taraf*), at least not until the basic needs of society were met.[33] Islamic finance was perceived as the key to economic development, providing long-term funding to businesses that would otherwise have no access to finance. More generally, it was supposed to bring about balanced economic development, social justice, and an equitable distribution of income and wealth.

Undoubtedly, the gap between promise and performance was greatest in the area of economic development. Despite the support and special privileges (such as guarantees against nationalization) obtained by Islamic banks, they behaved like risk-averse agents. The early goal of concentrating on PLS was soon abandoned. The objective of penetrating the hinterland and serving rural areas was not fulfilled.

Most evidence highlights the tendency of Islamic banks to invest in short-term commercial transactions as opposed to industry or agriculture. In Sudan, an agricultural country, only about 4 per cent of the investments were allocated to agriculture, while 90 per cent went to import–export operations.[34] In Egypt, statistics compiled between 1979 and 1991 compared Islamic banks unfavorably with conventional banks on matters of productive and domestic investment. There are no comprehensive or comparative surveys on the subject, but anecdotal evidence as well as a number of case studies suggest that the promise of bringing into the system a heretofore neglected segment of the market has not been fulfilled. Elias Kazarian's study of the Egyptian case suggests that much of the increase in Islamic bank deposits occurred at the expense of conventional banks (and was driven by the increase in the remuneration of accounts), that most of the activities of Islamic banks have been in large cities as opposed to the countryside where they most needed,[35] and that their main customers were likely to be the well-to-do, and not the poor or the lower middle class.[36] Not only were Islamic banks less likely to invest in industry or agriculture, but they were more likely to invest their money abroad and to keep it in foreign currency.[37] In fairness to Islamic banks, it should be said that the more rigorous and reliable surveys were conducted before what we refer to as the third stage of Islamic finance, when rapid growth combined with a greater concern for a return to the basics of Islamic finance may yet result with a better alignment of promise and performance.

3 Islamic Capital Markets

Islamic finance, with its long-term, equity-based orientation was supposed to be an acceptable substitute for capital and stock markets. But as we have seen, banks have been reluctant to finance mudaraba and musharaka operations. There is thus a renewed interest in creating and nurturing national financial markets – all the more so since capital and equity markets – usually considered to be the most efficient means of financial intermediation – are almost a prerequisite to participation in the global economy. A number of factors are driving the trend toward the creation of national capital and equity markets: the new ideological consensus; pressures from international organizations; privatization and deregulation; the emergence of large institutional investors, etc.[38] Such markets present a number of advantages: they broaden the options of investors; they attract and encourage national savings as well as the repatriation of funds held abroad; they attract foreign investment; they provide much needed liquidity; they encourage sound management and good corporate governance, etc.[39] At the same time, they present substantial risks. The Souk el-Manakh experience (the collapse of the informal Kuwaiti stock market in 1982) – whose financial fall-out (estimated at $40 billion) is felt to this day in the Kuwaiti banking system – is still a vivid memory. Foreign investment is sorely needed, but fickle short-term capital that comes and leaves suddenly increases volatility and can have a destabilizing effect on the economy as a whole.

One of the main problems with capital markets is their potential for speculative excess, which poses economic and religious objections. From an economic standpoint, John Maynard Keynes said it best: "Speculators may do no harm as bubbles on a steady stream of enterprise. But the position is serious when enterprise becomes the bubble on a whirlpool of speculation."[40] Products designed to hedge and minimize risk can themselves become instruments of speculation. From a religious standpoint, markets raise issues of gharar as well as riba. Increasingly, however, mainstream Islamic doctrine is reconciling itself to the idea of capital markets, even of certain types of speculative operations, provided that they do not amount to market manipulation. According to one specialist:

> Islam is not against speculation if it is made by genuine investors who have worked hard and analyzed the macro- and micro-economic and financial fundamentals, and, therefore, have the right to speculate once the environment at the stock exchange is conducive to do so. On the contrary, what Islam is against is insider trading and the role of rumours, whose main interests are to manipulate the market and force their counterparts (the genuine investors) to sell off their shares at lower prices.[41]

The dilemma of emerging markets is that while they lack the institutional experience and attendant financial culture that older financial centers have, they are expected to create, more or less instantly, a transparent and well-managed system that inspires confidence: a market with breadth and depth, with credible national players and regulators, and a state-of-the-art system for placing, processing, and settling orders; and a market that cross-lists securities from other regional markets, and that is open to foreign investors. This in itself is a tall order. But even more than laws and institutions, markets require an adequate culture, and this cannot be legislated.

4 Macro-economic Policies

Banking has a direct impact on money supply – as every economic textbook explains, "banks create money" – on government borrowing, and on most macro-economic aggregates. Three issues are of particular importance: one is regulatory control – how they are regulated and whether they are given special status[42] – which is discussed in Chapter 10. The others are related to the use by governments of the "interest-rate weapon" to regulate the economy, and to the public debt.

The "interest-rate weapon" is an essential tool of liquidity management, credit allocation, and, more broadly, macro-economic policy. By raising or lowering a variety of rates, regulators can directly influence the money supply. In an interest-free system, such a tool cannot in theory be used. Advocates of Islamic banking argue that other tools can be just as effective. Among such tools are the modification of reserve requirements for banks, the manipulating of budget surpluses or deficits, the imposition of new "lending ratios" (the proportion of demand deposits that commercial banks are obliged to lend out as interest-free loans), or "refinance ratios" (which refer to the central bank refinancing of a part of the interest-free loans provided by the commercial banks).[43] The problem is that such solutions are mostly theoretical constructs that vastly exaggerate the role of interest-free loans.

In reality, however, no Islamic regulatory system has completely eliminated interest. When it comes to relations with the outside world, interest is still used. The three pioneers of full Islamicization – Pakistan, Iran, and the Sudan – happen to be heavily indebted countries, whose foreign debt carries interest.

As for domestic borrowing, these countries have not been able to create sufficient Islamic financing instruments to cater for the financial needs of the public sector. A number of theoretical concepts – such as issuing bonds where interest would be replaced by a rate that would vary according to the economy's growth and inflation rate, or mudaraba schemes – have yet to be fully put into practice. One complication is that governments do not have the same criteria of profitability as the private sector, and social rates of return have yet to be operationalized in a way that can satisfy investors.

III Islamic Banks and Project Finance

In the 1970s and 1980s, project finance in the Islamic world was the preserve of governments – though often in conjunction with the IDB. It is only in the last few years that the private sector, following global trends, has greatly increased its involvement in infrastructure investment and, more broadly, project finance; an area which by virtue of its sociodevelopmental potential and its focus on real assets is very much in line with the original objectives of Islamic finance. In between those two periods there were, of course, crucial developments, including the greater involvement of global conventional institutions with experience in project finance (among them HSBC and Citigroup) in Islamic finance, the creation of a wide range of new Shariah-compliant products which could substitute for interest-based loans, and the appearance of an Islamic secondary market centered around sukuk.

The years between 2002 and 2008 saw an unprecedented boom in project finance in the Middle East, fueled primarily by the oil boom. In those years, the Gulf Cooperation Council (GCC), the economic bloc made up of Bahrain, Kuwait, Oman, Qatar, Saudi Arabia, and the United Arab Emirates, emerged as the world's biggest project finance market.[44] In a 2008 report, the IDB predicted that Islamic countries were expected to invest nearly $1.2 trillion in infrastructure projects over the following 10 years, especially in telecommunications, transportation, and power.[45] A number of challenges nonetheless remain. Increasingly, project finance deals, whether in oil and gas, petrochemicals, power and water sectors, infrastructure, transportation or telecommunications, include "Islamic tranches." Instead of typical interest-based loans, such tranches consist of Shariah-compliant instruments such as leasing, murabaha, istisnaa, sukuk, and the like. Typically, those tranches are entirely backed by physical assets. There have also been a few issues of muqarada bonds (Islamic instruments whose returns are based on the actual revenues generated by the projects), especially in connection with projects such as toll roads. Of course, the bigger the projects, the greater the uncertainties (legal and practical) and risks involved. Specific challenges involve structuring complex transactions while maintaining some measure of transparency, or coordinating the Shariah- and non-Shariah-compliant tranches. In addition, Shariah scholars have been paying increased attention to the environmental dimension of new projects, especially their carbon footprint, in order to minimize the impact of harmful greenhouse gas emissions.

Given its triple-A rating and its experience in complex development projects, the IDB has provided the lead in Islamic project finance. One of the highest profile projects (the world's largest energy project, and the third largest project ever[46]) was the $12 billion Qatar Gas II, a joint venture between Qatar Petroleum and Exxon Mobil Corporation designed to supply liquid natural gas from Qatar to the United Kingdom, which included a $530 million Islamic tranche,[47] based on the lender buying the asset and then leasing it back to the borrower for a fixed period

Following the recent credit crunch, a number of GCC projects were halted,[48] though the Islamic involvement in Islamic project finance is here to stay. As of June 2009, it was estimated that 24 per cent of the project finance sector in the Islamic world was structured Islamically.[49]

IV Islamic Banks and Poverty Alleviation

1 Zakat

Zakat, or almsgiving, has been regarded throughout Islamic history as the principal welfare system – a means of taking care of the needy in society, and of achieving some measure of income redistribution.[50] The importance and centrality of zakat cannot be overstated. It is one of the five pillars, or obligations, of the Islamic faith.[51] Some scholars have even asserted that zakat is quite simply the cornerstone of Islamic economics, and in that respect is even more significant than, say, riba.[52]

Although often assumed to be fixed and unchanging, the zakat system has evolved since the early days of Islam according to the Islamic community's revenue and welfare needs.[53] The proper recipients of zakat are specified in the Koran: the poor and the needy; zakat collectors; travelers in difficulty; and captives (9:60).[54] Although in theory consisting of voluntary almsgiving, it could be assimilated into a religious tax. Early Islam established elaborate rules as to amounts, collection practices, exemptions, and the like. Every Muslim possessing a certain amount of resources was expected to contribute. Zakat was to be levied on traded goods and revenues from agriculture and business transactions, but not on personal property or belongings. Different rates (from 2.5 to 10 per cent) applied to different categories of products (produce, livestock, etc.).

In the contemporary setting, there have been debates about the nature, relevance, and usefulness of zakat: should it be voluntary or compulsory?; should it be fused with the official tax system or kept separate?; what items should be imposed and at what rates, or should the categories and rates of early Islamic days be kept unchanged?; should individuals give their contributions directly to a beneficiary or else to a special institution set up to distribute the funds? As more countries Islamicize their economies, governments have tended to reintroduce zakat as a cornerstone of both the tax and the welfare systems.[55] Countries such as Saudi Arabia, Pakistan, Malaysia, and Kuwait run their zakat system in a centralized way.

Ever since the 1970s aggiornamento, zakat has been a part of modern Islamic finance. Indeed, most Islamic banks set aside a percentage of their profits for charitable activities. Most Islamic banks are involved in zakat at two different levels. First, they contribute a percentage of their profits – over and above secular taxes – to charity. Hence, the frequent mention in financial statements of "profits before taxes and zakat." Second, many banks administer zakat funds, collecting and distributing money, often on behalf of their clients, for the needy and for a variety of charitable and welfare organizations (schools, hospitals, etc.).

Some banks have a strict interpretation of zakat, and subsume under it only those uses of zakat specified by the Koran, and dedicate other charitable funds (such as those endowed by late fees) to other uses such as the relief of distressed debtors. It is indeed not unusual for banks to extend qard hassan to their own borrowers who are experiencing financial difficulties.[56]

A few Islamic banks are primarily, or even exclusively, "social banks" as opposed to being profit-making ventures. Thus, the Nasser Social Bank, one of the first Islamic banks, created in the early 1970s as a successor of sorts to the Mit Ghamr bank,[57] initially focused on the qard hasan (interest-free loans to underprivileged groups when faced with exceptional expenses arising from illness, weddings, or funerals), and on financing pilgrimages to Mecca, pensions, and welfare benefits. The bank also established a fund for administering social insurance. (In later years, the bank moved beyond such activities and started investing in economic projects.) Social banks, of course, raise questions of financing and regulation. The Nasser Social Bank was initially supervised by the Ministry for Social Affairs and the Ministry of Finance, and received 2 per cent of the net profits of public enterprises to finance its services.[58]

2 Micro-lending or Micro-finance

Although the concept was largely initiated by a Muslim in a Muslim country, micro-lending or micro-finance institutions (MFI) developed separately from Islamic banks. Indeed, the best-known experiment in micro-lending is Muhammed Yunus' Grameen Bank, which was initially started in Bangladesh and has since been replicated in dozens of countries.[59] Although interest-based and devoid of any explicit references to Islam, the Grameen Bank concept is based on a central tenet of the moral economy of Islam.

Micro-lending purports to provide a market-based solution to one of capitalism's thorniest problems: integrating the poor into the economy. The major difference with zakat-based schemes is that it focuses on moving people off the dole and into productive enterprise. Self-help and self-reliance are at the center of the system. The scheme turns the conventional banking logic on its head: rather than looking for creditworthy customers and basing lending decisions on credit history and collateral, MFIs lend small amounts of money to people – principally women – with no resources as a means of integrating them in the productive economy. The following statement about Islamic finance could have been written in connection with micro-lending: "To establish a grass-root foundation in the society and to narrow down the rich–poor gap, Islamic banks have a moral and social responsibility towards their economies by investing in long-term projects. This means channelling resources to the people who need them, especially the womenfolk and the poor."[60]

MFIs have largely fulfilled the ideal of self-help, preservation of local traditions, and entry into the productive economy.[61] According to Jacques Gélinas: "The MFIs are in the process of destroying several very old myths: the poor are not creditworthy; they are not reliable borrowers; they are not resourceful enough to make savings; they are bad investors and even worse entrepreneurs."[62] Grameen Bank boasts that 98 per cent of its loans are repaid on time.[63]

The micro-lending idea has gained a number of adherents, in particular among governments and international organizations in recent years. In 1997, a micro-lending summit chaired by then First Lady Hillary Clinton was held in Washington. The micro-lending idea got a big boost in 2006 when Dr Yunus and Grameen Bank were jointly awarded the Nobel peace prize "for their efforts to create economic and social development from below."

The main objection of Islamic scholars to micro-lending as practiced by Grameen Bank was the practice of lending at interest. For that reason, most Islamic banks steered clear of micro-lending, preferring instead to devote the bulk of their zakat funds to donations to Islamic charities. All this started changing in the wake of September 11, 2001, when a number of Islamic charities found themselves accused of funding terrorism. The fact that Islamic banks had heavily contributed to funding them shone a negative spotlight on them.

A number of Islamic banks were, for example, among the defendants in a massive 2002 lawsuit filed by a group calling itself "the 9/11 Families United to Bankrupt Terrorism."[64] By that time, most large Islamic banks had changed their policy of providing massive financial support to Islamic charities, and decided to do more of their poverty alleviation work in-house. Many Islamic banks, especially those operated in countries with endemic poverty, became active in Grameen-style micro-lending, albeit through Shariah-compliant instruments such as qard hasan, murabaha, ijara, and even mudaraba and musharaka, in lieu of interest-based lending.

Notes

1. Edward S. Shaw, *Financial Deepening in Economic Development* (Oxford: Oxford University Press, 1973), p. 3.
2. Ross Levine, "Foreign Banks, Financial Development, and Economic Growth," in Claude E. Barfield (ed.), *International Financial Markets: Harmonization versus Competition* (Washington, DC: The AEI Press, 1996), pp. 229–32.
3. Chapters 4 and 5.
4. See also Chapter 2.
5. Alan Richards and John Waterbury, *A Political Economy of the Middle East* (Boulder, CO: Westview Press, 1996), p. 181.
6. John Zysman, *Governments, Markets and Growth* (Ithaca, NY: Cornell University Press, 1983).
7. See Chapter 5.
8. Karen Pfeifer, "Is there an Islamic Economics?," in Joel Beinin and Joe Stark (eds.), *Political Islam: Essays from Middle East Report* (Berkeley, CA: University of California Press, 1997), p. 155.
9. Robert Springborg, "Egypt," in Tim Niblock and Emma Murphy (eds.), *Economic and Political Liberalization in the Middle East* (London: I. B. Tauris, 1992), p. 20.
10. Hicham Ben Abdallah El Alaoui, "Les régimes arabes modernisent … l'autoritarisme," *Le Monde diplomatique*, April 2008.
11. *The Economist*, April 12, 1997.
12. David Fairlamb, "Beyond Capital Adequacy," *Institutional Investor*, August 1997.
13. Ibrahim Warde, "Un capitalisme de compères," *Le Monde diplomatique*, November 1998.
14. *Forbes*, July 6, 1998.
15. *Institutional Investor*, August 1997.
16. Ibrahim Warde, "Financiers flamboyants, contribuables brûlés," *Le Monde diplomatique*, July 1994.
17. Ibrahim Warde, "Alternative, Informal and Underground Markets in the Islamic World", unpublished manuscript.
18. Hernando de Soto, *The Other Path: The Economic Answer to Terrorism* (New York: Basic Books, 1989) (with a 2002 preface), p. xxxix.
19. Ibrahim Warde, *The Price of Fear: The Truth behind the Financial War of Terror* (Berkeley, CA: The University of California Press, 2007).
20. Jonathan Randal, *Osama: The Making of a Terrorist* (New York: Alfred A. Knopf, 2004), p. 200.
21. Hernando de Soto, *The Mystery of Capital: Why Capitalism Triumphs in the West and Fails Everywhere Else* (New York: Basic Books, 2000), p. 21.
22. The World Bank, *World Development Report 1989* (Oxford: Oxford University Press, 1989), p. 114.

23. Christopher Capozzola, "The Informal Economy of the LDCs: Regulation and Reaction," *Harvard International Review* (Summer 1991).
24. Jacques B. Gélinas, *Freedom from Debt: The Reappropriation of Development through Financial Self-reliance* (London: Zed Books, 1998), pp. 101–8.
25. Edward F. Buffie. "Financial Repression, the New Structuralists, and Stabilization Policy in Semi-Industrialized Economies," *Journal of Development Economics*, 14 (April 1984).
26. Ronald I. McKinnon, *Money and Capital in Economic Development* (Washington, DC: The Brookings Institution, 1973).
27. See Kiren Aziz Chaudhry, *The Price of Wealth: Economies and Institutions in the Middle East* (Ithaca, NY: Cornell University Press, 1997), p. 254, and Khalid M. Midani, "Financing Terrorism or Survival? Informal Finance and State Collapse In Somalia, and the US War on Terrorism," *Mideast Report* (Summer 2002).
28. See Chapter 8.
29. *The Wall Street Journal,* January 8, 1998.
30. McKinnon, *Money and Capital in Economic Development*, pp. 68–9.
31. These issues are discussed in greater detail in Chapter 8.
32. Based on *Al Mausua al Ilmiya wa al Amaliya lil Bunuk al Islamiya* (*Handbook of Islamic Banking*) (Cairo: International Association of Islamic Banks, 1982), vol. 6.
33. *Handbook of Islamic Banking*, vol. 6, p. 293.
34. Khalid Medani, "Funding Fundamentalism: The Political Economy of an Islamist State," in Joel Beinin and Joe Stork (eds.), *Political Islam: Essays from Middle East Report* (Berkeley, CA: University of California Press, 1997), p. 169.
35. Yahya M. Sadowski, *Political Vegetables? Businessman and Bureaucrat in the Development of Egyptian Agriculture* (Washington, DC: The Brookings Institution, 1991), p. 201.
36. Elias Kazarian, *Islamic versus Traditional Banking: Financial Innovation in Egypt* (Boulder, CO: Westview Press, 1993).
37. Kazarian, *Islamic versus Traditional Banking*, pp. 217–26.
38. Miroslava Filipovic, *Governments, Banks and Global Politics: Securities Markets and Global Politics* (Aldershot: Ashgate, 1997).
39. William E. James, Seiji Naya, and Gerald M. Meier, *Asian Development: Economic Success and Policy Lessons* (Madison, WI: University of Wisconsin Press, 1989), pp. 59–88.
40. John Kenneth Galbraith, *A Short History of Financial Euphoria* (London: Penguin, 1990), p. 26.
41. Saad al-Harran, "The Islamic Stock Exchange," in Saad al-Harran (ed.), *Leading Issues in Islamic Banking and Finance* (Selangor, Malaysia: Pelanduk Publications, 1995), p. 150.
42. See Chapter 10.
43. See Mohammed Ariff (ed.), *Monetary and Fiscal Economics of Islam* (Jeddah: International Centre for Research in Islamic Economics, 1982), especially Mohammed Ariff, "Monetary Policy in an Interest-free Islamic Economy – Nature and Scope"; Mohammed Uzair, "Central Banking Operations in an Interest-free Banking System"; and Mohammed Siddiqi, "Islamic Approaches to Money, Banking and Monetary Policy: A Review."
44. Richard Dean and William Wallis, "Challenges and Opportunities in World's Hottest Market," *The Financial Times*, October 24, 2006.
45. P. K. Abdul Ghafour, "Islamic Countries to Invest $1.2t in Infrastructure," *Arab News*, June 11, 2008.
46. The two largest are the Channel tunnel linking the United Kingdom to the European continent, and a high-speed rail financing in Taiwan.
47. Gordon Platt, "Qatar Gas Project Pushes Bounds of Project Finance," *Global Finance*, February 1, 2005.
48. Mahmood Rafique, "GCC may Halt some of the New Projects," *Arab News*, November 27, 2008.

49. Ibrahim Warde, "Islamic Project Finance" (Boston, MA: AIU Financial Consulting, 2009).

50. Chibli Mallat, *The Renewal of Islamic Law: Muhammad Baqer as-Sadr, Najaf and the Shi'i International* (Cambridge: Cambridge University Press, 1993), p. 120.

51. The other pillars are: the *shahada*, or professing that "there is but One God, and Mohammed is his Messenger"; the *salat*, or praying five times a day; fasting from dawn to sunset for one month of the year, Ramadan; and, if a believer is able to do so, making at least one pilgrimage to Mecca.

52. Abdelhamid Brahimi, *Justice sociale et développement en économie islamique* (Paris: La Pensée Universelle, 1993). The author is a former Prime Minister of Algeria.

53. Timur Kuran, "The Economic System in Contemporary Islamic Thought: Interpretation and Assessment," *International Journal of Middle Eastern Studies* (May 1986), p. 149.

54. 9:60 "(Zakat) charity is only for the poor and the needy, and those employed to administer it, and those whose hearts are made to incline [to truth], and [to free] the captives, and those in debt, and in the way of Allah and for the wayfarer – an ordinance from Allah. And Allah is Knowing, Wise."

55. In many oil-rich states with no income tax, zakat is often looked at as an adequate substitute. In populous, non-oil states, zakat is typically looked at as a complement to other taxes.

56. Nabil Saleh, *Unlawful Gain and Legitimate Profit in Islamic Law* (Cambridge: Cambridge University Press, 1986), p. 99.

57. Michel Galloux, *Finance islamique et pouvoir politique: le cas de l'Egypte moderne* (Paris: Presses Universitaires de France, 1997).

58. Traute Wohlers-Scharf, *Arab and Islamic Banks: New Business Partners for Developing Countries* (Paris: OECD, 1983), p. 80.

59. Muhammed Younes, *Vers un monde sans pauvreté* (Paris: J. C. Lattès, 1997).

60. Saad al-Harran (ed.), *Leading Issues in Islamic Banking and Finance* (Selangor, Malaysia: Pelanduk Publications, 1995), p. xi.

61. Gélinas, *Freedom from Debt*, p. 108.

62. Gélinas, *Freedom from Debt*, p. 108.

63. *The Wall Street Journal Europe*, June 18, 1997.

64. Warde, *The Price of Fear*, p. 85.

10

REGULATORY ISSUES AND CHALLENGES: GLOBAL NORMS AND RELIGIOUS CONSTRAINTS

Modern Islamic finance came into existence shortly before a sweeping movement of deregulation transformed the landscape of global finance. In the early years of modern Islamic banking ambitious regulatory schemes were devised. There was talk of an Islamic Central Bank, of a global zakat fund, and of other ambitious collaborative schemes.[1] Scholars worked on an Islamic approach to bank regulation.[2] Most of these ideas were never put into practice, as they were simply overtaken by events. In the era of deregulation, national regulators gradually lost the margin of maneuver they once enjoyed. Most of the norms and practices of financial regulation were established internationally, with little input from regulators outside the industrial world.

Although Islamic banks have thrived in the global economy, their compliance with many of the new norms has sometimes been problematic. Increasingly, however, in recent years and in particular since the creation in 2002 of the IFSB, Islamic regulators have been coordinating their policies with other international financial regulators. Although the global financial collapse of 2008 set in motion attempts to re-regulate global finance, the outlines of such global re-regulation are not, as this book goes to press, yet clear.

I Financial Regulation

Financial regulators must perform a number of tasks: ensuring that the financial sector is safe and sound; mobilizing savings by channeling them toward the most productive uses; and devising an efficient conduit for payments around the economy. Before the disruptions of the 1970s, regulators performed a mostly technical task outside the political limelight. In recent years, however, virtually every country, including those with well-established regulatory authorities and traditions has been rocked by banking crises. The near-collapse of the global financial system in 2008 is likely to cost, according to the projections of the IMF, $4.1 trillion.[3]

Emerging markets – the category to which most Islamic countries belong – are even more vulnerable, since they often lack a regulatory framework and tradition, and suffer from a wide array of structural problems. Typically, they are over-banked and in need of consolidation. Many are plagued with a bad loan overhang, and suffer – to an even greater extent than industrial countries – from the "crony capitalism" syndrome, whereby cozy ties among politicians and bankers prevent effective compliance, let alone reform.[4] Whenever banking crises occur, their impact can be devastating.

Once confined to developed countries, the new rules of global finance have extended to the rest of the world. Four broad sets of factors account for this evolution: the spread of the liberal ideology; the integration of emerging countries into the global economy; the growing involvement of international financial institutions in emerging markets; and the proliferation of currency and banking crises. National and developmental goals were once central to financial policy. But the developmental orthodoxy has changed in line with the "Washington consensus," which favors free market solutions, export orientation, fiscal discipline, and, most recently, the overhaul of existing financial systems. Indeed, financial turmoil, most recently in Asia, has accelerated the push for bank reform. The IMF and the World Bank have determined that their programs were undermined by troubled financial sectors, and that institutional investors, given their increased exposure to emerging markets, have a lot more at stake than they did a few years ago. Since October 1998, regulators worldwide have been committed to the implementation of the "Core Principles of Banking Supervision" issued the previous year by the Basel Committee. Similarly, since March 1999, the 102 signatories of the December 1997 Free Trade in Financial Services Agreement (under the aegis of the World Trade Organization) are engaged in a massive liberalization effort.

II The Ideological Debates on Financial Regulation

Regulation is a balancing act. Different, often contradictory, goals – flexibility and consistency, freedom and strict controls, innovation and crisis avoidance, consolidation and conflicts of interest, efficiency and consumer protection, openness and protection of national firms – must be applied in proper dosages by people familiar with the political and cultural environment. The audit systems and incentive structures must be flexible yet strict enough to allow innovation but prevent rogue operations. In case of fraud or heavy losses, there is an enormous temptation to adopt a policy of "regulatory forbearance" – that is, bending the rules to avoid closing insolvent banks – as a way of preventing panic. But, as was the case with the recent financial meltdown, this often leads to distrust and simply postpones the day of reckoning. Yet overreacting can create a credit crunch. Other dilemmas are related to the need to ensure fair competition. The logic of economic freedom in a global economy tends to lead to the formation of huge conglomerates and thus unfair competition among firms of vastly different sizes. In addition, as firms are allowed to enter new lines of business, the potential exists for conflicts of interest that are detrimental to the interests of consumers and investors. For example, as financial institutions get involved in the financial advisory business, the need to sell their products compromises their commitment to impartial advice. Yet building firewalls between advisory activities and sales goes against the spirit of deregulation.

Such dilemmas are amplified by the transformations of global finance. Once clearly defined, financial functions are now blurred. Different types of finance – commercial banking, investment banking, securities, insurance – call for different forms of regulation. Yet the same financial institution can be a lender, an investor, a guarantor, a portfolio manager, etc. Balance sheets have changed beyond recognition. (Complicating matters further, a growing number of transactions do not even appear on balance sheets at all.) In addition, traditional bank products such as loans are being securitized, creating more headaches for regulators who must decide what is a bank, and what types of products need what type of controls. Insofar as financial institutions engage in a wide array of activities, regulators must resolve a number of issues. Should there be functional regulation whereby a financial institution would deal with different regulators for its commercial, investment banking, or insurance activities? Or should financial institutions have a single regulator which would oversee diverse functions? In one instance the financial institution would have to comply with complex and perhaps contradictory rules and be entangled in turf battles fought among regulators. In the other, the regulator may lack the expertise to oversee a wide array of activities and may risk being "captured" by the firms it regulates.

Debates on financial regulation, in addition to being influenced by historical traditions and regulatory cultures, tend to go through cycles and are ideologically loaded. In the wake of financial failures, regulatory authorities are likely to tighten the rules, only to relax them when the memory of such failures fades. Partisans of *laissez-faire* argue in favor of minimal supervision, claiming that strict supervision does more harm than good and that the "private provision of bank regulation through the marketplace" is far preferable to intrusive government regulation. The theory is that "the market" through its proxies – analysts, rating agencies, the business press, etc. – evaluates at all times financial institutions, thus imposing its own discipline on participants. Such an approach also takes a benign view of bank failures, seen as a cost of doing business, rather than a cause for panic – or a pretext to tighten regulation. Simply put, the ideological issue can be reduced to a trade-off: *laissez-faire* fosters financial innovation, but also encourages fraud and abuse; conversely, strict regulation can help to prevent problems but it stifles innovation and dynamism.

In sum, regulators must thus be strict yet flexible, collegial but not too cozy. The problem is that while lip service is often paid to the principle of independence, regulators not beholden either to politicians or to the industry they regulate are more an ideal than a reality. In most countries, bankers tend to be prominent figures, often involved in politics, or at the very least generous to politicians. Recent scandals suggest the many ways in which regulators can be influenced. In the case of the American savings and loans scandals, dubbed by Martin Mayer "the worst public scandal in American history," money paid by operators to politicians (in the form of campaign contributions or sweetheart loans) led to bad laws and lax regulation: insolvent institutions were kept in business, fraud and abuse ran rampant, etc. The more recent financial debacle was similar in its basic dynamics,[5] but far more significant in its magnitude and consequences.[6]

An additional problem of regulation is one of resources. The knowledge and skills necessary to be a competent regulator in today's complex, uncertain, and constantly changing environment are such that governments can seldom afford the best possible regulators. The private sector in contrast can afford those lawyers, strategists, and product innovators, who are in a position to keep the industry one step ahead of the regulators.

In Islamic countries, the complications arising from international pressure to adapt global regulatory norms are compounded by the added and often conflicting demands of religion. Religion is a touchy subject, and has on occasion been used as a cover for fraudulent activities.[7] Independence and integrity are all the more important since regulatory issues are even more likely than in a conventional setting to degenerate into major political crises. Furthermore, despite growing similarities with conventional ones, Islamic products and practices do not fit neatly into existing legal, regulatory, and accounting systems. In addition to establishing standard prudential rules (concerning capital and reserve requirements, capital/assets and other ratios), Islamic banking regulators have to devise rules to govern such issues as new finance methods, conditions of ownership of Islamic institutions (minimum capital, maximum individual ownership, etc.), fiscal status of income, and the like. In sum, they must operate under the watchful eyes of "markets" and religious authorities, while complying with international practices and standards.

III The Changing Paradigm of Financial Regulation: from National Control to Global Supervision

In 1944, John Maynard Keynes, who was then actively involved in shaping the post-war financial order, stated: "We intend to retain control of our domestic rate of interest, so that we can keep it as low as suits our own purposes, without interference from the ebb and flow of international capital movements or flights of hot money."[8] In the system of "embedded liberalism" that prevailed for much of the post-Second World War era, governments were committed to a liberal economic order, but reserved the right to control capital movements.[9]

Under such a system, the regulation of financial institutions was subject to strict controls, clearly defined boundaries, and limits on foreign participation in the national market. Cartel-like arrangements within sectors as well as stable relationships between borrowers and lenders prevailed. Financial markets were divided into distinct and clearly-defined segments: commercial banks; investment banks; securities firms; insurance companies, etc. Interest rates were "administered" as opposed to being left to market forces, and most financial operations were tightly regulated. Except for the United States and the United Kingdom, public ownership of banks (by federal or local governments) was common, allowing governments to channel credit to favored sectors of the economy.[10] Even when banks belonged to the private sector, the logic was not fundamentally different, since government–bank relations were defined by a quid pro quo: managers gave away some autonomy in exchange for protection from outsiders. To be sure, a measure of openness was allowed in many countries, but this did not prevent national firms from remaining somewhat insulated from foreign competition, since the occasional authorization given to a foreign firm to operate in the domestic market was designed not to upset existing cartels.

A chain of events, starting with the birth of "euromarkets" led to a gradual internationalization of financial markets.[11] Change has greatly accelerated in recent years, resulting in a global financial market – which in turn called for a global regulatory regime.[12] "Harmonization" of norms was seen as necessary, at a time when capital could move freely, to prevent "regulatory arbitrage" (the switch by investors and financial institutions to lower cost regulators). Also, there was a need to create a global "level playing field," so that investors and financial institutions from certain countries would not benefit from unfair advantages. Hence, the need to agree on common standards and close "loopholes," such as those provided by offshore financial centers.[13] Another rationale for consolidated global regulation was the fear of contagion. As financial systems became increasingly interconnected,[14] the possibility of problems spreading across the globe were ever-present, raising the specter of systemic risk – a wholesale collapse of the world's financial system.

The need to contain crises and ensure the integrity of the global system (based on the dubious but widely accepted view that markets operate fairly and safely in order to encourage the widest possible confidence in them, thereby promoting high levels of savings and investment) explains why since 1995, financial regulation has taken center stage in the annual summits of the Group of Seven (G7) heads of government. A succession of financial crises affecting firms – BCCI, Daiwa Bank, Sumitomo, Barings, etc. – or countries – Mexico, Thailand, Indonesia, Korea, Russia, etc. – has lent greater urgency to regulatory cooperation. With each crisis the new orthodoxy was refined and the reach of global regulators expanded.

The Asian financial crisis of 1997–8 led to a further consolidation of the new paradigm. Until July 1997, the "tiger economies" of southeast Asia were held out as models of well-run economies. Reports by the IMF and the World Bank praised their macro-economic management and predicted continuing growth and success. Rating agencies were still awarding high ratings to their debts. The successive crises that spread in domino fashion, starting in Thailand, caught the world by surprise.[15] Since the "fundamentals" of these economies were sound, a frantic search for new culprits ensued. A new consensus soon emerged, helped in no small part by the steady deterioration of the Japanese banking system: the financial systems of these countries were to blame. Rescues of Thailand, Indonesia, and South Korea by the IMF were directly linked to the transformation of these countries' financial systems which were said to epitomize "crony capitalism." Regulators from the developing world, including Islamic countries, were to be trained and counseled on an on-going basis by more experienced regulators. They had little choice, since the acceptance of new norms became the *sine qua non* to being allowed to expand abroad, or to have access to international financial markets.

IV The Making and Enforcement of the New Global Norms

An overlapping network of governments (directly and through the G7 and G10),[16] private corporations (including most large financial banks, securities companies, and insurance companies), and international organizations (the World Bank, the IMF, the Organization of Economic Cooperation and Development [OECD], the WTO, etc.) played a key role in promoting global financial standards.[17] This section focuses on two little known organizations, the Group of Thirty, a private think-tank, and the Bank for International Settlements (BIS), "the central bank of central banks," both of which were instrumental in shaping the new norms of financial regulation.

The Group of Thirty, established in 1978, describes itself as "a private, independent, nonpartisan, nonprofit body," whose aims are "to deepen understanding of international economic and financial issues, to explore the international repercussions of decisions taken in the public and private sectors, and to examine the choices available to market practitioners and to policymakers." It is "supported by contributions from private sources: foundations, banks, non-bank corporations, central banks, and individuals." In reality it is dominated by the large financial conglomerates, and its role could best be described as that of a consensus-making body on matters of global finance. Through its papers, conferences and symposia, study groups, and specialized committees, the Group of Thirty has in recent years produced the prevailing orthodoxy on matters of capital requirements, harmonization of rules and procedures, derivatives regulation, risk management, and cooperation among financial regulators. Because of its make-up, it is the ideal forum for discussions among regulators and practitioners and for consensus-making. Its membership is a who's who of leading financial institutions, central bankers, and mainstream economists.[18] It also works in close cooperation with the main trade groups and regulatory associations.[19]

The BIS, created in 1930 and based in Basel, Switzerland, is the oldest international financial organization, and perhaps the most mysterious.[20] The bank is primarily owned by the central banks of industrialized countries. Until recently, the Bank's Board was made up of representatives from eleven countries (Belgium, Canada, France, Germany, Italy, Japan, the Netherlands, Sweden, Switzerland, the United Kingdom, and the United States). In 1996–7, it extended its membership to nine emerging countries. Those nine countries, however, are not equal partners: they may join in some discussions, but may not attend G10 meetings unless invited. Yet the BIS has business and advisory relations with considerably more than its shareholding central banks, because some 140 central banks and international financial institutions use it as their bank. As of March 2006, currency deposits totaled approximately $186 billion, or about 7 per cent of world foreign exchange reserves.[21] Furthermore, the central banks or official monetary institutions of all but a few countries throughout the world are regularly represented at the Annual General Meeting of the BIS in June each year.

As with other international organizations such as the World Bank and the IMF, the power of the BIS grew with the successive financial crises starting in the 1980s. In 1982, for example, when the debt crisis erupted, the BIS, at the request of the leading central banks, and with their support (in the form of guarantees), helped to provide bridging finance to a number of central banks, mainly in Latin America and Eastern Europe, pending the disbursement of conditional credits granted by Western governments, the IMF, and the World Bank.

Of special interest to us is the Basel Committee on Banking Supervision which was created by the central bank governors of the G10 countries plus Switzerland and Luxembourg in December 1974, in the aftermath of the failures of Franklin National Bank in New York and Bankhaus Herstatt in West Germany. Although formally distinct, the BIS and the Basel Committee are often confused with one another. Indeed, the Secretariat of the Basel Committee is provided by the BIS, and the activities of the two organizations overlap considerably. Under the aegis of the Basel Committee, cooperation among bank supervisors has steadily increased. The first International Conference of Bank Supervisors was held in 1979. The Basel Concordat of 1975 – revised in 1983 and 1990 – clarified the sharing of supervisory responsibilities among national authorities with respect to banks' foreign establishments, the aim being to ensure effective supervision of banks' activities worldwide.[22] It is by virtue of those rules that bank regulators acted in concert to close down the BCCI in 1991. As will be discussed later, the Basel Committee also issued capital adequacy rues (usually referred to as Basel or Cooke ratios in 1988, updated in 2004 with the "Basel 2" guidelines). In 1997, the Basel Committee also issued its "Core Principles of Banking Supervision."

In addition to issuing papers and detailed compendia on implementation of sound supervisory standards, the Basel Committee and the BIS have been increasingly involved in the dissemination of global banking norms. There are frequent meetings of central bank economists and other experts on a variety of matters, such as economic and monetary issues of interest to central banks (monetary policy techniques, operating procedures, and netting arrangements), and on specialized topics (data bank management, security, automation, internal management procedures, collection of international financial statistics). The BIS also participates with the European Bank for Reconstruction and Development (ERBD), the World Bank, the IMF, and the OECD in the "Joint Vienna Institute," a training institution set up in 1992 to offer courses for central bankers and other economic and financial officials from economies that are "in transition" from central planning to free markets. In 1998, the BIS announced the creation, in association with the Basel Committee on Banking Supervision of an Institute for Financial Stability, whose purpose is to organize high-level seminars directed at key policy-making officials in central banks and supervisory agencies, provide training for the officials in charge of implementation, and act as a clearing house for the coordination and provision of technical assistance by central banks and supervisory bodies.[23]

A web of global regulation involving banking, securities, and insurance regulators has thus taken shape and is continually gaining in size and scope. A number of principles govern this web: home–host cooperation; information sharing; lead regulator principle; transparency; disclosure, etc. How are those norms enforced? Initially, the Basel Committee had no formal authority since its agreements were carried out on a voluntary basis by the member countries. Today, however, it has considerable power due to the new, albeit mostly indirect, powers of enforcement of private, public, and international organizations. Adopting certain norms – such as the successive capital ratios or the comprehensive home supervision requirement – is now a pre-condition to being part of the global financial system. The countries whose legislation inspired (in the case of the United States), or were inspired by, the Basel norms would not permit the operation on their territory of banks from countries that did not endorse such rules. Thus, in 1991, in the wake of the BCCI and Banco Nazionale del Lavoro (BNL)[24] scandals, the US Congress enacted the Foreign Bank Supervision and Enhancement Act (FBSEA), which added a new layer of control to its regulatory framework. The centerpiece of the legislation was the requirement that a foreign bank show that it is subject to "comprehensive supervision or regulation on a consolidated basis by the appropriate authorities in its home country" before any application to open a US office, or significantly expand its business in the United States, can be approved.[25] As for the "Core Principles of Effective Banking Supervision," their implementation is to be monitored by the IMF as part of its regular surveillance procedures. More generally, and especially since an increasing number of countries are now rated by international ratings agencies such as Standard & Poor's and Moody's, any refusal to apply the new norms is likely to result in being sanctioned or even "ostracized" by the international markets.

V Recent Developments in Global Financial Regulation

This section focuses on three sets of recent developments: the new rules on capital and risk management; the Core Principles of Bank Supervision; and the liberalization of trade in financial services.

1 Capital Standards and Risk Management

The Basel Accord concluded on July 12, 1988 was a landmark regulatory agreement. For the first time, regulations affecting banks in many different countries were jointly established: banks operating internationally had to have a minimum capital-to-assets ratio of 8 per cent; the capital was divided into three tiers, each subjected to different definitions and rules.

The idea of imposing strict ratios was related to the banking problems in the United States in the early 1980s in the wake of deregulation, and as a result of the exposure of major banks to the international debt crisis. In 1984 and 1985, the Federal Reserve Board and the Federal Deposit Insurance Corporation issued new capital guidelines, forcing banks into a choice between raising new capital and reducing their assets. The underlying logic was that in order to be able to weather bad economic times, banks needed a high ratio of capital to assets. In January 1987, an agreement between the United States and the United Kingdom extended the principle of uniform rules to the two countries.[26] The ostensible goals were to reduce the risk of the international banking system and minimize competitive inequality arising from differences among national bank capital regulations. A more political explanation lay in the attempt to eliminate the funding-cost advantage that had allowed Japanese banks to capture more than one-third of international lending for much of the 1980s.[27] Even before the 1992 deadline, thirty-three countries besides the G10, spurred by their central banks had chosen to adopt the 8 per cent rule, as it helped them establish credibility.[28] In the following years, virtually all countries had officially changed their capital requirements to conform with the Basel ratios.[29] In other words, although aimed initially at banks from the industrialized world that operated internationally, the standards soon became universal. In addition to the 8 per cent rule, The Basel Committee on Banking Supervision devised a risk-based capital framework: different asset classes (both on- and off-balance sheet) had to be weighted according to their riskiness. Five weights – 0 per cent, 10 per cent, 20 per cent, 50 per cent and 100 per cent – were attached to different types of assets (cash, OECD, and non-OECD government debt, secured and unsecured loans, etc.).[30] Increasingly, following the lead of the United States and the 1991 Federal Deposit Insurance Corporation Improvement Act (FDICIA), a two-tiered regulation system appeared in many countries: institutions that were well-capitalized would be subjected to a rather light, if not lax, regulatory regime, whereas the others would be subjected to tight controls.

A number of drawbacks appeared over the years, which modifications in the Basel standards attempted to address. Capital requirements have moved from being simple mechanical rules to becoming sophisticated risk-adjusted models. For one thing, the world of finance had changed considerably with new financial instruments being devised every day. The Basel ratios concentrated almost exclusively on credit risk, while other risks were ignored. Also, at least in the United States, the financial sector had recovered its health following a difficult decade (1982–92), and had become more assertive and politically influential.[31] The new paradigm, propounded in particular by the Group of Thirty became that of "self-regulation": the largest financial institutions would develop their own risk management models and tools, and regulators, rather than micro-managing risk, would have to be satisfied that those models were accurate and that internal risk controls and disclosure policies were adequate. In an influential report, the Group of Thirty argued that:

the fundamental responsibility of ensuring financial stability of financial institutions, and thereby limiting systemic risk, rests with the Board and management of global institutions themselves. It also implies that supervisors will be readier to rely on institutions that they supervise, and that the institutions themselves will accept the responsibility to improve the structure of, and discipline imposed by, their internal control functions.[32]

Since 1988, new guidelines on derivatives and off-balance sheets items have been issued on a regular basis as a new orthodoxy on risk management, which was regarded in financial circles as something of an exact science, took shape. Each firm had to have a thorough understanding of the risks it faced. In addition to the credit risk (the risk that a counterparty will fail to perform on an obligation to the institution), other risks had to be covered, with procedures drawn up for each category.[33] The new regulatory framework thus focused on an institution's risk control strategy, with risk control defined as the entire process of policies, procedures, and systems an institution needs to manage prudently all the risks resulting from its financial transactions, and to ensure that they are within the bank's risk appetite. To avoid conflicts of interests, risk control had to be separated from, and sufficiently independent of, the business units which execute the firm's financial transactions.

Needless to say, most of the underlying assumptions behind risk management and the safety of "sophisticated instruments" were proven to be woefully wrong by the 2008 financial meltdown, though it remains to be seen how these developments will affect future regulation.

2 The Core Principles of Bank Supervision

In 1992, the first minimum standards for cross-border supervision established four main principles. First, all international banks should be supervised by a home country that is capable of performing consolidated supervision. Second, the creation of a cross-border banking establishment should receive the prior consent of both the host country and the home country authority. Third, home country authorities should possess the right to gather information from their cross-border banking establishments. Fourth, if the host country determines that any of these three standards is not being met, it could impose restrictive measures or prohibit the establishment of banking offices.

With the proliferation of banking crises worldwide, the G7 pressed the Basel Committee to issue more detailed guidelines. Indeed, since 1995, G7 summit communiqués have repeatedly called for measures to strengthen banking regulation and supervision, in particular deeper cooperation among supervisors of global firms to "promote the development of globally-integrated safeguards, standards, transparency and systems necessary to monitor and contain risks," and improved supervision in the emerging market economies.

In 1997, the Basel Committee issued for comment a draft of its "25 Core Principles for Effective Bank Supervision." Among those principles are the following: all banks must have comprehensive risk management systems as well as management information systems that enable management to identify concentrations within their portfolio; supervisors must set prudential limits to restrict bank exposures to single borrowers or groups of related borrowers; they must also determine that banks have adequate policies, practices, and procedures in place, including strict "know-your-customer" rules that promote high ethical and professional standards in the financial sector and prevent the bank being used, intentionally or unintentionally, by criminal elements; and regulators must be able to supervise the banking group on a worldwide consolidated basis.

According to the press release, the Principles "have been drawn up by the Basel Committee in close collaboration with the supervisory authorities in fifteen emerging market countries and have benefited from broad consultation with many other supervisory authorities throughout the world." They were "intended to serve as a basic reference for supervisory and other public authorities worldwide to apply in the supervision of all the banks within their jurisdictions." Supervisory authorities throughout the world were "invited to endorse the Core Principles, not later than October 1998." The Principles were designed to be verifiable by national regulators, regional supervisory groups, and the market at large. The Basel Committee would monitor the progress made by individual countries in implementing the Principles. In addition, the IMF, the World Bank, and other international organizations were asked to use the Principles "in assisting individual countries to strengthen their supervisory arrangements in connection with their work aimed at promoting overall macroeconomic and financial stability." The Basel Committee also announced it was preparing a three-volume Compendium of its existing recommendations, guidelines and standards.

As of October 1998, emerging countries were expected to review their current supervisory arrangements and set a timetable to make changes in order to conform with the Principles. If legislative changes were needed, national legislators were requested to give urgent consideration to the changes necessary to ensure the application of the Principles. Some in the banking profession have criticized those Principles for being too vague – in effect for being guidelines and not strict rules. The Principles, say other critics, pay insufficient attention to several issues, such as the profitability, the quality of deposits (which is especially important in emerging markets), and earnings.[34] Implementation of the Principles was to be reviewed at the International Conference of Banking Supervisors in October 1998 and biennially thereafter.

3 Free Trade in Services

Financial services were left out of the Uruguay Round Agreement that created the WTO in 1994. At the time, countries such as South Korea, India, and Brazil feared that an onslaught of foreign competition would endanger their national firms. This unfinished business was taken up by the newly-created organization. In 1995, an agreement was arrived it, but was rejected by the United States on the ground that it did not going far enough in the direction of liberalization. For a time, the talks seemed deadlocked. It is in part as a result of the Asian financial crisis of 1997 that the deadlock over the financial services agreement was broken. By the end of that year, Asian countries had lost much of their bargaining power as they desperately needed the help of Western governments and international organizations such as the IMF.[35] And the United States and other developed countries, worried about the ripple effects of the crisis, were intent on drastic reform. In their view, the fastest way to cure a sick financial system and to reform it is to open it up to foreign competition. In the words of US Deputy Treasury Secretary Lawrence Summers: "Emerging markets' growing importance to the global economy gives the international community a particularly strong interest in strengthening their financial systems to insure against financial-sector crises like the one in Thailand."[36]

In December 1997, an agreement was finally signed, with 102 countries pledging to open, to varying degrees, their banking, insurance, and securities sectors to foreign competition. The agreement, effective as of March 1999, covers 95 per cent of the world's multi-trillion dollar financial services – which according to US negotiators involves $18,000 billion in global securities assets, $38,000 billion in international bank lending, and $2,500 billion in worldwide insurance premiums. Like other WTO agreements, the financial services agreement covers not just cross-border trade, but all the ways in which foreign suppliers can deliver services to a country's market, including the establishment of local subsidiaries and branches. The interests of foreign firms were to be protected by the rules of the world trade body.[37]

The WTO stressed the benefits of the new agreement to developing countries. Increased international competition in financial services would force domestic companies to reduce waste, cut costs, improve management, and become more efficient. Liberalization would improve service quality and benefit consumers, depositors, and investors. Open markets would encourage the emergence of new financial instruments, allowing companies to choose the optimal combination of equity, loans, or commercial paper to finance their activities. In addition, according to the WTO, broadening the volume of transactions and the spectrum of services would reduce the volatility of markets and their vulnerability to external shocks.[38]

VI Applying the New Norms in the Islamic World

While elaborating the "Core Principles of Effective Banking Supervision," the Basel Committee negotiators initially considered having two sets of principles, to be applied to developed and developing countries respectively. In the end, however, they settled for a single set of rules that would be applicable worldwide. Most Islamic countries were ill-prepared to implement these reforms. Only two Islamic countries – Malaysia and Indonesia – were nominally associated with the work of the Basel committee,[39] and both have since had their differences with the global financial community. At the time of the Asian financial crisis of 1997, both countries saw themselves as victims of speculative financial flows. Indonesia only reluctantly accepted the conditions imposed by the IMF in exchange for its rescue package. Malaysia, in the WTO negotiations, fought vigorously in favor of maintaining limits on foreign ownership of some of its financial firms. Indeed, one of the last-minute stumbling blocks concerned the new 30 per cent limit on foreign ownership of insurance firms as part of the "Malaysianization" program.[40] Since the signing of the agreement, the conflict between Malaysia and the international financial community has escalated. Prime Minister Mahathir blamed international speculators for his country's woes. In September 1998, Malaysia took drastic steps to insulate itself from the vagaries of the international markets, which, despite criticisms, may not have been a bad decision. Still, this remains the exception to the general rule that Islamic countries are expected to comply with many of the new norms of global banking, despite institutional, cultural, political and religious obstacles.

Although most Islamic techniques have conventional counterparts, they do not always fit conveniently within existing regulatory regimes. The main financing techniques often imply specific contractual obligations and different levels of risk than their conventional counterparts.[41] From the standpoint of Islamic bankers, Islamic financial techniques are fundamentally different from conventional loans, and they should, therefore, not be subjected to the same prudential ratios and capital requirements as conventional banks.[42] As for the attitude of many Western regulators, it can be summed up in a famous statement by Robin Leigh-Pemberton, the former Governor of the Bank of England, to the effect that Islamic banking is "a perfectly acceptable mode of investment, but it does not fall within the long-established and well understood definition of what constitutes banking in this country."[43]

From the standpoint of ownership and control, at least two major groups of Islamic banks have had a hard time complying with the "comprehensive consolidated supervision by the home country regulator" requirements, namely the Dar al-Maal al-Islami (DMI) and the Dallah al-Baraka group. DMI, controlled by Prince Mohammed al-Faisal al-Saud, is headquartered in the Bahamas and runs its network of banks out of Geneva. Commercial operations extend throughout the Islamic world, though not in Saudi Arabia. Similarly, the Dallah al-Baraka group is controlled by Saleh Kamel, a Saudi citizen, but does not operate a bank in his home country. Ever since the collapse of the BCCI, which had used loopholes within the global regulatory system to engage in illegal practices, regulators have frowned upon such structures. In 1993, the Bank of England ordered the closure of al-Baraka International Bank, the British subsidiary of the Dallah al-Baraka group, on the ground that the bank's true "mind and management" were in Saudi Arabia, although it did not operate as a bank there.[44]

Another set of issues faced by Islamic financial institutions is the new emphasis on internal risk management. Because of the religious injunctions against gharar,[45] financial institutions and their Shariah Boards tread carefully around all issues involving risk,[46] including complicated financial instruments designed to control risk. Thus, although such products are supposed to control risk and reduce it (although as we have seen, they sometimes have the opposite effect), they do not always pass muster with Shariah Boards. Islamic banks have thus generally lagged behind in their efforts to devise the risk management techniques required by regulators.

Other regulatory complications are posed by the nature of interest-free banking. In the United States, for example, Islamic financial institutions have found it hard to comply with the Truth in Lending Act, the federal regulation that governs full disclosure of terms and costs in lending transactions. The law requires the use of the term "annual percentage rate." Even replacing it, as some have suggested, by a "profit participation rate" would be tricky since it would mean the endorsement of the "fixed, pre-determined rate" concept to which many Islamic scholars object.

One of the flaws of the principle of global and compulsory norms is that it ignores the fact that banking structures are embedded within a religious, institutional, political, and cultural context that cannot, international prodding notwithstanding, be changed overnight. Consider, for example, the new norms of banking supervision: arms' length relations between banks and their customers; "Know-your-customer" rules;[47] limits on sizable exposure to a single client or to a group of connected clients; disclosure and transparency, etc. It is unrealistic to expect the successful implementation of such principles in countries where the business community is small and enjoys close ties with the political elite.

Matters of disclosure and transparency also have a cultural dimension. The openness with which the Americans discuss financial matters – such an executive's salary or an individual's net worth – comes in sharp contrast to the way such matters are discussed, or the fact that they are not discussed at all, in other cultures. The opacity extends to issues such as bank ownership, where the use of "fronts" is common and does not necessarily imply sinister intent. In the first high profile instance of application of the 1991 FBSEA, Saudi Arabia's National Commercial Bank, the largest bank in the Middle East was accused of helping the BCCI conceal its ownership and financial condition, and was ordered by the Federal Reserve Board to close its New York branch. In a compromise, it eventually chose a "voluntary liquidation," and a $170-million penalty was levied against its former head, Sheikh Khalid Bin Mahfouz.[48] His attorney, Laurence Tribe, the Harvard University constitutional law expert, undertook to rehabilitate him by arguing that the case highlighted a lack of cross-cultural understanding and an international financial and regulatory system more adapted to pursuing and controlling corruption than to defending individual rights.[49]

In the past few years, there have been great strides toward achieving greater coherence and bringing such regulation in line with the evolution of global financial regulation. The creation in 2002 of the IFSB in Kuala Lumpur was a major accomplishment, since it brought together central banks from the Islamic world and all the major players in Islamic finance. A principal role of the IFSB is to issue prudential standards to be adopted by various regulators. The IFSB, working in close cooperation with the Basel Committee and the IMF has issued standards on risk management, capital adequacy, and corporate governance. In 2005, the IFSB also issued a draft on the application of Basel 2 rules to Islamic institutions.

It should also be said that a greater coherence and harmonization has been achieved through informal and semi-formal means. As explained by Abdel Maoula Chaar, Shariah Board interlocks[50] – the fact that prominent Shariah advisors tend to belong to multiple Shariah Boards – and the *de facto* rule-making mechanisms achieved through close cooperation between central banks and universities offering programs on Islamic finance have played a significant role in shaping Islamic financial practices.

VII The Supervision of Islamic Financial Institutions

1 Prudential Regulation

Left to its own devices, the financial industry is prone to various excesses and types of fraud. These in turn undermine confidence and can shake the economy to its foundations.[51] A central function of the regulators is "prudential" – that is, making sure that financial institutions operate in a prudent manner. Confidence is instilled by establishing the right safeguards and enforcing strict supervision. A number of monitoring mechanisms – prudential ratios, accounting, auditing, and disclosure rules – are available and have far-reaching implications. The sudden liberalization of finance has revealed the predicament of regulators. On the one hand, they are dedicated to a free market and strive to encourage financial dynamism and innovation. But on the other hand, a freewheeling climate is highly conducive to fraud, in particular to speculative bubbles and "pyramid" schemes – whereby institutions pay dividends from new deposits, rather than from profits generated by legitimate business operations. In Egypt in the 1980s, billions of dollars "evaporated," and the fact that the IMMCs operated under the veil of Islam was particularly damaging.[52] Islamic financial institutions present special problems. Due to the potential for Islamic moral hazard and the lack of suitable Islamic investments, many banks have been prone to placing their excess liquidity in risky places. Insofar as they do not usually purchase Treasury Bonds, and that they often place their assets overseas, regulators are often unable to properly monitor the bank. Another potential problem has to do with profit-sharing ratios and the bank's relation to its customers. At times of low profits, banks sometimes choose to subsidize profit distributions to depositors out of the bank owners' share of profits, which is clearly unsustainable in the long run.[53]

2 The Question of Dual Regulation

Countries having a dual – conventional and Islamic – financial system must contend with a dilemma: should both types of banks be subjected to the same rules and regulations (on capital adequacy ratios, liquidity provisions, depository reserves, accounting and auditing standards, etc.)?; and should they be supervised by the same supervisory authorities? Given the current emphasis among international regulators on comprehensive regulation, a strong case can be made in favor of a single regulator that would be in a position to see the "big picture" of the financial system. Regulators may not accomplish their mission if a whole segment of the industry is beyond their reach.

Until a few years ago, Islamic banks tended to favor separate treatment. Their argument can be divided into two parts: a religious argument, based on the belief that religious factors should be paramount; and an economic argument, to the effect that Islamic operations are fundamentally different from conventional ones. It is unfair, in their view, to treat the main Islamic financing techniques – mudaraba, musharaka, and murabaha – as conventional loans since many such operations do not constitute lending, but merely financing, or even sales. Also, as they lobbied in favor of special treatment, Islamic banks argued that only by being treated separately could they be in a position to develop their identity and in turn create new products.

A related issue is that of discrimination – whether positive or negative. Conventional banks have repeatedly decried the "special privileges" enjoyed by their Islamic counterparts, which in their view amount to unfair competition. Conversely, at times Islamic institutions have complained about not having the same prerogatives as their conventional competitors. Consider, for example, the case of Faisal Islamic Bank of Egypt. Created in 1977 by a special law, it was given countless privileges that went far beyond the already considerable advantages provided to foreign investors by 1974 (Law No. 43). The new bank was exempted from foreign exchange controls, corporation regulations, credit control (except for credits in local currency), labor laws and social legislation, and customs duties. Also, for a period of 15 years, it would not be subject to income, corporate, or real estate taxes. It was further given iron-clad guarantees against nationalization or seizure of deposits. And it was placed above the law, since any conflict between the bank and any other party would be resolved solely by the bank's board of directors. Such an array of privileges (some of which were later rescinded) led to accusations that the bank would become a "state within the state."[54]

Similar criticisms were leveled at Turkish "Finance Houses"[55] (now known as participation banks) which, since their inception, were subjected to lower reserve requirements than their conventional counterparts.[56] In 1996, during the rule of Islamist Prime Minister Necmettin Erbakan, the six Islamic institutions were given a further boost when their performance bonds were deemed acceptable in state tenders. At the same time, however, Islamic institutions were arguing that they were in fact the ones discriminated against. As proof that they were victimized by a political vendetta led by the military-dominated political establishment, they put forth the following evidence: the authorities had made it nearly impossible for them to expand their branch network; an earlier increase in reserve requirements had already slowed down the flow of deposits; and they were more thoroughly inspected by the Treasury and the Central Bank than the conventional banks.[57] But soon after the Islamic Prime Minister was forced to resign in 1997, new legislation brought Islamic financial institutions under the jurisdiction of the banking law.

Worldwide, the current trend in bank regulation and central banking is toward "independence," meaning that regulators ought to be technocrats insulated from political pressures. A case can be made that such insulation is more difficult to achieve in the case of Islamic banks, as regulatory considerations are more likely to be overridden by politica and, of course, religious, considerations. Another issue is that of experience. The regulation of Islamic financial institutions requires an understanding of both Islamic and conventional finance. If anything, the novelty of Islamic financial products calls for greater vigilance, especially as rapid growth and competitive pressures are likely to lead financial institutions to take on greater risks.

The recent trend has been toward clarifying the status of Islamic banks through new dedicated legislation, and generally bringing them under the same regulatory framework as conventional banks, while generally recognizing their special status. In Kuwait, for example, Islamic banking was long subjected to special treatment: Kuwait Finance House, long the sole Islamic bank of the country was not regulated by the Central Bank but by the Ministry of Finance. In 2003, new legislation ended this near-monopoly, set up new conditions for the creation of Islamic banks, and brought Kuwait Finance House under the regulatory umbrella of the Central Bank.

3 Deposit Insurance and the Lender of Last Resort Issue

Another unresolved issue is that of deposit insurance. In most countries, if a bank fails, a government agency, drawing on a special insurance fund, steps in to reimburse depositors. The underlying philosophy is that certain types of deposits and certain groups of people deserve to be protected – in effect insulated from the ups and downs of the economic cycle. In the United States, deposits up to $200,000 are insured by the Federal Deposit Insurance Company (FDIC). In exchange for the protection customers accept a lower remuneration. Banks pay a premium and agree to strict controls by the FDIC.

Insofar as Islamic banking is supposed to be primarily based on PLS, deposit insurance should not normally apply. Depositors are shareholders of sorts, whose fortunes are tied to the institution's fate (or to the fate of the specific investment being financed). Only if the institution (or the investment being financed) makes a profit will they be entitled to a share of the profit. Potential losses carry a heavy political and economic cost. Typically, the government is likely to step in. No consensus exists among Islamic banks, which are caught in a dilemma: the logic of PLS accounts does not lend itself to deposit insurance; yet human psychology is such that depositors want to have it both ways – share in the profits and be insured against losses. The absence of "fixed, pre-determined" interest rates complicates the determination of premiums and, of course, such protection has the unfortunate consequence of discouraging the typically Islamic PLS accounts in favor of conventional demand deposit ones.

In reality, the share of PLS transactions has been very low.[58] On a number of occasions, Islamic banks (and thus indirectly their depositors) have had to be rescued, usually as a result of losses on commodities and foreign exchange markets and sometimes as a result of fraud. In most instance, there was one of three outcomes (or a combination thereof): temporary takeover by the Central Bank (it happened temporarily for Egypt's IIBID); injection of funds from the government (it happened in 1984 with the Kuwait Finance House); or emergency funds from consortia of Islamic banks, usually led by the IDB (it happened with the Dubai Islamic Bank in 1998).

There is, therefore, everywhere at least implicitly, some deposit insurance scheme and a lender of last resort. When South Africa's Islamic Bank Limited was liquidated in 1997, the South African Reserve Bank announced that, although the country does not have deposit insurance protection, it would compensate all depositors up to 50,000 rand ($11,000) each. The decision was taken "in the interest of financial stability of the country." The announcement also stated that "this arrangement should not be seen as creating a precedent."[59]

Such a caveat was to be a reminder that expecting bailouts can lead to reckless behavior – one example of the all-pervasive moral hazard, which extends to many aspects of financial supervision. The concept, which originated in the insurance industry, is that certain rules and practices tend to encourage reckless behavior. For example, once a business has obtained fire insurance, it may be inclined to reduce its expenditures on fire safeguards and prevention, thus increasing the likelihood of a fire as well as the size of the losses that the insurer may incur.[60] By the same token, insured depositors care little about the financial health of their bank, while unscrupulous financial operators may be invited to gamble with the public's money. For a slightly higher interest rate on insured deposits, a weak or even insolvent financial institution can obtain almost unlimited funds.[61] A similar incentive to engage in risky behavior occurs when management operates without substantial net worth or stockholder capital. Indeed, legislation aimed at allowing savings and loan corporations (S&Ls) to diversify their investments beyond financing home purchases, combined with lax supervision and an increase in the insured deposit amounts turned out to be an invitation to gamble with the insured public's money through real estate speculation or junk bonds.[62]

By the same token, announcing that the government will be a lender of last resort can encourage risky behavior. In most instances, there is an implicit "too big to fail" policy – an unspoken guarantee against failure given to the largest institutions for fear of either run contagion or a gridlock shutdown of the payment or banking system. The predicament of regulators in a free enterprise system is that they must act as if such a safety net did not exist – or else they would invite customers of small banks to transfer their deposits to largest banks – yet be ready to rescue those institutions whose collapse is likely to trigger a domino effect.[63]

A related question is that of the resources of a central bank in an interest-free setting. Assuming no deposit insurance scheme, where would the resources of the Central Bank come from? One suggestion was that the Central Bank should acquire some equity in the commercial banking sector, giving it access to the resources necessary for it to act as lender of last resort.[64]

VIII Conclusion

In the early years of Islamic finance, national regulators enjoyed wide autonomy. Islamic regulators could devise rules and practices with minimum interference from the outside world. This chapter has explained why this is no longer the case. Today, they are urged to comply with new international rules, as well as liberalize and open up their financial sector to foreign competition. Islamic regulators thus face a daunting task to which they are singularly ill-prepared: they must engage in consolidation and reform in the face of considerable obstacles before domestic banks confront the onslaught of foreign competition. As one analyst remarked:

> The terrible truth is that supervisors in developing countries, capable and well intentioned though they may be, typically lack the resources, independence and clout to do their jobs properly. As a result, the banks in their care are often able to expand recklessly, lend carelessly and run themselves unwisely. To make things worse, supervisors sometimes come under pressures to turn a blind eye to the imprudent practices of some bankers.[65]

At a time of harmonization of regulatory practices, the interest-free Islamic regulators have a hard time achieving convergence with interest-based conventional regulators. Interest rates have been an essential (and convenient) tool of regulation and control. By raising or lowering a variety of rates, regulators can influence the money supply and achieve specific policy goals. In an interest-free system, such a tool cannot in theory be used. Advocates of Islamic banking argue that other tools – such as modifying reserve requirements for banks; injecting liquidity into the system, for example, by manipulating surpluses or deficits; or imposing new "lending ratios" (the proportion of demand deposits that commercial banks are obliged to lend out as interest-free loans); or "refinance ratios" (which refer to the Central Bank refinancing of a part of the interest-free loans provided by the commercial banks) – can be used.[66] Original solutions have been offered to deal with issues such as deposit insurance or the ability to be lenders of last resort,[67] especially since the creation of the IFSB.

The main problem with one-size-fits-all approaches is that they ignore the fact that different countries have different institutional frameworks and regulatory cultures. To be sure, there are a number of escape clauses,[68] and the makers of the new global norms usually pay lip service to the notion that differences across regulatory systems should be part of rule making. Clearly, the timetables and expectations of the new global regulations are unrealistic. It remains that, given the firm deadlines associated with the implementation of the "Core Principles" and the WTO Agreement, and given the various surveillance and enforcement mechanisms discussed earlier, there is little doubt that the new norms – openness and transparency, free flow of capital, internal controls, better informed and more consistent supervision – will define, if not the extent of change, at least its direction. As countries build legal and regulatory infrastructures – especially with regard to nascent stock and financial markets – they will be bound by the new rules.

Finally, it should be said that following the credit crunch of 2008, a complete overhaul of regulation at the national and international levels is on the table. What kind of changes will be imposed (and how they will affect the Islamic sector) remains to be seen.

Notes

1. Ahmed Abdel Aziz El-Nagar, *One Hundred Questions & One Hundred Answers Concerning Islamic Banks* (Cairo: International Association of Islamic Banks, 1980), p. 8.
2. Mohammed Ariff (ed.), *Monetary and Fiscal Economics of Islam* (Jeddah: International Centre for Research in Islamic Economics, 1982).
3. "I. M. F. Puts Bank Losses From Global Financial Crisis at $4.1 Trillion," *The New York Times*, April 21, 2009.
4. Ibrahim Warde, "Regulatory Cultures," IBPC Working Papers, 1998.
5. Kevin Phillips, *Bad Money: Reckless Finance, Failed Politics, and the Global Crisis of American Capitalism* (New York: Viking, 2008).
6. Charles R. Morris, *The Trillion Dollar Meltdown: Easy Money, High Rollers, and the Great Credit Crash* (New York: Public Affairs, 2008).
7. See Chapter 8.
8. *The Economist*, September 19, 1992.
9. John Gerard Ruggie, "International Regimes, Transactions, and Change: Embedded Liberalism in the Postwar Economic Order," in Stephen D. Krasner (ed.), *International Regimes* (Ithaca, NY: Cornell University Press, 1983).
10. John Zysman, *Governments, Markets and Growth* (Ithaca, NY: Cornell University Press, 1983).
11. Susan Strange, *Casino Capitalism* (Manchester: Manchester University Press, 1997).
12. See Chapter 5.
13. Claude E. Barfield (ed.), *International Financial Markets: Harmonization versus Competition* (Washington, DC: The American Enterprise Institute Press, 1996).
14. François Chesnais, *La mondialisation financière: Genèse, coût et enjeux* (Paris: Syros, 1996).
15. Ibrahim Warde, "Les remèdes absurdes du Fonds monétaire international," *Le Monde diplomatique*, February 1998.
16. The G7 and the G10 refer, respectively, to the seven and the ten most industrialized countries. The G7 should more accurately be called the G8 since it now formally includes Russia.
17. Ethan B. Kapstein, *Governing the Global Economy: International Finance and the State* (Cambridge, MA: Harvard University Press, 1994).
18. See http://www.group30.org/members.htm.
19. Based on a variety of Group of Thirty publications, and on information from its website, available at: http://www.group30.org.
20. It was initially created upon the adoption of the Young Plan, which was designed to settle the problem of German reparations after the First World War at the Hague Agreements of January 20, 1930. Initially, it was owned by six European central banks and an American financial institution. The United States, although an active

   participant did not formally become a shareholder until 1994. The history of the bank
   has left it many quirks: although owned by central banks, its shares are trades on stock
   exchanges in Paris and Zurich; its also has its own "currency," the gold franc.

21. http://www.newyorkfed.org/aboutthefed/fedpoint/fed22.html.

22. Miroslava Filipovic, *Governments, Banks and Global Capital: Securities Markets in Global
    Politics* (Aldershot: Ashgate, 1997), p. 175.

23. Based on publications, press releases and website of the Bank for International Settle-
    ments.

24. The Atlanta (Georgia) branch of the Banca Nazionale del Lavoro had made illegal
    loans to the Iraqi government.

25. Raj K. Bhala, *Foreign Bank Regulation after BCCI* (Durham, NC: Carolina Academic
    Press, 1994).

26. Filipovic, *Governments, Banks and Global Capital*, p. 180.

27. John D. Wagster, "Impact of the 1988 Basle Accord on International Banks," *Journal
    of Finance* (September 1996).

28. *Global Finance* (November 1992).

29. Ibrahim Warde, *The Regulation of Foreign Banking in the United States* (San Francisco, CA:
    IBPC, 1998).

30. Basel Committee on Banking Supervision, "International Convergence of Capital
    Measurement and Capital Standards", Basel, 1988.

31. Kevin Phillips, *Arrogant Capital: Washington, Wall Street and the Frustration of American Politics*
    (Boston, MA: Little Brown, 1995), pp. 121–8.

32. The Group of Thirty, "Global Institutions, National Supervision and Systemic Risk,"
    Washington, DC, 1997.

33. John C. Braddock, *Derivatives Demystified: Using Structured Financial Products* (New York:
    Wiley, 1997), Lillian Chew, *Managing Derivative Risks: The Use and Abuse of Leverage* (New
    York: Wiley, 1996).

34. David Fairlamb, "Beyond Capital Adequacy," *Institutional Investor* (August 1997).

35. *The Wall Street Journal*, December 15, 1997.

36. *Far Eastern Economic Review*, October 2, 1997.

37. *The Financial Times*, December 15, 1998.

38. *Far Eastern Economic Review*, October 2, 1997.

39. The countries outside the G10 are Argentina, Brazil, Chile, China, the Czech Republic,
    Hungary, India, Indonesia, Korea, Malaysia, Mexico, Poland, Russia, Singapore, and
    Thailand.

40. *The Wall Street Journal*, December 10, 1997.

41. See Chapter 7.

42. Chibli Mallat, *Islamic Law and Finance* (London: Graham and Trotman, 1988).

43. *The Financial Times*, November 28, 1995.

44. *The Financial Times*, April 3–4, 1993.

45. Chapter 3.

46. Nabil A. Saleh, *Unlawful Gain and Legitimate Profit in Islamic Law: Riba, Gharar and Islamic
    banking* (Cambridge: Cambridge University Press, 1986).

47. The "know-your-customer" rule is primarily designed to make sure that the bank is
    not a conduit for illicit funds, such as those obtained from money laundering. Banks
    are expected to report suspicious transactions to regulators.

48. Ibrahim Warde, *Foreign Banking in the United States* (San Francisco, CA: IBPC, 1995).

49. *The Financial Times*, January 10, 1995.

50. Jean-Paul Laramée (ed.), *La finance islamique à la française: Un moteur pour l'économie, une
    alternative éthique* (Paris: Bruno Leprince, 2008), p. 69.

51. See the episodes described in James Grant, *Money of the Mind: Borrowing and Lending in
    America from the Civil War to Michael Milken* (New York: Farrar, Straus and Giroux, 1992);
    and John Kenneth Galbraith, *A Short History of Financial Euphoria* (New York: Viking,

1990).

52. Chapter 4.

53. Frank E. Vogel and Samuel L. Haye, III, *Islamic Law and Finance: Religion, Risk, and Return* (The Hague: Kluwer Law International, 1998), p. 8.

54. Michel Galloux, *Finance islamique et pouvoir politique: le cas de l'Egypte moderne* (Paris: Presses Universitaires de France, 1997), p. 57.

55. Turkish legislation did not allow the use of the word Islamic in either the name of the financial institution or the description of their operations.

56. Conventional banks must keep 8 per cent of all deposits and 11 per cent of all foreign exchange with the Central Bank. Islamic houses must keep 10 per cent of their current accounts held before June 1994 in cash and another 10 per cent with the Central Bank, among other requirements. *The Wall Street Journal*, January 8, 1998.

57. *The Wall Street Journal*, January 8, 1998.

58. See Chapter 7.

59. Agence France-Presse, November 21, 1997.

60. Kenneth E. Scott and Barry R. Weingast, *Banking Reform: Economic Propellants, Political Impediments* (Stanford, CA: Hoover Institution Press, 1992), p. 2.

61. Scott and Weingast, *Banking Reform*, p. 3.

62. Michael Lewis, *Liar's Poker: Rising Through the Wreckage on Wall Street* (New York: W. W. Norton, 1989), p. 218.

63. Scott and Weingast, *Banking Reform*, pp. 8–9.

64. Mohammed Uzair, "Central Banking Operations in an Interest-free Banking System," in Mohammed Ariff (ed.), *Monetary and Fiscal Economics of Islam* (Jeddah: International Centre for Research in Islamic Economics, 1982).

65. David Fairlamb, "Beyond Capital Adequacy."

66. See Mohammed Ariff (ed.), *Monetary and Fiscal Economics of Islam* (Jeddah: International Centre for Research in Islamic Economics, 1982), especially Mohammed Ariff, "Monetary Policy in an Interest-free Islamic Economy – Nature and Scope"; Mohammed Uzair, "Central Banking Operations in an Interest-free Banking System"; and Mohammed Siddiqi, "Islamic Approaches to Money, Banking and Monetary Policy: A Review."

67. Mohammed Uzair, "Central Banking Operations in an Interest-free Banking System."

68. Article 21 of the WTO Agreement, for example, allows members to take trade actions to protect their "essential security interests."

11

ISLAMIC FINANCE AND POLITICS: GUILT BY ASSOCIATION

Do Islamic banks have a domestic or international political agenda? Do they play a role in promoting radical Islam and international terrorism? The short answer is that they usually do not. Banks, by virtue of being part of the existing power structure, have a strong status quo orientation. There are, however, exceptions to that general rule. And as the next pages show, the benign view is not widely shared among authoritarian leaders who often see financial Islam as a destabilizing force.

This chapter addresses the connection between Islamic finance and politics in domestic and international contexts. Following a general discussion of the relation of money and politics, it compares the evolution of financial Islam in Saudi Arabia, Turkey, Egypt, the Sudan, and Indonesia. It later discusses the role of Islamic finance in the New World Order, and especially in the post-September 11 world, where Islamic financial institutions have often been considered "guilty by association."

Critics of Islamic finance nonetheless focus on the *potential* for political mischief, whether domestically or internationally. The suspicions surrounding Islamic banks rest on a syllogism: political Islam at the domestic and international level requires financial resources, Islamic banks are committed to Islam and have vast financial resources; therefore, Islamic banks are likely to advance the political goals of potentially subversive Islamic groups.

Any sweeping generalization about political Islam (and by implication about Islamic finance and politics) is likely to be misleading, if not outright wrong. Different, contradictory strands have coexisted at all times. One can find numerous examples of Islam as an ideology of protest against social injustice and a means to defend the rights of the disinherited and oppressed, or of Islam as the religion of the establishment, used to justify the status quo, or as an entirely non-political ideology.

A complicating factor is that relationships between religion and politics are fluid, dynamic, and dependent on contingent factors as well as external events. While it is easy to think of a government's relations with Islamic groups in terms of simple dichotomies – opposition/loyalism, co-optation/repression, etc. – the reality is more complex. Governments often apply successively, and sometimes simultaneously, contradictory policies. At times, governments fight Islam with Islam, co-opting Islamic groups as a way of keeping them under control. A complicating factor is that such policies often backfire. When the otherwise secular Zulficar Ali Bhutto tried to exploit Islam, he became all the more vulnerable to Islamic opposition group and their charges of hypocrisy.[1] Similarly, Anwar Sadat carefully cultivated his image of "believer-president" and patron of Islam. In conjunction with his overtures toward the Muslim Brothers, he amended Article 2 of the Constitution in 1971 and then again in 1980 – at a time when he was aggressively fighting Islamic fundamentalists – to proclaim that "the Islamic Shariah is the principal source of the Constitution." This did not prevent extremist groups launching a "jihad" against him, and assassinating him in 1981.[2]

I Business, Finance, and Politics

The connection between money and politics is well established. One can think of the old saying that "money is the sinew of war" or of California politician Jesse Unruh's famous dictum that "money is the mother's milk of politics," or of the advice given by the mysterious informant, "Deep Throat," to the journalists investigating the Watergate affair: "Follow the money." No wonder that Islamic financial institutions have on occasion been suspected of having a political agenda, domestically – working to establish a fundamentalist Islamic regime – or internationally – financing or serving as a conduit for "international Islamic terrorism," or even for the development of an "Islamic bomb."

Such claims, casually if sometimes hysterically made, have seldom been subjected to systematic scrutiny. It is important to distinguish the inadvertent from the intended, and the exception from the rule. Thus, it is probably true that the Islamic banks of the Sudan facilitated the advent of an Islamic state in that country. The significant issues are, first, whether it was the intended outcome of the creation of the Faisal Islamic Bank, and, second, whether such a scenario is likely to be replicated elsewhere.

Also, on occasion, Islamic financial institutions have been suspected of involvement in subversive activities. The most frequently cited example is that of the "Afghan warriors." Generously funded by Saudi Arabia and trained and organized by the CIA, a number of volunteers from Islamic countries fought, along with Afghan mujahideen, the Soviet forces in Afghanistan throughout the 1980s. The support was part and parcel of the Saudi effort to promote Islam worldwide by funneling, sometimes via Islamic financial networks, aid to a wide variety of Islamic groups, some of whom turned out to be, or became, radical and subversive.[3]

Helping the mujahideen was part of the US-led effort to overthrow the Communist regime of Kabul. Both Saudi Arabia and Pakistan, two "fundamentalist," yet pro-US, countries played an active part in that effort.[4] Unwittingly, the resistance movement sowed the seeds of a transnational anti-US and anti-Saudi political movement. Indeed, with the Soviet withdrawal, some of the non-Afghan Islamic volunteers – the so-called "Afghan Arabs" – found themselves in the position of hardened rebels without a cause, and ended up involved in a number of terrorist actions. The irony, of course, is that such attacks, which include anti-tourist attacks in Egypt, the bombing of the World Trade Center in New York in 1993, the Khobar attack on the US Air Force barracks in Saudi Arabia in 1996, the bombings of the American embassies in Nairobi and Dar es-Salam in 1998, the September 11 attacks in the United States, and many later attacks were aimed at the terrorists' former patrons. Saudi Arabia belatedly discovered that indiscriminate religious proselytizing could on occasion backfire, and has since modified its policy.

II Domestic Politics: the Power of Islamic Business and Finance

Are Islamic financial institutions part of an Islamic "civil society" working to de-legitimize governments? Are Islamists in business and finance bankrolling subversive activities? Are they tied to, or are they used by, radical groups? In every country, the answers to these questions are different. This section considers the political aspects of Islamic finance and the ties between Islamic financial institutions and political movements in Saudi Arabia, Turkey, Egypt, and Indonesia.

1 Saudi Arabia: Islamic Finance and the Possible Delegitimation of the State

Saudi Arabia is justifiably preoccupied by any challenge to its religious legitimacy. As the birthplace of Islam and as a country whose king decreed in 1986 that he should be known as the "Custodian of the Two Holy Shrines" (*Khadim al-Haramayn al-Sharifayn*), Saudi Arabia has been vulnerable to criticisms expressed over the years about the compatibility of its policies with Islamic ideals.[5] The ruling family was stunned when in late 1979 the Great Mosque of Mecca was seized, for a few weeks, by Muslim fundamentalists.[6] Underground opposition groups have since grown increasingly visible and vocal, calling for the overthrow of a regime accused of squandering the oil wealth, being too closely aligned with the United States and the West, and more generally of being un-Islamic.

The ruling family's legitimacy is based on its Islamic credentials, but the economy and the banking system are managed along Western practices. One can, therefore, understand why the Saudi Arabian regime is so sensitive about the subject of Islamic banking. The government plays up the fact that the inter-governmental Islamic Development Bank is headquartered in Jeddah, yet the two largest Islamic banking groups, Dar al-Maal al-Islami and Dallah al-Baraka, both owned by prominent Saudis, could not obtain licenses to operate commercial banks in the kingdom. And when the al-Rajhi Banking and Investment Company was authorized in 1985 to engage in interest-free banking, it was on the condition that it did not use the word "Islamic" in its name.[7]

Saudi Arabia does not officially recognize the concept of Islamic banking. The logic is that if one bank is recognized as an Islamic institution then all others, by implication, would be un-Islamic. The official line was that all banks operating in Saudi Arabia were by definition Islamic. In addition, the country's vast bank deposits and foreign holdings generated substantial interest income, and thus the Saudi authorities had to tread carefully around the issue of riba.[8] Saudi banks, for example, report interest income as "special commission income," as "service charges" or as "book-keeping fees."[9]

In the last few years, however, a new phenomenon has appeared: a creeping Islamicization from below, which was not resisted by regulators, in part because of the perceived need to be competitive with the Islamic sector of other Gulf Cooperation Council Countries (GCC) such as Qatar, Bahrain, Kuwait, and the United Arab Emirates.[10] Although the Islamic banking label was still not used by the banks, regulatory restrictions on the establishment of Islamic institutions and the sale of Islamic products were loosened. Thus, al-Rajhi lost its monopoly as the sole Islamic bank. At the time of writing, it is in competition with three other Islamic banks: Bank al-Jazeera, Bank al-Bilad, and Bank al-Inma, and a number of non-bank financial Shariah-based financial institutions. Furthermore, a growing number of conventional institutions offer Shariah-compliant products, and some of the major banks, most prominently the National Commercial Bank, have embarked on major efforts to Islamicize their operations. Overall, this Islamic sector has become a key driver of the growth of the financial sector.[11] By some estimates, 40 per cent of all Saudi accounts are Shariah-compliant, as is 75 per cent of the retail lending market.[12]

2 Turkey: the "Dangerous Relationships" between "Finance Houses" and Islamic Fundamentalists

Islamic banks have always had a special status in secular Turkey. They were once called "Special Finance Houses." Since the changes in Turkey's banking law in 2005 (at a time when the country was governed by the Justice and Development Party [AKP] of Recep Tayyip Erdogan, a party with Islamist roots), the four remaining Islamic institutions are known as "Participation Banks." They are Kuveyt Turk Participation Bank, al Baraka Turk Participation Bank, Asya Participation Bank, and Turkiye Finans Participation Bank. The role, status, and evolution of those banks can be understood only with reference to the country's recent history.

Almost alone among Islamic countries, since 1924 Turkey has adopted a staunchly secular political system. Despite strict rules against the political use of religion, Islamist groups have in recent years become increasingly visible. In 1996, for the first time in its history, Turkey had an Islamist Prime Minister. Necmettin Erbakan, leader of the Refah (or Welfare) Party, ruled for less than a year.[13] Throughout his long political career, Erbakan had advocated such measures as outlawing interest rates and replacing the Turkish lira with a vaguely defined "Islamic dinar." Yet as Prime Minister, he demonstrated great pragmatism. He was nonetheless forced to resign in 1997 under pressure from the military-dominated National Security Council, Turkey's highest decision-making body, which considered itself the guardian of Ataturk's ideal of secularization. The new government has since engaged in a crackdown on all forms of Islamism, particularly in business and finance.

Although certain segments of the business community have at certain times and in certain areas been associated with Islamic militancy,[14] the Islamicization of business is a rather recent phenomenon. Ironically, Islamic finance officially came to Turkey during the very secular Ozal years in the early 1980s.[15] At a time when the need for cash was pressing and the Islamist danger appeared remote, Turkey welcomed investments from oil-rich states and their citizens.

The election of a Welfare Party mayor in Istanbul marked a turning point. Small engineering, service, and contracting concerns which stressed their Islamic character won the business of the city. Islamic business networks grew bigger and more assertive.[16] In 1996, with the advent of an Islamist-led government, secularist groups led by the military launched an unrelenting campaign accusing the government and its allies of trying to establish an Islamic state. In the all-out war against Islamist groups, business and financial groups were a central target. By certain estimates, Islamic companies held $2.5 billion in investments in Turkey in textiles, media, chemicals, automotives, food, tourism, and transportation. The Islamist Independent Businessmen's and Industrialists' Association, also known as Musiad, founded in 1990, had 3,000 members by 1997, most of them small or medium businesses based in the Anatolian heartland. Military spokesmen alleged that 100 major businessmen controlling 1,000 companies were financing fundamentalists, undermining the "regime" and "planning to buy privatized companies." Six of the businessmen were said to be worth more than $700 million each. Kombassan, a thirty-five-company provincial cooperative that has grown rapidly on promises of a better than 25 per cent return on investments saw its bank accounts frozen. Hasim Bayram, the head of the cooperative responding to accusations that he was running a pyramid scheme declared: "This is not about ideology. It's political. This is about the old system, and old monopolistic capital, keeping the others out."[17] As for the Finance Houses, they were accused of having "a dangerous relationship" with the Islamists.[18]

The subsequent crackdown on Islamism included banning the Welfare Party, increasing penalties against the opponents of secularism, establishing new bodies in every province to guard against Islamic fundamentalism, and stepping up government control over schools. The army issued a blacklist of 100 prominent capitalists associated with Islamist groups and all 3,000 members of Musiad. The assets of Kombassan were temporarily frozen, and Islamic companies were subjected to harassment and punitive audits. Corporations identified as contributing to Islamic causes were prevented from receiving public contracts or subsidies, and new legislation brought the Special Finance Houses under stricter control and eliminated their special privileges.[19] During the banking crisis of 2000 and 2001, for example, the Special Finance Houses suffered greatly. The Savings Deposit Insurance Fund, a government agency, intervened during the crisis and took control of five banks with liquidity problems. According to one analyst, "the interference of the public authority with the banks resulted in general distrust of the banking sector. Speculations about the Finance Houses influenced the clients negatively, and the interest-free banking sector had to bear the most difficult period of the last 15 years."[20]

Ihlas Finance, an Islamic Finance House, was one of these Special Finance Houses with liquidity difficulties. Ihlas Finance eventually declared bankruptcy in 2001 and was taken over by the Banking Regulating and Supervising Agency. Thereafter, total assets in the Islamic financial sector plunged by 40 per cent due to the widespread concern over Ihlas Finance's bankruptcy and general mistrust of the banking sector.[21] Under Turkey's national banking law, deposits in Special Finance Houses, or with Islamic banks in general, are not insured by the Banking Regulating and Supervising Agency. Conventional banks, however, are given insurance for their assets.[22]

The wilderness years turned out to be relatively short for Turkish Islamists. Indeed, 2002 saw the coming to power of the AKP, a party with Islamist roots. That year, Recip Tayyip Erdogan, former Mayor of Istanbul, became Prime Minister. Five years later, Abdullah Gül, former Foreign Minister, was elected President in 2007. The debate about Islamism, secularism and Turkish nationalism took a new turn, yet on banking matters, despite the changes of name and status the old suspicions and perceptions persist.

3 Egypt: the Tensions between Secularism and Islamism

The Egyptian case is in one way unique: it is one of a few Islamic countries where the top religious establishment has approved of interest-based lending.[23] Yet from the standpoint of government suspicions about Islamic finance, the country is quite typical: the government worries about the potential of the Islamic sector, despite its heterogeneous and decentralized nature,[24] to destabilize the state.

Faisal Islamic Bank of Egypt (FIBE), the largest financial institution represents the dominant model. Since its inception, it has striven for inclusiveness and political respectability. Prince Mohammed al-Faisal al-Saud attempted to include among the bank's founders and shareholders the widest possible array of political, economic, and religious figures, ranging from Prime Minister Abd al-Aziz Hijazi (who later became a leading proselytizer of Islamic economics) to the most prominent infitah businessman Uthman Ahmed Uthman, to leading Islamist figure Tawfiq Mohammed al-Shawi. Most revealing were Prince Mohammed's efforts to include the Waqf ministry among the shareholders.[25]

The greatest political clash occurred with IMMCs.[26] Unlike the Islamic banks, they were unregulated entities working outside the official channels and thus escaped government control. Most serious analyses of the phenomenon show that with very few exceptions the IMMCs, just like other Islamic financial institutions, shied away from partisan politics. One notable exception was al-Sharif, the oldest IMMC, whose owner had ties to the Muslim Brothers.[27] The Muslim Brothers also controlled al-Taqwa ("Piety"), a bank registered in the Bahamas, but which was denied permission in 1988 to operate as a commercial bank in Egypt.[28] The IMMCs were nonetheless repeatedly accused by the government, particularly during the 1987 elections (which saw a strong showing of the alliance between the Wafd Party and the Muslim Brothers), of political meddling. Their meteoric growth caused concern. Not only did they have the resources to influence the electoral outcome, but the dynamic they had created and the symbolism they were using was considered to be subversive. One of the advertising slogans of the al-Rayyan group, the largest IMMC was "the blessings behind success" ("*al-baraka wara al-najah*"), which amounted to the economic version of the rallying cry of the Muslim Brothers and other Islamist groups ("Islam is the solution").

Authoritarian governments tend, usually for good reason, to have a nagging suspicion that agitation is occurring underground, and that it has the potential to turn into a groundswell. The operative word is "potential." The vast network of private voluntary organizations, given its size and resources has the potential to challenge the state. Low cost clinics and social welfare centers have been providing essential services to areas that have been all but abandoned by the government. The Islamic "civil society" was in a position to challenge the government to reform itself and open itself to greater democratization.[29]

The paranoia could be fed by selective evidence. Thus, the name of Sheikh Omar Abdul-Rahman, the spiritual advisor of Tanzim al-Jihad, the group accused of assassinating Anwar Sadat, and alleged mastermind of the 1993 World Trade Center bombing, has surfaced on a couple of occasions. He had been employed by one of the IMMCs as a middleman in a major business deal.[30] He was also one of the dozens of nominal "founders" of the FIBE.[31] Such "evidence," of course, proves nothing other than the need for financial institutions to surround themselves with religious figures as a means of asserting their religious legitimacy. Yet as subsequent examples will show, such isolated facts are on occasion dredged up to "prove" that Islamic financial institutions have ulterior political motives. Despite the government's inherent mistrust of the Islamic financial sector, it has continued to support the development of Islamic branches at Egypt's publicly-owned national bank, Banque Misr. Banque Misr established its first Islamic branch, al-Hussein, in 1979.[32] By 2003, Banque Misr had thirty-three Islamic branches.[33]

Presently, three major Islamic banks operate out of Egypt: FIBE, the IIBID, and the Egyptian-Saudi Investment Bank (ESIB). The state (represented by both the Ministry of Awqaf and public banks) possesses an estimated 20 per cent of the capital for FIBE, 40 per cent for ESIB and 80 per cent for IIBID.[34] Indeed, the state remains heavily involved in the Islamic financial sector. More importantly, it is attributed with influencing the sector's discourse and ideology. Al-Azhar University, for example, a public religious university whose president is appointed by Egypt's executive branch, runs the Saleh Kamel Center for Islamic and Commercial Research and Studies. The Center was established with support from Sheikh Saleh Kamel, the owner of al-Baraka Group and the primary shareholder in the Egyptian-Saudi Investment Bank. The Saleh Kamel Center has sponsored many conferences and symposiums on Islamic banking and finance in Cairo. More importantly, al-Azhar University has produced numerous religious scholars that now sit on various Shariah Boards at many Islamic banks.[35]

Islamic banking in Egypt still faces many critics. One of the stronger recent critiques came from Ahmed Kamal Abou El-Magd, a well-known Islamic scholar, who stated,

> The managers of these [Islamic] banks are neither honest nor efficient; that is why I transferred my money to conventional banks. I got the opportunity to see the contracts signed between an Islamic bank and the Bank of Credit and Commerce, and I discovered then that the managers of these banks lacked even the capacity to administer a financial institution.[36]

Sheikh Mohammed Sayed Tantawi, former Mufti of Egypt, has also been critical of Islamic banking in Egypt, and, as already discussed, issued fatwas stating that conventional banks were closer to Islam than Islamic banks.[37]

4 The Sudan: Islamicization of Politics, Politicization of Finance

When the Faisal Islamic Bank was licensed by President Nimeiri in 1978, it was under circumstances very similar to the licensing of the FIBE. In both countries, the bank obtained significant tax and regulatory breaks. But the evolution of the Sudanese bank was driven by the country's political and economic context. It quickly became the second largest bank, and developed close ties with Hassan al-Turabi (who had previously spent a number of years in exile in Saudi Arabia) and his National Islamic Front (NIF), playing a key role in promoting Islamic businesses and Islamic causes. By certain accounts, "Turabi virtually controlled the bank."[38]

The Islamicization of the entire banking sector in December 1983 further upset the country's delicate political, economic, and religious balance.[39] The Khatmiyya, a Sufi sect which since colonial rule had enjoyed considerable power among petty traders, was increasingly displaced economically and politically by the Muslim Brothers. According to one analysis:

> The investment pattern [of Islamic banks] encouraged the growth of small and medium sized businesses, and has effectively ensured support for the Muslim Brothers from the middle and lower strata of urban entrepreneurs. This has led to conflict with the traditional export-import merchants, mostly linked to the Khatmiyya order, who had previously dominated this sector and whose members have little access to Islamic bank financing.[40]

Both under Nimeiri and his successors, the Muslim Brothers and businessmen close to them, have enjoyed tremendous economic privileges. They have benefited from preferential allocations of bank loans, customs exemptions, and foreign currency for imports. They were the main beneficiaries of the privatization programs, and were given advance notice of currency devaluations.[41] To maintain their business activities, members of the Khatmiyya, unable to obtain bank loans, resorted to trading foreign currency. The government crackdown on "black market" currency traders (which included the death penalty against offenders) was justified by the need to curb inflation, but it was also interpreted as a way of maintaining the Islamic banks' (and by implication the Muslim Brothers') monopoly on commercial lending.[42]

In a bid to regain their monopoly of the country's retail trade and financial system, the Khatmiyya established the Sudanese Islamic Bank in 1982. But Nimeiri used both his ties to Saudi financiers and the domestic support of the Muslim Brothers to reconfigure the economy. By 1983, the Muslim Brothers were among Nimeiri's few remaining supporters,[43] and his decision to Islamicize the financial system was designed to benefit them.[44]

One of the consequences of the Islamicization of finance was a forced Islamicization of economic, political, and social life. Indeed, in order to qualify for an Islamic bank loan an aspiring businessman had to provide references from an already established businessman with a good record of support for the Muslim Brothers. "This has led to almost comic attempts on the part of many in the urban marketplace to assume the physical as well as religious and political guise of Islamists."[45] In sum, The Muslim Brothers initially obtained economic privileges for political reasons. This allowed them to become a state within the state, and in due course to overtake the state.

5 Indonesia: Co-optation and Pre-emption

It had long been assumed that Indonesia would not be hospitable to Islamic finance.[46] Although the country is inhabited by some 200 million Muslims (who account for some 90 per cent of the population), the country had a strong secular and multi-ethnic tradition. Full-scale Islamicization did not occur until the fifteenth century. The Indonesian brand of Islam, introduced primarily by merchants and imbued with Sufi influences, blended easily with local traditions and customs. Due to their somewhat diluted and syncretic beliefs and to the low level of religious practice, Indonesians have often been referred to as "nominal Muslims." In the political and economic system, the "primubis" (the ethnic or "native" Indonesians, most of them Muslims) historically played a marginal role.[47] Since the days of the Dutch occupation (1678–1942), economic power has belonged to the Chinese. To this day, although the Chinese constitute only about 3 per cent of the population, they own most of the leading conglomerates, and have maintained such close ties with the Suharto family that Indonesia has come to epitomize "crony capitalism."[48] Comparable in numbers, the Indonesian Christians have been disproportionately represented in the government and the military.

The delicate ethnic, religious, political, and economic balance was maintained through a system of "religious secularism." The Indonesian constitution affirms the belief in "One, Supreme Divinity" as the first of its "five principles" (pancasila), but it does not mention Islam or even Allah.[49] The system, whose motto is "unity through diversity" emphasizes the importance of consensus ("*mufakat*"), which is also used as a justification for authoritarianism.

For most of the rule of President Suharto (1965–98), neither the Islamic religion nor its leaders played any significant political role. But with the rise of Islamist opposition, Suharto started courting religious leaders and made openings to the more devout segment of the population. He gave his blessing to the creation of the Association of Moslem Intellectuals (ICMI), an influential grooming ground for leaders founded by B. J. Habibie (Suharto's successor and President from 1998 to 1999). The government relaxed restrictions on Islamic dress, and the Suharto family made a widely-publicized pilgrimage to Mecca. Islamic groups such as Nahdathul Ulama and the Muhammadiyah, both partisans of a moderate and non-political Islam, focusing instead on the expression of religious faith through social programs, education, and moral guidance were increasingly co-opted, in part as a way of undercutting extremist groups. A number of Christian figures in the army and in government were replaced by Muslims.[50]

Thus, Suharto became a patron of Islamic banking. Soon after the Indonesian Ulemas Council (MUI), the country's highest Muslim authority, resolved in August 1990 that an interest-free banking system should be established, it was the Amal Bhakti Muslim Pancasila Foundation (of which Suharto was chairman) which gave the MUI an interest-free loan of Rp3 billion as a deposit to establish Bank Muamalat Indonesia (BMI) and support its banking license application. Suharto also offered the presidential palace in Bogor, West Java as a venue for the sale of shares to the public. When the bank opened in 1992, it had shareholder commitments totaling Rp106 billion, an amount exceeding the paid-up capital of any Indonesian bank at the time. BMI was also to become the catalyst in the development of an Islamic financial sector. And indeed, soon afterwards, a number of rural Islamic banks and credit cooperatives were established. In 1994, together with the MUI and the Association of Indonesian Muslim Intellectuals, the bank launched the country's first Islamic insurance company, Syarikat Takaful.

True to the country's developmental orientation, the bank's mission was to help the government in the process of national economic development, particularly in relation to small- and medium-scale entrepreneurship. Interestingly, however, the BMI's articles of association do not limit its shareholders to Muslims, and a significant segment of its clientele consists of non-Muslims.[51] By 1999, only three Islamic banks, including Muamalat, existed in Indonesia. Almost a decade later, twenty-three Islamic banks operated, along with 456 Islamic windows at conventional banks.[52] Indonesia is the largest economy in southeast Asia, but it has been slow to develop the Islamic banking sector for its predominantly Muslim population. Indonesia's Islamic banking industry represents only 5 per cent of Indonesian domestic bank assets, for example, compared with 12 percent representation in Malaysia.[53] In 2006, however, Islamic banks published a 79 per cent year-on-year increase in business activity to $1.36 billion.[54]

Islamic banking and finance will likely continue to grow and thrive in Indonesia.

In the last four years alone, there has been a noticeable spike in Islamic banking and finance across Indonesia. This recent trend was helped in large part by a 2003 MUI decree stating that regular bank financial transactions are not compliant with the Shariah. After the declaration, many pious Muslims followed the ruling and opened accounts with Shariah-compliant banks.[55]

The Indonesian government and its Indonesian Islamic banks are catching on to the increased attraction and growth of the sector by offering new and innovative Islamic financial products. In 2006, for example, approximately twenty Shariah funds were in operation, and at least seventeen companies listed on the Jakarta Stock Exchange had issued Shariah-compliant bonds, or an estimated 10 per cent of the total number of listed companies that have issued debt instruments.[56] The government also issued its first ever sukuk.[57] Further, three primary banks (Bank Danamon, Bank Negara Indonesia (BNI), and Bank Mandiri) now issue Islamic credit cards.[58] In 2008, the Indonesian government increased its commitment to developing the Islamic financial sector by agreeing to support a new bill on Shariah law that would permit foreigners to establish Islamic banks across Indonesia.[59] HSBC is the only foreign bank currently licensed to conduct Islamic banking in Indonesia.[60]

The tsunami tragedy and devastation caused in Aceh Province provided a surprising new market for Islamic banks after 2004. According to one report:

> The tsunami that devastated Aceh Province in north Sumatra left countless people in need of bank loans but nothing to show as collateral to a regular bank. The tragedy has created a tremendous need for compassionate lending and an opportunity for Islamic financial services to settle deep roots in Indonesia.[61]

After the tragedy, many banks sought immediate permission to open branches. By the end of 2005, an estimated twenty-five Islamic bank branches operated regionally.[62]

III Islamic Finance and the Islamist Threat

Islamic banks have often been portrayed as having a global political agenda. In recent years, countless accusations – never backed up by any credible evidence – have surfaced, purporting to warn against the evil designs of Islamic institutions. Initially confined to the lunatic fringe, such views have, at a time when far right and supremacist circles are increasingly vocal,[63] made occasional inroads into the political mainstream. This section discusses the debate about political Islam, the "Sudanese exception," and the Islamophobic discourse on Islamic finance.

1 Perspectives on Global Islam

Fears over global Islam started with the Iranian revolution, and were later greatly amplified following the demise of communism and the search for a new enemy.

John Esposito offers a useful summary of the Western mind-set in the wake of the revolution:

> Amid the hysteria of the post revolutionary period, assessing the Iranian threat, separating fact from fiction, proved difficult if not impossible for the West and its allies. The shock of a revolution which had made the unthinkable a reality resulted in an overcompensation that saw both Iranian domestic politics and foreign policy through the lenses of Islamic radicalism and extremism.[64]

The collapse of communism made things worse. In January 1991, columnist William Pfaff wrote: "There are a good many people who think that the war between communism and the West is about to be replaced by a war between the West and Muslims."[65] Indeed, the "threat vacuum" made Islam the most likely candidate for "global enemy." Shortly after the fall of the Berlin Wall, columnist Charles Krauthammer had warned of an "unnoticed but just as portentous global intifada ... an uprising spanning the Islamic world."[66] Islam was all the more threatening since most influential pundits and academics posited a fundamental incompatibility between Islam and Western values. Thus, Amos Perlmutter, a professor at Washington's American University wrote: "There is no spirit of reconciliation between Islamic fundamentalism and the modern world – that is, the Christian–secular universe."[67]

The theme of Islam as new global enemy soon dominated foreign policy thinking.[68] The influential journal, *Foreign Affairs*, published by the Council on Foreign Relations, carried a debate: "Is Islam a Threat?" (Judith Miller answered "yes," Leon Hadar answered "no").[69] The debate was given, if not theoretical and historical depth, at least academic cachet when Harvard University's Samuel Huntington wrote his famous *Foreign Affairs* article "The Clash of Civilizations?," which argued that future conflicts would break out along civilizational lines, with Islam and Confucianism epitomizing those "civilizations" that were inherently hostile to Western values. Huntington later converted his article into a book which acted as an intellectual foundation for foreign policy makers that pitted the West against the rest of the world.

Huntingtonesque analyses are often based on a number of dubious yet oft-repeated axioms: Islam is a monolith and all Muslims are united in action; and all Islamists, perhaps even all Muslims, are at heart radical and anti-Western. As demonstrated throughout this book, Islam is extremely diverse and fragmented. Indeed, a number of pan-Islamic organizations whose rhetoric emphasizes cooperation, if not unity, exist today. In fact, most are allies of the United States. However, in addition to groups such as the OIC or the Arab League, there are a number of sub-groupings onto which superficial observers find it is easy to project unity of purpose and action. In 1997, for example, an initiative by Turkish Prime Minister Necmettin Erbakan designed to fight poverty and establish a "just world order" led to the first meeting of the "Developing 8" – Turkey, Pakistan, Indonesia, Iran, Bangladesh, Egypt, Malaysia, and Nigeria – countries with little in common other than their Islamic character. From the outset, representatives disagreed on all major issues, reflecting variations in ideology, global outlook, and economic priorities, yet the meeting ended with the requisite pledge of coopera-tion in several economic fields, including industrial development, research, banking, and agriculture.[70] Similarly, a meeting of the newly formed ten-country Organization of Economic Cooperation (OEC) brought together representatives from Turkey, Iran, Pakistan, Azerbaijan, Afghanistan, Kazakhstan, Kyrgyzstan, Tajikistan, Turkmenistan, and Uzbekistan.[71] Pledges of economic cooperation were overshadowed by deep political and religious differences.

Dubious, if common, assertions to the contrary, a common Islamic foreign policy is difficult to identify. Examples abound of the inability of Islamic countries to unite in the face of major crises. Relations between and among "fundamentalist" (in one way or another) states – Saudi Arabia, Pakistan, Iran, Sudan, Afghanistan – are anything but harmonious. At the time of the first Gulf War in 1990–1, for example, most Islamic countries sided with the US-led coalition against Iraq, while Iran abstained. Additionally, several Islamic governments supported the US-led coalition to invade Iraq and topple Saddam Hussein in 2003.

History is also replete with examples of Muslim rulers uniting with "infidels" to fight co-religionists. The great Abbassid caliph, Harun al-Rashid, whose reign is remembered as a golden age of Islamic achievement, carried on a friendly correspondence with his Christian contemporary, Charlemagne, at a time when the latter was engaged in hostilities against the Umayyad rulers of Spain. Later, in medieval Spain, alliances of Muslim princes with Christians, such as El Cid, against other Muslims, became quite commonplace.[72] Edward Mortimer, in challenging "the notion of the house of Islam as a single community of believers, whose members owed solidarity to one another in any conflict with outsiders" noted that even in the nineteenth century, "expressions of solidarity were gener-ally a matter of lip-service rather than statements of serious intent to take risks or make sacrifices where one's own interests were not directly threatened."[73]

2 Saudi Finance and Sudanese Politics

In the Sudan, Islamic finance played an important role in bringing about polit-ical Islamicization. Lest one be tempted to draw sweeping generalizations based on that case, one should keep in mind the specific context of Sudanese Islam, more specifically the facts that: (1) the Nemeiri regime had moved from Nasser-style Arab socialism to establishing an Islamic state; (2) for many years (roughly until 1993) the Islamic regime had been dominated by free market, pro-Western policies; and (3) the leading Islamic figures, especially Hassan al-Turabi were labeled as "moderate." Turabi was warmly supported by the Reagan Administra-tion for his staunch anti-communism. He visited the United States in 1992, and it was only in 1993 that the Sudan was added to the list of countries supporting terrorism.[74] Even after that date, the Sudan was on occasion helpful in the fight against global terrorism: it delivered terrorist Illich Ramirez Sanchez ("Carlos") to France, and expelled Usama bin Laden from its territory.[75]

Many analysts have conflated and compressed a complex series of events to show that Islamic banks were instrumental in bringing about a "rogue state." The role of the Faisal Islamic Bank of Sudan bolstered the argument that money collected in the name of Islam is in the final analysis used for political ends, and that even conservative, pro-Western regimes promote radical Islam. Thus, Judith Miller concludes that "Saudi and Gulf support, though diffuse and often ostensibly donated to cultural and charitable Islamic causes, has been equally, if not more, consequential for Islamist groups (than Iranian funding)."[76]

In reality, arguing that the Saudi regime wanted to create the kind of regime which later emerged would be tantamount to arguing that the United States conspired to create the rabidly anti-US "Afghan Arabs." The point is that unintended consequences should be distinguished from conscious agenda. Saudi Arabia has attempted to deal with the unwitting fallout from its indiscriminate generosity by enacting in 1993 and 1994 a number of changes in its proselytizing efforts. It set up a Supreme Council of Islamic Affairs, headed by Prince Sultan to consider aid requests from Islamic groups, and banned the collection of private money within the kingdom for charitable Muslim causes without Interior Ministry permit. Such efforts were considerably stepped up in the post-September 11 years.[77]

3 The Demonization of Islamic Finance

To those who were quick to associate anything Islamic with terrorism, Islamic banks and financial institutions provide a logical target. In a climate of generalized suspicion, Islamic banks – and more generally banks from the Islamic world – are often considered guilty until proven innocent. Virtually every work in the "secrets of terrorist financing" genre has made such allegations,[78] using broad unsubstantiated assertions or a six-degrees of separation logic (A knows B who knows C, and since C is suspected of terrorism, A too must be a terrorist).[79] So entrenched were the suspicions that the US Treasury asked foreign bank regulators, including the Saudi Arabian Monetary Authority (SAMA), to include Islamic banks among those institutions warranting close surveillance.[80]

The rationale for the financial focus of the "global war on terror" was three-fold. First, tracing financial flows held the promise of untangling money puzzles and yielding information about terrorist or otherwise objectionable groups. Second, the use of economic and financial tools – embargoes, asset seizures, and the like – was supposed to starve terrorism. Third, the financial front held the promise of "framing the guilty" through a host of derivative crimes, such as money laundering.[81]

The initial blow to Islamic banking and finance after September 11 was considerable since it had been well-integrated into the global economy, and had been widely regarded as a useful way of countering Islamic extremism.[82] At a November 2001 Islamic Banking Conference in Bahrain, two of the most prominent figures in Islamic finance expressed dismay at the smear campaigns against their institutions. Prince Muhammed al-Faisal, founder of the DMI Group, declared:

> We all condemn the September 11 attack on the World Trade Center and Pentagon as a heinous crime, which has nothing to do with Islam or Muslims as a whole. The West is raising various questions. But these questions are not raised with us, but with "experts" who do not know anything about this.

Asked about the freezing of assets of some Islamic institutions, he said: "If they wanted to do it merely on the basis of suspicion let them do it. Of course, it is fair to freeze anyone's assets if there is proof and there should be remedy if they do so without any proof." As for Sheikh Saleh Kamel, founder of the al-Baraka Group, and chairman of the General Council for Islamic Banks and Financial Institutions (CIBAFI), he declared:

> The concept of Islamic banking is one of the creative methods of Islam to serve the economic and social welfare of Muslims. But some circles tried to use the September 11 attacks to launch a campaign under the false pretext that these Islamic banks are the source for financing terrorism.[83]

The general level of ignorance on the subject is epitomized by a statement made by former National Security Advisor Sandy Berger shortly after September 11. The top official in charge of the surveillance of bin Laden's networks during his tenure at the White House (1996–2000) casually stated that it would be difficult to track down Usama bin Laden's money because it was hidden in "underground banking, Islamic banking facilities."[84] And it took six months for Treasury Secretary Paul O'Neill, the official in charge of the financial war on terror, to "learn," in March 2002 following meetings in Saudi Arabia, Kuwait, and Bahrain, that Islamic banking is "a legitimate way of doing business."[85] Since that time, the US Treasury has established a scholar-in-residence position to provide better understanding and awareness of Islamic finance,[86] and a growing number of regulators within the United States have expressed their "openness to Islamic financial products" – which in the Islamophobic literature was promptly called "playing into the hands of bin Laden."[87]

It later became clear that there was no credible evidence of any connection between Islamic banks and terror networks. The new visibility of Islamic finance in the early years of the twenty-first century has nonetheless generated new anxieties and led to a considerable expansion of the cottage industry dedicated to exposing the "evils" of Islamic finance. Websites purported to "explaining" Islamic finance and publicizing the dangers it poses sprouted everywhere, though the credentials of their promoters were dubious at best. One such "expert," who ran the blog "Shariah Finance Watch" was a former interior designer from Los Angeles who had "never balanced her checkbook" before dedicating herself to exposing the risks posed by Islamic finance.[88]

Like the anti-Semitic literature on Jewish finance,[89] such discourse has a paranoid streak. The range of attacks to which Islamic institutions have been exposed is mind-boggling. In addition to funding terrorism (old discredited allegations are endlessly dredged up), banks are accused of fraud, of "financing Islamism," and more ominously, of sinister political designs. One Alex Alexiev explained that "Islamo-fascist rules" of finance "were little more than a hoax perpetrated on its clients through a series of deceitful ruses."[90] In addition, Islamic finance is said to be a backdoor way of introducing the Shariah into the United States and establishing the "Dhimmitude [sic] of non-Muslims,"[91] of creating a "Caliphate of Toxic Assets,"[92] and finally as a means of infiltrating American capitalism in order to destroy it from within. One book even suggests an apocalyptic confrontation, a "final jihad," between the West and "the Leftist/ Marxist-Islamist Alliance."[93]

Many ideas on the perils of Islamic finance originated on the lunatic fringe, but were occasionally picked up by mainstream publications such as the *Investor's Business Daily*, and systematically recycled in ideologically-driven outlets such as *The National Review* and *Human Events*.

One of the more bizarre episodes was the lawsuit brought in December 2008 by the Thomas More Law Center, a non-profit law firm in Ann Arbor (Michigan) against Treasury Secretary Henry Paulson and the Federal Reserve Board to stop $40 billion in US bail-out aid from reaching American International Group (AIG), on the grounds that the company has a Shariah-compliant unit.[94] Richard Thompson, President of the Law Center, explained,

> Although widespread public anger has rightfully focused on bonuses AIG paid to top executives using taxpayers' money, that anger would be at an even higher pitch if the public knew that our tax dollars were being used by AIG to promote Islam and Shariah law, which provides support for terrorist activities aimed at killing Americans and destroying America.[95]

Many of the self-styled experts make up in zeal what they lack in knowledge on the subject. Frank Gaffney, a minor figure in the neo-conservative movement, has been engaged, through his Center for Security Policy "think tank," in a high profile jihad against Islamic finance. He warned US financial institutions engaged in Shariah-compliant financing that they were exposed to "criminal and civil exposure on the grounds of: securities fraud, consumer fraud, racketeering, antitrust violations, material support for terrorism and aiding and abetting sedition."[96] He also issued warnings to trustees of universities holding conferences on the subject and demanded to hold his own counter-conferences. In his words, "Shariah-compliant finance ... is a vehicle for effecting in America and in other Western capital markets, what its proponents have called 'financial jihad' – a kind of soft jihad, but one arguably going after the lifeblood of our capitalist system and economy." Gaffney defines the Shariah as "a totalitarian program for bringing about a global caliphate, for ruling the world, for governing religious conduct, personal practices and family relations." What will happen if his warnings are not heeded? "We will find ourselves dead or enslaved." [97]

Notes

1. Edward Mortimer, *Faith and Power: The Politics of Islam* (New York: Random House, 1982), p. 219.
2. Mohammed Hassanein Heikal, *Autumn of Fury: The Assassination of Sadat* (New York: Random House, 1983).
3. Steve Coll, *Ghost Wars: The Secret History of the CIA, Afghanistan and bin Laden, from the Soviet Invasion to 10 September 2001* (New York: Penguin, 2004).
4. Steve Coll, *Ghost Wars*.
5. Ibrahim A. Karawan, "Monarchs, Mullas, and Marshalls: Islamic Regimes?," in Charles E. Butterworth and I. William Zartman (eds.), *Political Islam: The Annals of the American Academy of Political and Social Science* (November 1992), pp. 107–10.
6. Yaroslav Trofimov, *The Siege of Mecca: The Forgotten Uprising in Islam's Holiest Shrine and the Birth of al-Qaeda* (New York: Doubleday, 200).
7. Michel Galloux, *Finance islamique et pouvoir politique: le cas de l'Egypte moderne* (Paris: Presses Universitaires de France, 1997), p. 103.
8. Another, less convincing explanation for Saudi Arabia's reluctance to endorse Islamic banking is that the experiment is still too new. Given the country's position in Islam, it has to wait until the concept is refined, and until the problems encountered by Islamic institutions are resolved. See Hamid Algabid, *Les banques islamiques* (Paris: Economics, 1990), p. 168.
9. Peter W. Wilson, *A Question of Interest: The Paralysis of Saudi Banking* (Boulder, CO: Westview Press, 1991), p. 112.
10. Stephen Timewell, "Saudi Arabia – New Dynamics Bolster Banking," *The Banker*, March 1, 2005. Available from LexisNexis, accessed June 21, 2008.
11. Stephen Timewell, "Saudi Arabia – Growth Levels Off," *The Banker*, April 1, 2008. Available from LexisNexis, accessed June 21, 2008.
12. Timewell, "Saudi Arabia – New Dynamics Bolster Banking."
13. Metin Heper, "Islam and Democracy in Turkey: Toward a Reconciliation," and Nilufer Gole, "Secularism and Islamism in Turkey: The Making of Elites and Counter-Elites," *Middle East Journal*, 51:1 (Winter 1997).
14. EMortimer, *Faith and Power*, p. 153.
15. See Chapter 4.
16. *The Financial Times*, May 26, 1997.
17. *The Wall Street Journal*, June 19, 1997.
18. *The Wall Street Journal*, January 8, 1998.
19. *The Wall Street Journal*, August 20, 1997.
20. Filiz Baskan, "The Political Economy of Islamic Finance in Turkey: The Role of Fethullah Gülen and Asya Finans," in Clement M. Henry and Rodney Wilson (eds.), *The Politics of Islamic Finance* (Edinburgh: Edinburgh University Press, 2004), p. 235.
21. Baskan, "The Political Economy of Islamic Finance in Turkey: The Role of Fethullah Gülen and Asya Finans," in Henry and Wilson (eds.), *The Politics of Islamic Finance*, p. 235.
22. "Full of Interest: A Turkish bank collapses," *The Economist*, February 17, 2001. Available from Expanded Academic Index, accessed July 7, 2008.
23. Chapter 3.
24. Sami Zubaida, "Religion, the State, and Democracy: Contrasting Conceptions of Society in Egypt," in Joel Beinin and Joe Stork (eds.), *Political Islam: Essays from Middle East Report* (Berkeley, CA: University of California Press, 1997), p. 51.
25. Galloux, *Finance islamique et pouvoir politique*, p. 57.
26. See Chapter 4.
27. See Chapter 4.
28. Clement M. Henry, *The Mediterranean Debt Crescent: Money and Power in Algeria, Egypt, Morocco, Tunisia and Turkey* (Gainsvillle, FL: University Press of Florida, 1996), p. 266.

29. Denis J. Sullivan, *Private Voluntary Organizations in Egypt: Islamic Development, Private Initiative, and State Control* (Gainsvillle, FL: University Press of Florida, 1994).

30. Yahya M. Sadowski, *Political Vegetables? Businessman and Bureaucrat in the Development of Egyptian Agriculture* (Washington, DC: The Brookings Institution, 1991).

31. Stéphanie Parigi, *Des banques islamiques* (Paris: Ramsay, 1989), p. 128.

32. Soliman, "The Rise and Decline of the Islamic Banking Model in Egypt," in Henry and Wilson (eds.), *The Politics of Islamic Finance*, p. 271.

33. Soliman, "The Rise and Decline of the Islamic Banking Model in Egypt," in Henry and Wilson (eds.), *The Politics of Islamic Finance*, p. 278.

34. Soliman, "The Rise and Decline of the Islamic Banking Model in Egypt," in Henry and Wilson (eds.), *The Politics of Islamic Finance*, p. 271.

35. Soliman, "The Rise and Decline of the Islamic Banking Model in Egypt," in Henry and Wilson (eds.), *The Politics of Islamic Finance*, p. 271.

36. Soliman, "The Rise and Decline of the Islamic Banking Model in Egypt," in Henry and Wilson (eds.), *The Politics of Islamic Finance*, p. 280.

37. Soliman, "The Rise and Decline of the Islamic Banking Model in Egypt," in Henry and Wilson (eds.), *The Politics of Islamic Finance*, p. 281.

38. Judith Miller, *God has Ninety-Nine Names: A Reporter's Journey through a Militant Middle East* (New York: Simon and Schuster, 1996), p. 151.

39. See Chapter 6.

40. Khalid Medani, "Funding Fundamentalism: The Political Economy of an Islamist State," in Joel Beinin and Joe Stork (eds.), *Political Islam: Essays from Middle East Report*, p. 169.

41. Medani, "Funding Fundamentalism," in Beinin and Stork (eds.), *Political Islam*, pp. 168–75.

42. Medani, "Funding Fundamentalism," in Beinin and Stork (eds.), *Political Islam*, p. 169.

43. Nimeiri's "September laws" imposing the Shariah on the country had been opposed by the Sufi sect on the ground that it was politically divisive in a country where 40 per cent of the population was not Muslim.

44. See Chapter 6.

45. Medani, "Funding Fundamentalism," in Beinin and Stork (eds.), *Political Islam*, p. 169.

46. Mohamed Ariff, "Islamic Banking," *Asian-Pacific Economic Literature*, 2:2 (September 1988).

47. Bernard Botiveau and Jocelyne Cesari, *Géopolitique des islams* (Paris: Economica, 1997), pp. 40–1.

48. Gabriel Defert, "Sous la houlette du président Suharto et de sa famille: Succès et impasses de l'ordre nouveau" indonésien," *Le Monde diplomatique*, March 1993.

49. William E. Shepard, "Islam and Ideology: Towards a Typology," *International Journal of Middle Eastern Studies*, 19 (1987), p. 309.

50. Gabriel Defert and Eléonore Defert , "Durcissement du Régime, Scandales Financiers: 190 millions d'Indonésiens en panne de modèle," *Le Monde diplomatique*, June 1995.

51. Ibrahim Warde, "Comparing the Profitability of Islamic and Conventional Banks," San Francisco, CA: IBPC Working Papers, 1997.

52. Bill Guerin, "Tapping Indonesia's Islamic Potential," *Asia Times*, June 26, 2007, available at www.atimes.com, accessed June 22, 2008.

53. Andreas Ismar and Muhamad al Azhari, "Update 1 – Indonesia MPs Agree to Pass Islamic Banking Bill," *Reuters*, June 5, 2008.

54. Guerin, "Tapping Indonesia's Islamic potential."

55. Yoichi Iwamoto, "Islamic Banking Taking Hold in Indonesia," *The Nikkei Weekly*, February 21, 2005. Available from LexisNexis, accessed June 22, 2008.

56. Guerin, "Tapping Indonesia's Islamic potential."

57. "Indonesia Plans to Issue Islamic Sharia Bonds," *BBC Monitoring Asia Pacific*, July 19, 2006. Available from LexisNexis, accessed June 22, 2008.

58. Iwamoto, "Islamic Banking Taking Hold in Indonesia."
59. Ismar and al Azhari, "Update 1 – Indonesia MPs Agree to Pass Islamic Banking Bill."
60. Guerin, "Tapping Indonesia's Islamic potential."
61. Iwamoto, "Islamic Banking Taking Hold in Indonesia."
62. Iwamoto, "Islamic Banking Taking Hold in Indonesia."
63. "Hate Crimes and Extremist Politics," *The New York Times*, June 11, 2009.
64. John Esposito, *The Islamic Threat: Myth or Reality* (Oxford: Oxford University Press, 1991), p. 114.
65. William Pfaff, "Help Algeria's Fundamentalists," *The New Yorker*, January 28, 1991.
66. *The Washington Post*, January 16, 1990.
67. *The Washington Post*, January 19, 1992.
68. Alain Gresh, "Quand l'islamisme menace le monde," *Le Monde diplomatique*, December 1993.
69. *Foreign Affairs*, Spring 1993.
70. The Associated Press, June 15, 1997.
71. Deutsche Presse-Agentur, May 11, 1998.
72. Mortimer, *Faith and Power*, pp. 89–90.
73. Mortimer, *Faith and Power*, p. 90.
74. Miller, *God has Ninety-Nine Names*, p. 148.
75. See Jonathan Randal, *Osama: The Making of a Terrorist* (New York: Knopf, 2004), pp. 115–62.
76. Miller, *God has Ninety-Nine Names*, p. 468.
77. Ibrahim Warde, *The Price of Fear: The Truth behind the Financial War on Terror* (Berkeley, CA: University of California Press, 2007), pp. 127–50.
78. Richard Labévière, *Dollars for Terror: The United States and Islam* (New York: Algora Publishing, 2000), pp. 86–7 and 134–40; Jean-Charles Brisard and Guillaume Dasquié, *Forbidden Truth: U. S.–Taliban Secret Oil Diplomacy, Saudi Arabia and the Failed Search for bin Laden* (New York: Nation Books, 2002), p. 81.
79. Warde, *The Price of Fear*, pp. 58–61. Consider the following line: "the *shari'a* finance boards setting 'Islamic banking' standards themselves employ highly objectionable 'authorities.' Both the Accounting and Auditing Organization for Islamic Finan-cial Institutions (AAOIFI) and Islamic Financial Services Board (IFSB) for example, include many representatives of nations, banks, and organizations implicated in terror-funding." Alyssa A. Lappen, "Investing in Jihad," FrontPageMagazine.com, February 4, 2009.
80. *The Wall Street Journal*, February 5, 2002.
81. For a detailed discussion of these issues, see Warde, *The Price of Fear*.
82. Clement M. Henry and Rodney Wilson (eds.), *The Politics of Islamic Finance* (Edinburgh: Edinburgh University Press, 2004).
83. *Gulf News*, November 12, 2001.
84. Gene J. Koprowski, "Islamic Banking Is Not the Enemy," *The Wall Street Journal Europe*, October 1, 2001.
85. *The Wall Street Journal*, March 12, 2002.
86. The position held by Rice University professor Mahmoud El-Gamal, lasted six months.
87. Rachel Ehrenfeld and Alyssa A. Lappen, "Financial Jihad," *Human Events Online*, September 22, 2005.
88. DarAlHarb Radio show, available at: http://www.blogtalkradio.com/RadioFree DaralHarb /2008/03/29/Funding-Terror. Thanks to Fletcher student Christopher DeVito for pointing it out to me.
89. Brad A. Greenberg, "An Ugly Bias is Back: Blaming Jews for Financial Woes," *The Christian Science Monitor*, February 27, 2009.
90. Alex Alexiev, "Playing by Islamofascist Rules," *The Washington Times*, January 27, 2007. See also Alex Alexiev, "Islamic Finance, or Financing Islamism?," The Center for

Security Policy, October 2007.

91. http://www.jihadwatch.org/dhimmiwatch/archives/011791.php.
92. Alyssa A. Lappen, "A Caliphate of Toxic Assets," FrontPageMagazine.com, June 29, 2009, available at: http://frontpagemag.com/readArticle.aspx?ARTID=35378.
93. David J. Jonsson, *Islamic Economics and the Final Jihad: The Muslim Brotherhood to the Leftist/ Marxist-Islamist Alliance* (Xulon Press, part of Salem Wb Network, 2006).
94. http://www.foxnews.com/story/0,2933,471004,00.html.
95. http://creepingsharia.wordpress.com/2009/03/20/obama-admin-files-motion-to-dismiss-sharia-promoting-lawsuit-against-aig/.
96. http://www.businesswire.com/portal/site/topix/?ndmViewId=news_view&newsId =20080416006198&newsLang=enm.
97. Pete Winn, "Shari'a-Compliant Financing Described as New Islamist Threat," *CNSNews.com*, April 21, 2008.

12

RELIGIOUS ISSUES AND CHALLENGES: DEFINING ISLAM AND INTERPRETING THE SHARIAH

The battle to define the parameters of Islamic finance – and more generally the struggle over the authoritative interpretation of Islam – is not exclusively or even principally about religion. Indeed, one of the themes developed in this book is that religion cannot be separated from other factors – economic, political, cultural, ideological, historical, etc. Yet since political and economic struggles are fought on the religious terrain and expressed in religious terms, we need to be able to isolate, insofar as it is possible at all, religious issues. This chapter provides a framework for understanding the religious challenges faced by Islamic banks. It seeks to answer three questions: what are the mechanisms by which financial institutions interpret religion?; what are the bases (scriptures, traditions) of the various possible interpretations?; what interpretations are likely to prevail? The chapter begins with a discussion of Shariah Boards and other mechanisms designed to interpret religion for banking purposes. It then broadens the discussion to contending views on religious interpretation, before adopting a comparative perspective designed to map the likely direction of change in religious interpretations. The final section of the chapter discusses current debates among Islamic finance scholars.

I Interpreting the Shariah

Since the aggiornamento of Islamic finance, one of the defining characteristics of an Islamic bank has been the existence of a "Legitimate Control Body," or "Shariah Board," whose purpose is to ensure that the bank operates in conformity with the Shariah. Such a religious supervisory board enhances the credibility of the bank in the eyes of its customers, and bolsters its Islamic credentials. The somewhat unexpected and haphazard appearance of the first Islamic institutions, respectively, the IDB and the DIB,[1] may explain why neither had, at their inception, a Shariah Board. Virtually all subsequent institutions did, and in due course, both the IDB and the DIB established Shariah Boards.

The general characteristics of the Shariah Board were described as follows in a document issued by the IAIB:

It is formed of a number of members chosen from among Jurists and men of Islamic Jurisprudence and of comparative law who have conviction and firm belief in the idea of Islamic Banks. To ensure freedom of initiating their opinion the following are taken into account: (a) They must not be working as personnel in the bank. That means: They are not subject to the authority of the board of directors. (b) They are appointed by the general assembly as it is the case of the auditors of accounts. (c) The general assembly fixes their remunerations. (d) The Legitimate Control Body has the same means and jurisdictions as the auditors of accounts.[2]

The exact characteristics and roles of Shariah Boards differ from one institution to another, and a number of controversies have occasionally plagued them. A 1998 survey of thirty Shariah Boards revealed their diversity.[3] In that sample, numbers of members varied from one to nine. (Odd numbers are often preferred as a means of breaking possible deadlocks.) All members were trained in Islamic law or religious studies, and about half of them also held degrees in business and economics. Boards met at least annually; many met quarterly and even monthly. Their recruitment, pay, and conditions of employment were usually decided at shareholders' meetings, although in a few cases such decisions were made by the bank's management.

In theory, the Shariah Board's opinions are authoritative in that their refusal to endorse a product should automatically result in the bank scrapping that product. Also in theory, Shariah Boards perform a religious audit of all accounts. The reality, however, is more complicated. Interviews revealed that in some cases the review is perfunctory, with Boards "rubber stamping" decisions already made by the bank's management or shunning controversial issues. The model for the role of the Shariah Board is that of the account auditors. Although remunerated by the bank, their members should retain their independence. Like the auditors, they "certify" at the end of the year that that the bank's operations were in conformity with religious teachings. They review the institution's products and policies and issue fatwas as needed and as requested by the institution or its customers. For example, they decide whether a new financial instrument is religiously acceptable, or whether a fee charged by the bank could be assimilated to riba.

A number of issues have been raised in connection with Shariah Boards. One is about their independence. Insofar as they derive what is frequently their principal income from their membership in a Shariah Board, some scholars may legitimate the most dubious operations. The debate on "fatwas for sale" raged in Egypt, especially at the time of the IMMCs.[4] The debate was ideological, political, and, of course, financial, as much as it was religious. It pitted "private clerics" in the employ of IMMCs and Islamic banks against "public clerics," functionaries of the state who were critical of these companies. In those "fatwa wars," each side had its backers. Some argued that in a country where from the days of Mohammed Ali (1805–49) to those of Gamal Abdel Nasser (1952–70), clerics were an appendage of the state, allowing private sector income would enhance their independence.[5] Others argued that clerics were in effect becoming mercenaries, ready to offer tailor-made fatwas that would legitimate certain practices on the most tenuous religious grounds in exchange for money. In 1989, the Egyptian press mentioned that some clerics were receiving a monthly stipend as high as $4,000. The implication was that bank clients were cheated in two ways: it was their money that was being siphoned off to make excessive payments; and the religious validity of fatwas that were essentially "bought" was in doubt.[6]

A related issue is the varying degrees of leniency of Shariah Boards. As a general rule, Shariah Boards in southeast Asia, especially Malaysia, tend to be more lenient than those of the Arab Middle East. One obvious factor is the different religious and historical traditions and practices. Another variable though may be the intensity of competition. The Kuwait Finance House was known for its strict rulings. Under the presidency of Mufti Abdel-Latif Batayban, it rejected various types of murabaha as constituting hiyal and consistently prodded the bank's management into increasing PLS arrangements.[7] Insofar as the Kuwait Finance House was until 2003 the sole Islamic bank in the country, thus enjoying a monopoly of sorts on a lucrative segment of the market, it could afford stricter religious rules.[8] So it may be that, at a time of heightened competitive pressures, banks try to compete on the basis of the leniency of their Shariah Boards.

Another criticism is that Shariah advisors are not truly necessary, and may be a drag, financial and competitive, on the operations of the financial institution. Insofar as most bank employees are versed in Islamic law and practices, and insofar as the largest banks have in-house research departments that study matters of religion and economics, Shariah Boards are perceived by some as being all the more superfluous since in the era of e-cash, Internet banking, and exotic derivatives, religious scholars may not be up-to-date on state-of-the-art strategic or technological matters. The typical retort of religious advisors is that the religious experience of bank staffers is insufficient and that religious rectitude should prevail over considerations of profitability and competitiveness. They invoke a merchant-faqih tradition in Islam and a quote by Abu Hanifa (founder of the Hanafi school) stating that "every merchant must be accompanied by a faqih whose advice will allow him to avoid riba."[9] Yet another line of analysis in the wake of the 2008 credit crunch is that Shariah scholars provided a much-needed system of checks and balances that shielded Islamic banks from the crisis.[10]

From the standpoint of Islamic banks as a collective group, the major criticism is that the practice of banks having their own Shariah Boards adds to the fragmentation of Islamic finance, making it difficult to arrive at a consensus on products and procedures, which in turn complicates the task of developing a secondary market for Islamic products. Different Boards have different interpretations of the Shariah, and no uniform rules apply to the industry as a whole. Hence, the attempts at national and transnational levels to develop common standards under the aegis of the IFSB and AAOIFI, which has issued guidelines on Shariah Boards.

To avoid fragmentation and the reliance on the opinions of lone scholars, "group ijtihad" has since the 1970s been encouraged, through international conferences, symposia, and convocation, as well as through permanent new bodies such as fiqh academies. A number of research institutes – among them the International Center for Research in Islamic Economics at King Abdul Aziz University in Jeddah, the Islamic Foundation in Leicester, the Islamic Research and Training Institute of the Islamic Development Bank in Jeddah, and the International Institute for Islamic Thought in Cairo and the Harvard Islamic Finance Information Program in Cambridge, Massachusetts – have been involved in research projects on Islamic finance. Increasingly, the old principle of ijmaa[11] was modified to signify broad consensus or even simple majority.

The most prestigious transnational body is the Islamic Fiqh Academy created by the OIC in Jeddah. Its members are appointed by governments belonging to the OIC. It holds annual meetings in various locations where reports of specialized experts on a specific issue are discussed. Following debates, a decision by a majority vote states the Academy's position on the issue. The fatwas, debates, and reports are published in the *Fiqh Academy Journal*.[12] Despite its multinational membership, the Islamic Fiqh Academy remains closely identified with Saudi Arabia. Other fiqh academies are associated with other countries and other fiqh traditions.

As for national level coordination, many Islamic countries have appointed Shariah advisors to their central banks. One of the most significant attempts at national harmonization occurred in Malaysia where a National Syariah [Shariah] Board was established in 1997 to harmonize financial practices and review the compatibility of new financial products with religion, as well as to advise the Central Bank on religious matters. The goal was to adopt a liberal, modernist bent that would be consistent with the developmental goals of the government.[13]

One of the risks faced by Islamic banks and investors is the Shariah-compliance risk, or the risk of being challenged on religious grounds. On occasion, bankers have been forced, under religious pressure, to change course. Instances where Shariah Board decisions lead to strategic changes are rare, but they do exist. In 1987, the FIBE had to put an end to its forward contracts in foreign exchange markets.[14] The same year, the IDB changed its practice of charging a fixed service fee of 2.5 to 3 per cent after an Islamic Fiqh Academy fatwa stated that fees should not be fixed arbitrarily, but based on the bank's real costs.[15] There have also been countless opinions on the question of tawarroq. Perhaps the most consequential statement was that of Sheikh Taqi Usmani, the chairman of AAOIFI's Shariah Board in November 2007 to the effect that up to 85 per cent of sukuk in existence may not be Shariah-compliant.[16]

II Religious Diversity

Religious diversity is a mixed blessing for Islamic banks. On the one hand, it provides flexibility and creates a benchmarking effect, whereby successful practices will be widely adopted and unsuccessful ones will fall by the wayside. On the other hand, it casts doubt on the religious validity of certain decisions and makes consensus more elusive. The exponents of both modern interpretations of Islam and those of traditional interpretations can draw on selected scriptures and precedents to bolster their views. Most debates on what the religion truly commands boil down to a few basic questions: "What is Islam?;" "Who is a true Muslim?;" "How does God Speak?;" and "Who speaks for God?"[17]

Different communities of Muslims have different answers. The literal definition of Islam is "submission" to God. The prescribed duties of Muslims are limited to the "five pillars" of the religion (shahada, prayer, fasting, zakat, pilgrimage). There is no Vatican-like authority (at least in Sunni Islam) that imposes rules and proclaims dogmas. The process of conversion requires no certification of religious knowledge. Thus, beyond a few basics, it is difficult to assess religious rectitude authoritatively. All this leaves significant room to accommodate many interpretations, each claiming authenticity. Furthermore, the Islamic tradition posits the absolute equality of all Muslims, with the degree of piety (which can be assessed only by God) being the only differentiating factor.

Every major belief system has contradictory strands. Ideologues and theologians find coherence through exegesis, but they still disagree among themselves on issues of "essence" and original meaning. In Islam, one can choose to focus on the Prophet's original role as political ruler and military conqueror and on the role of holy wars in Arab conquests and in the propagation of Islam. Or one can choose to concentrate on the peaceful, tolerant side of the religion, on the Koranic verses saying that there is no compulsion in religion (2:256),[18] that diversity in religious beliefs is part of God's overall plan (10:99),[19] or that relations with non-Muslims should be marked by kindness and equity (60:8).[20]

A wide spectrum of intellectual, moral, and theological traditions is still in existence today. Different strands of Islam claim lineage from different leading Islamic figures. In addition to the concept of shura (consultation), which is mentioned in both the Koran and the Sunna, early Islamic thinkers devised a number of concepts designed to control political power. Al-Mawardi (d. 1058) advanced the concept of separation of functions via delegation from the ruler (tawfid).[21] The philosopher Abu al-Walid Ibn Rushd, known to the West as Averroes (1126–98), developed the theory of ta'weel (allegorical interpretation), placing reason above all other considerations. He argued that religious texts have an exoteric and an esoteric meaning. If the exoteric meaning is at variance with reason, the text must be interpreted according to reason. Following Aristotle, Averroes gave priority to demonstrative proof (burhan), the highest form of certainty, over the dialectical and rhetorical arguments of theologians. In his lifetime, he lost his intellectual battle. He was tried for kufr (unbelief), his books were burned, and he was banished to his village. Ali Abd al-Raziq's al-Islam was-usul al-hukm, published in Cairo in 1925, the best-known advocacy of strict separation of the religious and the secular realm, led to violent attacks on the book. The author was defrocked by al-Azhar. This stifled the debate for years to come. Such fates were not dissimilar to those of Galileo and countless other Church dissidents. Amazingly (considering common stereotypes about Islam being about din wa dawla [fusion of mosque and state], while Christianity is supposedly inherently secular[22]) Averroes' ideas were

used in the West to propound the separation of Church and state. More specifically, Frederick II (1194–1250), Emperor of Germany and King of Sicily, ordered
Averroes' works translated so that he could use his arguments in his war against
the religious authorities.

Averroes' views were in line with the Islamic tradition of awareness (*wai'i*)
which implies that Muslims should be exerting a permanent effort of education
and reasoning "so that their knowledge can be applied for the benefit of society,
including the economic order."[23] The flourishing cultural and intellectual life
of Baghdad and Spain kept science and rationalism alive during Europe's Dark
Ages, and medieval Islam was a vital link between the ancient world of Greece
and Rome and the Renaissance.

The other, traditional, puritanical, and literalist strand is epitomized by Ibn
Taymiyya (1268–1328), who spent his life trying to strip Islam of alien accretions and influences. In recent decades, a number of Islamic revivalists have
embarked on similar crusades.[24] Both Abul Ala Mawdudi (1903–79), who created
the Jamaat-i Islami in India in 1941 and Egyptian Muslim Brother Sayed Qutb
(1906–66) associated modern society with the *Jahiliyya*, the pre-Islamic society,
with its connotation of ignorance and paganism.[25] Qutb's views were radicalized
following his imprisonment and torture by the Egyptian government (he was later
executed). In his influential book *Maalim fi al-Tariq*, he set up a stark dichotomy:
a political system could be either Islamic (*nizam Islami*) or pagan (*nizam Jahili*). A
syllogism of sorts followed: since it is the duty of devout Muslims to establish an
Islamic government, it is also their duty to wage a jihad against all other governments.[26] The notion of *takfir* (an excommunication of sorts) is central to his and
his radical followers' thinking. The group, Jamaat al-Jihad (Holy War), which
assassinated Anwar Sadat on October 6, 1981, maintained that jihad was the sixth
pillar of Islam, and that it was the religious duty of Muslims to wage holy war
against Egypt's un-Islamic state and its leader.[27]

Often the same Koranic verse, or even the same word, is open to contradictory
interpretations. As to differing interpretations of certain words, the best example
is jihad (usually followed by "in the path of God").[28] Some adopt a militaristic
interpretation – that of a holy war against enemies. Others adopt a spiritual
interpretation – that of the jihad of the soul. Another ambiguous term is towhid.
For some it is a strictly theological concept about the "oneness" of God (often
used in contrast to the Christian doctrine of the Trinity). For others, it is an
all-encompassing concept meaning that religion, politics, economics, and society
should all be one.[29] For others still, it refers to the unification of mankind.[30]

By the same token, the notion of *hukumiyya* (sovereignty or power) has elicited
contradictory interpretations. The fundamentalist slogan "*la hukma illa li-Llah*"
(sovereignty belongs to God alone) was first used by the Kharijites, a marginal
and secessionist sect, when they opposed Ali's decision to seek arbitration in the
conflict with Muaawiya, the founder of the Umeyyad dynasty. Nowadays, it can
be used either to justify a theocracy, or on the contrary to separate temporal
and spiritual matters. In Iran, the roles of the *Velayat-e Faqih*, of the Council of

Guardians, and of the Assembly of Experts reflect the view that clerics should hold high political offices to keep control over the political system. The view was opposed, at the time of the Iranian revolution by many leading clerics.[31] Indeed, the Iranian Shia tradition had both a strong anti-political tradition (since unlike the mainstream Sunnis, they rejected the political system that followed the death of Ali, the fourth Caliph) and a messianic one. Many clerics argued that in the absence of the hidden Imam, no religious leaders were entitled to claim his mantle. (In that respect, their views resembled those of a minority of ultra-Orthodox Jews who opposed Zionism on the grounds that the return to Israel would be legitimate only if led by the Messiah.) It took the Ayatollah Khomeini's remarkable rhetorical and political skills to impose his interpretation, whereby the supreme jurist would assume power pending the return of the Imam.[32]

Throughout the Islamic world, there are also well-established traditions that regard the state not as a direct expression of Islam, but as a secular institution whose duty is to uphold Islam.[33] Other strands, deriving mostly from Sufi perspectives, and paralleling similar Christian strands, are decidedly apolitical, if not anti-political. They claim that authenticity lies within the soul of the individual and that it manifests itself in righteous behavior within the Islamic community. Insofar as temporal power is perceived as inherently violent and corrupt, it should be shunned. Islam would then be circumscribed to a personal and social ethos.[34] A related argument is that Islamic rule cannot be imposed on a society that is not yet Islamicized or permeated by Islamic values, or that an Islamic government can exist only when virtue prevails.[35]

As for the question of "who speaks for Islam?" (or whose answer is authoritative) it is not easily answered either. Edward Mortimer wrote:

> Is it the ruler, who holds power by God's grace? But rulers also fall from power and are replaced by others with different opinions. Does Islam change with every coup d'état? Surely not. Then is it the ulema – those who have devoted their lives to studying Islam and its law? Many believe so, particularly among ... the ulema themselves. But are the ulema infallible, even when they all say the same thing? The example of the ban on coffee suggests that they are not;[36] and anyway infallibility is an attribute of God. To attribute it to a group of human beings, even the wisest, may involve the cardinal sin of shirk – associating others with God.[37]

One should add that most contemporary fundamentalist movements, starting with al-Afghani, have been characterized by revolts against established ulema, who were accused either of distorting the faith or of being too closely associated with the existing political-economic order.[38] Paradoxically, many revivalists have invoked independent reasoning as a weapon against the status quo. They posited that it was up to the individuals themselves to conduct their own ijtihad and make up their mind using their own conscience and intelligence under God's guidance. (Once in a position of power, though, such revivalists have usually suspended that right of individual interpretation.)

On a number of occasions, this somewhat "Lutheran" approach to the interpretation of the scriptures was used by leaders such as Libya's Moammar Qaddafi. He rejected the ulema's interpretation of Islam by stating: "As the Muslims have strayed from Islam, a review is demanded. The [Libyan revolution] is a revolution rectifying Islam, presenting Islam correctly, purifying Islam of the reactionary practices which dressed it in retrograde clothing not its own."[39] He also instructed the "popular committees" of the Libyan *Jamahiriyya* to seize the mosques and rid them of "paganistic tendencies" and of religious leaders who have been "propagating heretical tales elaborated over centuries of decadence and which distort the Islamic religion."[40] But Qaddafi then imposed his own idiosyncratic interpretations of the Koran, with the most controversial decision being changing the Islamic calendar so that it would start in 632 AD, the year of the death of the Prophet. He even called for the disregarding of the sunna on the grounds that it had been corrupted and misinterpreted.[41]

Similarly, Sudan's Hassan al-Turabi in his opposition days had stated that it was up to ordinary Muslims to conduct their own independent reasoning.[42] He also expressed the difficulty of finding an appropriate and applicable political model: "Muslims themselves sometimes don't even know how to go about their Islam. They have no recent precedent of an Islamic government."[43] Not surprisingly, once in power, he tried to impose his own Islamic vision, and even to export it. Indeed, every government that calls itself Islamic tends to view its own interpretation of Islam as being the correct one. This has resulted in a greater diversity of beliefs worldwide, but also in authoritarianism at home. Indeed, linking religion and politics is not without certain political advantages for an authoritarian regime. In Iran, the criterion of Islamic rectitude has been more likely "to verify political reliability and loyalty rather than faith and piety."[44] As was noted in connection with the Zia regime in Pakistan, when the regime is linked to religion, "any deviation becomes both a religious heresy and treason against the state ... political rebellion and religious dissent become indistinguishable."[45]

To use Max Weber's categories, religion has been reinterpreted by saints, scholars, and warriors. And to use Ibrahim Karawan's typology, monarchs, mullahs, and marshals have claimed religious rectitude, attempting to discredit if not "excommunicate" rival regimes. One of the most enduring rivalries has been that of Iran and Saudi Arabia. In a famous statement, the Ayatollah Khomeini attacked Saudi Islam as "the Islam of money and power ... deception, compromise, and captivity, the Islam of the sovereignty of capital and capitalists over the oppressed ... in a word the American Islam."[46]

III Finance and Religion in Comparative Perspective

In order to predict the likely evolution of Islamic finance, it is useful to consider the ways older but related religions have evolved over time. Will Islam – the youngest of the Abrahamic religions – evolve in the same way that Judaism and Christianity did in political and economic matters and more specifically with

regard to money and finance? Needless to say, all comparisons can be treach-
erous. Not only can areas of convergence and divergence be equally significant
(thus, confusing as much as enlightening), but superficial resemblance often hides
fundamental differences. Consider, for example, the notion of clergy as intermediary between God and the faithful. All clerics preach and interpret the word
of God. But there are wide variations in the exact role, importance, and status
of clerics. The primary function of Catholic priests is to administer sacraments,
whereas Protestant ministers are predominantly preachers, Jewish rabbis are more
akin to moral teachers and Islamic ulema are essentially legal scholars. Another
complication arises from variations within a specific faith and over time. Even
broad generic categories (for example, dividing the Jewish faith into Orthodox,
Conservative, and Reform) can hide significant differences within each category.
Yet the opposite position – because no comparison is ever perfect means that all
comparative endeavors are futile – would severely limit our understanding.

Perhaps the most enduring cliché in discussions about Islam is the alleged
difference between the essence of Christianity, which is said to accommodate,
even encourage, secularism and separation of church and state, and Islam, which
cannot. Hence, the formulation of Huntington: "In Islam, God is Caesar."[47] The
general argument has been summarized by Bernard Lewis as follows: "The notion
of church and state as distinct institutions, each with its own laws, hierarchy, and
jurisdiction, is characteristically Christian, with its origins in Christian scripture
and history. It is alien to Islam."[48] For some reason, the early Islamic experience is
supposed to be "indelibly stamped"[49] on the mind of every Muslim. It is true that
Christianity and Islam started under sharply differing circumstances. Early Christians placed themselves outside the existing political order, preaching a message
antithetical to existing Judaic and Roman practices. Unlike Jesus, Mohammed
was a military and political leader. Under his rule and that of his four immediate
successors, political, military, and religious leadership were not differentiated.
But even in the early days of both religions, the religious position on matters of
politics was sometimes comparable. Consider, for example, St. Paul's injunction:
"Every person must submit to the supreme authorities. There is no authority but
by act of God, and the existing authorities are instituted by him; consequently
anyone who rebels against authority is resisting a divine institution, and those
who so resist have themselves to thank for the punishment they will receive." Or
his statement that "[The authorities] are God's agents working for your good."[50]
They are not fundamentally different from the Koranic injunction to "obey Allah
and obey the Messenger and those in authority from among you" (4:59). The
three religions have tended to evolve over time. In the words of John Esposito:
"The Judaeo-Christian tradition, while once supportive of political absolutism,
was reinterpreted to accommodate the democratic ideal. Islam also lends itself to
multiple interpretations; it has been used to support democracy and dictatorship,
republicanism and monarchy."[51]

It is true, however, that modern concepts of secularism appeared in the Christian West. The seeds of such thinking were introduced with the sixteenth century

Reformation. A more systematic political and theoretical formulation occurred during the Enlightenment, and starting in the late eighteenth century, such views started to be implemented in much of the Western world. Since that time, the principle of separation of church and state has by and large become the norm. The word "secularism" is seldom used in the Islamic context. Also, a certain amount of intellectual intimidation (the equation by radical fundamentalists of secularism with unbelief) has somewhat chilled the debate. For one thing, the concept – as are the categorization of religious traditions and the "naming of other religious systems or isms" – is a creature of the post-Enlightenment West.[52] The argument that Islam cannot accommodate secularism is more about language than about history and praxis. As we have seen, the practice of early Islamic societies often provided for a separation of mosque and state. But despite linguistic and rhetorical differences, secularism does have its Islamic "functional equivalents." Some leading intellectuals such as Egyptian, Mohammed Said al-Ashmawi, have argued that "Islamism was against Islam."[53] Others have argued in favor of a sort of "religious secularism" which would keep institutionalized religion outside the political structure, while developing policy in the context of Islamic values.[54] In Indonesia, the constitution provides for a broad religious framework, but separates the state from any specific faith. Turkey is the most famous case of explicit, assertive secularism. Even there though, secularism was justified in religious terms. In 1924, the same year that he abolished the Caliphate, Mustafa Kemal in a speech to the Turkish Assembly expressed the need to "cleanse and elevate the Islamic faith, by rescuing it from the position of a political instrument, to which it has been accustomed for centuries."[55]

The essentialist analysis conveniently omits what happened between the fourth century and the advent of modern secular state. Indeed, with the Christianization of the Roman Empire, church–state relations were fused. The obligatory judicial coincidence of Christian and Roman citizenship has been established since 379 AD.[56] Whether one looks at the last Roman emperors, at the Byzantine emperors, at the symbiotic relations between pope and emperor in the Holy Roman empire, or at the "divine rights of kings" in Western states, one sees that separation of church and state was not the norm, and that theocratic (the subordination of political authority to religious authority) and Caesaro-papist (the subordination of religious authority to political authority) tendencies alternated for most of the history of Christianity. The paradigmatic jihads were the Crusades, which were perceived by Muslims at the time in much the same way as many manifestations of "radical Islamic fundamentalism" are perceived nowadays in the West.[57]

The advent of secularism was neither swift nor peaceful. It took centuries of religious wars and intellectual debates before the issue of separation of church and state was resolved. An essentialist reading of religion ignores the evolution of ideas and interpretations. The scriptural basis for the separation of the two realms is Jesus' famous saying: "Then render unto Caesar what is due to Caesar, and render unto God what is due to God" (Matthew 22:21). But as was noted by Charles Butterworth, "not until sometime after Marsilius of Padua (c. 1275–1342) were Paul's strictures and the famous advice offered by Jesus about distinguishing between the things belonging to Caesar and those belonging to God raised to the elevated rank it occupies today."[58]

In Islam the evolution was almost opposite. The early tradition as well as recent "radical fundamentalist" movements do not distinguish the religious from the political realms. Yet historically, from the time of the Umeyyad empire, some measure of secularization started to appear,[59] and over the centuries the power of the caliph became increasingly nominal. (The caliphate was abolished in 1924.) Olivier Carré has argued that the "long tradition of Islam" was one characterized by some measure of separation of the two realms (though not by a Western-style secularism).[60] Only with the Islamic revival that started in the late eighteenth century and persists to this day, did Islamist regimes resort to the "deviant orthodoxy" based on a return to the "ideal" of Islam – that of Muhammed and the four "rightly-guided Caliphs." It is Carré's hope that a return to this great tradition, which is commonly accepted by traditional Islamic jurisprudence in both Sunni and Shi'i doctrine could open the way to what he calls a "post-Islamist Islam."

This section as well as the historical and comparative discussions in Chapters 2 and 3 have shown that Islam, like other successful religions, has undergone significant change and proved itself capable of adjusting to changing circumstances. In terms of the traditionalist–modernist dichotomy, traditionalist backlashes are possible in response to certain political, economic, or financial developments, but they are likely to be short-lived. The long-term trend in Islamic finance is clearly toward increased pragmatism and the prevalence of modernist interpretations, although the specific nature of such interpretations – whether they take the form of simply mimicking conventional finance or seeking guidance in the moral economy of Islam – remains to be seen.

Notes

1. Chapter 4.
2. Ahmed El-Nagar *et al.*, *One Hundred Questions & One Hundred Answers Concerning Islamic Banks* (Cairo: Islamic Banks International Association, 1980), p. 20.
3. Ibrahim Warde, *The Role of Shariah Boards: A Survey*, IBPC Working Papers (San Francisco, CA: IBPC, 1998).
4. Chapter 4.
5. Michel Galloux, *Finance islamique et pouvoir politique: le cas de l'Egypte moderne* (Paris: Presses Universitaires de France, 1997), pp. 39–45.
6. Galloux, *Finance islamique et pouvoir politique*, p. 46.
7. Galloux, *Finance islamique et pouvoir politique*, p. 59.
8. Ibrahim Warde, "Comparing the Profitability of Islamic and Conventional Banks," IBPC Working Papers (San Francisco, CA: IBPC, 1997).
9. Galloux, *Finance islamique et pouvoir politique*, p. 47.
10. See Conclusion.
11. Based on the saying of the Prophet: "my community will never agree on an error."
12. *Majallat Majmaa al-Fiqh al-Islami*.
13. Chapter 6.

14. *Al-Ahram al-iqtissadi*, March 3, 1987.

15. Hamid Algabid, *Les banques islamiques* (Paris: Economics, 1990), p. 126.

16. See Chapter 7.

17. Daniel Brown, *Rethinking Tradition in Modern Islamic Thought* (Cambridge: Cambridge University Press, 1996).

18. 2:256 "There is no compulsion in religion – the right way is clearly distinct from error – So whoever disbelieves in the devil and believes in Allah, he indeed lays hold on the firmest handle which shall never break. And Allah is Hearing, Knowing."

19. 10:99 "And if thy Lord had pleased, all those who are in the earth would have believed, all of them. Wilt thou then force men till they are believers?"

20. 60:8 "Allah forbids you not respecting those who fight you not for religion, nor drive you forth from your homes, that you show them kindness and deal with them justly. Surely Allah loves the doers of justice."

21. Gudrun Kramer, "Islamist Notions of Democracy," in Joel Beinin and Joe Stork (eds.), *Political Islam: Essays from Middle East Report* (Berkeley, CA: University of California Press, 1997), p. 77.

22. Chapter 1.

23. Rodney Wilson, Economics, *Ethics and Religion: Jewish, Christian and Muslim Economic Thought* (New York: New York University Press, 1997), p. 115.

24. Ibrahim M. Abu Rabi', *Intellectual Origins of Islamic Resurgence in the Modern Arab World* (Albany, NY: State University of New York Press, 1996).

25. Seyyed Vali Reza Nasr, *Mawdudi and the Making of Islamic Revivalism* (Oxford: Oxford University Press, 1996).

26. John L. Esposito, *The Islamic Threat: Myth or Reality?* (Oxford: Oxford University Press, 1992), pp. 127–8.

27. Esposito, *The Islamic Threat*, p. 134.

28. Bernard Lewis, *Islam and the West* (Oxford: Oxford University Press, 1993), p. 9.

29. See Chapter 6.

30. Stéphanie Parigi, *Des banques islamiques* (Paris: Ramsay, 1989), p. 119.

31. Olivier Roy, *L'échec de l'islam politique* (Paris: Editions du Seuil, 1992), p. 46.

32. Chibli Mallat, *The renewal of Islamic law: Muhammad Baqer as-Sadr, Najaf and the Shii International* (Cambridge: Cambridge University Press, 1993), pp. 84–96.

33. Ira M. Lapidus, "The Golden Age: The Political Concepts of Islam," in Charles E. Butterworth and I. William Zartman (eds.), *Political Islam, The Annals of the American Academy of Political and Social Science* (November 1992), p. 17.

34. Lapidus, "The Golden Age: The Political Concepts of Islam," in Butterworth and Zartman (eds.), *Political Islam*, p. 7.

35. Roy, *L'échec de l'islam politique*, pp. 10, 42 and 56.

36. With the spread of coffee drinking in the seventeenth century, the ulema almost unanimously took the view that it was unlawful and punishable with the same penalties as wine drinking. This even resulted in some executions. But the prohibition was ignored and the ulema eventually gave up the fight. See Mortimer, p. 98.

37. Edward Mortimer, *Faith and Power: The Politics of Islam* (New York: Random House, 1982), p. 123.

38. Roy, *L'échec de l'islam politique*, p. 45.

39. Lisa Anderson, "Tunisia and Libya: Responses to the Islamic Impulse," in John L. Esposito (ed.), *The Iranian Revolution: Its Global Impact* (Tampa, FL: Florida International University Press, 1990), p. 171.

40. Lisa Anderson, "Qaddafi's Islam," in John L. Esposito (ed.), *Voices of Resurgent Islam* (Oxford: Oxford University Press, 1983), p. 143.

41. Ann Elizabeth Mayer, "In Search of Sacred Law: The Meandering Course of Qaddafi's Legal Policy," in Dirk Vandewalle (ed.), *Qaddhafi's Libya, 1969–1994* (New York: St. Martin's Press, 1995).

42. Judith Miller, *God Has Ninety-Nine Names: A Reporter's Journey Through a Militant Middle East* (New York: Simon and Schuster, 1996), p. 162.
43. Ibrahim A. Karawan, "Monarchs, Mullas, and Marshals: Islamic Regimes?," in Butterworth and Zartman (eds.), *Political Islam*, p. 115.
44. Sami Zubeida, "Is Iran an Islamic State?," in Beinin and Stork (eds.), *Political Islam*, p. 111.
45. Mumtaz Ahmad, "Pakistan," in Shireen Hunter (ed.), *The Politics of Islamic Revivalism* (Bloomington, IN: Indiana University Press, 1988), p. 231.
46. Karawan, "Monarchs, Mullas, and Marshals: Islamic Regimes?" in Butterworth and Zartman (eds.), *Political Islam*, p. 107.
47. Samuel P. Huntington, *The Clash of Civilizations and the Remaking of World Order* (New York: Simon and Schuster, 1996), p. 70.
48. Bernard Lewis, *Islam and the West* (Oxford: Oxford University Press, 1993), p. 135.
49. Bernard Lewis, *Islam and the West*, p. 135.
50. Letter to the Romans, 13:1–2 and 13:14.
51. Esposito, *The Islamic Threat*, p. 186.
52. Esposito, *The Islamic Threat*, p. 199.
53. Muhammad Said al-Ashmawy, *L'Islamisme contre l'Islam* (Paris: La Découverte, 1989).
54. Nimat Hafez Barazangi, M. Raquibuz Zaman and Omar Afzal (eds.), *Islamic Identity and the Struggle for Justice* (Gainesville, FL: University Press of Florida, 1996), pp. 69–71.
55. Mortimer, *Faith and Power*, p. 137.
56. Olivier Carré, *L'Islam laïque ou le retour à la Grande Tradition* (Paris: Armand Colin, 1993), p. 51.
57. Amin Maalouf, *Les croisades vues par les Arabes* (Paris: J. C. Lattès, 1992).
58. Charles E. Butterworth, "Political Islam: The Origins," in Butterworth and Zartman (eds.), *Political Islam*, p. 27.
59. See Chapter 2.
60. Carré, *L'Islam laïque ou le retour à la Grande Tradition*.

CONCLUSION: ISLAMIC FINANCE
AND THE GLOBAL FINANCIAL MELTDOWN

When it first appeared in the mid-1970s, Islamic finance was generally dismissed as an inconsequential epiphenomenon of the oil boom. Introducing the religious factor in what was perceived as a quintessentially secular area struck many as bizarre, and many critics asserted that the growth of Islamic banks was bound to remain stunted.[1] In reality, for most of its existence, Islamic finance experienced growth rates in the double digits. In fact, the rate of growth accelerated from an average of 14 per cent a year in 1994–2002 to 26 per cent a year in 2003–2009.[2]

The overall record is nevertheless mixed. On the one hand, Islamic finance by becoming a permanent feature of the global financial system has proven its viability. It did not, however, quite live up to its original billing. Rather than being a different financial system, based on partnership finance, which would bring social and economic development to the Islamic world, Islamic banks have generally mirrored conventional finance and concentrated on short-term financial transactions.

Islamic institutions thus raise the inevitable question: is Islamic finance necessary? Stated differently, does it add anything of value to the conventional banking system? Before discussing the issue, two points should be stressed. One is that the gap between promise and performance could be attributed to the youth of the industry. Modern Islamic finance started in earnest only in the mid-1970s. Its evolution has been marked by a constant process of trial and error, and its shortcomings may be unavoidable growing pains. The second point is that it would be unfair to judge Islamic institutions too harshly, considering that the world's most prominent conventional institutions have not proven to be exemplars of either probity or strategic acumen. Although it could be argued that Islamic finance could still fulfill its original objectives, the argument of this concluding chapter is that the recent financial meltdown has recast the debate about the role and contributions of the Islamic sector.

The near-collapse of global finance brought to light the consequences of nearly three decades of unbridled deregulation and the unprecedented "financialization" of the economy and society.[3] Financiers were the main actors and beneficiaries of the new "gilded age" that preceded the meltdown. In the words of Sanford I. Weill, who had assembled the Citigroup conglomerate, "People can look at the last 25 years and say this is an incredibly unique period of time.

We didn't rely on somebody else to build what we built, and we shouldn't rely on somebody else to provide all the services our society needs."[4]

The language is interesting, first because of the building metaphor, but also because it suggests that finance, once seen as providing a service to the economy, had become a self-contained, self-centered, and dominant realm. In the years preceding the credit crunch, "financial engineers" were at the cutting edge of finance.[5] Indeed, since the 1980s investment banks and other financial institutions have engaged in a massive effort to hire Ph.D. graduates in physics, engineering, mathematics, and other such disciplines to create increasingly complex and highly lucrative new financial instruments. The trend toward abstraction and the heavy use of mathematical symbols had created the illusion of scientific precision. More worrisome, many in the financial community started taking the engineering metaphor literally. To quote finance professors-turned bankers Eric Briys and François de Varenne: "On what grounds can one reasonably expect that a complex financial contract solving a complex real-world issue does not deserve the same thorough scientific treatment as an aeroplane wing or a micro-processor?"[6]

Perhaps, as later events would show, the house of cards metaphor[7] would have been more apt, but there are other advantages to the talk about engineering. It is value-neutral, and makes preoccupation with ethics or morality superfluous, if not counterproductive. In an amazing display of groupthink, the seemingly irresistible rise of finance was cheered on by an overwhelming majority of every group that mattered – the financiers themselves, of course, but also regulators, academics, analysts, and journalists. It is no surprise then that the financial meltdown of 2008 seemed to take just about everybody by surprise.[8] The world of finance seemed to proceed on the assumption that, as Alexander Pope would have put it, "whatever is is good."

It became easy to forget that models were only as good as their underlying assumptions. At the height of the boom, the same finance experts asserted that "there is no divorce between the real economy and the financial economy," just as they marveled at "the vast panoply of solutions offered by international finance," railed at "fallacies, such as the supposedly demonic trend of financial specula-tion and its destabilizing effects," and mocked those who "express deep concerns and denounce the ascendancy of the financial economy over the so-called real economy."[9]

We saw in this book that the early objective of an alternative, partnership-based, financial system was not fulfilled, and that Islamic finance chose instead to mimic many aspects of conventional finance (and there is nothing inherently wrong with this since Muslims have the same financial needs as non-Muslims), albeit through Islamic contracts and within boundaries imposed by religion. Yet given the tendency in the world of finance to think in broad-brush and binary terms, this caveat is often ignored. Differences between conventional and Islamic finance may, by the standards of the early promoters of Islamic finance, be modest; they are nonetheless real. And those differences, as revealed by the recent crisis, now cast Islamic finance in a different light.

So, to answer the question asked earlier, Islamic finance does offer an alternative. To be sure, it is mostly by default, since for the past 30 years or so finance has been moving toward a single model, aggressively exported throughout the world,[10] and whatever checks and balances existed previously, through regulatory agencies, consumer groups, academics, or the media have, whether for reasons of ideological hegemony or co-optation, ceased to function properly.[11] The large Wall Street firms became the superstars and the guiding lights of that system, stressing the goals of efficiency, convergence, leverage, and deregulation. Governments stayed out of the way to allow the magic of the marketplace to operate.[12] Yet innovation was not pursued, despite the underlying rhetoric, for the benefit of the economy and society. It was pursued for its own sake – and for the fat fees it generated. It is this unanimity (here we are reminded of Margaret Thatcher's assertion of TINA: There Is No Alternative) that in hindsight made the Islamic sector appear as one of the few organized systems of alternative finance.

Many critics of the Islamic finance industry have asserted that Islamic finance is simply conventional finance dressed up in Islamic garb. Others have criticized Islamic finance for not going all out to replicate the conventional sector, thus losing in efficiency. Some have made both criticisms simultaneously.[13] Differences between Islamic and conventional finance once looked so minor as to be insignificant. Yet they were greatly magnified by the excesses of conventional finance. This explains why, as the following pages show, the principles, if not the actual practice, of Islamic finance have come to hold undeniable attraction well beyond Islamic circles.

Three elements could be singled out. The first has to do with Islamic products and instruments, which despite their relative lack of originality, retain specific features. Even as they sought in their broad outlines to mimic conventional products, Islamic products, such as murabaha, have specific contractual features stressing ethics and risk-sharing. These can be consequential when problems arise, and the debtor is unable to pay. In contrast to conventional finance, where banks have no qualms about taking advantage of distressed borrowers, the attitude of Islamic institutions is that they must in such circumstances forsake some of their profits, typically by extending a qard hasan to help the distressed borrower.[14]

Second, a number of financial products and practices, often among the most lucrative ones – from selling debt to exotic derivatives, from short-selling to highly-leveraged transactions – are simply off-limits to Islamic institutions. Nor are practices deemed to be predatory, such as payday loans or "vulture funds" acceptable. Third, are screening mechanisms which prevent Islamic companies from investing in, or doing business with, companies belonging to non-halal sectors, or companies whose financial ratios or ethical practices are not deemed to be acceptable.[15]

Because of those limits set on allowable transactions, Shariah Boards have been criticized for being hopelessly old-fashioned, for being unaware of the latest innovations, and for causing efficiency losses. Yet at a time when conventional finance was unable to be self-critical or resist the lure of easy profits, Shariah

Boards, by scrutinizing every innovation on the basis of criteria other than profit-ability, provided badly needed checks and balances – always the best way of reining in excesses.[16] By insisting on ethical and prudential guidelines at a time when Wall Street was playing Pied Piper, they may have played a salutary role.

The question of leverage provides an interesting illustration of differences between the Islamic and the conventional sectors. Islam favors equity and is suspicious of debt. The requirement that loans be fully backed by an asset greatly reduces the potential for leverage. The "one-third rule" (limiting the debt to market value ratio to one-third), is where the Dow Jones Islamic indexes and other screening mechanisms drew the line. In contrast, conventional finance has since the findings of Modigliani and Miller to the effect that the debt to equity ratio has no bearing on value, has been agnostic on the issue. Yet with the increased focus on profitability and the steady weakening of prudential rules, conventional finance became increasingly partial to debt at the expense of equity. Indeed, the single-minded focus on profitability favored pushing leverage to the limit. It is thus no surprise that conventional firms on the eve of the credit crunch were still, with the acquiescence of regulators, finding creative ways of piling debt upon debt to increase their leverage. In 2004, the Securities and Exchange Commission (SEC) decided to permit investment banks to increase their permitted leverage from 10 to 1 to 30 to 1.[17] Shortly before its collapse, leverage at Lehman Brothers was at 44 to 1, with $748 billion in assets standing atop $17 billion in equity.[18]

More generally, since the dawn of the age of financial deregulation, which roughly corresponds to the entire lifespan of modern Islamic banking, conventional banking has been transformed almost beyond recognition. Beyond the question of leverage a number of changes are worth noting. Since 1978, caps on usury ceilings (usury in the conventional banking sense of excessive interest) were effectively removed opening the door to considerable abuse.[19] The relationship between debtor and creditor was transformed by the practice of securitizing loans. In 2001 the value of pooled securities in America overtook the value of outstanding bank loans. The market for derivatives, which barely existed before deregulation, grew exponentially, with a corresponding increase in complexity and opacity. According to the BIS, in 1997, the notional value of derivatives contracts was $75 trillion, or 2.5 times global GDP. A decade later it mushroomed to $600 trillion or 11 times global GDP.[20] The whole incentive structure within the financial industry changed, favoring reckless and short-term behavior which generated bonuses yet ignored the impact of such open-ended innovation on the economy and society.

The Islamic approach in contrast favored, in theory of not always in practice, a conservative and ethical approach to finance, two qualities that came to be prized following the financial meltdown. The excesses revealed in its wake were accompanied by a backlash and calls for a return to the basics of banking, to de-leveraging and simplifying finance.[21] Whereas finance is prone to overkill and hubris, religion – any religion and for that matter any durable secular philosophical system – stresses temperance and is likely to object to the conceit of omniscience.

Nassim Taleb, in response to those who sought comfort in financial models, stated that "It's easier to say 'God knows' than 'I don't know.'"[22]

On the specific matter of ethics, the world of finance had adopted a cynical attitude. As told by a Stanford business school professor: "In the early eighties, the faculty here started getting snotty comments about how they were contributing to greed on Wall Street and training modern day pirates and buccaneers. After a while it got hard to laugh off. So the faculty said, 'Hey, let's just put an ethics unit in the curriculum. That'll shut everybody up.'"[23] A whole generation of what may be called non-practicing ethicists arose, whereby talking a lot about ethics provided cover for the perpetuation of ethical lapses.

The same is true about governance, transparency, risk control, and other reassuring concepts. In an Orwellian twist, high-sounding principles were invoked just as they were violated in practice.[24] On the eve of a massive destruction of value, all the talk was about how financial innovations were creating value. Risk management took on the airs of an exact science just as risk managers were about to prove that they had been clueless all along.[25]

Just as excesses spawned an interest in simplifying finance, the "amorality" of contemporary finance has generated an interest in "moralizing" it. And whereas Western or Judeo-Christian finance had become thoroughly secularized (the religious origin of many financial institutions has long receded from the public consciousness),[26] Islamic finance stood apart in still asking age-old questions about the dangers of making money with money, the need to tether finance to the real economy, and more generally questions of ethics and morality. In the quest for a free enterprise system that is circumscribed by moral norms and codes, religion, and Islam in particular – a religion that holds positive view of economic activities while providing for strict guidelines – came to hold some attraction. The Vatican newspaper *l'Osservatore Romano* recently wrote: "The ethical principles on which Islamic finance is based may bring banks closer to their clients and to the true spirit which should mark every financial service."[27]

Even secular observers have noted that Islamic finance could be a restraining factor in the rise of transnational criminal networks and other unsavory phenomena that came to be associated with globalization[28] – what some have called "rogue economics." In the words of Loretta Napoleoni: "Above all, Islamic finance represents the sole global economic force that conceptually challenges rogue economics. It does not allow investment in pornography, prostitution, narcotics, tobacco, or gambling. Since the fall of the Berlin Wall, all these areas have blossomed thanks to globalization outlaws under the indifferent eyes of the market-state."[29]

In sum, as the financial crisis has brought about a rare moment of reflection and critical thinking, the logic of Islamic finance can no longer be dismissed out of hand. At the same time, it may be dangerous to overstate the virtues of Islamic finance and present it as a panacea, especially since its principles state what is permissible and not what is necessarily advisable. To quote Mahmoud El-Gamal: "The claim that Islam has the perfect solution is questionable in economics, just as in politics."[30] Islamic finance is still in its early stages of development and is still beset by tensions and problems.[31] And one of the lessons of the recent crisis is about the dangers of complacency.

Notes

1. Timur Kuran, *Islam and Mammon: The Economic Predicaments of Islamism* (New Haven, CT: Princeton University Press, 2004), p. xii.
2. Author's database.
3. Gerald F. Davis, *Managed by the Market: How Finance Reshaped America* (Oxford: Oxford University Press, 2009).
4. Louis Uchitelle, "The Richest of the Rich, Proud of a New Gilded Age," *The New York Times*, July 15, 2007.
5. Sharon Reier, "Financial Engineers Thrive Despite the Subprime Mess," *International Herald Tribune*, August 1, 2008.
6. Eric Briys and François de Varenne, *The Fisherman and the Rhinoceros: How International Finance Shapes Everyday Life* (New York: Wiley, 2000), p. 76.
7. William D. Cohan, *House of Cards: A Tale of Hubris and Wretched Excess on Wall Street* (New York: Doubleday, 2009).
8. There were only a handful of dissenters such as Nassim Taleb, Nouriel Roubini, and Robert Shiller.
9. Briys and Varenne, *The Fisherman and the Rhinoceros*, pp. 8, 5, 2 and 8.
10. Paul Krugman, "America the Tarnished," *The New York Times*, March 29, 2009.
11. Andrew Ross Sorkin, *Too Big to Fail: The Inside Story of how Wall Street and Washington Fought to Save the Financial System – and Themselves* (New York: Viking, 2009).
12. See Chapter 10.
13. See Dr Muhammad Saleem, "Islamic Banking: A $300 Billion Deception," Xlibris Corporation, 2006.
14. Rodney Wilson, "Why Islamic Banking is Successful? Islamic Banks Are Unscathed Despite of Financial Crisis," February 15, 2009, IslamOnline.net.
15. See Chapter 7.
16. For examples of religious scholars providing checks and balances in the political realm, see Noah Feldman, *The Fall and Rise of the Islamic State* (New Haven, CT: Princeton University Press, 2008).
17. Andrew Leonard, "Mr. Paulson goes to Washington," *Salon*, September 3, 2009.
18. Lawrence G. McDonald with Patrick Robinson, *A Colossal Failure of Common Sense: The Inside Story of the Collapse of Lehman Brothers* (New York: Crown Business, 2009), pp. 287–8.
19. Thomas Geoghegan, "Business as Usury," *The American Prospect*, May 6, 2008.
20. "Taming the Beast," *The Economist*, October 9, 2008.
21. Robert Kuttner, "Back-to-Basics Banking," *The Boston Globe*, October 11, 2008.
22. David Ignatius, "Humbled Economic Masters at Davos," *The Washington Post*, February 1, 2009.
23. Peter Robinson, *Snapshots from Hell: The Making of an MBA* (New York: Warner Books, 1994), p. 217.
24. Gillian Tett, *Fool's Gold: How the Bold Dream of a Small Tribe at J. P. Morgan was Corrupted by Wall Street Greed and Unleashed a Catastrophe* (New York: Free Press, 2009). See also Hernando de Soto, "Toxic Assets Were Hidden Assets," *The Wall Street Journal*, March 25, 2009.
25. Justin Fox, *The Myth of the Rational Market: A History of Risk, Reward, and Delusion on Wall Street* (New York: HarperCollins, 2009).
26. See Bernard Taillefer, *Guide de la Banque pour tous: Innovations africaines* (Paris: Karthala, 1996), p. 19. See also Chapter 1.

27. Lorenzo Totaro, "Vatican Says Islamic Finance May Help Western Banks in Crisis," *Bloomberg*, March 4, 2009.
28. See Moises Naim, *Illicit: How Smugglers, Traffickers, and Copycats Are Hijacking the Global Economy* (New York: Doubleday, 2005).
29. Loretta Napoleoni, *Rogue Economics: Capitalism's New Reality* (New York: Seven Stories Press, 2008), p. 241.
30. Carla Power, "Faith in the Market," *Foreign Policy*, January/February, 2009.
31. Roula Khalaf, "Islamic Finance must Resolve Inner Tensions," *The Financial Times*, March 30, 2009.

GLOSSARY

adl: justice.

alim (pl. **ulema**): learned man or religious scholar.

al-wadiah: safekeeping.

arbun: common Islamic practice of non-refundable down-payment similar to modern "options."

awqaf (sing. **waqf**): religious endowments.

Ayatollah: honorific title given to leading Shia clerics in Iran (literally, "sign of God").

bay' al 'ina: selling goods for cash and buying back at higher price for deferred payment.

bay' dayn: sale of debt.

bay' muajjal: deferred-payment sale.

bay' salam: pre-paid purchase.

bidaa: innovation.

daawa: missionary activities (literally, "call").

darura: overriding necessity.

falah: wellbeing.

faqih (pl. **fuqaha**): jurist, expert in Islamic law.

fatwa: legal opinion, religious edict.

fiqh: jurisprudence.

gharar: deception, hazard, speculation, uncertainty, risk (literally, "peril/hazard").

ghosh: fraud.

Hadith: stories about and sayings (specific pronouncements, deeds, or approvals of other people's actions) of the Prophet.

haj: pilgrimage.

haja: need.

halal: lawful or permissible (see **haram**).

haram: unlawful or forbidden (see **halal**).

hisbah: an office which in traditional Islam supervised markets, provided municipal services and settled petty disputes.

hiyal (sing. **hila**): ruses, used in reference to crafty ways of circumventing the prohibition of riba.

hudud: punishments such as dismemberment and death by stoning.

hukumiyya: sovereign power.
ibadat: acts of worship.
ijara: leasing.
ijmaa: consensus.
ijtihad: devout and careful reflection and effort; use of independent judgment or original thinking in interpreting the Koran and the Sunna.
ilm: science.
infitah: open-door policy pursued by Anwar Sadat in the early 1970s.
islah: reform.
israf wa taraf: luxury activities; profligacy.
istisnaa: commissioned manufacture.
jahiliyya: pre-Islamic era (literally, "state/age of ignorance").
jahl: ignorance, or lack of knowledge.
jihad: holy war or spiritual exertion.
Koran: Islam's holy book.
madhab: school of religious and moral interpretation.
makrub: reprehensible.
manfaa: usufruct.
maslaha: the general interest.
Maysir: a game of chance condemned by the Koran.
muamalat: transactions.
mubah: morally neutral.
mudaraba: trustee finance, or commenda partnership.
mudarib: managing trustee.
mufti: chief religious cleric, usually government-appointed.
muqarada: loan participation.
murabaha: contract whereby a financial institution buys goods or commodities on behalf of a borrower and then sells it on a deferred basis at a mark-up.
musawama: bargaining.
musharaka: joint venture between a financier and an entrepreneur.
mustahabb: meritorious.
niyya: intent.
qadi: judge.
qard hasan: interest-free loan usually given for charitable purposes (literally, "good loan").
qimor: speculation and gambling.
qirad: see **mudaraba**.
qiyas: reasoning by analogy or by logical inference.
rabb al maal: beneficial owner or sleeping partner.
riba: interest or usury (literally, "increase/addition").
sadaqa: pious work of charity.
sakk (pl. **sukuk**): Islamic bonds.
salaf: the "pious ancestors", usually includes the Prophet Mohammed and the first four "rightly guided" caliphs.

salam: advance purchase.

salat: prayer.

shahada: proclamation of faith.

Shariah: Islamic law.

shirka: see **musharaka**.

shura: consultation by the ruler of the community notables.

Sunna: practices and rulings deduced from the deeds, utterances and unspoken approvals of the Prophet and his companions.

tajdid: renewal.

takaful: mutual guarantee/Islamic insurance.

takfir: excommunication.

talfiq: patching.

taqlid: imitation.

tawarroq: synthetic **murahaha**, whereby a commodity is bought on credit and immediately sold for cash.

towhid: oneness of God.

ulema (sing. **alim**): learned men or religious scholars.

umma: community of believers or nation of Islam.

urf: custom.

ushr: title.

usufruct: benefit derived from use of an item.

usul el fiqh: principles of Islamic jurisprudence.

waad: promise made by buyer to purchase an item.

wajib: obligatory.

wakala: agency.

waqf (pl. **awqaf**): charitable trusts; property endowed to Islam for the benefit of Muslims.

zakat: voluntary almsgiving (literally, "purification").

INDEX